CW01667346

The
Watford Football Club
Illustrated Who's Who

The
Watford Football Club
Illustrated Who's Who

by

Trefor Jones

"..... all sorts and conditions of men ....."
(The Book of Common Prayer)

TGJ

Published by T.G. Jones, 10 Brook House,
143 London Road, Twickenham, Middlesex, TW1 1EQ

ISBN 0-9527458-0-1

Designed and typeset by the author and Amanda Beckley

Printed by Ian Allan Printing Ltd, Coombelands House,
Coombelands Lane, Addlestone, Surrey, KT15 1HY

CONTENTS

ILLUSTRATIONS

Front cover: F.A. Sargent; L.L. Blissett

Half-title page: P.A. Jennings

Back cover: Watford FC 1905/6 Standing, from left - J. Goodall (manager), D. McCartney, W. Lindsay, W. Biggar, J. Brooks, J.W. Richardson, J. Upton (trainer); Sitting, from left - A. Main, G.H. Badenoch, J. Reid, R.A. Thorpe (chairman), J. Foster, P. Turner, F. Kelly

FA Cup Final squad 1984 Back row, from left - J.C.B. Barnes, K.F. Jackett, G.G. Reilly, S.G. Terry, L. Sinnott; Middle row, from left - L. Taylor, M.J.G. Johnston, N.I. Callaghan, S. Sherwood, D.J. Bardsley, P.G. Atkinson, N. Price; Sitting, from left - W. Hails (physiotherapist), G. Taylor (manager), J.P. Ward (coach)

Acknowledgements

COMPILING any half-decent book of this kind depends heavily on the interchange of information amongst the widespread network of football researchers and historians, and in this connection the author is deeply indebted most of all to Jim Creasy, Douglas Lamming and Mike Davage.

The many other specialists who have been particularly helpful include Wilf Armory, Loek Bertels, Chris Bethell, John Blackmore, Michael Braham, Gary Chalk, Mark Chapman, Dennis Clarebrough, Bill Cook, Garth Dykes, Cris Freddi, Ian Garland, Peter Grace, Marshall Gillespie, Roger Harris, Andy Howland, Colin Jose, Richard Lindsay, Dick Middleton, Gerald Mortimer, Robert Reid, Ceri Stennett, Dave Sullivan, Paul Taylor, Roger Triggs, Alex White and Tony Woodburn.

More parochially, a major source of information, advice and help of various kinds over a long period of time has been the *Watford Observer*'s assistant editor, Oliver Phillips, author of the official Watford FC history and supremely dedicated and authoritative chronicler of the club's affairs for more than three decades. And being able to draw constantly on Robert Smith's extraordinary knowledge of clubs and players at all levels of the contemporary game has been a godsend.

On behalf of Watford Football Club, vitally important assistance was provided by Ed Coan. Mark Devlin and Gabriela Lang are also due a sincere expression of thanks.

Extensive use was made of various public records and official football archives, notably those of the Football Associations and Football Leagues of both England and Scotland, the General Register Office, the Public Record Office, the Principal Probate Registry, the British Library Newspaper Library, the National Library of Scotland, the General Register Office (Scotland), the Society of Genealogists, Watford Central Library, and many other libraries and institutions from here to Timbuktu - and beyond.

Countless ex-players and their relatives and descendants have courteously, and more often than not enthusiastically, answered queries and provided details which would otherwise have been lost for ever - and in some cases also supplied photographs.

The book's production stages were smoothed immeasurably by the support and professional expertise of Mandie Beckley.

PHOTOGRAPHS

Many of the photographs in the book are reproduced by kind permission of Watford Football Club, the *Watford Observer*, Malcolm Fox, Action Images, and photographers Alan Cozzi, Mark Leech and Martin Wolmark.

Note on Appearances and Goals

Throughout the book, figures following '+' denote games in which players appeared as a used substitute, and '1p', '2p', etc, indicate goals scored from penalty kicks.

Foreword by Elton John, CBE

THE wealth of information in this book, and its photographs, provide a comprehensive record of the identities and deeds of Watford FC players and managers of all eras. It not only covers the big names of the past, and the players on the current staff, but gives equal prominence to all the 'one-appearance' men and the forgotten players of long ago.

Since I first stood and watched games from 'the bend' between the old Shrodells Stand and the Rookery End at Vicarage Road, I have seen a great many players in action in a Watford shirt - and, like everyone else who has followed the club's fortunes, I have a personal store of memories associated with those players. The book offers all of us a source of endless nostalgic pleasure and interest, and serves as a tribute to the hundreds of personalities who have done their bit for Watford Football Club.

Enjoy it!

Chronology

1881	The club is formed, as Watford Rovers.
1882	Home games begin in Vicarage Meadow.
1883	Rose & Crown Meadow becomes the venue for home matches.
1886	The first competitive match - an FA Cup tie. Rovers also enter the Herts County Cup and reach the final.
1889	The club moves to Colney Butts when Rose & Crown Meadow is lost to urban development.
1890	Rovers become the football section of the newly-formed West Herts Club & Ground at Cassio Road.
1893	After three years of internal conflict over the club name, 'West Herts' is universally accepted.
1896	West Herts join Division 2 of the Southern League.
1897	Professionalism adopted.
1898	Rival club Watford St Mary's is absorbed by West Herts, and the name 'Watford' is adopted.
1900	Promoted to Division 1 of the Southern League.
1903	Relegated to Division 2 of the Southern League. John Goodall appointed as the club's first manager.
1904	Promoted to Division 1 of the Southern League.
1909	The club becomes a limited company, and its committee is replaced by a board of directors.
1915	The Southern League championship is won.
1917	After two seasons of wartime activity as a member of the London Combination, the club suspends operations for two years.
1919	Post-war football begins.
1920	The Southern League's First Division (including Watford) becomes Division 3 of the Football League. It is styled 'Division 3 (South)' a year later, when a corresponding Northern section is added.
1922	Vicarage Road becomes the club's new home ground.
1939	Normal competitions cease when war is declared, and the club embarks on seven seasons of football under wartime regulations.
1945	The FA Cup competition is resumed.
1946	Normal League activity is resumed.
1958	Watford are founder-members of Division 4 as the League's lower sections are reorganised.
1960	Promoted to Division 3.
1969	Champions of Division 3, and promoted to Division 2 for the first time.
1970	The club reaches the FA Cup semi-finals for the first time.
1972	Relegated to Division 3.
1975	Relegated to Division 4.
1978	Division 4 champions, and promoted to Division 3.
1979	Promoted to Division 2.
1982	Promoted to Division 1.
1983	By finishing second in Division 1, Watford qualify for entry to the UEFA Cup.
1984	The club's first FA Cup Final appearance.
1988	Relegated to Division 2.
1992	Division 2 of the Football League becomes Division 1, as the top-flight clubs break away to form the FA Premier League.
1996	Relegated to Division 2 (formerly Division 3).

Part One

The Players Before 1896/7

IN 1881 the concept of league football, involving a regular programme of organised home-and-away fixtures, was as yet unknown, and Watford Rovers' very earliest matches were exclusively of a 'friendly' nature, opposition being provided by clubs and schools from the Watford area and nearby towns such as Berkhamsted, St Albans and Uxbridge. An increasingly stronger fixture list was built up as the club grew in stature, with opponents of a higher standard being drawn from the London area and elsewhere.

Rovers first entered organised competitions in 1886/7, when they took part in the Herts County Cup and the FA Cup, both of which they were to contest regularly in the coming seasons, making little impression in the national competition but winning the county cup five times in the next decade. They also played in the Hennessey Cup, a local tournament, for three seasons from 1888/9, and flirted with the FA Amateur Cup four times in the '90s. Outside these knockout competitions, the club continued to play only friendlies until they joined the Southern League in 1896.

The Rovers' founder-members, and most of those who represented the club in the early days, were sons of property-owning, middle-class families, and for some years the pupils and old boys of Aldenham School, including several Cambridge blues, were to provide an additional rich seam of talent. Only gradually were artisans and labourers absorbed into the playing strength, until eventually the 'Victorian gentlemen' image disappeared for ever when the decision to turn professional - a highly contentious one - was taken in 1897.

The following list of players, with their appearance and goalscoring totals, encompasses first-team games - both friendlies and cup matches - played from the club's formation until its acceptance into the Southern League. In the early '80s match details reported in the local press were often much less than comprehensive, and although coverage became more thorough and consistent from 1885, the list is inevitably incomplete and in some cases not totally accurate.

*Names in **BOLD CAPITALS** indicate players who went on to represent the club in Southern League and/or other competitive matches from 1896/7, and who are therefore featured in Part Two. Names underlined indicate others who appeared in friendly matches from 1896/7, and are listed in Part Four. Of the rest, four in particular (marked with an asterisk) have a significant place in the club's history, and are the subject of brief biographies at the end of the list.*

First App	Last App		Apps	Goals
1884	1884	- Abercrombie	1	
1892	1892	G. Adams	3	
1884	1885	R. Adcock	6	
1891	1892	A.B. Anderson	3	1
1896	1896	**H.G. ANDERSON**	10	1
1893	1894	J.O. Anderson	9	10
1894	1896	**A.O. ARDLEY**	39	1
1891	1892	B.A.F. Astley	3	
1888	1889	G.R. Bacot	5	2
1890	1890	C.H. Baker	1	
1892	1892	W. Baker	1	
1896	1896	J. Baldwin	1	
1894	1894	A. Bartlett	1	
1890	1890	B. Bateman	1	
1893	1893	C.H. Baylis	1	
1888	1888	- Beaumont	1	

Part One

First App	Last App		Apps	Goals
1889	1892	E. Beevor	8	2
1895	1895	W.H. Bentley	1	
1892	1892	J. Black	1	
1895	1896	**R. BLYTH**	20	3
1892	1892	H.R. Bradstreet	1	
1894	1895	J. Brandon	4	
1894	1895	W. Brandon	1	
1887	1887	E. Brennan	1	
1886	1887	E. or H.B. Broughton	3	
1885	1886	- Brown	3	1
1888	1890	J.A. Brown	5	5
1883	1883	T. Brown	1	
1890	1891	**W.W. BRUNT**	14	
1893	1894	A. Burr	7	
1892	1892	A. Burton	1	
1891	1893	A. Butler	20	7
1888	1888	G. Butler	1	
1893	1896	**J.T. BUTTON**	3	
1882	1888	H.J. Capell	59	
1884	1884	J. Capell	1	
1894	1894	H.S. Cartmell	1	1
1893	1893	G. Cashmore	1	
1887	1887	W.E. Chadwick	1	
1882	1884	H.O. Chatterton	4	1
1882	1885	A. Christmas	3	
1888	1891	G.C. Clark	7	
1891	1891	R. Clarke	1	
1896	1896	**T.W. CLARKE**	1	1
1883	1883	H. Clegg	2	1
1889	1894	A. Coles	14	
1887	1895	P. Coles	98	47
1887	1895	*W.S. Coles	146+1	195(4p)
1895	1895	J.O. Conquest	3	
1890	1892	G.P. Cooper	2	
1892	1895	M.J. Cottam	9	4
1892	1892	P. Cottam	2	
1892	1892	J.G. Coulter (or Coulton)	1	
1895	1895	H.T. Cronk	1	
1886	1886	- Cross	1	
1895	1895	R.R. Cruise	2	1
1889	1892	H. Culverhouse	14	3
1886	1886	A. Curtis-Brown	1	
1892	1892	G. Dalley	1	
1892	1892	J. Danks	1	
1896	1896	**G. DAVENPORT**	5	
1889	1895	H.J. Dewey	32	2
1888	1890	J.W. Dickson	8	4
1891	1891	W.H. Dixon	3	
1891	1895	W. Dodds	10	5
1893	1893	- Doggett	1	
1895	1895	**H.J. DOW**	4	1

First App	Last App		Apps	Goals
1892	1892	F.B. Downer	2	1
1895	1895	**C.F. DRAKE**	1	
1888	1889	J.R. Dukes	2	
1888	1892	A.T.B. Dunn	4	8
1888	1888	A. Dyer	1	
1883	1887	F. Fairman	4	
1896	1896	A.S. Fish	1	2
1886	1886	E. Fisher	4	
1895	1895	C. Fishwick	1	
1886	1887	E. Foster	3	1
1893	1893	P.G.C. Foster	2	
1884	1885	J. Gale	7	
1885	1886	A. or J. or H. Gardner	6	
1886	1890	W.E. Gardner	4	1
1894	1894	H.H. Gaylard	1	
1886	1886	- Gibson	1	
1891	1891	H. Gibson	1	
1888	1889	W. Gibson	8	2
1895	1895	W. Giddens	1	2
1882	1887	H. Grace	17	3
1882	1885	W. Grace	5	
1895	1895	**J.J. GRAN**	1	
1892	1896	**G.E. GREEN**	40	2
1884	1885	H. Green	4	
1893	1895	C. Griffiths	3	1
1883	1883	- Grou	1	
1882	1890	*H.W. Grover	72	1
1889	1889	J.R. Hainsworth	2	
1886	1889	C.H. Halsey	3	1
1885	1887	E. Halsey	24	12
1892	1895	H.M. Harford	47	
1894	1894	A. Harrison	1	
1892	1894	C. Harrison	32	13
1891	1891	C. Harvey	1	
1890	1890	- Harvey Smith or Walker Smith	1	
1890	1893	W. Hatch	6	2
1893	1894	A. Heath	8	
1893	1893	W. Heath	7	
1889	1889	- Heaton	1	
1891	1892	J.C. Hibbert	9	
1887	1887	W.H. Hill	1	
1891	1892	W.H. Hinton	2	
1894	1896	**S.G. HOBBS**	39	39
1888	1888	E. Hockliffe	1	1
1893	1893	J. Hodgins	1	
1885	1885	T. Holford	1	
1889	1890	F.E. Holt	2	
1894	1894	H.O. Holt	1	
1894	1894	A. Hopkings	1	
1890	1892	A. Horton	30	6
1882	1884	H.T. Horton	4	1

First App	Last App		Apps	Goals
1882	1891	W. Horton	43	1
1891	1893	A.J. Houghton	24	
1892	1892	C. Houghton	2	
1891	1891	W. How	1	
1896	1896	F. Hughes	2	
1892	1892	H. Hughes	1	
1896	1896	R. Hughes	1	2
1892	1892	W. Hughes	2	1
1890	1890	G. Humphrey(s)	1	
1884	1885	A. Hunt	6	
1895	1895	B.H. Hunter	1	
1882	1883	W. Hurndall	5	2
1896	1896	H.A. Hutchings	2	
1890	1891	F.H.S. Iles	11	3
1884	1885	H.W. Iles	5	
1895	1896	**J.H. ILES**	3	3
1892	1893	E.G. Jackson	2	
1893	1895	R.H. James	4	
1888	1888	- Johnson	1	
1892	1892	H.L. Jones	2	
1892	1892	W. Jones	1	
1893	1893	B.C. Joy	1	1
1895	1895	B.H. Joy	7	
1889	1889	Rev J. Kennedy	2	
1883	1885	W. Kinder	7	
1896	1896	J.C. King	1	
1892	1896	**S. KING**	87+1	
1895	1896	I.H. Kitchin	5	1
1892	1892	J. Lamb	1	
1883	1892	W.S. Large	18	4
1892	1893	W.L. La Touche	8	9
1883	1883	- Lawrence	1	
1883	1885	G. or H. Lea	3	
1886	1886	- Leeson	1	
1889	1889	J. Leeson	1	
1883	1883	H.V. Lemenager	1	
1896	1896	R. Leslie	1	
1893	1893	F.J. Lidderdale	2	
1893	1895	J.S. Lidderdale	22	
1892	1892	J. Lockwood	1	
1895	1895	W. Lovett	3	1
1889	1891	A.M. Low	6	1
1891	1894	R.A. Low	2	
1886	1886	B. McGregor	2	1
1895	1895	L.H. Mackenzie	1	
1894	1896	**C.F. MACLACHLAN**	35	14
1894	1894	W.A. Macready	1	
1888	1888	F. Madder	1	
1895	1895	D.C. Mahoney	1	
1889	1894	E.H. Mariette	35	1
1896	1896	F.M. May	7	2
1888	1888	J. Mayfield	1	

First App	Last App		Apps	Goals
1890	1890	W.H. Meadows	1	
1889	1889	A.J. Millar	2	
1892	1892	R. Mills	5	1
1888	1888	S.F.P. Moore	2	2
1889	1892	G.D. Morrison	17	2
1887	1888	P.H. Morton	8	5
1891	1896	J. Munn	8	4
1892	1892	**J.E. MYERS**	2	
1893	1895	J.G. Neal	5	1
1891	1891	J. Neate	1	
1892	1892	R. Newman	1	
1892	1892	L. Orr	1	1
1885	1891	F. Parkes	32	8
1883	1888	W.H. Parkhouse	13	
1892	1892	**R.B.J. PATEN**	1	
1888	1888	H. Paul	1	
1892	1896	**J.R. PAULL**	66	1
1884	1894	*C.H. Peacock	177	10
1887	1889	T.J. Peacock	3	
1892	1892	R. Peel or J. Pell	1	
1892	1892	J. Pender	1	
1891	1895	J. Penney	100+1	3
1886	1887	W.J. or H.J. Pickin	8	2
1895	1895	F.E. or W. Pitkin	1	
1885	1885	H. Plumb	1	
1888	1888	H. Poulton	1	
1885	1891	S.J. Poulton	88	6
1892	1892	C. Pretty	1	1
1895	1895	- Pryce-Whyte	1	
1895	1895	W. Racklyeft	1	
1894	1895	H.A. Rauthmell	2	
1896	1896	W.H. Rawcliffe	1	
1895	1895	J. Reed	6	1
1893	1895	F. Reeves	3	1
1893	1893	O. Reeves	1	
1892	1892	C. Regan	1	
1883	1887	H. Richardson	5	
1895	1895	**J.W. RICHARDSON**	1	
1895	1896	F.F. Ritchie	2	1
1895	1896	G. Ritchie	2	
1892	1892	F.W. or T.W. Roach	1	
1891	1891	R.K. Robertson	1	
1894	1896	**F.C. ROBINS**	54	3
1887	1888	W.N. Roe	9	
1892	1892	C. Rowe	1	
1885	1888	J.A. Ryding	3	
1889	1889	E.J. Sainsbury	1	
1885	1890	A.A. Sargent	92	
1885	1885	E.J. Sargent	1	
1884	1895	*F.A. Sargent	151+1	161
1883	1892	W.A. Sargent	139	10

First App	Last App		Apps	Goals
1895	1896	**W. SAUNDERS**	9	3
1884	1887	H. Scrivener	12	
1892	1892	J. Seborne or Seaborne	1	
1884	1884	- Seabrook	1	
1892	1892	A.V. Sedgwick	1	
1895	1895	E.V. Sedgwick	1	1
1889	1889	- Selby	1	
1887	1887	A. Seymour	1	
1890	1891	J.W. Sharpe	6	4
1890	1890	H. Sherlock	1	
1893	1896	**R. SLAUGHTER**	15	3
1882	1887	T. Smith	22	6
1892	1893	W. Spearing	25	
1888	1888	S.M. Stanley	2	
1890	1890	H. Stokes	1	
1890	1890	J. Stokes	3	2
1890	1890	E.M. Strouts	1	
1893	1895	R.C.M. Strouts	8	1
1887	1888	A.K. Stuart	3	2
1890	1890	J. Stuart	2	
1889	1891	J.A. Stuart	22	10
1887	1887	T. Stuart	1	
1886	1886	- Taskers	1	
1893	1896	S.S. Taylor	12	12
1895	1895	W. Tearle	1	
1883	1883	- Thomas	1	
1890	1890	- Thomas	1	
1885	1886	G. Thompson	7	2
1884	1884	- Tomkins	1	
1889	1889	A. Tooms	1	
1887	1887	A.H. Town	3	1
1892	1892	F.P. or T.P. Trew	1	
1894	1894	C. Tucker	1	
1896	1896	**A.D. TURNER**	3	
1884	1889	W.B. Tyler	5	
1890	1890	E.J.A. Tyrrell	2	
1882	1887	S.J. Valentine	61	24
1888	1892	E.E. Villiers	70	3
		(for Walker Smith, see Harvey Smith)		
1894	1894	H.F. Ward	1	
1893	1894	L.E.S. Ward	4	
1891	1892	H.G. Wardale	2	
1894	1894	H.M. Washbourne	2	
1882	1888	G. Waterman	72	12
1889	1892	W. Waterman	4	
1894	1895	F. Watson	4	
1895	1896	J.G. Weall	3	
1888	1888	T. Weatherhead	1	
1883	1887	W.H. Wellings	50	14
1892	1892	W. Wells	1	
1892	1895	C. Wheeler	76	38
1892	1894	F. Wheeler	3	
1882	1888	H. Wheeler	53	22
1887	1887	M. Wheeler	1	
1894	1894	D.L. White	1	
1891	1891	F. White	1	1
1896	1896	H.E. White	1	
1888	1890	J.B. Wildman	14	1
1896	1896	E. Wilkins	2	
1892	1892	J. or T.B. Wilkinson	1	
1892	1892	S.C. Wilks	2	4
1890	1890	E. Williams	1	
1892	1896	F.J. Williams	5	
1896	1896	R. Williams	1	
1894	1894	W. Williams	1	
1892	1892	A. Wilson	2	
1892	1892	G.R. Wilson	1	
1895	1895	**J. WILSON**	5	
1894	1896	**R.K. WISE**	3	
1890	1890	A.A. Woodhouse	1	
1894	1895	**H. WOOD**	2	
1888	1893	J. Woods	75	
1890	1890	W. Woodward	11	1
1894	1895	**A.R.L. WRIGHT**	11	1
1894	1896	**R.G. WRIGHT**	37	21

Historic penalty kick

Walter Selby COLES
b Watford, Herts 14/6/1869
d Watford, Herts 5/10/1932

HE scored freely for the club from the age of 18, and peaked in 1891/2 with a return of 61 goals in 26 appearances, including the club's first-ever penalty as part of an FA Cup hat-trick at Maidenhead. He was appointed captain for the next two seasons, but then stood down in 1894, due to his forthcoming absence from the town. Educated at both Cranleigh and Aldenham, he was the son of a county councillor prominent in Watford's civic affairs, and was partnered in the forward line on many occasions by his younger brother Percy, a future captain of West Herts Golf Club. Walter's son Theo was to make a Football League appearance for Watford in 1921, and sporting distinction extended into the third generation when Theo's son scored a century for Eton v Harrow at Lord's.

The founder

Henry William GROVER
b Bovingdon, Herts 28/10/1865
d Watford, Herts 22/3/1949

WHEN a group of youths who had been given permission to kick a ball about in Cassiobury Park subscribed to form a club which they called Watford Rovers, it was Henry Grover who purchased the ball and who was acknowledged as the founder. After playing at full-back and then half-back for nearly a decade, he faded from the scene, and although he continued to live just a short walk from each of the five sites which have provided the club with its home grounds, when he died an old man his identity as Watford FC's founder had long gone unrecognised. The son of a prosperous wine-merchant and ex-farmer with many properties in the Watford area and elsewhere, he became the financial partner in a building firm.

Watford Observer man

Charles Herbert PEACOCK
b Watford, Herts 11/11/1867
d Watford, Herts 11/11/1930

YOUNG Charlie Peacock was one of Grover's pals who were in at the start in 1881, and for years he was a formidable presence at the heart of the club's defence, also representing the county. He became a central figure in the affairs - footballing and otherwise - of West Herts Club & Ground from its formation in 1890, and was proprietor of the *Watford Observer*, his name surviving until 1991 in the title of the company which publishes the newspaper. He organised an annual horse-and-carriage show at Vicarage Road in the early 1920s, which did nothing to enhance the quality of the playing surface. His son Kim was a co-founder of West Herts Rugby Club, but became much more widely known as the actor who portrayed Paul Temple in the popular 1950s radio detective series.

Frederick Albert SARGENT
b Watford, Herts 10/3/1858
d Watford, Herts 13/4/1942

Hertfordshire's best

ONE of three brothers conspicuous in the club's early history, Freddie Sargent was widely regarded as the finest player in the county. A fast, skilful and (although physically no giant) robust goalscoring forward, he made his reputation with Herts Rangers and St Albans before throwing in his lot with Rovers. He also played cricket for Herts, won many trophies as a sprinter and hurdler, and was a noted bass singer. Cantankerously opposed to hotly debated decisions involving the loss of the name 'Watford Rovers', the seeking of Southern League membership, and the embracing of professionalism, he was nevertheless held in great esteem and affection. He was awarded the OBE after nearly 50 years' service as a railway official with the LNWR, latterly as its London Traffic Superintendent.

Part Two

League and Cup Football - 1896 to 1996

THIS main section of the book consists of brief biographies of all the players who have represented Watford in competitive matches under peacetime conditions from 1896/7 to 1995/6, inclusive.

NAME

The part of the name shown in **BOLD CAPITALS** *is that by which the player is or was commonly called. (If no first name is given in capitals, this information is not known.) Nicknames are signified only in cases where they are/were better-known than the first name. Some players are known by surnames which are different from those with which they began their lives. In such cases a desire to balance the aims of a factual reference book with proper regard for an individual's privacy has resulted in a compromise: players' previous names are given only in respect of those no longer alive. The dates in brackets after a player's name represent the years of his first and last Watford appearance, including any wartime games.*

BIRTH / DEATH DETAILS

Places of birth and death reflect their administrative location at the time of the event; hence, for example, Arthur Woolliscroft - born Salford, Lancs, but died Salford, Greater Manchester.

APPEARANCES / GOALS

Appearances and, in brackets, goals are given for each competition - see key overleaf. Figures following '+' denote games in which players appeared as a used substitute, and 'inc 1p', 'inc 2p', etc, indicate goals scored from penalty kicks. Where applicable, cup appearances and goals prior to 1896/7 have been included, with the year of first such appearance indicated accordingly. End-of-season Test Matches (1899/1900, 1900/1 and 1902/3) and Play-Off matches (1988/9) have been included in Southern League and Football League totals, respectively. Abandoned matches, and those which were completed but subsequently declared void, have been excluded, as have goals scored in penalty shoot-outs used as a means of deciding drawn cup matches.

OVERALL CAREER

Dates of joining and leaving each club are denoted as month and year - eg 6/57 = June 1957. Known transfer fees are stated, but it should be borne in mind that this is a topic on which, especially in the past, clubs have been notoriously cagey. Published figures have often been inaccurate but, wherever possible, reliable or official sources have been used for this book.

REPRESENTATIVE HONOURS

If a player has achieved international or other major representative status, this is recorded in CAPITAL LETTERS below his list of clubs. In this connection it should be noted that 'Scotland Junior' and 'Ireland Junior' refer not to schools or youth football, but to representative matches involving players from outside the major national leagues of those countries. 'Youth' honours refer to matches at levels from Under-16 to Under-20, inclusive.

Part Two

KEY TO COMPETITIONS

(Listed in chronological order of Watford's first involvement)

FAC	**FA Cup** (including 1945/6 - see introduction to Part Three)
HSC	**Herts County Cup / Herts Senior Cup**. The club's re-entry into this competition in modern times has been essentially on a reserve-team basis, and only those matches which were played in the Victorian era are included.
FAAC	**FA Amateur Cup**
SL	**Southern League**
BCCL	**Bucks & Contiguous Counties League**
SEL	**South-Eastern League**. For some fixtures in this competition, the club fielded its first team, and for others the reserve team. Appearances in the latter have been disregarded.
UL	**United League**
SCC	**Southern Charity Cup**
FL	**Football League**. In recent years, under temporary commercial sponsorships, the competition has also been known at various times as the Canon League, the Today League, the Barclays League and the Endsleigh Insurance League.
3SC	**Football League Division 3 (South) Cup**
WW1	**All first-team matches played from 1915/6 to 1918/9, inclusive**
WW2	**All first-team matches played from 1939/40 to 1945/6, inclusive** (except FA Cup matches in 1945/6 - see 'FAC', above)
SFC	**Southern Floodlight Cup**
FLC	**Football League Cup**. In recent years, under temporary commercial sponsorships, the competition has also been known as the Milk Cup, the Littlewoods Cup, the Rumbelows Cup and the Coca-Cola Cup.
FLT	**Football League Group Cup / Football League Trophy**
UEFA	**UEFA Cup**
FMC	**Football League Full Members Cup**. Under temporary commercial sponsorships, the competition was also known at various times as the Simod Cup and the Zenith Data Systems Cup.
AIC	**Anglo-Italian Cup**

OTHER ABBREVIATIONS

am = amateur (until 1974 - see below)

appr = apprentice (a status introduced by the Football League in 1960)

b = born

cs = close season

d = died

pro = professional

sch = associated schoolboy (a status introduced by the Football League in 1963, under which clubs may register boys from the age of 14)

tr = trainee (replaced the 'apprentice' status in 1986)

WW1 = First World War

WW2 = Second World War

Amateur status

Until the Football Association abolished the distinction in 1974, amateur and professional football were quite separate. An amateur could play in a professional team, but the reverse did not apply, and a player's decision to relinquish amateur status and 'turn professional' was a significant step. It meant that, unless he successfully applied for permission to play as a 'permit player' or a reinstated amateur, he could never again take part in amateur football at any level. Few did so, and even then they appeared only in local leagues which would accept former professionals.

Appealed for his release

<u>*CHRIStopher James*</u> <u>***ADAMS***</u> *(1954-1956)*
b Hornchurch, Essex 6/9/1927
FL 75 (5), FAC 6 (1), SFC 1 (-)
Essex Schools; Suttons; Leytonstone; Romford; Tottenham Hotspur (am 6/47, pro 11/48); Norwich City (player-exchange 12/52); <u>Watford</u> (4-figure fee 3/54 until cs 1956); Dartford (11/56 until 1964)
His two-and-a-half-year Vicarage Road stay ended when he refused the part-time terms offered for the 1956/7 season. On appeal to the Football League he was granted a free transfer, and spent several years in the Southern League. A shortish, stocky outside-left, he had turned pro with Spurs, for whom he played a handful of First Division games.

Début as a soldier

<u>*Laurence Edward **(LAURIE)*** ***ADAMS***</u> *(1952)*
b Barnet, Herts 14/2/1931
FL 1 (-)
<u>Watford</u> (am 1/52, pro 7/52 until cs 1953); Whipton (permit player 10/55)
One of ten amateurs to play League football for Watford between the Second World War and the abolition of the amateur/professional distinction. He made his one appearance at inside-left whilst in the army, and turned professional on being demobbed three months later, but was only a reserve thereafter. He later played in the Exeter area.

Big Sheff Utd profit

<u>*Patrick Anthony Olazinka **(TONY)*** ***AGANA***</u> *(1987-1988)*
b Bromley, Kent 2/10/1963
FL 12+3 (1), FAC 2 (-), FLC 1+1 (2), FMC 1 (-)
Welling Utd (cs 1981); Weymouth (£4,500 3/84); <u>Watford</u> (£22,000 8/87); Sheffield Utd (valued at £35,000 in exchange deal involving M.Kuhl and P.Hetherston 2/88); Notts County (£750,000 11/91); Leeds Utd (loan 2/92)
ENGLAND SEMI-PROFESSIONAL
A late starter in League football, he left Watford to join Dave Bassett for the second time in six months, as part of a complex transfer deal. He was later sold by Bassett for big money, but then ran into injury problems. A pacy left-winger or striker, he's best remembered at Vicarage Road for a virtuoso performance against Manchester United.

Top Arsenal manager

<u>*VICtor David*</u> <u>***AKERS***</u> (1975)
b Islington, London 24/8/1946
FL 22 (-), FAC 1 (-), FLC 3 (-)
Fulham youth team; Tonbridge; Bexley Utd (5/69); Cambridge Utd (£5,000 7/71); Tooting & Mitcham Utd (free 1/75); <u>Watford</u> (£1,000 or £2,000 7/75); Dartford (free 7/76); Hayes (1978); Slough Town (by 10/80); Carshalton Athletic (by 3/84); Arsenal administrative staff (cs 1984)
He had half a season as Watford's ever-present left-back after sharing in Cambridge United's first Football League promotion with Eades, Greenhalgh and his subsequent Vicarage Road coach, John Collins. He later helped Dartford win the Southern League Cup with Craker and Greenhalgh, and at Highbury became manager of Arsenal's successful women's team.

Part Two

Edward (NED) **ALLAN** *(1902-1903)*
b Montrose, Angus 31/8/1875
SL 20 (-), FAC 1 (-), SEL 3 (-)
Dundee Wanderers (by 9/96); Millwall (10/99); Newcastle Utd (5/00); Dundee (5/01); Watford (7/02 to cs 1903)
In his Watford season, which ended in relegation, he captained the side from full-back. The son of a Crimea veteran, he'd had three League games at the top level with Newcastle after playing in Millwall's FA Cup semi-final team of 1899/1900. Dundee retained his Scottish League registration until 1905, although he left the club three years earlier.

No luck as captain

Walter (WATTY) **ALLAN** *(1900-1901)*
b Scotland
SL 18 (1), FAC 1 (-)
Fairfield (1894/5); Chorley (5/95); Stalybridge Rovers (10/95); Northfleet; Kettering (2/97); Berrys (7/97); Manchester City (6/98); Thames Ironworks (1/99); Loughborough (free 3/99); Watford (8/00 to cs 1901); Blackpool (11/01)
One of many pros who spent but a single Southern League season at Watford, he held the inside-left position for much of a campaign which ended with First Division survival being secured only in the wake of a goalless Test Match. After playing in a drawn FA Cup tie v QPR, he travelled to Scotland for his father's funeral and missed the replay.

DOUGlas Stewart **ALLDER** *(1977)*
b Hammersmith, London 30/12/1951
FL 1 (-)
Millwall (appr 4/68, pro 10/69); Orient (player-exchange 7/75 to cs 1977); Torquay Utd (a month's trial 8/77); Watford (a month's trial 9/77); Brentford (10/77); Tooting & Mitcham Utd (cs 1980); Staines Town (3/81); Walton & Hersham; coach at Millwall Centre of Excellence (circa 1992)
ENGLAND YOUTH
Extensive League action as a left-winger (332 games in all) included just one chance as a Watford trialist - and even then he was substituted at half-time, at Rochdale early in Graham Taylor's first season. He became a regular in the Brentford team which accompanied Watford up into the Third Division a few months later.

Became promotion rival

DERRICK Sydney **ALLEN** *(1956)*
b Luton, Beds 18/4/1930
d Luton, Beds 30/11/1978
FL 6 (1), FAC 2 (-), SFC 2 (-)
Limbury Boys' Club, Luton; Alton Town; Luton Town (1/52); Watford (5/56); Folkestone (free 2/57); Sunday football in Luton (until death)
He had a brief first-team run at outside-left after being signed from Kenilworth Road, where he was nicknamed 'Sos' and had played as a part-timer whilst working as a lorry driver. He left Watford for Folkestone with Bryan Atkinson in mid-season, and was still playing Sunday football in Luton when he died.

A footballer to the end

International at 18

MALCOLM ALLEN *(1985-1988)*
b Deiniolen, Caernarvonshire 21/3/1967
FL 27+12 (5 inc 1p), FAC 6+8 (6), FLC 4+1 (2)
Watford (appr 7/83, pro 3/85); Aston Villa (loan 9/87); Norwich City (£175,000 8/88); Millwall (£400,000 3/90); Newcastle Utd (£300,000 8/93 until 12/95)
WALES YOUTH, 'B' and FULL
A Welsh-speaking forward who broke into the Full international side at 18 after only a handful of League appearances. He scored Watford's only goal in the 1985 FA Youth Cup Final, and in the first team achieved a healthy scoring rate in cup football. His career ended when long-term injury problems forced his early retirement.

Scored goals elsewhere

WAYNE** Anthony **ALLISON *(1989-1990)*
b Huddersfield, Yorks 16/10/1968
FL 6+1 (-)
Halifax Town (tr 8/86, pro 6/87); Watford (£250,000 7/89); Bristol City (valued at £150,000 in part-exchange for M.W.Gavin 7/90); Swindon Town (£475,000 7/95)
The last of three players signed by Steve Harrison from Halifax Town for what was very big money for the Yorkshire club, for whom Allison first played League football as a trainee. Unable to establish himself at Watford, this big striker left in part-exchange for Mark Gavin and became a consistent scorer for his West Country clubs.

Youth-team skipper

JULIAN ALSFORD *(1992-1993)*
b Poole, Dorset 24/12/1972
FL 9+4 (1), FLC 1 (-), AIC 2 (-)
Watford (sch 12/88, tr 7/89, pro 5/91); Kingsbury Town (loan 1/92); Staines Town (loan 1/92); Slough Town (loan 3/94); Chester City (free 8/94, but Watford to receive a third of any 'sell-on' fee)
After captaining the youth team, he established himself in reserve-team football and was loaned out for experience at non-League level. With senior defenders ahead of him in the queue, there were only limited opportunities of a first-team place at centre-half, and he was tried as a striker in the Reserves before being released.

H.G. (ANDY) ANDERSON *(1896)*
SL 8 (2), FAC 1 (-), FAAC 4 (-)
West Herts (1896)
Frequently on view as a winger in the first team throughout 1896, he scored in the club's first Southern League game, which saw Wycombe Wanderers beaten 5-0 in front of an estimated 400 at Cassio Road, and had featured regularly in the first team in the latter half of the previous season. He played in the club's last four Amateur Cup ties.

Part Two

Thomas Cowan (**TOMMY**) **ANDERSON** *(1957-1965)*
b Haddington, East Lothian 24/9/1934
FL 73 (14), SFC 2 (2)
Heart of Midlothian (am); Queen of the South (pro 9/55 until 11/56); Watford (1/57); Bournemouth & Boscombe Athletic (£1,000 6/58); Queens Park Rangers (11/58); Torquay Utd 7/59); Stockport County (6/60); Doncaster Rovers (11/61); Wrexham (3/62); Hellas, Australia; Barrow (12/63); Hellas, Australia (2/64); Watford (1/65); St Mirren (free 10/65 until 12/65); Melbourne George Cross, Australia; Orient (7/67 until 12/67); Limerick player-manager (1/68)
SCOTLAND SCHOOLS
A nimble forward of blistering pace, an attribute which brought him second place in the 1957 Powderhall Sprint. He wandered far, wide and frequently in his football career, and eventually settled in Australia, where he became a Sydney soccer reporter and was given his own radio programme.

Flying Scotsman

Leonard Thomas Alford (**LEN**) **ANDREWS** *(1924-1925)*
b Reading, Berks 9/12/1888
d Southampton, Hants 21/1/1969
FL 38 (6), FAC 2 (1)
Reading University College; Reading Amateurs; Reading; Southampton (by 8/13); Reading (cs 1919); Southampton (8/21); Watford (free 8/24 until cs 1925)
He arrived at Watford as a veteran of 35 and became a first-team regular at inside-forward or on the left wing, but was nevertheless released after only one season. During his second Reading spell he was picked for the last Southern League representative XI (v Corinthians) to be fielded before its First Division was absorbed by the Football League.

Signed on at 35

WAYNE Michael Hill **ANDREWS** *(1996)*
b Paddington, London 25/11/1977
FL 0+1 (-)
Watford (sch 10/92, tr 7/94)
Taking a speedy and direct approach to the art of forward play, he was still a trainee when given his League début in March 1996, as a substitute. The previous season he had an eventful outing with the youth team when, having accomplished a South-East Counties League hat-trick against Portsmouth, he was harshly sent off.

Hat-trick and red card

Henry Augustus (**HARRY**) **ANSTISS** *(1923-1924)*
b Hampstead, London 22/8/1899
d Isleworth, Middx 9/3/1964
FL 18 (5), FAC 4 (-)
Hammersmith Athletic; Brentford (am 8/20, pro 11/20); Millwall (£650 5/22); Watford (£150 6/23); Rochdale (free 6/24); Sheffield Wednesday (£1,000 7/26); Port Vale (player-exchange 2/27); Swansea Town (5/31); Crewe Alexandra (7/33); Gillingham (7/34 until cs 1935); Tunbridge Wells Rangers (9/35); Cray Wanderers (1/37)
A survivor of the Battle of Jutland, and much-travelled in

Jutland survivor

his football career, he was one of the many one-season men at Watford. He scored at a healthy rate for Rochdale, his 39 League goals in two years earning him a spell in the big-time at Hillsborough, and his Port Vale service brought him a Third Division (North) championship medal.

Boundless energy

Arthur Oliver **ARDLEY** *(1894-1898)*
b Long Melford, Suffolk 22/7/1870
d Colchester, Essex 4/10/1958
SL 10 (-), FAC 3 (-), FAAC 5 (-), HSC 3 (-)
Long Melford (1886 until 1889); several London clubs; West Herts (1894 until 1900); also Crouch End (from 1895/6); also Watford St Mary's (4/97)
Having learned the game at Halstead School in Essex, he later won a Suffolk County Cup-winner's medal and also represented his native county before moving to Watford. Although lacking finesse, he displayed boundless energy as a wing-half and had plenty of first-team action in his first two seasons. He captained the Reserves in 1899/1900.

World Cup stardom

Gerard Joseph ***(GERRY)*** **ARMSTRONG** *(1980-1983)*
b Belfast 23/5/1954
FL 50+26 (12), FAC 5+2 (2), FLC 5+2 (3), FLT 6+1 (2)
St Paul's Swifts; Cromac Albion; Bangor, Northern Ireland; Tottenham Hotspur (£25,000 11/75); Watford (£250,000 11/80); Real Mallorca, Spain (£200,000 8/83); West Bromwich Albion (free 8/85); Chesterfield (loan 1/86, free 3/86); Brighton & Hove Albion (free 8/86); Millwall (loan 1/87); Brighton & Hove Albion player-coach (cs 1988); Crawley Town player-coach (2/89 until 3/90); Glenavon (3/90); also Bromley for mid-week games (4/90); Worthing player-manager (11/91 until 1995); Sussex FA youth coach (3/96); also Northern Ireland national-team coach (from 1994)
NORTHERN IRELAND FULL
A powerful and direct forward whose performances in the 1982 World Cup Finals were internationally acclaimed. He scored Watford's first First Division goal, and was frequently used as an invigorating substitute. He left both Brighton and Crawley after uncharacteristic altercations with spectators, one of which led to a criminal conviction for assault.

Commanding pivot

James Harris ***(JIMMY)*** **ARMSTRONG** *(1933-1940)*
b Lemington, Northumberland 8/3/1904
d Watford, Herts 13/4/1971
FL 187 (2), FAC 14 (-), 3SC 15 (-), WW2 52 (-)
Easington Colliery; Clapton Orient (11/26); Queens Park Rangers (5/28); Watford (free 5/33 until 1941)
A tall, commanding centre-half who was prominent in Watford's good seasons in the late 1930s, he continued to turn out for the club regularly on the outbreak of war, but in 1941 took a job with Universal Asbestos, who employed him for the remaining 28 years of his working life. His brother Dick made a wartime guest appearance for the club.

Part Two

Walter Bedford (**WALLY**) **ARMSTRONG** *(1927)*
b Bolton, Lancs 1906
d Westbury, Wilts 24/9/1950
FL 1 (-)
Bolton Wanderers (am 3/27); Atherton; Watford (am 10/27, pro 11/27 until early 1928/9); Atherton; BTH (London) (permit player 10/34)
After coming south to join the club as an amateur, he was given a League chance at centre-forward in a 3-1 away defeat at Bristol Rovers. He was soon taken on the professional staff, but had no further first-team action. Although released at the end of the season, he was taken on trial briefly at the start of 1928/9, but nothing came of it.

League career soon over

Thomas Edwin **ASHBRIDGE** *(1913-1914)*
b Maryport, Cumberland 1890
d Newcastle-upon-Tyne, Northumberland 1964
SL 21 (9), FAC 2 (5)
Wallsend; Watford (5/13); Sheffield Utd (£350 5/14 until cs 1915)
This inside-forward scored five in an FA Cup tie (still the club's best haul), four for the Reserves two days later, and four against West Ham in a Southern League game. His sale to Sheffield United with Harry Pantling was forced by the need to raise money for summer wages. He was only a reserve at Bramall Lane, whilst Pantling became an England player.

Record scorer

BARRY *John* **ASHBY** *(1989-1994)*
b Park Royal, London 21/11/1970
FL 101+13 (3), FAC 4 (-), FLC 6 (-), FMC 0+1 (-), AIC 2 (-)
Middlesex Schools; London Schools; Parkfield; Watford (sch 10/85, tr 7/87, pro 12/88); Brentford (valued at £35,000 in part-exchange for K.D.Millen 3/94)
He formed an impressive centre-half pairing with Jason Soloman when Watford won the FA Youth Cup in 1988/9, having been associated with the club since he signed schoolboy forms at the age of 14. Some of his first-team experience was at full-back. His first League goal was one of seven scored against Bradford City in December 1989.

Excelled in Youth Cup

William George **ASHMOLE** *(1916-1920)*
b Winshill, Staffs 1892
d Burton-on-Trent, Staffs 1968
SL 1 (-), WW1 6 (3)
Burton; Stockport County (5/13 until cs 1915); Watford (9/19 until cs 1920). Guested for Watford and West Ham Utd in WW1.
In half a dozen appearances as a guest player during the First World War he made enough of an impact to be taken on the staff when normal footballing activities were resumed. His one Southern League game was at outside-right in a 3-0 defeat at Exeter. His wartime games were followed by selection for Colonel Blizzard's XI in May 1919.

Trouble with a dog

Charles Lane **(CHARLIE) ASTON** *(1905-1908)*
b Bilston, Staffs 1875
d Leytonstone, Essex 9/1/1931
SL 104 (1), FAC 6 (-), SEL 6 (-), UL 23 (-)
Bilston Utd; Walsall (12/95); Aston Villa (4/98); Queens Park Rangers (6/01); Burton Utd (8/02); Gresley Rovers (cs 1903); Burton Utd (6/04); Watford (5/05); Leyton (6/08)
His 13 games during Villa's League championship win of 1898/9 were due mainly to the illustrious Howard Spencer's absence through injury. Aston dominated the right-back position at Cassio Road and hardly missed a game in his three seasons, during which his wife was reprimanded for her behaviour when spoken to about bringing a dog into the ground.

Crossed the county

BRYAN *Herbert* **ATKINSON** *(1955-1956)*
b Saffron Walden, Essex 15/4/1934
d Hunsdon, Herts 10/8/1989
FL 20 (-), FAC 1 (-)
Bishops Stortford; Watford (am 1/54, pro 6/54); Folkestone (free 2/57 until at least 7/60)
He was doing his National Service and playing for Bishops Stortford when he signed amateur forms for Watford, and turned pro five months later, after being demobbed. A sturdy half-back, he left for Folkestone at the same time as Derrick Allen. He represented Herts in the 1953/4 Southern Counties Amateur Championship.

Tribunal nonsense

PAUL *Graham* **ATKINSON** *(1983-1984)*
b Otley, Yorks 14/8/1961
FL 8+3 (-), FAC 0+2 (-)
Yorkshire Schools; Oldham Athletic (appr 8/77, pro 8/79); Watford (£175,000 7/83); Oldham Athletic (£30,000 8/85); Swansea City (loan 12/86); Bolton Wanderers (loan 2/87); Swansea City (loan 3/87); Burnley (free 7/88 until cs 1990); Northwich Victoria (3/91); RUS Binchoise, Belgium (7/91); Altrincham (8/93); Frickley Athletic; Farsley Celtic (by 11/94)
A left-winger who broke an ankle at the start of his Watford career, which never got off the ground, although he did play as a substitute in the FA Cup Final - his last competitive game. Earlier a farcical transfer-tribunal decision, after the clubs had failed to agree on a fee, left Watford to pay more than Oldham had asked for in the first place.

DUNCAN *Stewart* **AULD** *(1897)*
b Govan, Lanarks 16/7/1878
d Staines, Middx 1911
SL 2 (-), FAC 1 (-)
Watford Church Institute; West Herts (1897/8)
Unlike the vast majority of his compatriots who have represented the club down the years, he was living and playing in the Watford area when he got the call from Cassio Road. A wing-half or forward, he was a member of the last all-amateur line-up to be fielded by the club in the Southern League. The game was at Uxbridge, and the home side won 2-0.

Part Two

A.W. **AYLING** *(1896-1897)*
West Herts (1896/7)
SL 3 (-), FAAC 1 (1)
A forward in the club's first season of Southern League football, he was on the losing side in each of his three games. He was also picked for an FA Amateur Cup tie, and scored in the 3-1 win against Bradfield Waifs - the club's last-ever victory in the competition. He was employed by André & Sleigh, the Bushey firm which became Sun Printers.

Ernest Frederick **BACON** *(1920-1921)*
b Leicester 19/2/1896
d Aylestone, Leics 9/1/1972
FL 12 (-)
St Andrews, Leicester; Leicester City (8/19); Watford (free 5/20); Charlton Athletic (free 7/21); Nuneaton Town (5/23); Barwell Utd (1924); Erith & Belvedere (1928); Callendar Athletic (1929). Guested for Coventry City in WW1.
ENGLAND SCHOOLS
Watford's right-half in their first Football League match, he was in and out of the side before being released at the end of the season, never having made more than three consecutive appearances. After winning schoolboy honours he had a longish wait for his peacetime début in senior football, which came when he was 23, once the Great War had finished.

Early schoolboy cap

GEORGE Huntly **BADENOCH** *(1903-1906)*
b Castle Douglas, Kirkcudbrightshire 9/4/1882
d Givenchy, France 15/6/1915
SL 80 (9), FAC 9 (1), SEL 22 (3), UL 14 (4)
Douglas Wanderers; Glossop (10/01); Watford (8/03); Tottenham Hotspur (5/06); Northampton Town (5/07 until cs 1909); Indian Head, Canada
John Goodall, when captain of Glossop, discovered him in Scotland. Badenoch was a popular wing-half at Watford, and later played on the right wing. His only Southern League game for Tottenham was against Watford. He emigrated to Canada, where he played football with Micky Wood, and was killed in the trenches whilst serving with a Canadian regiment.

War casualty

HerBERT Osborne **BADGER** *(1906-1908)*
b Islington, Middx 4/10/1882
d Colchester, Essex 1965
SL 54 (5), FAC 2 (-), SEL 2 (-), UL 11 (2)
Clacton Town; Colchester Town (one season); Ilford; Tottenham Hotspur (am 11/03); Woolwich Arsenal (pro 9/04); Watford (8/06); Brentford (7/08); Nottingham Forest (cs 1909); Brentford (12/10)
He didn't make the first team at Arsenal, but was a senior player for the greater part of his two Watford seasons, mainly as a long-striding wing-half. He later had a couple of First Division games during his Forest spell. An accomplished violinist, he was wounded in a shooting accident near Clacton in December 1932.

Accomplished fiddler

Two Division 2 titles

John James **BAGSHAW** *(1921)*
b Derby 25/12/1885
d Nottingham 25/8/1966
FL 14 (-)
Fletcher's Utd; Graham Street Primitives; Derby County (10/06); Notts County (2/20); Watford (£200 5/21); Ilkeston Utd (free, cs 1922); Grantham; Nottingham Forest, Notts County and Coventry City scout, and Nottingham Forest training staff (WW2). Guested for Notts County in WW1.
ENGLAND FULL
That long period at the Baseball Ground encompassed two Second Division championships, in the first of which he was one of five participants who were past or future Watford players. He'd played anywhere in the half-back line, but at Watford was used only as the pivot. He played twice for England (including an 'unofficial' Victory International) at 33.

Returned to score goals

DENNIS *Lincoln* **BAILEY** *(1994)*
b Lambeth, London 13/11/1965
FL 2+6 (4)
Watford (youth team and Reserves 1982 until 1984); Barking; Fulham (non-contract 11/86); Farnborough Town (2/87); Crystal Palace (£10,000 12/87); Bristol Rovers (loan 2/89); Birmingham City (£80,000 8/89); Bristol Rovers (loan 3/91); Queens Park Rangers £175,000 7/91); Charlton Athletic (loan 10/93); Watford (loan 3/94); Brentford (loan 1/95); Gillingham (£25,000 8/95)
He had two seasons in the youth team and a few reserve-team games, but was 28 before he played in Watford's first team, scoring valuable goals on loan during a successful fight against relegation, including one in each of three successive games as a substitute. Easily the high point of his career was a hat-trick for Queens Park Rangers at Old Trafford.

Theatrical connections

Alfred **GUTHRIE BAKER** (1897-1900)
b Camberwell, Surrey 25/12/1871
d Watford, Herts 11/10/1945
SL 51 (-), FAC 9 (-), BCCL 16 (-)
Old Wilsonians (until cs 1897); Clapham Rovers; Bowes Park; Upton Park; Vampires; Old St Stephens; Watford St Mary's; Watford (am 1897); Harrow Athletic (by 11/01)
A goalkeeper who played for both Surrey and Herts and was a familiar figure on the amateur circuit in and around London. He had connections with music-hall greats, his sister having married Harry Tate and Baker himself having trodden the boards as a young man with George Robey. In later years he was well-known in Watford as a dog breeder and exhibitor.

James Seymour **(JIMMY) BAKER** *(1925-1926)*
b Aston Clinton, Bucks 24/11/1897
d Hemel Hempstead, Herts 13/4/1975
FL 9 (2)
Aylesbury; Wycombe Wanderers; Watford (am 8/24, pro

11/24); Wolverton Town (free 7/26)
A versatile performer who played at wing-half, centre-half and inside-forward in his occasional first-team games at Vicarage Road. His two goals contributed to narrow victories against Merthyr Town and Bristol Rovers, but he was less successful on two visits to Exeter City, where he suffered defeat by 4-0 and - in his final League game - 6-1.

Bad trips to Devon

John David **(DAVE) BAMBER** *(1988)*
b Huyton, Lancs 1/2/1959
FL 16+2 (3), FLC 2 (1), FMC 2 (-)
Leicester University; Blackpool (9/79); Coventry City (£50,000 6/83); Walsall (£20,000 3/84); Portsmouth (free 12/84); Swindon Town (loan 11/85, £12,500 3/86); Watford (£105,000 6/88); Stoke City (£240,000 12/88); Hull City (£130,000 2/90); Blackpool (loan 11/90, £25,000 1/91 until cs 1995)
He turned pro after representing Britain in the World Student Games in Mexico. A tall forward who possessed more all-round skill than most players of his height, he fetched a healthy profit for Watford on becoming one of several men purchased and then quickly sold by Steve Harrison. He scored heavily after rejoining Blackpool, well into his thirties.

Represented Britain

Herbert Ernest **(BERTIE) BANKS** *(1903-1904)*
b Coventry, Warwicks 1874
d Smethwick, Staffs 1947
SL 19 (21), FAC 2 (1), SEL 11 (11)
72nd Seaforth Highlanders; Everton (10/96); St Mirren (1/97); Everton (2/97); Third Lanark (cs 1897); Millwall (3/99); Aston Villa (4/01); Bristol City (11/01); Watford (5/03); Coventry City (7/04); Stafford Rangers (12/05); Verity's Athletic (10/06); reinstated am (5/07 until 1910/1)
ENGLAND FULL
Although once reported for being drunk during a game, he shared with Harry Barton over a hundred goals in all games in 1903/4, and no Watford player can equal his career record of more than a goal a game in Southern League/Football League matches. He had twice helped his regiment to victory in the Simla Cup in India, and later played once for England.

Unequalled scoring rate

William George **(BILL) BARBER** *(1957-1960)*
b Bushey, Herts 19/9/1939
FL 25 (-), FAC 1 (-), SFC 2 (-)
Watford Schools; Watford (am 7/56, pro 3/57); Aldershot (free 8/62); Hillingdon Borough; Amersham; Melbourne George Cross, Australia (2/67)
A sturdy wing-half who developed in local schools football and was in the club's first team at 17, but who failed to stay the course, making only six of his League appearances, plus one for Aldershot, after his 19th birthday. His professional service was as a part-timer, and he spent his last two seasons with the club as a National Serviceman.

Promise unfulfilled

Good day at Chelsea

DAVID John **BARDSLEY** *(1983-1987)*
b Manchester, Lancs 11/9/64
FL 97+3 (7), FAC 13+1 (1), FLC 6 (1), FMC 1 (-)
Coventry City (sch 1/79 until 4/81)); Blackpool (sch 5/81, appr 7/81, pro 11/82); Watford (£150,000 11/83); Oxford Utd (£250,000 9/87); Queens Park Rangers (valued at £500,000 in player-exchange 9/89)
ENGLAND YOUTH and FULL
A long-striding full-back of great pace who was ever-present in the FA Cup run to Wembley. He scored the first two League goals of his career in his 100th appearance, as a substitute in a 5-1 win at Chelsea. His England Youth manager was Graham Taylor, who then signed him for Watford and another nine years on capped him at senior level.

Cecil **BARNARD** *(1921)*
FL 2 (1)
Cubitts; Aylesbury Utd; Rotherham County (trial 9/21); Watford (am 11/21)
As a trialist he scored six times in a reserve-team friendly against Amersham, and was signed on amateur forms a few weeks later. He went straight into the first team at centre-forward, scored on his League début in a 2-1 win against Charlton Athletic, and played in the return fixture a week later, but was never picked again.

Made history at Luton

C. **BARNES** *(1904-1906)*
b Chesham, Bucks, circa 1879
SL 5 (1), FAC 1 (1), SEL 2 (-), UL 1 (-)
Chesham Generals (by 11/99); Chesham Town; Reading (3/00); Bristol City (6/02); Watford (free 8/04 until cs 1906)
Essentially a reserve-team player during his two seasons at Cassio Road, he made spasmodic appearances in the senior side, performing in either of the wing positions. His two first-team goals contributed to handsome victories (7-1 and 5-1) and for the Reserves he recorded the first goal ever scored at Luton Town's Kenilworth Road ground.

Forgotten man

DAVID **BARNES** *(1994-1996)*
b Paddington, London 16/11/1961
FL 16 (-), FAC 1 (-)
Coventry City (appr 8/78, pro 5/79); Ipswich Town (free 5/82); Wolverhampton Wanderers (£35,000 10/84); Aldershot (£25,000 8/87); Sheffield Utd (£50,000 7/89); Watford (£60,000 1/94 until cs 1996)
ENGLAND YOUTH
He'd been a League pro for 15 years when he was signed to solve a left-back problem arising from Jason Drysdale's lengthy absence through injury. Barnes's own Watford career became dominated by injury, which rendered him something of a forgotten man for long periods. He helped England to win the UEFA International Youth Tournament in 1980.

Part Two

Edward **BARNES** *(1920)*
SL 1 (-)
Tibshelf Colliery; Watford (am late-1912/3); Croxley Green (1913); Southend Utd (am 7/20); Charlton Athletic (am 8/21); Queens Park Rangers (am 6/22)
An amateur goalkeeper whose one Southern League outing came seven years after his association with the club began. Deputising on the occasion of one of Skilly Williams's rare absences, he took part in a 1-0 defeat at Norwich. A few months earlier he'd made his only other first-team appearance, helping the club to a 3-1 win in a benefit match at Luton.

GEORGE Henry **BARNES** *(1919-1924)*
b Chesham, Bucks 22/5/1899
d Chesham, Bucks 1/6/1961
FL 5 (1), WW1 1 (1)
Chesham Utd; Watford (am 4/19); Brentford (am 3/30); Chesham Utd chairman (by 9/32)
Well-known in his home town both as a footballer and a boot manufacturer, he was Chesham United's left-winger for many years, including a lengthy spell as club captain, and later became its chairman. He also played for the Berks & Bucks representative side, and for the Spartan League. His brother Maurice was killed in a game in which they both played.

Footballing tragedy

John Benjamin (JACK) **BARNES** *(1931-1933)*
b Atherstone, Warwicks 1908
FL 75 (11), FAC 8 (-)
Atherstone Town; Coventry City (3/28); Walsall (6/29); Watford (7/31); Exeter City (£100 6/33); York City (8/34); Atherstone Town (7/35); Wilstaff Sports, Birmingham (permit player 11/36)
He held the outside-left position throughout his two seasons at Vicarage Road, with Harry Lowe as his regular inside partner, before being transfer-listed with a fee of £300 on his head. This was reduced by the Football League on appeal, and Exeter City took him on at the revised figure. He'd been a miner before taking up the game professionally.

Knock-down price

JOHN Charles Bryan **BARNES** *(1981-1987)*
b Kingston, Jamaica 7/11/1963
FL 232+1 (65 inc 1p), FAC 31 (11), FLC 21 (7), FLT 4 (2), UEFA 6 (-), FMC 1 (-)
Sudbury Court; Watford (7/81); Liverpool (£900,000 6/87)
ENGLAND UNDER-21 and FULL; FOOTBALL LEAGUE
He rose rapidly from parks football to Watford's first team, Full caps at 19 and a famous solo goal in Rio. Always conducting himself with dignity, he often disappointed in a very long international career, but at club level reached great heights of personal and collective achievement. His ball-skills and athleticism were by used mainly on the left wing by Watford.

Great heights

Call-up held him back

PETER ***BARNES*** *(1960-1962)*
b St Albans, Herts 29/6/1938
FL 10 (-)
Sun Sports Juniors; Watford (am 7/56); Hemel Hempstead Town; Watford (pro 3/57 until cs 1963); Banbury Utd (by cs 1966); Hatfield Town
A local wing-half who came through the youth team and then served as a part-time pro, being employed in the printing trade. National Service interfered with his progress, but he eventually had two short spells in the first team. As a junior he'd played in the South-East Counties League representative side with Micky Benning and Chelsea's Jimmy Greaves.

Major Watford player

Thomas Andrew ***(TOMMY) BARNETT*** *(1928-1944)*
b Salford, Lancs 11/11/1908
d Watford, Herts 9/7/1986
FL 395 (144), FAC 36 (16), 3SC 11 (3), WW2 99 (26)
Longsight; Manchester Utd (10/27); Watford (free 5/28 until 3/43); Scammells (1941/2); Watford Reserves (reinstated am until 1947/8)
Mainly a creator for others, this gifted inside-forward, who was never entrusted with a penalty, nevertheless hit more goals for the club than anyone except Luther Blissett. He was content to see out his career at Watford, despite obvious potential for a higher grade of football. As a masseur he later served the Wembley Lions speedway and ice-hockey teams.

Spanned the Great War

Robert John ***(BOB) BARNSHAW*** *(1914-1921)*
b Hebburn, Co Durham 14/3/1889
d Watford, Herts 30/1/1974
SL 46 (3), FL 12 (1), FAC 3 (-)
Hebburn Argyle; Sheffield Wednesday (11/10); Hebburn Argyle; Sheffield Utd (£80 5/13); Watford (£50 5/14); Aberdare Athletic (free 6/21 until cs 1922). Guested for Darlington and Leeds City in WW1.
One of five Hebburn players transferred simultaneously to Bramall Lane, he was a centre-half for whom Watford were due to pay another £75 if they engaged him for a second season. The intervention of the Great War probably meant that this was forgotten. He played eleven times in the club's Southern League championship win in 1914/5.

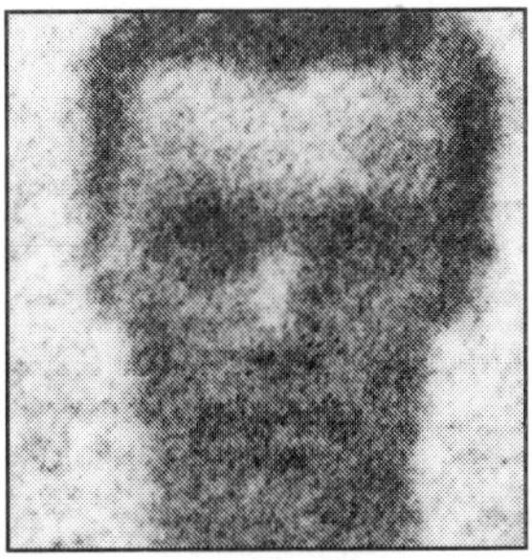
Stand-in defender

Ernest ***BARSBY*** *(1909-1910)*
b Stanton, Derbys 1886
SL 4 (-)
Overseal; Burton Utd (am 8/06); Midway Albion (pro 1/07); Birmingham (5/08); Watford (8/09 until cs 1910)
After a season in Birmingham's reserve team, he made four appearances for Watford as a stand-in defender in the 1909/10 season, in which team changes were a conspicuous feature. Twice he filled in at right-half, once at centre-half, and once at left-back. Only six goals were conceded in the four games, but these were thrice the number scored.

FRANK **BARSON** *(1928)*
b Sheffield, Yorks 10/4/1891
d Birmingham, Warwicks 13/9/1968
FL 10 (1)
Albion, Sheffield; Cammell Laird, Sheffield; Barnsley (7/11); Aston Villa (£2,700 10/19); Manchester Utd (£5,000 8/22); Watford (free 5/28); Hartlepools Utd (free 5/29); Wigan Borough (7/30); Rhyl Athletic player-manager (6/31); Stourbridge manager (7/35); Aston Villa coach (10/35 until WW2); Swansea Town trainer (cs 1947 until cs 1954); Lye Town trainer (9/54 until 1956)
ENGLAND FULL
A powerful centre-half, renowned for his brushes with authority, which may well be why he failed to win more than one England cap. Soon after joining Watford he was sent off and banned for the rest of the season, both decisions owing a great deal to his reputation and little to the incident which provoked them. Massive petitions for justice were rejected.

Enemy of authority

HARRY **BARTON** *(1903-1905)*
b Northwich, Cheshire 1874
d Northwich, Cheshire 6/2/1954
SL 34 (26), FAC 5 (-), SEL 18 (17)
Castle True Blues (circa 1895); Fairfield (am 11/96); Grimsby Town (pro 9/97 until 12/97); reinstated am (5/98); Witton Albion; Middlewich Athletic Rangers (by 1902/3); Northwich Victoria; Watford (pro 8/03 until cs 1905); Witton Albion (2/06 until at least 1908/9)
He shared a bucketful of goals with Bertie Banks *en route* to the Southern League Second Division championship in 1903/4, and himself scored six in one game. His Watford career ended after a series of club suspensions for, *inter alia*, drunkenness and, finally, making no effort whatever in a reserve game. He was a prize-winning middle-distance runner.

Goals and indiscipline

Edward John (TED) **BASSETT** *(1919-1921)*
b Deptford, London 1/1/1889
d Watford, Herts 25/11/1970
SL 37 (6), FL 33 (3), FAC 3 (-)
Deptford Invicta; Dartford (1/09); Croydon Common (trial 9/09); Metrogas (10/09); Charlton Albion (1910); Millwall (11/11); Newark Stanley Works (1912); Dartford (cs 1912); Notts County (9/13); Watford (6/19); Luton Town (£200 6/21); Dartford (8/22); Fordsons, Cork; Finchley (11/30). Guested for Fulham and Tottenham Hotspur in WW1.
He won a Second Division championship medal with Notts County before spending two seasons as a small and tricky crowd-pleasing character on Watford's right wing. After moving to Luton Town he was reported to the League for demanding, in writing, a share of the transfer fee. He settled in Watford, and for a time ran a snooker club in the town.

Tricks on the wing

Followed his brother

COLIN **BATEMAN** *(1954-1957)*
b Hemel Hempstead, Herts 22/10/1930
FL 50 (-), FAC 6 (-)
Hemel Hempstead Town; Watford (3/53); Sittingbourne (7/58)
The younger of two brothers, he both arrived at and left Vicarage Road a year after Ernie, whom he followed from and to the same clubs. A fair-haired right-back with a powerful kick, Colin had good runs in the first team, but then played only twice in two seasons after becoming a part-timer, at the same time as his brother, in 1956.

Hemel defender

Ernest (ERNIE) **BATEMAN** *(1955-1956)*
b Hemel Hempstead, Herts 5/4/1929
FL 23 (-), FAC 1 (-), SFC 1 (-)
Hemel Hempstead Town; Watford (3/52); Sittingbourne (free 8/57); Hemel Hempstead Utd joint-coach (10/60)
A tall centre-half who, like his brother Colin, became one of the many Watford players of the 1950s who ended their careers in the Kent League. He later joined Hemel Hempstead United to become joint-coach with former Vicarage Road colleague Frank Jackett. The Batemans were the last brothers for over thirty years to play League football for Watford.

Christmas gift from Luton

William Henry (BILLY) **BATES** *(1942-1949)*
b Eaton Bray, Beds 13/1/1922
FL 13 (1), WW2 1 (-)
Waterlows; Luton Town (am 5/39, pro 9/41); Watford (7/48 until cs 1949); Dunstable Town (by 10/55). Guested for Watford in WW2.
His Watford début was on Christmas Day 1942 - six years before he joined the club - when, as a Luton Town player, he was loaned to the visitors when they turned up at Kenilworth Road a man short. He played on both wings in his first-team run at Watford, at a time when things were not going well. Only two of his games were won, and eight lost.

Good times at Ipswich

William Alexander (BILL) **BAXTER** *(1971-1972)*
b Edinburgh 23/4/1939
FL 11 (-), FLC 1 (-)
Broxburn Athletic (7/57); Ipswich Town (£500 6/60); Hull City (£12,500 3/71); Watford (loan 10/71); Northampton Town (free 6/72, player-manager 10/72 until 5/73); Nuneaton Borough (10/73 until 1975)
A tough and accomplished defensive half-back who won a First and two Second Division championship medals with Ipswich Town, where he later came to blows with Bobby Robson as the latter set about establishing his authority early in his managerial career. Baxter's three-months loan period at Watford was during the disastrous 1971/2 season.

John Thomas **BAYLEY** *(1900)*
SL 4 (-), BCCL 2 (-)
Walsall Swifts (1887); Small Heath (1890); Walsall Town Swifts (7/93); Gainsborough Trinity (6/95); Small Heath (8/99); Watford (3/00 until cs 1900); Leamington Town
A late-season signing, he was transferred in time to take part in the run-in to the Southern League Second Division championship, being used at centre-half and in both full-back positions in his four games in the competition. He'd earlier been a first-team regular for several years with Gainsborough Trinity in the Second Division of the Football League.

Helped in title win

DARREN Shaun **BAZELEY** *(1990-1996)*
b Northampton 5/10/1972
FL 99+44 (13), FAC 7+1 (-), FLC 9+4 (2), FMC 1+1 (-), AIC 2 (-)
Watford (sch 12/86); Northamptonshire Schools; Watford (tr 7/89, pro 5/91)
ENGLAND UNDER-21
Given his League début whilst still a trainee, he was one of the dozen youngest players who have represented the club in competitive first-team football. Although originally a sprightly right-winger and occasional striker, he became a full-back under Glenn Roeder after five months out of action following an injury sustained in the opening game of 1993/4.

Converted to full-back

Thomas Henry (TUGGY) **BEACH** *(1897-1902)*
b Uxbridge, Middx 20/2/1872
d Watford, Herts, February 1940
SL 40 (16 inc 1p), FAC 9 (2 inc 1p), BCCL 12 (4)
Uxbridge Caxtonians; Southall; Uxbridge (9/92); Polytechnic (11/93); Uxbridge (4/94); West Herts (pro 11/97 until cs 1900, and 9/02 until cs 1903)
A popular centre-half at Uxbridge, he became one of the first professionals at Cassio Road, where he began as a goalscoring forward and was later used in various defensive positions. After a two-and-a-half- year gap he reappeared for an isolated FA Cup replay in 1902. Of his nine footballing sons, the eldest and youngest were both League professionals.

Nine footballing sons

PETER Clifford William James **BEADLE** *(1994-1995)*
b Lambeth, London 13/5/1972
FL 12+11 (1), FLC 1 (-)
Lordswood Boys' Club, Chatham; Gillingham (sch 12/86, tr 7/88, pro 5/90); Tottenham Hotspur (£300,000 6/92); AFC Bournemouth (loan 3/93); Southend Utd (loan 3/94); Watford (£5,000 plus 20% of 'sell-on' profit 9/94); Bristol Rovers (£40,000 11/95, plus possible additional payment)
A big-money transfer to a top club held the promise of great things, but his career came to a complete halt at White Hart Lane, where his first-team experience amounted to a few friendlies. At Vicarage Road this big striker was dropped for good after 24 Watford appearances. A 25th would have cost the club a further £20,000 under the transfer agreement.

Cost Spurs £300,000

Well-known local player

ROGER John **BEAMENT** *(1957)*
b Croxley, Herts 28/9/1937
FL 1 (-)
Watford Schools; Croxley Boys Club; Watford (am 5/55); Tring Town (12/57); Hemel Hempstead Utd (7/60); Wealdstone; St Albans City; Tudor Corinthians; Croxley Casuals; Watford College of Technology (by 4/77); Rolls Royce
For many years his burly frame was a familiar sight in goal at various levels of the amateur game locally, after he'd played in one League match as a 19-year-old, being beaten four times in Watford's final game of 1956/7, away to Bournemouth. He'd earlier made representative appearances locally as a schoolboy, and also at youth level for the county.

Blackpool manager

SYDney **BEAUMONT** *(1909-1911)*
b Wrestlingworth, Beds 8/10/1883
d Southport, Lancs 12/5/1939
SL 27 (1), SCC 3 (3)
Biggleswade; Colchester Town; Lincoln City (am 11/04, pro 12/04); Biggleswade & District FC (9/06); Watford (9/09); Preston North End (£25 7/11); Merthyr Town (free, cs 1912); Troedyrhiw (cs 1913); Barry manager (8 years); Llanelly (secretary, then manager 5/24); Aberdare Athletic manager (cs 1924); Blackpool manager (6/27 until 5/28); Chester assistant-trainer (1936 until death)
After scoring twice on his Watford début, in the Southern Charity Cup, he was in and out of the side for two seasons as a wing-half or forward, before moving to Preston, who gave him one First Division game. He played in Chelsea's pre-season trial matches in 1907, shortly after applying unsuccessfully for reinstatement as an amateur.

Waited over six years

William (BILL) **BECKETT** *(1945-1947)*
b Liverpool, Lancs 4/7/1915
FL 7 (1), FAC 8 (1), WW2 18 (6)
Litherland; New Brighton (am 6/34, pro 11/34); Tranmere Rovers (6/36 until 9/36); South Liverpool; Blackpool (4/37); Bradford City (7/38); Watford (free 5/39); Northampton Town (free 6/47 until cs 1948). Guested for South Liverpool and Walsall in WW2.
After joining the club he had to wait over six years for his début, first of all in games which were still being played under wartime-league conditions in 1945/6, and then in the FA Cup when it resumed in earnest in the same season. An inside-forward, he made 22 appearances in his first season of League football, for New Brighton, but very few thereafter.

MARTIN **BECTON** *(1909-1910)*
b Preston, Lancs 1883
d Fulwood, Lancs 18/4/1965
SL 20 (2), FAC 1 (-), SCC 3 (-)

Christ Church, Preston; Lytham; Preston North End (8/06); Nelson (8/08); Watford (7/09 until cs 1910)
A right-winger or inside-right who, after helping Lytham to win the Lancs Amateur Cup, played in the First Division for Preston, as had his brother (an England international) some years earlier. He married the sister of another England man who was his rival for a first-team place at Deepdale. Transfer-listed by Watford after one season, he didn't re-sign.

England connections

John ***BELL*** *(1924-1926)*
b Tannochside, Lanarks
FL 20 (6), FAC 1 (-)
Ashfield; Dundee (10/19); Albion Rovers (7/22); Hamilton Academical (2/23); Albion Rovers (4/23); Newport County (7/23); Watford (free 7/24); Arbroath (free 7/26 until cs 1927)
He played army football during the Great War, and then scored freely through four seasons in the Scottish First Division. At Watford a useful start at centre- or inside-forward was not maintained, and a broken toe suffered in mid-season did nothing to help. When he left the club he'd made only two League appearances in the last season-and-a-half.

Heavy-scorer in Scotland

Robert McDicken ***(BOBBY) BELL*** *(1957-1964)*
b Ayr 16/9/1934
FL 268 (2), FAC 23 (-), SFC 3 (-), FLC 9 (-)
Whitletts Victoria (am 7/53); Falkirk (pro 8/54); Ayr Utd (free 5/56); Watford (free 5/57); Folkestone (free 7/65 until cs 1969); Wealdstone; Rolls Royce (permit player 10/69, reserve-team manager by 7/79); Leverstock Green coach (by 10/81); Mill End coach (6/88); Hammer (Sunday football) trainer (by 1992)
Released by Bob Shankly at both Falkirk and Ayr, and signed by Neil McBain for both Ayr and Watford, he was a curly, fair-haired and determined right-back who, for more than seven seasons, was rarely absent from the first team, until new manager Ken Furphy took the No 2 shirt himself. Bell's father had been an Ayr United professional.

Seven good seasons

*Her****BERT BELLAMY*** *(1921-1923)*
b Kettering, Northants 6/4/1896
d Grimsby, Lincs 1978
FL 36 (2), FAC 1 (-)
Kettering White Cross (before WW1); Kettering Town (1919); Watford (free 5/21); Swansea Town (free 6/23); Brentford (5/26); Wellingborough player-manager (6/27); United Counties Bus Co, Irthlingborough (permit player 2/28); Kidderminster Harriers (8/28)
Having developed in army football, he joined Kettering on being demobbed. He performed outstandingly as a left-half at the start of his Watford career, but his form soon fell away and he was in and out of the side for the remainder of his two seasons at Vicarage Road. In the Fifties he kept a pub in the Folkestone area.

Form fell away

Olympic competitor

Edward Ernest (TED) ***BENNETT*** *(1953-1956)*
b Kilburn, Middx 22/8/1925
FL 81 (-), FAC 5 (-)
Southall; Queens Park Rangers (am 2/49); Southall; Watford (pro 12/53); Gravesend & Northfleet ("small fee" 9/56)
ENGLAND and GREAT BRITAIN AMATEUR
After winning eleven England Amateur caps and keeping Great Britain's goal in the 1952 Olympics, he immediately became Watford's first choice on turning professional, when Dave Underwood left for Liverpool. From his début, Bennett missed only one League game in 86 before breaking a finger early in 1955/6. He went on the 1955 FA tour of the West Indies.

Holton's wing partner

Michael David (MICKY) ***BENNING*** *(1959-1962)*
b Croxley Green, Herts 3/2/1938
FL 103 (14), FAC 14 (1), FLC 5 (-)
Watford Schools; Luton Town (am 5/55 until 8/55); Croxley Boys Club; Watford (am 7/56, pro 9/56); Cambridge City (7/62); Bedford Town (6/64 - Watford received £200); Dunstable Town; Hatfield Town (by 4/68); Tudor Corinthians (1/70, later manager); Ambassadors
He attracted much attention as a pacy part-time right-winger (he was employed in the print industry) for his contribution to the Holton/Uphill goalscoring exploits. Transfer talk came to nothing, but Watford listed him at £7,500 and retained his Football League registration when he went to Cambridge City, whom he helped to the Southern League championship.

Cost Newcastle £150

ARTHUR Charles ***BETTS*** *(1907-1910)*
b Scunthorpe, Lincs 2/1/1886
d Scunthorpe, Lincs 1967
SL 93 (-), FAC 7 (-), SEL 2 (-), SCC 3 (-)
North Lindsey; Gainsborough Trinity (5/05); Watford (5/07); Gainsborough Trinity (free 5/10); Newcastle Utd (£150, of which Watford received a share, 6/11); Derby County (10/11); Hull City (5/14); Scunthorpe & Lindsey Utd (6/20); Normanby Park Steelworks player-coach (5/23); Lysaght Sports coach
Showing a fair turn of speed, he had three good seasons as Joe Brooks's replacement at left-back, after representing Lincolnshire. He left Newcastle without having made the first team, but settled in immediately at the Baseball Ground and won a Second Division championship medal in 1911/2. He was a stonemason by trade.

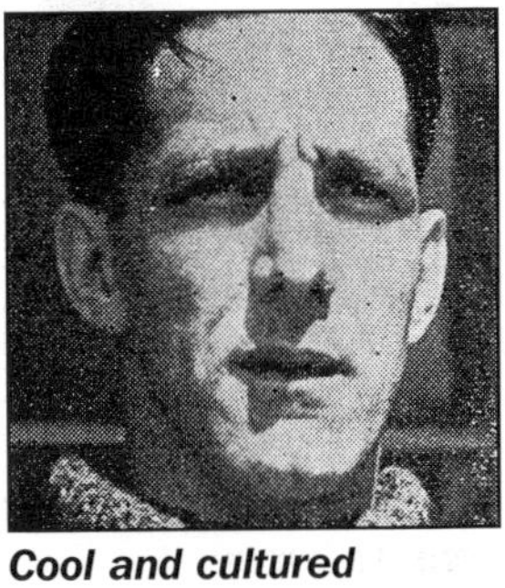
Cool and cultured

David George (DAVE) ***BEWLEY*** *(1953-1956)*
b Bournemouth, Hants 22/9/1920
FL 113 (1), FAC 7 (-)
Bournemouth Schools; Poole Town (am); Bournemouth & Boscombe Athletic (pro 9/37 until cs 1939); Gravesend; Fulham (5/45); Reading (3/50); Fulham (11/50); Watford (£500 5/53); Folkestone (free 6/56); Hemel Hempstead Town coach (10/57 until 1/59); Fulham scout (4/63). Guested for Aldershot and Southampton in WW2.
Although considered for international honours as a

schoolboy, he was 26 before he played League football. Ever-present in his first two seasons at Vicarage Road, he was a cool, cultured full-back. He also captained Oxhey Cricket Club, and after leaving full-time football was employed by Kodak at Hemel Hempstead for 26 years.

*William (**BILLY**)* **BIGGAR** *(1904-1910)*
*(formerly William **BIGGERS**)*
b Mexborough, Yorks 16/10/1874
d Croydon, Surrey 11/7/1935
SL 217 (1p), FAC 17 (-), SEL 16 (-), UL 29 (1p), SCC 4 (-)
Birtley (pro 3/00); Sheffield Utd (3/00); West Ham Utd (5/02); Fulham (cs 1903); Watford (5/04); Rochdale (5/10 until cs 1917, trainer from 8/16); Leyland Motors (1919/20)
A goalkeeping giant, in every sense, of the Southern League era, he made a club-record number of appearances in that competition and was captain for 15 months. In 1909 he performed the extraordinary feat of both scoring and saving a penalty in the same Southern League match. He'd earlier understudied the celebrated Fatty Foulke at Bramall Lane.

Amazing penalty feat

*Charles Roy (**CHARLIE**)* **BILLINGTON** *(1957)*
b Chesterfield, Derbys 8/11/1927
d Newbold, Derbys 19/11/1985
FL 14 (-), FAC 1 (-), SFC 2 (-)
Chesterfield (am); Aldershot (am 6/46, pro 12/46); Norwich City (1/56); Watford (6/57); Mansfield Town ("small fee" 6/58 until 1/59); Burton Albion (5/59)
His nine seasons with Aldershot, whom he joined from army football, encompassed over two hundred League appearances. A big, old-fashioned centre-half, he announced himself at Vicarage Road by being awarded the captaincy and then getting himself sent off on his début, at Bournemouth. All his League experience was at Third Division level.

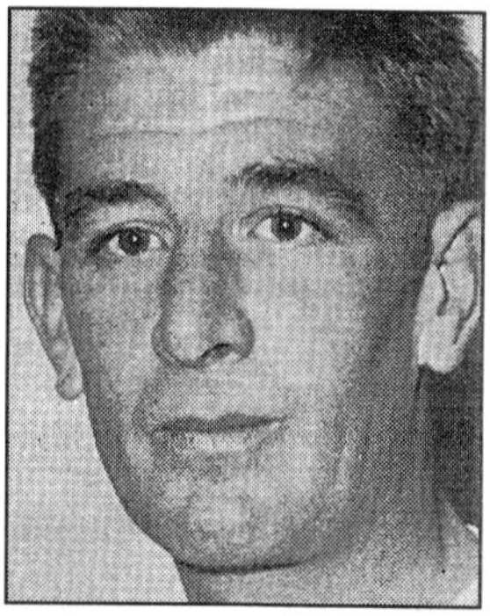
Ignominious start

CHARLIE *Duncan Valentine* **BIRSE** *(1946-1947)*
b Dundee, Angus 26/10/1916
FL 7 (-), FAC 2 (-)
Broughty Ex-Service (am 5/35, pro 5/35); Hibernian (3/37); Watford (5/46); Northampton Town (free 7/47 until cs 1948). Guested for Darlington and Middlesbrough in WW2.
SCOTLAND JUNIOR
He spent the war years on Hibs' books, having attracted their attention and won Junior honours when playing closer to home. He was a tall centre-half, but with Les Farnen monopolising the No 5 shirt he was used only at right-half and on the right wing in the first team at Vicarage Road, and was unable to command a regular place.

Nine years with Hibs

*William (**BILL**)* **BLACK** *(1937-1938)*
b Airdrie, Lanarks 15/1/1916
FL 16 (3), 3SC 4 (4)
Airdrieonians (8/32); Blantyre Victoria (free 8/33); Wishaw (6/34); Hibernian (10/34); Watford (free 5/37); Dunfermline Athletic ("small fee" 10/38 until cs 1946)

Scored 4 in a cup tie

Although small for a centre-forward, he went straight into the first team after moving south. He later scored four in a Division 3 (South) Cup tie against Notts County, but this was more than half his tally in 20 games. After refusing terms for a second season, he was transferred back to Scotland. His brother Dick played centre-forward for Manchester United.

Released twice

<u>ALBERT</u> <u>George</u> ***<u>BLAKE</u>*** *(1929-1933)*
b Fulham, London
FL 28 (-), FAC 1 (-)
Fulham (5/28); <u>Watford</u> (free 7/29); Queens Park Rangers (free 8/33); Tunbridge Wells Rangers (8/36)
The latter part of his Vicarage Road career followed a strange pattern, in that he was re-engaged for 1932/3 after being given a free transfer, recalled for the final game of the season after two years out of the first team, and then released again (for good) immediately afterwards. A wing-half who looked classy in distribution, he was less proficient when defending.

Emergency signing

<u>George PATrick</u> ***<u>BLAND</u>*** *(1945-1946)*
b Tutbury, Staffs 24/2/1915
d Peterborough, Northants 1970
FAC 1 (-), WW2 1 (-)
Horncastle Town; Lincoln City (am 5/36, pro 6/36); Bradford Park Avenue (5/38 until 12/38); <u>Watford</u> (free 1/39); Ransome & Marles (free, cs 1946 until 4/47); Spalding Utd. Guested for Notts County in WW2.
A tall goalkeeper who was an emergency signing - at first on a month's trial - to understudy the promoted Jock McHugh following injury to Jim McLaren. He made his début seven years later, in the club's first post-war FA Cup tie, and subsequently made his only other first-team appearance in one of the competitions played under wartime conditions.

Records galore

<u>LUTHER Loide</u> ***<u>BLISSETT</u>*** *(1976-1992)*
b Falmouth, Jamaica 1/2/1958
FL 369+46 (148 inc 22p), FAC 32+2 (15 inc 2p), FLC 41+3 (17 inc 2p), FLT 8 (6 inc 2p), FMC 1+1 (-)
<u>Watford</u> (youth team, pro 6/75); AC Milan, Italy (£1 million 6/83); <u>Watford</u> (£550,000 8/84); AFC Bournemouth (£60,000 11/88); <u>Watford</u> (£40,000 8/91); West Bromwich Albion (loan 10/92); Wimborne Town (free 7/93); Bury (free 8/93); Derry City (free 10/93); Bury (11/93); Mansfield Town (loan 12/93); Southport (loan 3/94); Fakenham Town (free 7/94 until 2/96); also <u>Watford</u> marketing assistant (6/95); <u>Watford</u> (joint-coach 2/96, assistant-manager 5/96)
ENGLAND UNDER-21, 'B' and FULL
Unsurpassed in popularity, he epitomised Graham Taylor's Watford with a combination of attacking flair and athleticism which brought him 14 Full caps and a major transfer to Italy. Although not always used as an outright striker, he set a string of goalscoring and appearance records, both for the club and among black players in English football.

Michael John (MIKE) **BLOCK** *(1966-1967)*
b Ipswich, Suffolk 28/1/1940
FL 11+2 (2)
Chelsea (am 5/55, pro 2/57); Brentford (1/62); Watford (10/66); Chelmsford City (free 7/67)
ENGLAND YOUTH
After playing in the League whilst on two months' trial, he was taken on for the remainder of the season, but not retained. A left-winger, he'd been one of the clutch of England Youth internationals produced by Chelsea in the mid-1950s, and played in the First Division before enoying the bulk of his League experience with Brentford.

Chelsea production-line

Alfred **BLYTH** *(1896-1897)*
b Norwood, Surrey 6/8/1878
d Watford, Herts 26/2/1958
SL 3 (-)
West Herts (1896/7)
He played at left-back on three isolated occasions in the club's first season of Southern League football, including the opening away game in the competition - a 3-2 defeat at Chesham. His brother Reuben was in the team on each occasion. Only seven other pairs of brothers have lined up together in a Watford eleven in the Southern and Football Leagues.

REUBEN **BLYTH** *(1895-1897)*
b Bromley-by-Bow, Middx 26/1/1872
d Watford, Herts 10/4/1953
SL 18 (-), FAC 2 (-), FAAC 4 (-), HSC 2 (-)
West Herts (1894/5 until cs 1897); also Bushey Grove (1895/6); also Queens Park Rangers; also Watford St Mary's (1896/7)
Already established in the first team when the club entered the Southern League, he was a versatile member of the side in that first season of competition, mainly at wing-half. The captaincy was offered to him for 1897/8, but he declined as he would frequently be unavailable. He was employed in the print trade, and became a colour etcher.

Declined the captaincy

John (JOHNNIE / JACK) **BLYTHE** *(1911-1913)*
b Berwick-upon-Tweed, Northumberland
SL 44 (-), FAC 5 (-), SCC 1 (-)
Delavel Villa; Blyth Spartans (pro 11/96); Jarrow (8/98); Everton (2/99); West Ham Utd (5/02); Millwall (5/04); Watford (free 9/11); Blyth Spartans player-trainer-groundsman (8/13 until circa 1926)
His first match for Watford ended in a six-goal defeat by the club he'd just left, and a few months later he became the only Watford player to be sent off between 1902 and 1923. On his return to Blyth Spartans his responsibilities were various; he was even used as an experimental goalkeeper, although his Watford service had been exclusively at left-half.

Rare sending-off

Money well spent

__IAN__ Robert **__BOLTON__** *(1977-1983)*
b Leicester 13/7/1953
FL 233+1 (28 inc 8p), FAC 15 (2 inc 1p), FLC 29+1 (5 inc 2p), FLT 5 (1), UEFA 3 (-)
Birmingham City (appr 9/68 until 10/70)); Notts County (3/72); Lincoln City (loan 8/76); __Watford__ (£12,000 7/77); Brentford (£5,000 12/83); Barnet (free, cs 1984); Kettering Town (10/84); Chalfont (7/85 until 3/86); Kingsbury Town (mid-1986/7); Hayes (cs 1987)
Graham Taylor had him on loan at Lincoln and brought him to Watford for what proved an absurdly small fee. In both midfield and defence, the tall and powerful Bolton was a master of the long driven pass and the explosive shot, and played a conspicuous role in the club's rise to prominence, encompassing all four divisions and the UEFA Cup.

Midfield class

__DENNIS__ Joseph Thomas **__BOND__** *(1964-1977)*
b Walthamstow, Essex 17/3/1947
FL 271+1 (38 inc 8p), FAC 13 (2 inc 1p), FLC 16 (2)
__Watford__ (appr 5/62, pro 3/64); Tottenham Hotspur (£30,000 3/67); Charlton Athletic (£25,000 10/70); __Watford__ (loan 2/73, £15,000 7/73); Dagenham (free 6/78); Highfield Sports player-manager (by 10/81); Boreham Wood (1982/3); Waltham Abbey player-manager; Mount Grace Old Boys manager (by 11/88)
ENGLAND SCHOOLS and YOUTH
Oozing class from a very early age, this little midfielder played League football at 17 and had a good career, which however failed to reach heights that reflected his ability. The fee received from Tottenham was a Watford record at the time, and altogether he had three spells at Vicarage Road, including one as a loan player.

Three Taylor promotions

__DENNIS__ **__BOOTH__** *(1977-1980)*
b Stanley Common, Derbys 9/4/1949
FL 97+3 (2), FAC 6 (-), FLC 11 (-)
Derbyshire Schools; Charlton Athletic (sch 6/64, appr 7/64, pro 4/66); Blackpool (£7,000 7/71); Southend Utd (£7,000 3/72); Lincoln City (loan 2/74, £9,000 8/74); __Watford__ (£10,000 10/77); Hull City (£40,000 5/80, acting-manager 5/84, reserve-team player-coach 6/84, assistant-manager until 5/89, also acting-manager 4/88 until 6/88); Aston Villa coaching staff (7/89 until cs 1991); Stafford Rangers assistant-manager (11/91, manager 1/92); Bristol Rovers assistant-manager (4/93); Huddersfield Town assistant-manager (7/95)
The midfield anchorman in Graham Taylor's Fourth Division championship-winning teams at both Lincoln and Watford, he then captained the latter to a second successive promotion. After a long League career as a player, he resumed former Lincoln/Watford links by serving under both Taylor (at Aston Villa) and John Ward (at Bristol Rovers).

*James Duncan (**JIMMY**)* ***BOWIE*** *(1952-1955)*
b Kintore, Aberdeenshire 9/8/1924
FL 125 (39 inc 13p), FAC 5 (1), SFC 1 (-)
Aberdeen Parkvale (am 6/42, pro 10/43); Chelsea (£25 2/44); Fulham (valued at £20,000 in player-exchange 1/51); Brentford (part-exchange 3/52); Watford (7/52); Bedford Town (about £500 1/56); Headington Utd (2/57); Fulham (5/57); March Town (free, cs 1958); Wisbech Town (12/59). Guested for Hounslow Town and Middlesbrough in WW2.
The typical skilful and canny little Scottish inside-forward, he prompted Watford's attack for three-and-a-half years, both creating and scoring a healthy share of the goals. His signing with Frank Mitchell and others had prompted a surge of expectation and big gates, but the euphoria was short-lived. He played in the 1944 South Cup Final at Wembley.

Made and scored them

STUART *Clive* ***BRACE*** *(1965-1966)*
b Taunton, Somerset 21/9/1942
FL 16 (4), FAC 2 (2)
Taunton Town; Plymouth Argyle (11/60); Watford (£1,000 9/65); Mansfield Town (free 7/66); Peterborough Utd (£5,000 11/67); Grimsby Town (£4,000 10/68); Southend Utd (£6,000 10/73); Falmouth Town (free, cs 1976); Liskeard Athletic coach (by 1982)
He accumulated what was, for a right-winger, a formidable total of more than 150 goals in League football, being particularly successful in his five-year stint at Grimsby, where he won a Fourth Division championship medal. His stay at Vicarage Road was brief, the free transfer he was given seeming ill-advised in the light of his subsequent record.

Unwisely released?

ARTHUR *Danby* ***BRADFORD*** *(1896)*
b Bromley, Kent 1/9/1876
d Little Kingshill, Bucks 6/6/1953
SL 1 (-)
Clapham Rovers; West Herts (1896)
He was elected a member of West Herts Club & Ground in February 1896 and played left-back in a Southern League home game against Uxbridge the following December, in which the visitors scored the only goal. A fortnight later he made his only other first-team appearance, in a friendly. He became chairman of the family firm in the City.

Something in the City

HENRY BRADFORD *(1896)*
b 20/11/1872
SL 1 (-)
Clapham Rovers; West Herts (1896)
After being elected a member several months after his cousin (Arthur Bradford), he played in the same two first-team games, once on each wing. The second match was a Boxing Day meeting with Watford St Mary's, which produced record Cassio Road gate receipts approaching £50. The Bradfords both played for the prominent amateur club, Clapham Rovers.

Selected with cousin

John Henry (JACK) **BRADSHAW** *(1919)*
b Burnley, Lancs 28/6/1892
d King's Lynn, Norfolk 1970
SL 1 (-)
Southend Utd (am, cs 1913); Watford (am by 10/19); Luton Town (am by 2/20); Aberdare Athletic; Queens Park Rangers (pro 8/21 until cs 1922)
Small and red-haired, this member of a prominent footballing family played inside-right in his one Southern League game for Watford, having been stationed locally with The Kensingtons. His manager at Southend was his brother Joe, and when he played for Watford his father, who managed Arsenal and Fulham, was secretary of the Southern League.

C. **BRAY** *(1905)*
SEL 1 (-)
Berkhamsted (by 11/03); Watford (am)
Only Croom can match his first-team record. Just once he played, at left-back against Hastings & St Leonards United in the South-Eastern League in January 1905, and the result was a six-goal win. Joe Brooks, who was otherwise a fixture in the side, made way for Bray on this one occasion, and the Berkhamsted man didn't play again.

Footballing family

BENjamin **BRELSFORD** *(1928-1930)*
b Sheffield, Yorks
d Oldham, Lancs 1968 (aged 71)
FL 25 (1)
Sheffield Wednesday (11/22); Barrow (£150 7/24); Oldham Athletic (5/26); Watford (free 5/28); Shelbourne (free 8/30); Bray Unknowns; Manchester North End (12/30); Rossendale Utd (10/31); Larne; Newton Heath Loco (permit player 1/33); New Mills (permit player 1/34); Chamber Colliery coach (after WW2)
One of a well-known Sheffield footballing family, he had two seasons at Hillsborough as a reserve-team player before setting off on his considerable travels, which included spells in Ireland. He played left-back in all his League games for Watford, possessing both height and brawn, with a corresponding ability to kick and tackle strongly.

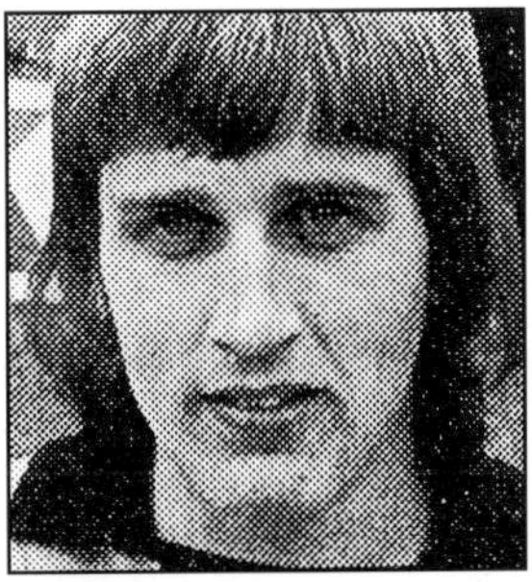
Success in Norway

GUY Austin **BRISTOW** *(1974-1976)*
b Kingsbury, Middx 23/10/1955
FL 18+5 (-)
Watford (appr 7/71, pro 7/73 until cs 1977); Lillehammer, Norway (by 3/78)
In Norway he and Kevin McCarthy helped Lillehammer to progress from the Fourth Division to a high position in the Second within two years - an echo of simultaneous events at Vicarage Road. He was a centre-half whose father, George, had eleven years as a pro with Brentford. After returning to England Guy had a milk round in the Sarratt area.

Sacked

*James (**JIMMY**)* ***BROAD*** *(1926)*
b Stalybridge, Cheshire 10/11/1891
d Chelmsford, Essex 22/8/1963
FL 1 (1), FAC 1 (-)
St Mark's, West Gorton; Stalybridge Celtic; Manchester City (11/09); Oldham Athletic (free 8/13); Corunna, Spain, coach; Millwall ("big fee" 4/19); Las Palmas, Spain, coach (10/20); Stoke City (£2,000 6/21); Barcelona, Spain, coach (8/24); Sittingbourne (10/24); Everton (£1,400 to Stoke City 11/24); New Brighton (£200 12/25); Watford (8/26 until 2/27); Caernarvon Town (10/27); Taunton Utd (9/28); Geneva, Switzerland, coach (1930); coach in Italy (1931); Fleetwood (8/31); coach in Turkey, South America and The Netherlands; Chelmsford groundsman. Guested for Blackburn Rovers and Morton in WW1.
A veteran centre-forward who was sacked for an incident which also involved Jack Swan. He'd previously fallen out in mid-season with the Millwall management and gone off to Spain, having scored 32 Southern League goals (the club's next highest total - four) in 1919/20. His father and two brothers were well-known in the game.

All-round sportsman

*Joseph (**JOE**)* ***BROOKS*** *(1903-1907)*
b Stalybridge, Cheshire
SL 106 (-), FAC 8 (-), SEL 28 (1), UL 25 (1)
Stalybridge Rovers (am); Glossop (pro, cs 1902); Watford (8/03); Sheffield Utd (£275 4/07); Stalybridge Celtic (free, cs 1912 until at least cs 1915); Hurst manager (by 1921)
Ever-present in Southern League games in his first two seasons at Cassio Road. he was a very popular and powerfully-built left-back who would later have five seasons at the top level at Bramall Lane before returning to the Southern League with his home-town club. Earlier he'd been a prominent athlete and amateur cycling champion.

MATThew ***BROUGHTON*** *(1904-1907)*
b Grantham, Lincs 8/10/1880
d Grantham, Lincs 23/1/1957
SL 14 (-), SEL 1 (-)
Nottingham Forest (am 11/01, pro 12/01); Notts County (am 10/04); Watford (am 11/04)
A well-known sportsman in Grantham, he played in the First Division for both the Nottingham clubs. All of his Watford appearances were on the right wing, except two when he occupied the inside position. They were spread over two-and-a-half years, and he travelled from Lincolnshire on each occasion. He captained Grantham Cricket Club for many years.

Soon fell away

*G.F. (**GEORGE**)* ***BROWN*** *(1905-1906)*
SL 3 (-), SEL 1 (-), UL 1 (-)
Wolverton Town (1902); Northampton Town (5/04); Watford (5/05); Northampton Town (9/06); reinstated am (5/09)
A Southern League centre-forward and inside-left at 17, he subsequently joined Watford whilst still serving a trade apprenticeship in Northampton, which he continued. His promise was not fulfilled, and he twice applied for reinstatement as an amateur, the FA at first refusing (in 1907), but then granting the second request two years later.

Brother of Lord Mayor

Henry ***ROY BROWN*** *(1953-1957)*
b Stoke-on-Trent, Staffs 20/12/1923
d Bushey, Herts 8/11/1989
FL 142 (40), FAC 5 (1), SFC 1 (-)
Stoke City (am 5/39, pro 8/42); Watford (£5,500 6/53); Chelmsford City (7/58). Guested for Chester and Shrewsbury Town in WW2.
One of the very few black professionals of his day, he also stood out for the distinguished service he gave Watford as centre-half, winger and centre-forward, being known especially for his speed and heading ability. His only hat-trick was the club's first at home in the League for eight years. His brother became Lord Mayor of Stoke-on-Trent.

Sent off in fifth game

Joseph ***(JOE) BROWN*** *(1937-1943)*
b Troon, Ayrshire 10/4/1913
FL 6 (2), 3SC 3 (1), WW2 17 (4)
Troon Athletic (5/32); Shawfield (7/35); Aberdeen (9/35); Watford (free 9/37); Frickley Colliery (free 7/39); Watford (11/40)
He was taken on following a trial period early in the 1937/8 season, and after being released the following summer was eventually re-engaged on part-time terms for a second season. He was also to rejoin the club during the war. A forward who played mainly on the left wing at Vicarage Road, he was sent off in his fifth League match.

Amateur in Division 1

Robert Henry ***(BOBBY) BROWN*** *(1961-1963)*
b Streatham, London 2/5/1940
FL 28 (10), FAC 2 (1)
Barnet; Fulham (am 9/60); Watford (pro 11/61); Northampton Town (part-exchange for B.R.Jones 11/63); Cardiff City (10/66 until 10/69); Hull City (youth development officer 1982, assistant-manager); Wales assistant-manager; Yate Town assistant-manager (1992)
ENGLAND and GREAT BRITAIN AMATEUR
Prominent as an amateur forward who played in the 1960 Olympics, and in the First Division for Fulham, he was hampered by injury during his two years at Vicarage Road. It was also an injury, sustained on Boxing Day 1967, which eventually forced his retirement. He once scored four goals in ten minutes for Watford Reserves.

Skilful lightweight

Thomas Graham ***(TOMMY) BROWN*** *(1949-1953)*
b Cowdenbeath, Fife 11/8/1924
FL 108 (11 inc 1p), FAC 5 (1)
Kelty Our Boys (pro 9/40); Kelty Rangers (10/41); Dunfermline Athletic (9/43 until 9/46); Worcester City; Portsmouth (10/46); Watford (£1,000 7/49 until cs 1954); Nelson; Northwich Victoria
A highly popular inside-forward who could also play at half-back and on the wing, he was small (weighing nine-and-a-half stones) and skilful in the Scottish style. His experience before reaching Vicarage Road included representative football for the RAF and First Division appearances for Portsmouth. He left Watford whilst on the transfer list at £1,000.

*William (**ROLAND**) **BROWN*** *(1901-1904)*
b Luton, Beds 1874
d Luton, Beds 6/1/1940
SL 57 (4), FAC 4 (1), SEL 12 (2)
Luton Town (late-1891/2); St Albans Town (reinstated am 9/95, pro 5/98); Luton Town (cs 1899); Watford (5/01); Luton Town (8/04)
First choice as Watford's outside-right for most of his three seasons at Cassio Road, he also had a thriving straw-hat-making business in his home town. Although not known for goalscoring, he enjoyed a hat-trick in a friendly against Luton, with whom he had three spells He also served the short-lived professional club, St Albans Town.

A Luton hatter

*William (**BILL**) **BROWN*** *(1928-1935)*
b Bishop Auckland, Co Durham 27/2/1907
d City of London 17/8/1976
FL 220 (-), FAC 21 (-), 3SC 8 (-)
Bishop Auckland; Crook Town; Huddersfield Town (5/27); Watford (free 5/28); Exeter City (exchange for R.Robinson 6/36); Darlington (8/39); Dickinson's, Apsley coach (1948); Hemel Hempstead Town coach (cs 1950)
No other Watford outfield player has made as many as 249 first-team appearances without a goal, but his defensive qualities and consistency at right-back were formidable. He was also a professional sprinter. Although transferred west and then back to the North-East, he had married a Watford girl and retained his home in the town, where he settled.

Goalless full-back

*William Willson (**BILLY**) **BRUNT*** *(1891-1900)*
b Watford, Herts 1869
d Watford, Herts 1942
SL 6 (-), HSC 2 (-), BCCL 1 (-)
The Grove (by 1889/90); Watford St Mary's (early-1890/1); Watford Rovers (1890/1); Church Institute (1891/2); Watford St Mary's (9/97); Watford (pro 9/98)
He became Guthrie Baker's understudy after turning professional, but had been the club's regular 'keeper back in 1890/1, after helping St Mary's to win the Herts County Cup the previous season. In 1894 he sustained severe facial injuries when he fell from a 26-rung ladder at Broad Street Station in the course of his employment as a painter.

Cup win with rivals

*Cecil (**CHRIS**) **BULLING*** *(1911-1914)*
b Tuxford, Notts 12/7/1886
d Nottingham 1968
SL 60 (4 inc 1p), FAC 8 (-), SCC 2 (-)
Heanor Town (1909); Watford (5/11 until cs 1913, and 2/14 until cs 1914); Luton Town (a month's trial 10/14)
The elder of two brothers signed simultaneously, he became club captain for 1912/3, but then had a cartilage operation in the summer and was not re-engaged until February 1914, when it became clear that his best days as a defensive half-back had gone. He played in a Southern Charity Cup tie against Watford whilst on trial at Luton.

Cartilage victim

Two title wins

HAROLD Montagu ***BULLING*** *(1911-1917)*
b Martin, Lincs 29/9/1890
d West Bridgford, Notts 9/11/1933
SL 99 (1), FAC 4 (-), SCC 5 (-), WW1 1 (-)
West Bridgford Boys; Heanor Town; Watford (5/11); Nottingham Forest (unspecified fee 8/19 until cs 1926). Guested for Nottingham Forest in WW1.
Outlasting his brother at Cassio Road, he played regularly at full-back in the 1914/5 Southern League triumph. Reluctant to leave Nottingham, where he was working for his father, a builder, he was sold to Forest in 1919 and was ever-present when they won the 1921/2 Second Division championship. A third brother and a nephew were also professionals.

First youth cap

Frederick (FREDDIE) ***BUNCE*** *(1955-1962)*
b Bushey, Herts 16/2/1938
d Victoria, Australia 9/10/1991
FL 150 (34), FAC 19 (3), SFC 4 (2), FLC 4 (3)
Herts Schools; Watford Boys Club; Watford (am 9/55, pro 10/55); Cambridge Utd (4-figure fee 11/62); Cambridge City; Highlands Park, South Africa (2/64 until 12/64); Germiston Callies, South Africa; Bedmond coach (1967); Whilmena, Australia (1969); Ringwood, Australia (by 9/74); youth coach in Australia
ENGLAND YOUTH
A flying left-winger with a bustling, energetic style which endeared him to the crowd and brought the club's first England honours since Tiny Fayers was capped in 1910. He helped Highlands Park to win their national league title, and later coached under Brian Garvey in Australia, where he was employed in a sportswear company by Willie Devine.

Pioneer apprentice

ERIC Robert Charles ***BURGESS*** *(1964)*
b Edgware, Middx 27/10/1944
FL 3 (-)
Watford (appr 9/60, pro 6/62); Torquay Utd (free 7/65); Plymouth Argyle (free 7/68 until 9/69); Plymouth City; Colchester Utd (12/70); Wealdstone (free 7/72 until 4/75)
After captaining Middlesex Schools as a cricketer, he became one of Vicarage Road's first two apprentices, and was a strongly-built defender whose career was ended by injury. His brother Les was also a Watford youth-team player, and a Queens Park Rangers professional, before playing in the FA Amateur Cup Final for Chesham United.

R. ***BURGESS*** *(1897)*
FAC 1 (-)
Royal Artillery; West Herts (1897/8)
He made his only appearance immediately after being discharged from the army, lining up at left-back in an FA Cup Preliminary Round tie against 3rd Grenadier Guards. It was one of only two cup games in the club's history which have produced eleven goals, and seven of them went to the visitors - a unique occurrence in cup football at Watford.

E. ***BUSBY*** *(1897)*
SL 10 (2), HSC 2 (-)
Watford St Mary's; West Herts (1896/7)
The regular outside-left for a spell late in 1896/7, he was in the side which won the Herts Senior Cup, but didn't get a look-in once the paid men were brought in the following autumn. During his first-team run the committee instructed the hon secretary to tell Busby and Dabber Harrison that "...they should take care not to infringe the offside rule...".

Offside problem

DAVID ***BUTLER*** *(1970-1975)*
b Thornaby-on-Tees, Yorks 23/3/1945
FL 168 (2), FAC 8 (1), FLC 10 (-)
Stockton; Workington (am 8/64, pro 11/64); Watford (£12,000 11/70, assistant-trainer-coach 11/75, first-team trainer cs 1976); Crystal Palace physiotherapist (9/79); Queens Park Rangers physiotherapist (by 12/80); Tottenham Hotspur physiotherapist (by 3/90); England joint-physiotherapist (2/94)
Replacing the long-established Duncan Welbourne at right-back, he gave consistently good service before a knee injury ended his playing career. He nevertheless stayed in the game to become a respected physiotherapist who was used by England frequently at Youth and later at Full level. He also assisted the Rest of the World team at Wembley.

England physio

STEVEn ***BUTLER*** *(1991-1992)*
b Birmingham, Warwicks 27/1/1962
FL 40+22 (9), FAC 1 (-), FLC 4+3 (-), FMC 1 (-), AIC 1+1 (-)
Windsor & Eton; Wokingham Town (cs 1983); Brentford (12/84); Maidstone Utd (loan 11/85, free 6/86); Watford (£150,000 3/91); AFC Bournemouth (loan 12/92); Cambridge Utd (£75,000 12/92); Gillingham (£100,000 12/95)
ENGLAND SEMI-PROFESSIONAL
A striker who had a good career in army football and represented the Combined Services. His scoring rate at Watford was a disappointment, with only one goal at home, but he amassed impressive totals with both Maidstone United and Cambridge United in the lower divisions, and hit an extraordinary eight in two League games, 48 hours apart, at Easter 1994.

Two games, eight goals

John Tinsley ***BUTTON*** *(1897)*
b Portsmouth, Hants 1874
d St Albans, Herts 24/7/1955
SL 3 (-)
Watford Church Institute (by 9/91); West Herts (from 1892/3); Melrose
The last of his three games at wing-half was surrounded by complications. The 1st Coldstream Guards were fined two guineas for scratching on the morning of the original date. They then forfeited home advantage for an undisclosed amount, and the game took place at Cassio Road - result 3-3. Button was appointed reserve-team captain for 1897/8.

Kiss-of-death goal

<u>*DAVID Stuart*</u> <u>**BYRNE**</u> *(1990-1991)*
b Hammersmith, London 5/3/1961
FL 16+1 (2), FMC 1 (-)
Brentford (sch); Southall; Hounslow; Chiswick Albion; Harrow Borough; Hounslow; Kingstonian (10/83); Gillingham (7/85); Millwall (£5,000 7/86); Cambridge Utd (loan 9/88); Blackburn Rovers (loan 2/89); Plymouth Argyle (free 3/89); Bristol Rovers (loan 2/90); <u>Watford</u> (£50,000 11/90); Reading (loan 8/91); Fulham (loan 1/92); Shamrock Rovers (free 1/93); St Johnstone (3/93); Partick Thistle (free 7/93); Walsall (loan 2/94); St Mirren (2/95); Tottenham Hotspur (non-contract 6/95); Ayr Utd (8/95); Albion Rovers player-coach (player-exchange 1/96)
After hitting a spectacular and vitally important last-minute winner at Middlesbrough, he was never picked again in two further years at Watford, during which he was converted from a right-winger into a full-back. That goal was his last kick for the club in first-team competitions. Very few players can boast even half his total of clubs.

Shots and crosses

<u>*NIGEL Ian*</u> <u>**CALLAGHAN**</u> *(1980-1991)*
b Changi, Singapore 12/9/1962
FL 215+19 (42 inc 1p), FAC 25+1 (3), FLC 20+3 (4), FLT 8 (2), UEFA 6 (1), FMC 1 (-)
Scorpions, Hemel Hempstead; Herts Schools; <u>Watford</u> (sch 11/77, appr 5/79, pro 7/80); Derby County (£140,000 2/87); Aston Villa (£500,000 2/89); Derby County (loan 9/90); <u>Watford</u> (loan 3/91); Huddersfield Town (loan 1/92); Stafford Rangers (free 3/92); Millwall Reserves (1/93); Berkhamsted Town (2/93); Walton & Hersham (10/93); also Leavesden Aerodrome S&S (on Sundays 10/93); Berkhamsted Town (12/93); Hellenic, South Africa player-coach (2/94 until 3/94); Borrowash Victoria (2/95); Beaconsfield Sycob (10/95)
ENGLAND UNDER-21 and 'B'
He made his League début as an apprentice and became an integral part of the successes in the early 1980s. He flourished on the right wing as a gifted striker of the ball, providing potent shots and crosses in profusion, and perhaps could have achieved more before allowing his career to drift. In 1984 he helped England to win the UEFA Under-21 tournament.

Nearly 41 when signed

<u>*Joseph William Herbert (JOE)*</u> <u>**CALVERT**</u> *(1948)*
b Beighton, Derbys 3/2/1907
FL 5 (-)
Owston Park Rangers; Bullcroft Colliery; Frickley Colliery; Bristol Rovers (5/31); Leicester City (5/32); <u>Watford</u> (one of four players signed for £4,750 1/48); Brush Sports (free 7/48). Guested for Northampton Town in WW2.
One of five players signed simultaneously from Filbert Street (one of them on loan), he briefly replaced Tommy Rigg in goal for a run of five games which constituted his entire first-team career at Vicarage Road. He's the oldest player ever to appear in the Football League for Leicester, and the second-oldest for Watford.

Manager's father-in-law

Thomas Albert Edward (**TOMMY**) **CARPENTER** *(1950-1951)*
b Carshalton, Surrey 11/3/1925
FL 4 (-)
Harrow Town (1940); Wembley (1946); Watford (am 11/46); Harrow Town (1948); Watford (pro 11/50); Headington Utd (free, cs 1951); Ashford (mid-1952/3 until 1954)
He began his association with Vicarage Road more than four years before he eventually signed professional forms at the age of 25. Engaged on a part-time basis, he understudied Geoff Morton, for whom he deputised in goal on four occasions before being released. His daughter was to marry a future Watford manager, Dave Bassett.

Serious car accident

David (**DAVE**) **CARR** *(1965)*
b Wheatley Hill, Co Durham 19/1/1937
FL 10 (3)
Ludworth; Huddersfield Town youth team; Spennymoor Utd; Darlington (5/57); Workington (£1,500 7/62); Watford (£2,000 plus K.Oliver 2/65 until 7/66)
A goalscoring forward well-known to Ken Furphy, Carr played with him at Darlington and then signed for him at both Workington and Watford. Just before moving to Vicarage Road he took part in the Cumberland club's greatest triumph - a 5-1 League Cup win at Blackburn. His career was ended by serious injuries sustained in a car crash.

Empire Games at 60

James Edward Charles (**JIMMY**) **CARR** *(1913-1914)*
b Glasgow 18/12/1893
d Harrow, Middx 26/6/1980
SL 18 (-), SCC 1 (-)
Pinner; Watford Orient (cs 1912); Watford (am 2/13, pro 8/13); West Ham Utd (free 5/14); Reading (cs 1919); Southampton (6/23); Swansea Town (5/26); Queens Park Rangers (free 10/27 until cs 1928). Guested for Portsmouth in WW1.
A winger who played for Herts and, with his brother Jack, was a founder-member of the Watford Orient club. He was still an amateur when he made the first three of his Southern League appearances for Watford. For a great many years he kept the *Red Lion Hotel* at Southall, and he represented England at bowls in the 1954 Empire Games in Vancouver.

Chances limited

John Henry (**JACK**) **CARTER** *(1933-1934)*
b Aylesbury, Bucks 11/11/1910
d Reading, Berks 2/7/1992
FL 15 (7), FAC 2 (1)
Hazells; Aylesbury Utd; Watford (am 11/31, pro 11/31); Reading (8/35); Ipswich Town (7/36); Yeovil & Petters Utd (8/38)
His first-team chances as Billy Lane's understudy at centre-forward were limited, but he scored in nearly half of them. A five-goal performance as a trialist in Reading's reserve team helped to get him an engagement at Elm Park, where he was employed as a steward four decades later. Mick O'Brien signed him soon after taking over at Ipswich.

County cricketer

*Wilfred (**WILF / BILL**) **CARTER*** *(1920-1925)*
b Annesley, Notts 19/6/1896
d Watford, Herts 1/11/1975
FL 126 (4), FAC 5 (-)
Bolsolver Colliery (by 1915); Watford (6/20 until cs 1926)
An accomplished wing-half who also played cricket for Derbyshire and as late as 1939 hit 206* in an hour and three quarters for Watford LMS. He was a cricket pro in Scotland and coached at Repton School before becoming football coach and caretaker at Callowland School in Watford. He died next door to the Vicarage Road ground, in Shrodells Hospital.

Irish League honour

NORMAN CASE *(1950-1951)*
b Prescot, Lancs 1/9/1925
d Watford, Herts 1973
FL 10 (4)
Sheffield Utd (8/48); Leyton Orient (10/48); Rochdale (11/48 until 2/49); Ards; Sunderland (10/49); Watford (12/50); Yeovil Town (loan 8/51); Rochdale ("small fee" 2/52); Canterbury City (by 8/53)
IRISH LEAGUE
He moved to Sunderland shortly after being capped by the Irish League following a five-goal performance for Ards v Coleraine. After a run at centre-forward when he moved to Vicarage Road, he was transfer-listed at £1,000 at the end of the season, but spent much of the next winter on loan to Yeovil, for whom he scored 23 times.

Winning England captain

DARREN** Mark **CASKEY *(1995)*
b Basildon, Essex 21/8/1974
FL 6 (1)
Tottenham Hotspur (sch 12/88, tr 8/90, pro 3/92); Watford (loan 10/95); Reading (£700,000 2/96)
ENGLAND SCHOOLS and YOUTH
He'd led England to success in the 1992/3 European Under-18 championship and had more than 30 Premier League games under his belt before his loan spell at Vicarage Road. He scored on his home début for Watford, and the characteristics of his assiduous link-play bore a marked resemblance to those of Kevin Richardson.

Wembley to Wembley

KEITH** Barrington **CASSELLS *(1978-1980)*
b Islington, London 10/7/1957
FL 6+6 (-), FAC 1+1 (-), FLC 2+1 (-)
Wembley; Watford (trial 5/77, £500 10/77); Peterborough Utd (loan 1/80); Oxford Utd (valued at £50,000 in part-exchange for L.Taylor 10/80); Southampton (£80,000 3/82); Brentford (£25,000 2/83); Mansfield Town (£17,000 8/85); Herts Police (12/89)
A lively forward who couldn't establish himself in Watford's first team, but made progress elsewhere. He scored a hat-trick in his first League game for Mansfield, whom he helped to win the Associate Members Cup at Wembley, a stone's throw from his first club. He later resumed match-day duties at Vicarage Road - as a uniformed Pc.

Part Two

<u>FRANCIS</u> *<u>James Augustine</u>* **<u>CASSIDY</u>** *(1983)*
b Watford, Herts 20/8/1964
UEFA 0+1 (-)
<u>Watford</u> (sch 6/79, appr 6/80, pro 5/82); Plymouth Argyle (loan 2/84); Peterborough Utd (free 6/84); Bishops Stortford (free, cs 1986); Harrow Borough (by 10/88); Chesham Utd (£15,000 11/89); Harlow Town (loan 3/91); Aylesbury Utd (4-figure fee 8/91); Hayes (by 4/92); Yeading; Berkhamsted Town (1994/5); Saffron Walden Town (1/95); Tring Town (by 4/95); Hemel Hempstead (cs 1995); London Colney (by 4/96)
One of the very few Watford-born players to turn out for the club in recent decades, he was even more unusual - unique, in fact - in playing out his entire first-team career more than six hundred miles from Vicarage Road. It amounted to a few minutes of substitute action in Prague. He was a midfield player, and took part in the 1982 FA Youth Cup win.

Career with a difference

<u>GEORGE</u> *<u>Charles</u>* **<u>CATLEUGH</u>** *(1954-1964)*
b Horden, Co Durham 11/6/1932
d Watford, Herts 5/4/1996
FL 293 (15), FAC 19 (1), SFC 9 (1), FLC 6 (-)
King's Lynn (am); Nuneaton Borough (am by 1953/4); also Bury (am 1953/4); <u>Watford</u> (pro 5/54); Folkestone (free 7/65 until at least 4/68)
He took the eye as the only amateur in Nuneaton's convincing FA Cup win against Watford in 1953, and became a Vicarage Road professional the following May. Eleven seasons of full-hearted commitment, mostly at right-half, earned him great popularity. He suffered a broken leg in 1962, and when he was with Folkestone a similar injury ended his career.

Commitment for 11 years

<u>Walter</u> **<u>CATLIN</u>** *(1898)*
BCCL 1 (-)
Luton Town (10/97); <u>Watford</u> (5/98 until cs 1899)
After scoring in his only Football League game, at the end of his one season as a professional with Luton Town, he spent the following winter as a Watford player. He was selected at inside-right or centre-forward for three friendlies and a Bucks & Contiguous Counties League game at Wycombe, but couldn't get on the scoresheet.

<u>James</u> **<u>(JIMMY) CHALMERS</u>** *(1901-1902)*
b Old Luce, Wigtownshire 3/12/1877
SL 30 (5), FAC 2 (1)
Morton (7/96); Sunderland (5/97); Preston North End (10/98); Notts County (6/99); Beith (9/00); Partick Thistle (10/00); <u>Watford</u> (7/01); Tottenham Hotspur (4/02); Swindon Town (5/04); Norwich City (5/06); Beith (1907/8 until cs 1913)
Good enough to have enjoyed three seasons of fairly regular First Division football, he was a left-winger whose style was once described as "impetuous and dashing". Returning to Cassio Road with Norwich Reserves in 1907, he was sent off and subsequently suspended for two months. A compositor by trade, he worked for a time on the *Watford Observer*.

Worked on the Observer

Barnett's partner

*William (**BILLY**)* ***CHAPMAN*** *(1928-1934)*
b Murton, Co Durham 21/9/1902
d Murton, Co Durham 2/12/1967
FL 210 (10), FAC 22 (-), 3SC (1 (-)
Democratic Club (Wearside League); Sheffield Wednesday (5/23); Manchester Utd (£250 4/26); Watford (less than £750, 6/28); Murton Colliery Welfare (free 8/34 until mid-1937/8)
By the time his six-year stint at Watford ended, the Chapman-Barnett right-wing pairing had long been a familiar feature at Vicarage Road, with Chapman on the flank. Fast, tricky and consistent, he'd been on the Old Trafford staff with Barson, McPherson and Barnett, all of whom were to play for Watford. He began his working life as a coalminer.

Peterborough profit

KENney ***CHARLERY*** *(1992-1993)*
b Stepney, London 28/11/1964
FL 45+3 (13), FAC 1 (-), FLC 3 (-), AIC 0+1 (-)
Essex Schools; Beckton Utd; Basildon Utd; Fisher Athletic; Maidstone Utd (£35,000 3/89); Peterborough Utd (£35,000 3/91); Watford (£350,000 10/92); Peterborough Utd (£150,000 12/93); Birmingham City (£350,000 7/95); Southend Utd (loan 1/96); Peterborough Utd player-coach (valued at £150,000 in player-exchange 2/96)
Peterborough did well financially out of his moves to and from Watford. A striker and a very popular figure at London Road, he hit two play-off goals at Wembley to take the club to its highest League status. He was nearly 25 when he made his Football League début - at Peterborough, for newly-elected Maidstone alongside Steve Butler.

Wartime paratrooper

*Charles Thomas (**CHARLIE**)* ***CHASE*** *(1946-1948)*
b Steyning, Sussex 31/1/1924
FL 16 (1)
Brighton & Hove Schools; Brighton & Hove Albion (am 9/40); Watford (pro 11/46); Crystal Palace (free 6/48 until cs 1950)
After serving as a paratrooper in the war, he turned pro at Vicarage Road after two months as a trialist. He was a versatile player whose spasmodic League appearances for Watford were all in the forward line. He later became head groundsman in The Parks, home of Oxford University CC, between two spells in a similar position at Brighton College.

Lengthy loan period

DENIS CHENEY *(1948)*
b Coalville, Leics 30/6/1924
FL 18 (5)
Coalville Town; Leicester City (am 3/40, pro 11/41); Watford (loan 1/48 until 7/48); Bournemouth & Boscombe Athletic (10/48); Aldershot (7/54); Dorchester Town (8/56)
The odd man out when five players were signed from Leicester, he came only on loan, but was ever-present on the left wing until he returned to Filbert Street. He was soon back in Division 3 (South), however, where he had a further two hundred games with the Hampshire clubs. In the war he served in Singapore with the Cameron Highlanders.

STEVE Reginald **CHERRY** *(1995)*
b Nottingham 5/8/1960
FL 4 (-)
Derby County (sch 11/75, appr 8/76, pro 3/78); Port Vale (loan 11/80); Walsall (£25,000 8/84); Plymouth Argyle (£17,000 10/86); Chesterfield (loan 12/88); Notts County (£70,000 2/89); Watford (free 7/95); Plymouth Argyle (loan 2/96, free 5/96)
ENGLAND YOUTH
Signed at the age of 34, he came to Watford in the unfamiliar role of second-choice goalkeeper, having enjoyed a long first-team career with his other clubs which brought him over six hundred League and cup appearances. More than half of them were for Notts County, whom he helped to win three times at Wembley, where he also enjoyed victory with Plymouth Argyle.

Four Wembley wins

GARY Paul Stephen **CHIVERS** *(1987-1988)*
b Stockwell, London 15/5/1960
FL 14 (-), FAC 4 (-), FLC 1 (-)
Chelsea (appr 7/76, pro 8/78); Swansea City (free 8/83); Queens Park Rangers (2/84); Watford (free 9/87); Brighton & Hove Albion (£40,000 3/88 until cs 1993) AFC Bournemouth (non-contract 11/93); Stamco (1/95)
Somewhat surprisingly sold only six months after being signed, he had begun to look an accomplished right-back in a relegation-doomed side, after being used at first in midfield. He was already an experienced player, having started with a good career at Chelsea, and after leaving Watford ran up over two hundred League appearances for Brighton.

Quickly discarded

Cyril (SAMMY) **CHUNG** *(1957-1965)*
b Abingdon, Berks 16/7/1932
FL 220 (22 inc 1p), FAC 19 (2), SFC 2 (-), FLC 4 (-)
Abingdon Town; Reading (am 8/49); Headington Utd (1950); Reading (pro 7/51); Norwich City (£5,000 1/55); Watford (6/57, player-coach from cs 1962); Ipswich Town assistant-manager (7/65); Wolverhampton Wanderers (trainer-coach 1969, assistant-manager 1972, manager 6/76 until 11/78); Vasteras, Sweden manager (1980 until 1982); coach in United Arab Emirates; Stoke City coach (7/85); Colchester Utd assistant-manager (1/90); Blackburn Rovers chief scout (cs 1990 until 9/71); Oldswinford manager (12/91); Tamworth manager (2/92 until 1/93); Doncaster Rovers manager (7/94)
Highly adaptable in his long spell at Vicarage Road, he turned out in all three half-back positions, and at centre-forward and inside-forward, before following manager Bill McGarry and becoming his coach at Ipswich and then Wolves. He was to succeed McGarry at Molineux and lead Wolves to the Second Division championship in 1976/7.

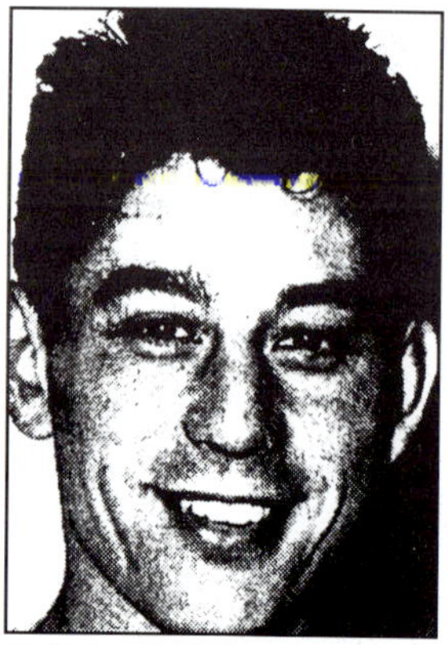
Followed McGarry

No contract offered

CHRIStopher Elliott **CLARKE** *(1966)*
b Battersea, London 11/12/1946
FL 1+1 (-)
Chelsea (appr 8/62); Millwall (12/63); Watford (trial 8/66); Dartford; Margate; Hastings Utd; Tonbridge; Hastings Utd

After serving a Stamford Bridge apprenticeship he was taken on by Millwall, but managed only 19 League appearances in two-and-a-half years. As a trialist he was used in Watford's pre-season friendlies in 1966 and selected at outside-left for the opening League game. He played once more, as a substitute, but wasn't given a contract.

Pro career cut short

TRACEY William **CLARKE** *(1897-1898)*
b Fenny Stratford, Bucks 1876
d Watford, Herts 1949
SL 12 (2), FAC 1 (2)
Watford Rangers (1892/3); Church Institute (by 11/93); Watford Permanent Way (by 9/94); Watford St Mary's; Watford Wanderers; West Herts (am, pro 10/97 until 1898)

A forward who liked to move around the local clubs, and in fact was once stopped from doing so by the West Herts FA, who refused to sanction a move from Permanent Way to Watford Wanderers. Soon after West Herts adopted professionalism he joined the paid ranks, but it wasn't long before his career was ended by a knee injury.

Hard work and energy

FREDerick Louis **CLEAVER** *(1908-1910)*
b Ashbourne, Derbys 22/4/1885
SL 39 (8), FAC 2 (1), SCC 3 (-)
Ashbourne Town; Derby County (2/06); Preston North End (5/07); Watford (8/08); Redditch (cs 1910); Atherstone; Washford Mills (permit player 9/21)

In his two seasons at Cassio Road he gave good service as an extremely hardworking and energetic forward or half-back. It was from the left-half position that he scored when Leicester Fosse visited Watford in the FA Cup - the first First Division team to do so - and were held 1-1. As well as playing for Redditch, he later became the groundsman there.

Long-distance transfers

Archibald Ernest (ARCHIE) **CLEMENT** *(1930-1931)*
b Grays, Essex 27/11/1901
d Chatham, Kent 9/5/1984
FL 14 (-)
Grays Athletic; Whitstable (1924); Chatham Town; Dartford; Millwall (6/28); Watford (free 6/30); New Brighton (free 8/31); Yeovil & Petters Utd (8/33); Southport (6/34 until cs 1935)

After playing army football in the First World War he stayed close to the Thames whilst developing his early career, but then embarked on a sequence of long-distance moves when he left Watford. His first-team experience as a full-back at Vicarage Road included 5-1 and 6-2 wins in successive games against Newport County (away) and Bristol Rovers.

<u>PETER</u> <u>Terence</u> **<u>COFFILL</u>** *(1975-1977)*
b Romford, Essex 14/2/1957
FL 56+7 (6), FAC 3 (1), FLC 1+2 (-)
<u>Watford</u> (sch 2/72, appr 7/73, pro 2/75); Torquay Utd (£4,000 11/77); Northampton Town (£5,000 7/81); Aylesbury Utd (free 7/83); Kidderminster Harriers (by 12/84); Chelmsford City coach (by 1988/9); Brantham (by 9/90); Bury Town (by 11/91); Gravesend & Northfleet assistant-manager (12/91)
He had a useful career at Vicarage Road after completing his apprenticeship, but moved on after a handful of games early in Graham Taylor's reign. An attacking midfield player, he took his career total of League matches past two hundred before finding his way around the lower leagues. He scored the winner on his final appearance for Watford.

Hit winner in last game

<u>Ephraim</u> **<u>COLCLOUGH</u>** *(1900-1901)*
b Stoke-on-Trent, Staffs 1875
d Stoke-on-Trent, Staffs 1914
SL 17 (1)
Stoke (1/99); <u>Watford</u> (7/00); Brighton & Hove Albion (8/01 until cs 1902)
A Potteries man with a fine Potteries name. He was at Cassio Road for one season, in which Watford gained only one point from their 14 away games in the Southern League, but at home achieved their best-ever result to date, beating Tottenham Hotspur, winners of the FA Cup that season. Colclough, a versatile forward, was playing at inside-left.

Helped to beat Spurs

<u>Walter</u> <u>**THEO**dore</u> **<u>COLES</u>** *(1921)*
b Bedford Park, Middx 17/8/1895
d Bushey Heath, Herts 11/3/1969
FL 1 (-)
Cambridge University; Corinthians; <u>Watford</u> (am 8/20)
Tall and well-built, he won a blue in 1919, and later captained Herts. Soon after his Watford appearance, at left-half, he gave up football for a time, on medical advice. He belonged to a prominent sporting family: his father (Walter) and uncle (Percy) were major figures in the club's very early years, and his son scored a century for Eton v Harrow at Lord's.

Sporting family

<u>Ernest (**ERNIE**)</u> **<u>COLLEDGE</u>** *(1924)*
b Chesterfield, Derbys 12/5/1902
d Bricket Wood, Herts 10/1/1974
FL 1 (-)
Bolsover Colliery; <u>Watford</u> (8/24 until cs 1925); Leavesden Hospital (permit player 10/27 until 5/33)
His one League appearance was on the left wing in a 2-0 away defeat against Bristol Rovers. He came from the same Derbyshire colliery team as Wilf Carter and settled in south-west Herts, being employed at Leavesden Mental Hospital. He got the FA's permission to play for the hospital, which had a strong amateur team between the wars.

Settled in the area

Took Rochdale to final

Anthony Norman (TONY) ***COLLINS*** *(1950-1957)*
b Kensington, London 19/3/1926
FL 107 (9), FAC 5 (1), SFC 1 (1)
Acton Utd; Sheffield Wednesday (11/47); York City (7/49); Watford (£250 8/50); Norwich City (£3,500 7/53); Torquay Utd (7/55); Watford (unspecified fee 6/57); Crystal Palace (free 11/57); Rochdale (6/59, manager 6/60 until 9/67); Bristol City (chief scout 12/67 until 1972, assistant-manager 1976 until 1980, caretaker-manager 9/80 for 19 days); Leeds Utd chief scout (until 10/81); Manchester Utd chief scout (by 2/83 until 6/88); Queens Park Rangers chief scout (9/88); Newcastle Utd chief scout (2/89); Millwall scout
A skilful and elegant left-winger who had wide experience as a player and then in various capacities after retiring, including key backroom posts at Elland Road and Old Trafford. In 1962 he took Rochdale of the Fourth Division to the final of the Football League Cup. He first signed professional forms, for Sheffield Wednesday, whilst on army service in Italy.

Sidelined

Ronald Michael (MIKE) ***COLLINS*** *(1958-1959)*
b Middlesbrough, Yorks 8/6/1933
FL 43 (-), FAC 3 (-), SFC 3 (-)
Redcar Albion; Chelsea (11/51); Watford (7/57); Folkestone (free 6/59)
He spent nearly six years as one of Chelsea's goalkeepers, but played only once in their First Division side. After joining Watford he was again kept on the sidelines, understudying Johnny Curran for six months before getting the first-team jersey, which he then kept for nearly a year. He subsequently trod the well-worn path to Folkestone.

Full cap at 18

DAVID James ***CONNOLLY*** *(1995-1996)*
b Willesden, London 6/6/1977
FL 7+6 (8 inc 2 p), FAC 1+2 (-)
Bushey Rangers (by 1989); Watford (sch 11/91, tr 7/93, pro 11/94)
REPUBLIC OF IRELAND FULL
Small and sprightly, he was a prolific scorer for the youth team and became the club's youngest-ever player in the FA Cup. Following injury problems, and with only brief first-team experience, he scored two League hat-tricks and won Full international status at 18.

League Cup's first goal

MAURICE ***COOK*** *(1953-1958)*
b Hemel Hempstead, Herts 10/12/1931
FL 208 (68), FAC 10 (9), SFC 6 (4)
Herts Schools; Potten End; Berkhamsted Town; Watford (am 10/52, pro 5/53); Fulham (£15,000 1/58); Reading (5/65); Banbury Utd player-coach (7/66)
A hard-running, no-frills centre-forward or winger who was Watford's major player of the mid-1950s and left for a club-record fee after prolonged transfer gossip. He was the only Watford player to represent Division 3 (South) against its northern counterpart, and for Fulham scored the Football League Cup's first-ever goal. He also played cricket for Herts.

Robert Kenneth **(BOBBY) COOK** *(1951-1952)*
b Letchworth, Herts 18/6/1924
FL 53 (8), FAC 3 (1)
Letchworth Town; Reading (3/48); Tottenham Hotspur (7/49); Watford (8/51); Canterbury City (7/53); Northampton Town (3/56); Biggleswade Town (6/57)
A part-time pro at Tottenham and Watford, he played outside-right for most of his first-team career at Vicarage Road, which ended abruptly when he lost his place in December 1952, never to be picked again. He at first joined Canterbury on loan, whilst on the transfer list at £1,000, but Watford eventually cancelled his registration.

Never picked again

William Henry **(BILLY) COOKE** *(1954)*
b Whittington, Derbys 7/3/1919
d Luton, Beds 22/9/1992
FL 10 (-)
Bournemouth & Boscombe Athletic (4/38); Luton Town (1/46); Shrewsbury Town (7/53); Watford ("small fee" 7/54); Bedford Town (free 7/55 until at least 3/57). Guested for Crewe Alexandra, Luton Town, Millwall and York City in WW2.
This rugged, determined left-back was 35 when he came to Vicarage Road. He played in the first ten games of the season, but was replaced first by Lionel Smith (who was himself 34) and then Dave Bewley (also 34). Cooke didn't play again. The vast majority of his League experience was with Luton Town, for whom he played over two hundred games.

Veteran left-backs

Edwin **(EDDIE) COTHER** *(1898-1899)*
b Uxbridge, Middx 1878
d St Albans, Herts 1961
SL 8 (1), FAC 1 (-), BCCL 6 (-)
Watford Athletic; Watford St Mary's (1896); West Herts (am by 12/97, pro 9/98)
A versatile footballer, the younger Cother was frequently in trouble and his career was ruined by criminal convictions, although he did reappear briefly in the Reserves in 1903. He also played cricket. His last days were spent in the Watford and St Albans workhouses, and he lies in a pauper's grave. Like Jack, he was widely known as 'Darkie'.

Sad end

John William **(JACK / DARKIE) COTHER** *(1898-1905)*
b Uxbridge, Middx
d Watford, Herts 2/12/1946 (aged 73)
SL 111 (-), FAC 12 (-), BCCL 13 (2), SEL 5 (1)
Colne Valley (by late 1891/2); Watford Rangers (by 1/93); Melrose (1894); Watford St Mary's (am, cs 1894, pro 10/97); Watford (6/98 until cs 1905)
The elder of the two dark-skinned brothers whose father was born in India, he was a beefy full-back and a great favourite of the Cassio Road crowd. He was employed by Watford Council, and later became a programme-seller at Vicarage Road. Rumours that he was illegally playing for Colne Valley as a professional as early as 1892 were denied.

Beefy crowd-pleaser

Two eventful débuts

Anthony Philip (TONY) ***COTON*** *(1984-1990)*
b Tamworth, Staffs 19/5/1961
FL 235 (-), FAC 32 (-), FLC 18 (-), FMC 6 (-)
Tamworth; Mile Oak Rovers; Birmingham City (£1,000 10/78); Hereford Utd (loan 10/79); Watford (£300,000 9/84); Manchester City (£1 million 7/90); Manchester Utd (£500,000 1/96)
ENGLAND 'B'
A high-class goalkeeper who in the opinion of many was unlucky not to have played for England. He saved a penalty in the first minute of his League career, but conceded five goals at home on his first appearance for Watford. Before Manchester City paid that million-pound fee, no Watford goalkeeper had attracted a sum above £27,000.

FRANK ***COTTERILL*** *(1909-1916)*
b Wolverhampton, Staffs 1885
d Watford, Herts 1952
SL 13 (4), FAC 2 (2), SCC 1 (-), WW1 1 (-)
Bilston Utd (9/04); Cannock Town (6/05); Aston Villa (5/06); Halesowen (6/07); Redditch (11/07); Maidstone Utd (2/08); Southend Utd (4/08); Watford (9/09); Croydon Common (3/10); Nelson (10/10). Guested for Watford in WW1.
He came to Watford to follow his trade at Sun Printers, and was taken on as a forward at Cassio Road, but was one of three men suspended *sine die* in February 1910 for "utterly disgraceful and demoralising conduct". He made a wartime guest appearance, and scored, against Arsenal in 1916, and one of his sons played for the Reserves in 1946/7.

Died on the terraces

Ernest Herbert ***COTTRELL*** *(1901-1903)*
b Grantham, Lincs 31/1/1876
d Watford, Herts 12/1/1929
SL 38 (12), FAC 1 (-), SEL 2 (-)
Newark (11/95); Hucknall St John's (2/96); Sheppey Utd (5/96); Stockport County; Woolwich Arsenal (5/98); Watford (5/01); Fulham (6/03); Workington (10/04); Coventry City (2/07); Nuneaton Town (11/07)
A versatile forward with Football League experience before he joined Watford, where he settled once his football wanderings were over. Gassed in the Great War, he suffered from heart trouble, and collapsed on the Vicarage Road terraces at the end of a famous FA Cup win over Preston North End. He was carried to the boardroom, where he was found to be dead.

Seaside goals

Albert Cowley ***COUSINS*** *(1911)*
b St Pancras, London 1890
SL 2 (-), SCC 1 (-)
Tottenham Hotspur (11/07); Hastings & St Leonards Utd (free 8/08); Chelsea (5/09); Watford (8/11 until cs 1912)
His 27 first-team goals in a season for Hastings induced Chelsea to sign him, but he didn't make their League team. Watford failed to score in his three competitive games on the wing, which included a six-goal Southern League defeat at Millwall. With reserve-team player Sam McClure he was suspended for 28 days in March 1912, for alleged misbehaviour.

<u>Wilfred John **COUTANCHE**</u> *(1921-1923)*
b Sherborne, Dorset 1895
d Bournemouth, Hants 1/7/1960
FL 6 (-)
Watford Schools; Callow Land (by early 1913); Watford Orient (by 4/14); St Albans City; <u>Watford</u> (am 5/21); Tufnell Park; Ilford
A stoutly-built amateur full-back of courage and resource - attributes which earned him the soubriquet 'The Old Warhorse'. He played in a good standard of amateur football for several clubs, was for a time a regular Watford reserve, and also represented Herts. Late in 1923/4 he was suspended for misconduct whilst playing for Ilford.

'The Old Warhorse'

<u>Robert (BOB) **COWAN**</u> *(1928-1929)*
b Wheatley Hill, Co Durham 1907
FL 6 (1)
Crook Town; Durham City (am 3/26, pro); Huddersfield Town (£800 1/27); <u>Watford</u> (free 5/28); Rhyl Athletic (free 8/30); Blackhall Colliery; Leavesden Mental Hospital (permit player 9/32)
He joined the club from Huddersfield with Bill Brown, unlike whom he made little impact, although he did score on his first-team début. He was picked at both centre-forward and right-half. After being granted an FA permit to play for Leavesden as an amateur, he turned out only briefly for the hospital, whom he also represented at cricket in 1932.

Quickly off the mark

<u>JOHN Michael **COWEN**</u> *(1965-1967)*
b Lewisham, London 1/12/1944
FL 17 (-)
Chelsea (am 5/60, appr 5/61, pro 10/62); <u>Watford</u> ("small fee" 10/64 until 10/67); Gravesend & Northfleet (until 9/76)
ENGLAND YOUTH
He was highly regarded in his apprentice days at Stamford Bridge, and earned wider recognition when selected to play in goal for the national side. Unable to break through into Chelsea's first team, he had nearly three years at Vicarage Road before leaving full-time football at 22 and taking up an appointment with a security firm.

Peaked in youth football

<u>A.G. **COX**</u> *(1899)*
b Luton, Beds
SL 1 (-)
Christ Church, Luton; Staines; Folkestone; Grays; Gravesend; St Albans (pro until cs 1899); <u>Watford</u> (11/99); Luton Town (5/00); St Albans (am by 3/03); Hitchin Town (cs 1904)
Captain and hon secretary of Christ Church, Luton, and one of the founders of the Staines club after he'd moved there, he also played with the old professional club in St Albans until its demise. His one Southern League game for Watford was at right-half in a 4-0 victory over Shepherds Bush. He was later allowed to play as an amateur again.

Jo'burg to Watford

*Laurence David (**LAURIE**)* ***CRAKER*** *(1973-1976)*
b Aylesbury, Bucks 1/3/1953
FL 60+6 (4), FAC 2+1 (-), FLC 3 (-)
Bucks Schools; Chelsea (appr 4/69); Jewish Guild, Johannesburg, South Africa (one season); Watford (11/72 until 3/77); Dartford (loan 2/77); Hayes (cs 1977 until at least 11/79); Staines Town; Chesham Utd player-manager (cs 1982 until 11/82); Staines Town; Maidenhead; Windsor & Eton (by 12/84, assistant-manager, manager by 11/85); Chalfont St Peter manager (6/86 until 2/89); Marlow coach (cs 1989); Slough Town assistant-manager (cs 1994)
Taken on after a two-months trial period when he returned from South Africa, he had several good first-team runs in midfield or defence. Whilst on loan to Dartford he won a Southern League Cup winner's medal alongside Vic Akers and Brian Greenhalgh, and subsequently served a succession of clubs in the Bucks/Thames Valley area, some of them as manager.

J. ***CRAMB*** *(1913)*
SCC 1 (-)
Kilburn; Barnet Alston; Watford (am)
He made reserve-team appearances as a goalkeeper over a period of several seasons, but played only once for the first team. The occasion was a 3-0 defeat at Luton in the Southern Charity Cup, a knockout competition for Southern League clubs. He came to Watford's notice whilst with the club which is now known as just Barnet.

Starred in California

RON*ald James* ***CRISP*** *(1961-1965)*
b Datchet, Bucks 24/9/1938
FL 89 (14), FAC 5 (-), FLC 7 (3)
Dulwich Hamlet; Luton Town (am 11/59); Watford (am 7/60, pro 1/61); Brentford (£2,000 8/65); Los Angeles Toros, USA (12/66); San Diego Toros, USA (3/68); Orient (briefly 3/69); Juventus, South Africa, manager (by 1993)
Comfortable both at right-half and in the forward line, he played for Herts before turning professional on completion of his National Service. He was elected the Northern Professional Soccer League's Player of the Year in 1967, and two years later went to South Africa, where he settled and became managing director of a company supplying office machinery.

FA Cup winner

PETER *Harry Lucas* ***CROKER*** *(1952-1953)*
b Kingston, Surrey 21/12/1921
FL 23 (-), FAC 3 (-)
Kingston YMCA; Leyland Motors, Kingston; Charlton Athletic youth team; Bromley; Charlton Rovers; Charlton Athletic (am 3/41, pro 1941/2); Watford (£300 6/52); Gravesend & Northfleet (7/53); Harvey Sports, Greenwich (permit player); Charlton Athletic (youth team manager, chief scout, assistant-manager 10/65 until 7/66); Blackpool scout (by 1972); South-East Counties League fixtures secretary for ten years, chairman by 12/86). Guested for Brentford in WW2.

He was a goalkeeper until after he left school, and made the odd appearance in goal for Watford Reserves, but was otherwise a full-back throughout his senior career. In 1947 he won an FA Cup winner's medal and was an England reserve. He also played cricket in the Durham Senior League, and his brother Ted became the FA's Chief Executive.

W. **CROOM** *(1905)*
SEL 1 (1)
Waltham Glendale; Watford (am)
One of nine players (compared with only three in the seasons immediately before and after) who occupied the outside-right position in competitive first-team games in 1904/5. His sole appearance was in a 6-0 home win over Hastings & St Leonards United in the South-Eastern League, to which Croom contributed one of the goals.

*Her***BERT CROWNSHAW** *(1909-1916)*
b Sheffield, Yorks 1880
d Watford, Herts 27/5/1954
SL 1 (-), SCC 1 (-), WW1 3 (-)
Wycliffe (pro 11/04); Leavesden Asylum (am by 4/06); Watford (am 9/09)
After playing professionally in Sheffield, he came south and took employment at Leavesden Asylum, in whose footballing and cricketing affairs he was a prominent figure for many years. He helped them to win the Herts Senior Cup twice, represented the county, and was a commanding centre-half with many sterling performances for Watford Reserves.

Stalwart of local sport

James Freshwater **(JIMMY) CRUSSELL** *(1925)*
b Watford, Herts 19/2/1904
d Ottery St Mary, Devon 11/12/1983
FL 1 (-)
Old Fullerians; Leavesden Road Baptists; Sun Engraving; Watford (am 8/24); Tufnell Park; Clapton (cs 1925)
ENGLAND AMATEUR
A member of the Crussell family which ran a dairy in Leavesden Road, he went to Watford Grammar School before embarking on a successful football career as an amateur. As a Clapton player he won county and international honours, and his one League game was at inside-left in Watford's last game of 1924/5 - a goalless draw with Charlton Athletic.

A capped Fullerian

Reginald **HORACE CUMNER** *(1948-1950)*
b Cwmaman, Glam 31/3/1918
FL 62 (7), FAC 4 (-)
Swansea Town youth team; Arsenal (5/36); Margate (loan cs 1936 until 1/38); Hull City (loan 1/38); Notts County (part-exchange 7/46); Watford (£2,200 7/48); Scunthorpe & Lindsey Utd (3-figure fee 9/50); Bradford City (8/53); Poole Town (cs 1954); Bridport. Guested for Cardiff City, Clapton Orient, Fulham, Liverpool, Morton, Plymouth Argyle, Portsmouth, Port Vale and Swansea Town in WW2.

Scourge of England

WALES SCHOOLS and FULL
A left-winger who scored on his First Division début, as understudy to the great Cliff Bastin. His career was in doubt following a wartime accident in which he suffered burns when a hydrogen container exploded, but shortly afterwards he scored both goals for Wales at Wolverhampton in a 2-1 win against a very strong England side.

Hampden Park triumph

*John (JOHNNY) **CURRAN** (1957-1958)*
b Glasgow 22/6/1924
d Milltimber, Grampian 24/3/1985
FL 30 (-), FAC 1 (-), SFC 2 (-)
Queens Park (9/45); Aberdeen (pro 5/48); East Fife (2/51); Shrewsbury Town (free 8/56); Watford (unspecified fee 6/57 until cs 1958)
He had plenty of goalkeeping experience in Scotland before moving south to Gay Meadow. A memorable match-winning display at Vicarage Road the following February, in a match dignified by live radio coverage, led to his transfer to Watford a few months later. He helped East Fife to win the Scottish League Cup in 1953/4, when they were in the Second Division.

Railway transfer

*PATrick Joseph **CURRAN** (1939-1946)*
b Sunderland, Co Durham 13/11/1917
FAC 4 (-), WW2 16 (3)
Sunderland St Joseph's; Sunderland (am 1/36, pro 10/36); Ipswich Town (£750 10/38); Watford (£300 6/39); Bradford City (free 6/47). Guested for South Shields in WW2.
His transfer from Ipswich Town took place in unusual circumstances, when manager Bill Findlay travelled to the north-east, obtained the player's signature on Sunderland station, and immediately returned to Watford. The inside-forward's League début for the club was nullified by the declaration of war the next day.

Started with goal-burst

*Anthony William (TONY) **CURRIE** (1967-1968)*
b Edgware, Middx 1/1/1950
FL 17+1 (9), FAC 2 (-), FLC 0+1 (-)
Hendon Schools; Queens Park Rangers (sch 11/64); Chelsea youth team; Watford (appr 2/66, pro 5/67); Sheffield Utd (£26,500 2/68); Leeds Utd (£250,000 6/76); Queens Park Rangers (£400,000 8/79); Toronto Nationals, Canada (£60,000 5/83 until club folded 6/83); Chesham Utd (8/83); Southend Utd (9/83); Chesham Utd (11/83); Torquay Utd (3/84); Goole Town player-coach (9/87); Sheffield Utd community officer (by 2/89)
ENGLAND YOUTH, UNDER-23 and FULL; FOOTBALL LEAGUE
One of the country's most gifted midfielders during the 1970s, artistic on the ball and blessed with great vision. He had emerged spectacularly from his Watford apprenticeship with six goals in his first four League matches, but soon after his 18th birthday he was lost to the bigger clubs, and to a career by no means free of brushes with authority.

George H. **CUTTS** *(1921-1923)*
b Hucknall, Notts
FL 5 (-), FAC 1 (-)
New Hucknall Colliery; Arnold Town; Mansfield Town (cs 1919); Watford (5/20 until cs 1923); Sutton Town; Grantham Town; Hucknall Byron (permit player 9/27); Hucknall British Legion (permit player 10/30)
For the first three Football League seasons at Watford he was Skilly Williams's deputy - a thankless task at a time when the long-serving goalkeeper was rarely absent from first-team duty. Like so many players during Harry Kent's 16 years at the helm, Cutts was recruited from the East Midlands coalfields, and he later ended his career there.

Thankless task

BENjamin Edwin **DABBS** *(1938-1940)*
b Oakengates, Salop 17/4/1909
FL 3 (-), WW2 4 (-)
Oakengates Town (by 8/26); Liverpool (6/32); Watford (6/38 until cs 1945); Rickmanworth Town coach (1949/50)
After his six years at Anfield (54 games in the First Division) he found it difficult to wrest the Watford right-back shirt from the well-established Vic O'Brien. Dabbs was still on the club's books after the war, being transfer-listed at £250 in 1945, but had made what was to be his last appearance in a South Regional League fixture back in 1940.

Six years at Anfield

William **DACKERS** *(1902-1903)*
b Dalkeld, Perthshire 20/10/1874
SL 26 (1p), FAC 2 (-), SEL 1 (-)
St Johnstone; Victoria Utd; New Brighton Tower (by cs 1898); Aberdeen (11/01); Watford (5/02 until cs 1903)
Capped several times by Perthshire before turning professional, he held a regular first-team place during his one winter at Cassio Road. He played in various defensive positions in a season which ended with Watford relegated to the Second Division of the Southern League after an eventful Test Match which they lost 5-3 after equalising from 0-3 down.

Perthshire honours

MALCOLM Owen **DALRYMPLE** *(1974)*
b Bedford 8/10/1951
FL 5 (-)
Luton Town (am 9/68 until cs 1970); Margate; Bristol Rovers (10/71); Watford (free 7/73); Hendon (free cs 1975)
ENGLAND YOUTH
Despite national recognition as a junior goalkeeper, he failed to make the grade at senior level at Kenilworth Road. His League career eventually amounted to 12 games in the Third Division, including the last five of Watford's 1973/4 fixtures, the first three of which were won. He was kept out by Andy Rankin throughout the rest of his two seasons.

Luton international

Demob signing

<u>***RON**ald George* **DALY**</u> *(1950)*
b Clerkenwell, London 22/7/1930
FL 3 (-), FAC 1 (-)
<u>Watford</u> (am 9/50, pro 10/50); Dover (free 8/52)
He signed amateur forms for Watford immediately after being demobbed from the RAF, and soon turned professional, as a part-timer. His single run of first-team appearances was in the inside-right position, at a time when the No 8 shirt was frequently changing hands, and it included an FA Cup defeat at Norwich in front of over 21,000.

Mancunian influx

<u>***ARTHUR* DANIELS**</u> *(1926-1930)*
b Manchester, Lancs
FL 136 (16 inc 1p), FAC 10 (1)
Salford Lads Club; West Salford; Mossley; Manchester City (am 8/20, pro 2/21); <u>Watford</u> (5/26); Queens Park Rangers ("small fee" 6/30 until cs 1931)
A forward who was fast and clever, but lacked consistency and didn't relish the rough stuff. His Watford career was spent mainly on the left wing, and having travelled south from Maine Road with Jack Warner he was one of a succession of good players recruited from the two Manchester clubs in the late 1920s. He was Bill Sheppard's best man.

Heavy defeat

<u>*Alfred Ronald* **DARVILL**</u> *(1925)*
b Berkhamsted, Herts 27/10/1897
d Ilford, Essex 1960
FL 1 (-)
Watford Corinthians (by 2/20); Ilford (by 9/20); <u>Watford</u> (am 6/23, pro 9/24 until cs 1925)
One of three brothers from Harwoods Road who made a name for themselves in local football. His only League game was a 4-0 defeat at Exeter, in which he played at centre-forward. A few weeks earlier his brother Harvey had died as a result of injury sustained in a collision with Leicester City's goalkeeper while he was playing for Fulham.

Good start to married life

<u>***GEORGE* DAVENPORT**</u> *(1896-1899)*
b Tarporley, Cheshire 19/12/1876
d St Pancras, London 1910
SL 47 (1), FAC 1 (-), FAAC 2 (-), HSC 1 (-), BCCL 2 (-)
Watford Permanent Way (by 10/94); <u>West Herts</u> (am 12/95, pro 11/97 until cs 1899)
A versatile defender who missed only two games in the club's first two seasons in the Southern League. He enjoyed an eventful day on 15th January 1898, being married in the morning and then helping to beat Warmley 4-0 in front of a record Cassio Road crowd of 3,000. Before turning professional he'd represented Herts.

__GRAHAM__ *Golding* **DAVIES** *(1947-1948)*
b Swansea, Glam 3/10/1921
FL 9 (-)
Swansea Town (am 11/40, pro 2/42); Watford (6/47); Colchester Utd (trial 4/49)
WALES SCHOOLS
Although playing second fiddle to other goalkeepers during his two seasons as a part-time player at Vicarage Road, he conceded only eleven goals in his nine League appearances. He was outstanding as a schoolboy, and got his professional career going during the Second World War. When he left Swansea he was a Flight Lieutenant in the RAF.

RAF officer

Robert **DAVIES** *(1910-1911)*
b Chirk, Denbighs
SL 15 (-), FAC 2 (-), SCC 1 (-)
Cammell Laird; Stafford Rangers; Watford (am 9/10, pro 9/10); Manchester City (8/11); Pontypridd (free 6/12)
WALES AMATEUR
Signed soon after being capped, he turned pro after one friendly appearance as an amateur. A right-half, he was on stand-by as reserve for the Full international side three months later, but didn't travel. He shared a birthplace with the immortal Billy Meredith of Manchester City, a club which Davies himself represented in the First Division.

Amateur cap

Thomas *(TOM)* **DAVIES** *(1933-1937)*
b Troedyrhiw, Glam
FL 58 (3), FAC 3 (-), 3SC 7 (-)
Luton Town (am 7/24, pro 9/24 until cs 1925); Bournemouth & Boscombe Athletic (10/25 until cs 1928); Columbia; Chelsea (8/29); Watford (free 7/33); Exeter City (free 5/37); Walsall (8/38 until cs 1939)
After he'd dropped into minor football, his professional career was resurrected by Chelsea, although he was only a reserve-team player in his four years at Stamford Bridge. A wing-half sound in tackling and distribution, he played League football for four clubs, most of it for Watford and all of it in the Third Division (South).

Div 3(S) was his level

William *(TAFFY)* **DAVIES** *(1931-1950)*
b Troedrhiwfuwch, Glam 24/6/1910
d Watford, Herts 30/10/1995
FL 283 (69 inc 7p), FAC 29 (3 inc 1p), 3SC 13 (3 inc 1p), WW2 128 (56 inc 12p)
New Tredegar; Watford (am 4/30, pro 7/30 until cs 1950). Guested for Bradford City, Grimsby Town and Notts County in WW2.
WALES WARTIME
A forceful, skilful and two-footed winger or inside-forward, he was one of very few men who have spent 20 seasons with one League club. His international honour came while he was guesting for Grimsby. At the age of 39 he was denied what was widely regarded as a valid opening goal against Manchester United in the FA Cup. Watford lost 1-0.

20 years' service

J. **DAVIS** *(1903-1904)*
SL 1 (-), SEL 1 (-)
Watford (am)
There were very few team changes during Watford's Southern League Second Division championship-winning season in 1903/4, but Davis appeared once - in a 3-1 home win over Chesham Town. A right-back who hailed from Bushey, he also played in a South-Eastern League home game against Hitchin, who turned up two men short and were beaten 9-0.

Promotion skipper

Joseph (JOE) **DAVISON** *(1927-1931)*
b Byers Green, Co Durham 6/7/1897
FL 135 (2 inc 1p), FAC 12 (-)
Durham Schools; Byers Green; Willington Juniors; Middlesbrough (10/19); Portsmouth (5/23 until cs 1927); Watford (9/27 until cs 1932)
He started his professional career after war service in Palestine, and was an experienced and accomplished full-back when he reached Vicarage Road, where he spent five seasons before retiring to become licensee of the *Sebright Arms* at Boxmoor. He skippered Portsmouth to the Division 3 (South) championship in his first season at Fratton Park.

Cup-final hat-trick

ALBERT **DAY** *(1949)*
b Camberwell, London 7/3/1918
d Brighton, Sussex, January 1983
FL 4 (1)
Preston Rovers; Fulham (am 11/37 until 2/38); Hastings & St Leonards; Brighton & Hove Albion (am 4/38, pro 8/38); Ipswich Town (5/46); Watford (free 6/49); Folkestone (free, cs 1950); Ashford (by 8/54); Crawley Town (9/55 briefly). Guested for Ipswich Town, Lincoln City and Reading in WW2.
His only League goal for Watford in a single run of four appearances at centre-forward came at Portman Road, from whence he had just been transferred. That goal was the only one scored by Watford in his four games. As a pre-war amateur he had represented Sussex and scored a hat-trick for Hastings & St Leonards in the 1938 Sussex Senior Cup Final.

Watford-born forward

Burcombe James (JIMMY) **DAY** *(1952)*
b Watford, Herts 9/5/1931
FL 3 (-)
Berkhamsted Town; Watford (pro 12/51); Dover (free 7/53); Ashford Town (by 8/54); Chatham; Leavesden Hospital (8/57 until 1961/2)
A local forward who had a season-and-a-half at Vicarage Road. His brief first-team experience came not long after he signed, during a season in which Watford avoided by one point having to seek re-election for a second year running. He did the rounds in Kent before dropping back into local amateur football with Leavesden in the County League.

ROGER Arthur **DAY** *(1962)*
b Romford, Essex 3/12/1939
FL 1 (-)

Dagenham Schools; Ilford Boys; Briggs Sports; Leytonstone; Enfield; Watford (am 12/61); Slough Town; Enfield; Ilford; Enfield; Hayes; Wycombe Wanderers; Walton & Hersham; Hendon player-coach; veterans football
ENGLAND AMATEUR
An inside-forward of class and vision who had an immensely distinguished amateur career, captaining England in nearly half his 43 internationals. He was also an Amateur Cup-winner with Enfield in 1967 and (as captain) 1970. For two seasons he played in mid-week games for Watford Reserves, and the club offered him professional terms, which he declined.

Distinguished amateur

Edward John **(EDDIE) DENTON** *(1991)*
b Oxford 18/5/1970
FL 0+2 (-)
Oxford Utd (sch 12/84, tr 7/86, pro 7/88 until cs 1989); Witney Town; Watford (2/91) Newbury Town (free, cs 1992); Chesham Utd (2/95)
Having trained with Watford as a 12-year-old he linked up with Oxford United, where he became known to Steve Perryman, who was to sign him for Watford after Denton had been forced out of the game by an injury sustained against Watford Reserves. His League career as a midfielder amounted to two substitute appearances for each of his clubs.

Injured against Watford

William Gemmell **(BILL) DEVAN** *(1933-1937)*
b Whitletts, Ayrshire 23/2/1909
d Paddington, London 12/12/1966
FL 90 (33), FAC 5 (1), 3SC 6 (1)
Ayr Utd (5/28 until 2/29); Ards (12/29); Sanquhar (5/31); Coleraine (6/31); Linfield; Watford (8/33 until cs 1938, reserve-team trainer 1958/9). Scammells (permit player) in WW2.
IRISH LEAGUE
He enjoyed the unusual distinction, for a Scot, of playing for the Irish League v the Scottish League and the Football League. He scored in both games - and got goals for Watford too, at a healthy rate for an inside-left, including a hat-trick in eight minutes. He received compensation for injury sustained as a pro, before being allowed to play for Scammells.

Opposed his compatriots

William **(WILLIE) DEVINE** *(1958-1959)*
b Whitletts, Ayrshire 22/8/1933
FL 30 (6), SFC 1 (-)
Whitletts Victoria (7/55); St Mirren (3/56); Watford (3/58); Partick Thistle (11/59); Accrington Stanley (5/60 until 2/62); Cambridge City (1962/3)
By a remarkable coincidence, he was born in the same tiny corner of Scotland as his alphabetical predecessor. One of a succession of Caledonians brought to Vicarage Road by Neil McBain, he scored on his début, at Southend. He emigrated to Australia, where he employed Freddie Bunce, who'd been his rival for the Watford No 11 shirt.

Crossed the border twice

Stylish international

ALAN Ernest **DEVONSHIRE** *(1990-1991)*
b Park Royal, Middx 13/4/1956
FL 23+2 (1), FAC 1 (-), FLC 1 (-)
Southall & Ealing Borough; West Ham Utd (£5,000 10/76); Watford (free 6/90 until cs 1992); Cippenham Sports player-coach; Osterley manager (cs 1995); Brentford Ladies manager
ENGLAND 'B' and FULL
Following his father into League football, he had a long and excellent career in West Ham's midfield, fast and stylish in possession, before injury took its toll. He was in the Second Division side which lifted the FA Cup in 1980, and won eight Full caps. As a trialist with Wycombe Wanderers after leaving Watford, he suffered a depressed cheek-fracture.

Wore specs in goal

Leonard Frederick (LEN) **DEWICK** *(1924)*
b Watford, Herts 24/2/1900
d Worthing, Sussex 8/3/1981
FL 7 (-)
Watford (am 11/23); Chesham Utd (6/25); Tufnell Park (1926); Chesham Utd (1927); Barnet (1929)
He kept goal wearing spectacles, and although never a professional he was the club's second choice for a while, at a time when Skilly Williams reigned supreme. After conceding ten goals in his first three League games, he kept clean sheets in the next three. Whilst playing for Chesham in 1925/6 he was picked for the Spartan League representative side.

13 seasons at Brighton

PERRY Michael **DIGWEED** *(1993-1995)*
b Westminster, London 26/10/1959
FL 28+1 (-), FAC 1 (-), FLC 1 (-)
Fulham (appr 9/76, pro 8/77); Brighton & Hove Albion (£150,000 1/81); West Bromwich Albion (loan 10/83); Charlton Athletic (loan 1/85); Newcastle Utd (loan 12/87); Chelsea (loan 2/88); Wimbledon (loan 3/93, free 8/93); Watford (free 12/93 until cs 1995)
An apprentice when he started his Football League goal-keeping career, he then had to wait two-and-a-half years for a second game. His 13 seasons at Brighton were littered with injuries and loan transfers, and in only half a season at Vicarage Road in 1993/4 he achieved his third-highest seasonal total of League appearances in a very long career.

Rejected by Tottenham

KERRY Michael **DIXON** *(1996)*
b Luton, Beds 24/7/1961
FL 8+3 (-)
Chesham Utd; Tottenham Hotspur (appr 7/78); Dunstable Town; Reading (£20,000 7/80); Chelsea (£175,000 8/83); Southampton (£575,000 7/92); Luton Town (loan 2/93, free 8/93); Millwall (£5,000 3/95); Watford (£25,000 1/96)
ENGLAND UNDER-21 and FULL
One of English football's outstanding strikers of the 1980s, he came to Vicarage Road very late in a career that brought him well over two hundred League goals after he'd been rejected by Tottenham Hotspur at the end of his apprenticeship. Fast, and athletically built, he enjoyed his best years with Chelsea, and won eight England caps.

Part Two

Top scorer twice

*Thomas (**TOMMY**) **DIXON** (1911-1913)*
b Cramlington, Northumberland
d 1941
SL 72 (21), FAC 8 (4), SCC 2 (1)
Bedlington Utd (5/06); Middlesbrough (1/07); Watford (£25 6/11); Bristol Rovers (£100 4/13); Blyth Spartans (cs 1914)
Top scorer in both his Watford seasons, he was then sold with Jack English to raise £600 to finance a summer wage-bill which retained players who would otherwise have been free to move on. It was a regular end-of-season necessity for the club at that time. He returned to the North-East in 1914 because of his wife's ill-health. She died a few months later.

Cup win led to transfer

***DAVID** Morgan **DONALD** (1913-1914)*
b Coatbridge, Lanarks 21/7/1885
d Derby 19/1/1932
SL 22 (3), FAC 2 (-)
Albion Rovers (7/05); Bradford Park Avenue (6/08); Derby County (£350 3/10); Chesterfield Town (6/12); Watford (£70 6/13); Queens Park Rangers (cs 1914 until cs 1921); Hamilton Academical (7/22 until cs 1923). Guested for Derby County and Leicester Fosse in WW1.
Bought to replace Arthur Squires at outside-left, he'd played in the Chesterfield side which beat Watford in the FA Cup only months earlier. His three Watford goals all came in two Easter fixtures on successive days. He played regularly in the same forward line as the great Steve Bloomer at Derby, before losing his place to Ivan Sharpe, signed from Watford.

Non-League double

***GARY DONNELLAN** (1981)*
b Westminster, London 3/7/1962
FLT 0+1 (-)
Chelsea (appr 9/78, pro 7/80); Watford (free 12/80); Reading (£5,000 11/81); Wealdstone (free, cs 1983). Yeovil Town; Slough Town (by 1/91); Hendon (6/92)
A winger who didn't get any League action with his first two clubs, although he did once spend 90 frustrating minutes on the bench at Watford. He had the satisfaction of scoring a Football League Trophy hat-trick against the club after being sold to Reading, and in 1984/5 he helped Wealdstone to achieve the major non-League equivalent of the Double.

Old Fullerians founder

*Herbert James **DOW** (1896-1897)*
b Watford, Herts 13/7/1874
d Westminster, London 21/9/1922
SL 5 (-)
The Grove (by 1889); West Herts (late-1893/4); also Old Fullerians (1894); Crouch End Vampires (by 2/97)
The son of a Watford High Street saddler, he was a founder and leading light of the Old Fullerians. He also skippered the Reserves at Cassio Road and went on several tours to the Channel Islands with both clubs. His few first-team games on the left wing were not appreciated by his colleagues - he was dropped at their request. He served on the Herts FA committee.

Valued by Taylor

*Robert David (**BOBBY**)* **DOWNES** *(1974-1979)*
b Bloxwich, Staffs 18/8/1949
FL 192+7 (18), FAC 9 (-), FLC 21+1 (4)
West Bromwich Albion (youth team, pro 8/66); Peterborough Utd (free 9/67); Rochdale (free 8/69); Watford (£10,000 5/74); Barnsley (£10,000 3/80); Blackpool (free 6/82, player-coach by cs 1983); Aston Villa youth-team manager (7/87); Port Vale (youth-team coach cs 1991, coach by cs 1993); Wolverhampton Wanderers (assistant-manager 6/94, caretaker-manager 11/95, director of youth football 12/95 until 2/96); Watford director of youth football (6/96)
Well-established after three seasons at Vicarage Road, he was then used by Graham Taylor on the left wing for two successive promotion seasons. Taylor also employed him in his managerial teams at Villa Park and Molineux and back at Watford. Downes had once been a full-back. Some of his shooting was spectacular.

C.F. **DRAKE** *(1902)*
SL 1 (-)
Hitchin Town; Casuals; West Herts (am)
He played only twice for the club's first team, those two Easter-weekend games being seven years apart, the first of them a friendly against Wolverton. His second appearance was at outside-right in front of one of Cassio Road's biggest attendances at the time - nearly 5,000 - as Portsmouth won 5-0 *en route* to the Southern League championship.

Wartime signing

*Charles John (**CHARLIE**)* **DRINKWATER** *(1941-1947)*
b Willesden, Middx 25/6/1914
FL 1 (-), FAC 9 (-), WW2 46 (5)
Golders Green (by 10/32); Walthamstow Avenue; Middlesex Wanderers; Brentford (am 6/34); Aston Villa (11/35); Charlton Athletic (7/38 until cs 1939); Watford (2/41 until cs 1947); Pinner trainer-coach (2/48); Ruislip Manor (player-manager by 4/52, until 10/53)
A diminutive left-winger whose peacetime Football League career was restricted to just six games - five of them in the First Division - with three clubs. He did, however, play wartime football after signing for Watford in 1941, and was ever-present in the 1945/6 FA Cup run, when all ties except the final were played over two legs.

Poor return for £2,500

***GEORGE** Benjamin* **DRURY** *(1948-1949)*
b Hucknall, Notts 22/1/1914
d Hucknall, Notts 19/6/1972
FL 35 (3), FAC 1 (-)
Hucknall Colts; Hucknall Congregationalists; Hucknall Villa; Loughborough Corinthians; Heanor Town; Sheffield Wednesday (9/34); Arsenal (3/38); West Bromwich Albion (10/46); Watford (£2,500 7/48 until cs 1950); Linby Colliery (11/50); Darlaston; South Normanton (until retirement circa 1954). Guested for Burnley, Bury, Doncaster Rovers, Liverpool, Nottingham Forest, Notts County and Sheffield Wednesday in WW2.
During his tour of minor clubs before turning professional he had a trial at The Hawthorns, but didn't sign for Albion until 12 years later. In the meantime he'd been a First

Division player at Hillsborough and Highbury. Watford used him in a number of attacking positions, but his performances didn't justify the big fee they'd paid.

*William (**BILLY**)* ***DRYDEN*** *(1913-1914)*
b Amble, Northumberland
SL 20 (8 inc 1p), SCC 1 (-)
Broomhill (8/06); Blyth Spartans (9/07); Ashington (5/08); Choppington; Clapton Orient (11/12); Watford (£25 7/13); Portsmouth (£100 1/14)
He occupied all three inside-forward positions in his few months at Watford, and hit four goals in his last three games before that £100 took him to Hampshire. In an earlier game he'd scored within seconds of the start, before an opponent had touched the ball. He was nicknamed 'Squash' for reasons now unknown, and his son played for Bristol City in the 1930s.

Scored within seconds

JASON DRYSDALE *(1989-1994)*
b Bristol, Glos 17/11/1970
FL 135+10 (11 inc 5p), FAC 2 (-). FLC 8+1 (2 inc 1p), FMC 2 (-), AIC 2 (-)
Watford (sch 3/85); FA School of Excellence; Watford (tr 7/87, pro 9/88); Newcastle Utd (£425,000 8/94); Swindon Town (£340,000 3/95)
ENGLAND YOUTH
Always fielded wide on the left, he served Watford sometimes in midfield, but usually in defence, his great strength being an ability to strike venomous left-foot shots and crosses. Despite the big fee, he didn't make Newcastle's first team, and moved on after only a few months. His father played in over 500 League games as a full-back.

Short stay at Newcastle

KEITH** Barry Lenoux **DUBLIN *(1990-1994)*
b High Wycombe, Bucks 29/1/1966
FL 165+3 (2), FAC 4 (-), FLC 12 (-), FMC 2 (-), AIC 4 (-)
Chelsea (sch 9/81, appr 7/82, pro 1/84); Brighton & Hove Albion (£50,000 8/87); Watford (£275,000 7/90); Southend Utd (valued at £100,000 in exchange for D.R.Payne 7/94)
ENGLAND YOUTH
His dependability as a central defender improved greatly after an error-strewn start to his Watford career, when his strength and speed were often negated by moments of over-confidence when in possession. He was a first-teamer at Vicarage Road almost without interruption for four seasons, in the second and third of which he was ever-present.

Two seasons ever-present

REGinald** Arthur **DUDLEY *(1950)*
b Hemel Hempstead, Herts 3/2/1915
d Cambridge, February 1994
FL 1 (-)
Boxmoor St John's; Apsley (cs 1934); Millwall (am 12/34, pro 3/35); Queens Park Rangers (player-exchange 12/46); Watford (£200 7/50); Dover (free 8/51); Margate (11/52 until 12/53); also Hemel Hempstead Town coach (cs 1953,

Apsley honour

manager 12/53 until 10/55)
ENGLAND AMATEUR
He put off turning professional until he'd won his expected Amateur cap with Apsley, and years later, as a veteran full-back, was brought to Vicarage Road to captain the Reserves. He was dismissed as Hemel Hempstead Town (formerly Apsley) manager in the light of financial irregularities, in connection with which he had been acquitted of criminal charges.

Record pre-war fee

William Leonard **(LEN) DUNDERDALE** *(1938-1948)*
b Willingham-by-Stow, Lincs 6/2/1915
d Saxilby, Lincs 11/1/1989
FL 74 (34), FAC 7 (4), WW2 8 (5)
Goole Town (1933); Sheffield Wednesday (am 3/34, pro 5/34 until cs 1935); Walsall (3/36); Watford (£1,000 5/38); Leeds Utd (£3,750 3/39); Watford (4/46); Sittingbourne (1948/9); Berkhamsted Town coach (cs 1949 until 2/54); also Sun Sports coach (by 8/50); Watford scout (2/54); Berkhamsted Town coach (by 10/56 until cs 1957, and from 6/60). Guested for Grimsby Town, Lincoln City, Mansfield Town and Watford in WW2.
In that one pre-war season his dashing centre-forward play and ferocious shooting were the talk of Vicarage Road and beyond, and the directors were unable to resist a club-record transfer fee. His second spell, after the war, was an unhappy one in which the home crowd turned against him. He once scored seven in a game for Walsall Reserves.

£1.25 million at 18

BRUCE *Antonio* **DYER** *(1993-1994)*
b Ilford, Essex 13/4/1975
FL 29+2 (6), FAC 1 (-), FLC 4 (2), AIC 2 (1)
Watford (sch 9/90, tr 7/91, pro 4/93); Crystal Palace (£1.25 million plus 20% of any 'sell-on' profit, 3/94)
ENGLAND UNDER-21
Spectators quickly responded to his exuberant and direct forward play in both wide and central positions, but soon he'd left the club as Britain's costliest teenager and was scoring important goals in Under-21 internationals. He's often wrongly been described as a relative of former Watford apprentice Alex Dyer, who forged a League career elsewhere.

Early goal-burst

John **BARRY DYSON** *(1968)*
b Oldham, Lancs 6/9/1942
d Layer de la Haye, Essex 26/2/1995
FL 38 (19), FAC 1 (-), FLC 1 (-)
Bury (am 8/59, pro 9/60); Tranmere Rovers (7/62); Crystal Palace (£15,000 9/66); Watford (£9,000 1/68); Orient (£8,000 12/68); Colchester Utd (7/73 until cs 1975); Chelmsford City (loan 2/75)
Four goals against Northampton Town took his Watford total to 13 in 13 League games, but a failure to produce the high work-rate demanded by Ken Furphy was to lead to the striker's departure as his goalscoring fell away. It was Tranmere who benefited from his most sustained scoring efforts - 99 goals in 174 League games.

Part Two

Terence Gerald (**TERRY**) **EADES** *(1976)*
b Bambridge, Co Down 5/3/1944
FL 4 (-)
Chelmsford City (by 1963); Cambridge Utd (2/69); Watford (loan 9/76); Chelmsford City (free 7/77); Histon
An Ulsterman who played Southern League football for both Chelmsford and Cambridge United. Following the latter's elevation to Football League status, he remained a pillar of their defence, rarely absent from the centre-half position in their first six seasons of League football. His loan appearances for Watford were as Alan Garner's partner.

East Anglian Ulsterman

Walter (**WALLY**) **EAMES** *(1901-1907)*
b Watford, Herts 21/12/1883
d Leavesden, Herts 11/3/1941
SL 61 (11), FAC 5 (6), SEL 9 (9), UL 8 (7)
Crescent Ramblers; Melrose (until 1902); Watford (am, pro 2/03); Tottenham Hotspur (£20 5/06); Watford (8/07); New Brompton (10/08 until 1911)
Only four younger players have represented Watford in a Southern League or Football League game. He was picked for the county before turning pro at 19, had a season at White Hart Lane, and later sustained an injury which at one time was thought likely to cost him the sight of an eye. He turned out for the club in all five forward positions.

To Tottenham for £20

Michael (**MIKE**) **EARLY** *(1946)*
b Dumbarton, Dunbartonshire 4/4/1928
d Dumbarton, Strathclyde 26/5/1995
FL 5 (1)
Strathleven; Watford (6/46 until cs 1948); Clydebank Juniors (6/50 until cs 1951)
A slightly-built, fast right-winger who was brought south at the age of 18 and went straight into the first team. He scored on his home début, against Mansfield Town, but a cartilage injury sustained soon afterwards led to an operation, and he never again played in the senior side before being released at the end of his second season.

Cartilage setback

RAYmond John **EASTWAY** *(1951-1952)*
b Croydon, Surrey 12/4/1929
d Wandsworth, London, January 1989
FL 12 (-), FAC 2 (-)
Manchester Utd 'A' team; Watford (8/49 until cs 1953); Hartlepools Utd (8/55 until 10/55); South Wimbledon Athletic (permit player 10/56)
He joined Watford on being demobbed from National Service in the army. Sturdy and two-footed, he had four seasons at Vicarage Road, but his only first-team action - all in the No 2 shirt - came in the 1951/2 season. The club transfer-listed him at an unrealistic £750 at the end of the following season, at which point he left the game for a while.

Few opportunities

Non-scorer in 10-1 win

SAMuel Llewellyn L. **EATON** *(1905-1906)*

b Derby 1878

SL 11 (1), FAC 1 (1), SEL 2 (1), UL 10 (1)

Derby Schools; Derby St James; Derby County Reserves (two seasons); Hinckley Town (1897); Leicester Fosse (2/98); Hinckley Town (8/00); Stockport County (5/01); Leicester Fosse (1/02); Luton Town (5/03); Watford (5/05); Earlestown (8/06); Accrington Stanley (10/06); Maidstone Utd (12/06 until at least 1908/9)

Having captained Derby Schools at 13, he enjoyed a professional career as a forward which incorporated a fair amount of League experience in Division 2 at both Leicester and Stockport. In his Watford season he failed to get on the scoresheet in a 10-1 United League win over Grays United, when seven of his colleagues scored, including the goalkeeper.

Stand-in amateur

A.W. (DOSS) **EBDEN** *(1907)*

SEL 2 (-)

St John's, Hitchin; Hitchin Town (by 8/04); Biggleswade (1906/7); Hitchin Town; Watford (am, cs 1907); Hitchin Town (3/08 until 4/08)

He was at the centre of Watford's defence in two South-Eastern League matches, the experienced Alf Hitch being one of several regulars rested from first-team duty. Both games were against Clapton Orient, who took maximum points with victories by 4-2 and 3-2. Alongside Ebden at left-half on each occasion was another reserve, George Howard.

Furphy's captain

KEITH **EDDY** *(1966-1972)*

b Barrow-in-Furness, Lancs 23/10/1944

FL 239+1 (26 inc 14p), FAC 19 (3p), FLC 15 (2 inc 1p)

Holker Old Boys; Barrow (6/62); Watford (£1,500 7/66); Sheffield Utd (£50,000 8/72 until 1/76); New York Cosmos, USA (4/76 until 1977); Toronto Blizzard, Canada coach (3/79 until 1981)

One of the outstanding transfer bargains in Watford's history. He was a cool, commanding defender or midfield player and influential captain during the Ken Furphy era, leading the club into the Second Division and to an FA Cup semi-final - both new experiences. Furphy later took him to the USA, where he stayed and became successful in business.

Clean sheets

DEREK James **EDMONDS** *(1971)*

b Newcastle-upon-Tyne, Northumberland 9/10/1950

FL 15 (-)

Leeds Utd (appr 5/66, pro 11/67); Watford (free 5/70); Cape Town City, South Africa (free 5/72); Southport (trial 7/74 until 10/74)

ENGLAND YOUTH

After nearly three years as a pro goalkeeper at Elland Road without getting into the first team, he finally made his League début well into his first season at Watford, and was then beaten only once in his first five games - and in a struggling side. Southport didn't sign him after his trial period, as Cape Town, who still held his registration, wanted £5,000.

Top-scored in title win

GEORGE William Neville **EDMONDS** *(1913-1927)*
b Finsbury, London 4/4/1893
d Ryde, Isle of Wight 10/12/1989
SL 85 (45 inc 2p), FL 22 (12), FAC 5 (3), WW1 6 (7)
Watford Schools; St Stephens (by 4/09); André & Sleigh (1910/1); Watford Wednesday (by 3/12); St Albans City (1912); Watford (am 2/13, pro 7/14); Wolverhampton Wanderers (£1,500 5/20); Fulham (10/23); Watford (£250 9/26 until cs 1927); Northfleet (10/27); Bushey United coach (8/31). Guested for Crystal Palace in WW1.
Employed in Watford's print industry throughout his career as a professional centre-forward, he nevertheless top-scored when the club won the Southern League championship, played in the 1921 FA Cup Final, and was an England reserve. His transfer fee in 1920 (Val Gregory went to Wolves simultaneously for the same amount) was easily a Watford record.

H.R. (HARRY) **EDWARDS** *(1899)*
SL 7 (-), BCCL 2 (1)
Singers (cs 1891); Small Heath (8/92); Ryton Rovers (8/93); Leicester Fosse (10/93); Derby County (8/94); Wolverton LNWR (cs 1895 until cs 1898); Watford (12/98); Bedford Queen's Engineering Works (12/00 until at least cs 1903)
He'd refused Wolverton's renewed terms and was out of training when he turned out in a friendly for Watford on Boxing Day 1898, but did well enough to earn an engagement for the remainder of the season. He represented the club at both right-half and inside-right, and had previously played alongside his brother for Wolverton.

Best of Leicester job-lot

Thomas (TOMMY) **EGGLESTON** *(1948-1952)*
b Consett, Co Durham 21/2/1920
FL 177 (6), FAC 9 (-)
Derby County (am 12/36, pro 2/37); Leicester City (the lesser portion of a joint £5,000 transfer 7/46); Watford (one of four players signed for £4,750 1/48 until 7/53); Brentford trainer (9/54); Watford trainer (5/57); Sheffield Wednesday trainer-coach (10/58); Everton coach (6/61); Mansfield Town manager (8/67); Ethnikos, Greece manager (7/70); Panahaiki, Greece manager (1971); Everton (youth-team manager cs 1972, assistant-manager 5/72 until 6/73, also caretaker-manager 4/73); Plymouth Argyle physiotherapist; Ipswich Town trainer (12/78 until retirement). Guested for Coventry City, Lincoln City and Southampton in WW2.
Of the Filbert Street consignment he proved easily the most successful, and stayed to give stylish service at wing-half or full-back until an injury sustained in September 1952 eventually ended his playing career. His coaching and physiotherapy qualifications stood him in good stead, and by 1957 he was the Football League's only qualified remedial gymnast.

Decades at Loftus Road

James Arthur E. (JIMMY) **EGGLETON** *(1923-1926)*
b Heston, Middx 1897
d Hillingdon, Middx 13/1/1963
FL 48 (2), FAC 4 (-)
The Army; Slough (am); Charlton Athletic (am 9/21, pro 1/22); Watford (£500 12/23); Queens Park Rangers (10/26 until 1931, assistant-trainer, trainer until retirement)
As a gunner in the Royal Artillery he played for The Army in representative matches in 1920/1. He was a strong-tackling centre-half who had several bursts of first-team action in his three years at Vicarage Road, and then began an association with Queens Park Rangers which lasted until the 1960s and encompassed a variety of roles during the war.

Cost money at 38

Albert John (JACK) **ELKES** *(1933)*
b Snedshill, Shropshire 31/12/1894
d Colchester, Essex 22/1/1972
FL 9 (1)
St Georges Amateurs; Wellington Town (1911); Stalybridge Celtic (1914); Shifnal Town; Birmingham (1/18); Southampton (player-exchange involving F.H.Foxall and others 3/22); Tottenham Hotspur (£1,050 5/23); Middlesbrough (£500 8/29); Watford (£150 8/33); Stafford Rangers (cs 1934); Oakengates Town (1935 until 1937); Ford Motor Works coach
ENGLAND 'UNOFFICIAL'; FOOTBALL LEAGUE
One of Watford's oldest signings - he was 38 - he'd had a highly respectable career as a big inside-forward or centre-half which incorporated three games for England in Australia and three for the Football League. It was in the defensive position that he made his League appearances for Watford, in the first nine games of 1933/4.

Beat ex-colleagues twice

FREDerick Charles **ELLIS** *(1931-1932)*
b Isle of Sheppey, Kent 7/10/1900
d Isle of Sheppey, Kent 1970
FL 30 (1), FAC 7 (-)
Sheppey Utd; Gillingham (6/25); Watford (free 6/31); Clapton Orient (free 7/32); Ashford Town (10/33)
He was an Aston Villa trialist in 1924/5, but it was with his local club that he started his League career, spending six years at Priestfield. A fairly regular choice at wing-half in his one Watford season, he had the satisfaction of taking part in a League double over his former colleagues. His only goal contributed to a 3-0 win over Cardiff City.

Led two Div 4 triumphs

SAMuel **ELLIS** *(1977-1978)*
b Ashton-under-Lyne, Lancs 12/9/1946
FL 30+4 (4 inc 3p), FAC 1 (-), FLC 5 (1p)
Snipe Wanderers; W.H.Smith, Manchester; Sheffield Wednesday (9/64); Mansfield Town (£10,000 1/72); Lincoln City (5/73); Watford (£6,000 7/77, coaching staff cs 1979, reserve-team manager); Blackpool manager (6/82 until 3/89); Bury manager (5/89); Manchester City assistant-manager (12/90 until 8/93); Lincoln City manager (5/94 until 9/95); Bury assistant-manager (11/95)

ENGLAND UNDER-23
A strong, tough-tackling centre-half who captained Graham Taylor's Fourth Division championship-winning teams at both Lincoln and Watford. Injury problems brought his playing career to an end, but he stayed in the game in coaching and managerial posts. His long Hillsborough stint encompassed an FA Cup Final appearance at the age of 19.

BARRY ENDEAN (1968-1971)
b Chester-le-Street, Co Durham 22/3/1946
FL 72+5 (28), FAC 13 (8), FLC 2+1 (1)
Pelton Fell; Watford (8/68); Charlton Athletic (£10,000 2/71); Blackburn Rovers (player-exchange 10/71); Huddersfield Town (3/75); Workington (loan 10/75); Hartlepool (3/76 until cs 1977); Workington manager (4/79 until cs 1980); Chester-le-Street (youth-team manager by 12/84, manager 3/88)
Plucked as a raw, enthusiastic striker from local football in the north-east, he spearheaded Watford's first rise to the Second Division, becoming a Vicarage Road cult figure in the process. His goals included a dramatic diving header against Liverpool which took the club into the 1970 FA Cup semi-finals - again, hitherto uncharted territory.

Swashbuckler

John Cogal (JACK) ENGLISH (1912-1913)
b Hebburn, Northumberland 13/12/1886
d Northampton 21/1/1953
SL 33 (-), FAC 3 (-), SCC 1 (-)
Hebburn Argyle (9/07); Wallsend Park Villa; Preston North End (5/10); Watford (under £100 8/12); Sheffield Utd (£500 4/13); Darlington manager (by 12/19); Nelson manager (cs 1928); Northampton Town manager (1/31); Exeter City manager (10/35 until 1939); Darlington manager (1945/6)
FOOTBALL LEAGUE
Watford received five times what they'd paid for him nine months earlier, the sale being needed to finance the club's summer wage-bill. He was a full-back who was good enough to play First Division football for Preston and then Sheffield United, whom he helped to win the FA Cup in 1915. His son scored 135 League goals for Northampton Town - a club record.

Quick 400 % profit

GEORGE Arthur EPHGRAVE (1951)
b Reading, Berks 29/4/1918
FL 4 (-)
Guernsey Rangers; Tottenham Hotspur (am 10/35); Northfleet (loan); Aston Villa (10/36); Swindon Town (3/39); Southampton (4/46); Norwich City (£500 7/48); Watford (8/51); Deal Town (8/52); March Town (8/53)
A Channel Islander from boyhood. Although not the club's most prominent goalkeeper in other ways, he was physically an imposing one, standing over 6'4" and wearing size-12 boots. He conceded seven goals at home on his Watford début - against one of his former clubs, Swindon. After being captured on Crete, he spent four years as a POW in Germany.

Memorable début

Soon discarded

Bernard **ROY**den **EVANS** *(1951)*
b Rotherhithe, London 7/10/1929
FL 2 (1)
Millwall (3/50); Watford (free 8/51); Canterbury City (free, cs 1952 until at least 9/53)
He couldn't get into Millwall's first team, and after being released he spent two months on trial at Vicarage Road before being engaged. He made his début straightaway - it was Shrewsbury Town's first-ever League game - and scored in a 3-2 away win. Although he kept the No 10 shirt for the next fixture, he was never picked again.

Christmas Day threesome

Denzil **RALPH EVANS** *(1937-1948)*
b Hungerford, Berks 9/10/1915
d Langley, Bucks 20/2/1996
FL 88 (30), FAC 8 (2), 3SC 5 (4), WW2 7 (1)
Yeovil & Petters Utd; Bury (am 2/34, pro 7/35); Halifax Town (7/36); Watford (free 7/37 until cs 1948, assistant-trainer cs 1950 until 1952)
An enthusiastic forward whose long Watford service, spanning the Second World War, was ended by injury, as a result of which he received £300 compensation. He was the club's top scorer in 1946/7, when he scored a Christmas Day hat-trick v Southend United, who avenged the 4-0 defeat with a 5-0 victory on Boxing Day.

Began with a goal

HUGH EVANS *(1952-1953)*
b Llanwonno, Glam 12/12/1919
FL 7 (2)
Redditch Utd; Birmingham City (am 11/47, pro 12/47); Bournemouth & Boscombe Athletic (6/50); Walsall (8/51); Watford (free 8/52); Bedford Town (7/54)
Signed by Watford when he was in business in Luton, where he had been brought up, he had a single run in the first team, in mid-season in the No 10 shirt, and scored on his début in a 2-0 win against Crystal Palace. Six games and one more goal later, he was replaced by Jimmy Bowie, returning from an absence caused by injury, and didn't play League football again.

Expectations unfulfilled

Jethro **EVANS** *(1912-1913)*
b Irchester, Northants 2/1/1887
d Mitcham, Surrey 12/5/1967
SL 11 (1), FAC 3 (-), SCC 1 (-)
Raunds St Peter; Sheffield Utd (am 2/08, pro 2/08 until cs 1909); Sutton Junction; Watford (5/12 until cs 1913)
Brought to Watford on the strength of his 30 goals in 1911/2 for Notts & Derbys League club Sutton Junction, he fell well short of expectations at centre-forward, scoring only once for the first team, in a Southern League win at Stoke. He was only a reserve for Sheffield United, who made a grant of £10 to Raunds St Peter after signing Evans and a colleague.

CHARLIE **EWINGTON** *(1934-1936)*
b Willesden, Middx 1/1/1914
d Watford, Herts 2/2/1978
FL 12 (-)
Greycaine Athletic; North Watford Athletic; St Albans City (9/32); Watford (am 5/32, pro 10/32 until cs 1938); Greycaines (permit player, cs 1947); other local teams until 1958
After developing locally in amateur football, he became a pro at Vicarage Road, but in six seasons on the staff he had very little first-team experience, being used as a stand-in full-back. He had a hand amputated in an industrial accident at Greycaines in 1942, but continued to play in local football until he was 44. He died in a car accident.

Rarely in the first team

JOHN **FAIRBROTHER** *(1959-1963)*
b Cricklewood, Middx 12/2/1941
FL 40 (19), FAC 3 (2), SFC 1 (-), FLC 2 (1)
Bennetts End Youth Club; Luton Town (am 11/58); Watford (am 6/59); Hemel Hempstead Town; Watford (pro 8/59); Worcester City (under £1,000 8/63); Peterborough Utd (£5,000 5/65); Northampton Town (2/68); Mansfield Town (9/71); Torquay Utd (6/73); Bath City (free 7/74); Barnet (1976 until 1978); Hemel Hempstead Town; Berkhamsted Town; Leverstock Green (by 12/84); Garston Veterans (by 2/94)
A sensational start in the Reserves (four goals in his first game, whilst still an amateur, and 40 in his first season) were no guarantee of first-team opportunities, for which he had to wait. He actually played in three different cup competitions before embarking on a long, free-scoring League career, which continued at senior non-League levels.

Always scored goals

MARK *Peter* **FALCO** *(1986-1987)*
b Bethnal Green, London 22/10/1960
FL 33 (14), FAC 7 (2), FMC 1 (-)
Tottenham Hotspur (sch 11/75, appr 7/77, pro 7/78); Chelsea (loan 11/82); Watford (£350,000 10/86); Rangers (£350,000 7/87); Queens Park Rangers (loan 12/87, £350,000 1/88); Millwall (£175,000 8/91 until 6/92); Enfield (11/92); Worthing (11/92); Enfield (12/92); Cornard (1/94); Worthing (8/94); Hitchin Town (3/96); Worthing assistant-manager (3/96)
ENGLAND YOUTH
Although lacking pace, he had enough strength and guile to enjoy a top-class career as a striker, mainly with Tottenham, whom he helped to win the UEFA Cup in 1984. He scored once in his first game for Watford - at Highbury - and then three times at home in his second, against Aston Villa. A spinal injury ended his career in full-time football.

European success

Shared Aberdeen triumphs

*William Henry (**WILLIE**)* ***FALCONER*** *(1988-1991)*
b Aberdeen 5/4/1966
FL 87+13 (12), FAC 6 (1), FLC 5 (-), FMC 2+3 (-)
Lewis Utd; Aberdeen (4/82); Watford (£300,000 6/88); Middlesbrough (£305,000 8/91); Sheffield Utd (£425,000 8/93); Celtic (£375,000 2/94); Motherwell (£200,000 1/96)
SCOTLAND SCHOOLS and YOUTH
As a teenager he got into Aberdeen's first-team squad during the great years at Pittodrie. A versatile player, he spent most of his Vicarage Road spell as an attacking midfielder capable of strong, surging runs. Watford benefited from his move to Bramall Lane, 5% of Middlesbrough's 'sell-on' profit being included in the £305,000.

Went to Division 1

JOHN *Denis* ***FARLEY*** *(1971-1974)*
b Middlesbrough, Yorks 21/9/1951
FL 97+8 (8), FAC 5+1 (1), FLC 4 (-)
Stockton; Watford (6/69); Halifax Town (loan 9/71); Wolverhampton Wanderers (£40,000 5/74); Blackpool (loan 10/76); Hull City (£30,000 5/78); Bury (8/80 until cs 1981)
One of a clutch of players from the North-East who were brought to Vicarage Road as a result of Ken Furphy's intimate knowledge of the area. The club was on the slide when he was establishing himself as a left-winger of League status, but he survived the bad times well enough to attract a useful fee eventually from Wolves, then in the First Division.

Not a happy ending

*Thomas (**TOT**)* ***FARNALL*** *(1900-1902)*
SL 30 (1), FAC 4 (1p), SEL 1 (-)
Eastville Rovers; Small Heath (9/93); Eastville Rovers (6/97); Small Heath (5/99); Watford (7/00); Bristol Rovers (5/01); Watford (5/02 until 12/02); Bradford City (5/03); Walsall (11/05); Barrow-in-Furness (5/06); Gloucester
His career encompassed two spells with each of three different clubs. The second Cassio Road stint ended with his being sacked, and he then got at loggerheads with his next employers and walked out. His first Watford game ended 1-6 (although he did score the goal), and his last 0-11. A wing-half, he had represented Gloucestershire before turning pro.

Began as an ever-present

Austin ***LES****lie* ***FARNEN*** *(1946-1949)*
b St Helens, Lancs 17/9/1919
d Harrow, Middx, January 1985
FL 77 (-), FAC 4 (-), WW2 1 (-)
Watford (am 4/46, pro 5/46); Bradford City (5/49 until 11/49)
Watford signed him on amateur forms, then as a pro, just after he'd returned from service abroad. He went straight into the first team for 1946/7, and was ever-present at centre-half, but his good fortune with fitness ran out the following season, during which he broke a collar-bone. His Bradford City engagement ended early, after eight League appearances.

ALEC ***FARRALL*** *(1966-1967)*
b Hoylake, Cheshire 3/3/1936
FL 47+1 (8), FAC 5 (3), FLC 3 (-)
Everton (am 7/51, pro 3/53); Preston North End (5/57); Gillingham (7/60); Lincoln City (6/65); Watford (free 6/66 until cs 1968)
ENGLAND SCHOOLS
A midfield player with over 13 seasons' experience as a professional by the time he moved to Vicarage Road, including a brief taste of First Division football at Goodison Park early in his career. He was part of Ken Furphy's team-building which was to take the club into the Second Division, but was released a year before the prize was attained.

Shone as a schoolboy

ALBERT Ernest ***FARROW*** *(1908-1909)*
b Gainsborough, Lincs 1886
d Gainsborough, Lincs 28/9/1916
SL 9 (-)
Working Men's Club & Institute, Gainsborough; Gainsborough Trinity (5/06); Watford (8/08): Worksop (cs 1909 until at least cs 1912)
Used both at half-back and on the wing, he was a young left-sided player who didn't appear on a winning side in his first six Southern League matches, but was recalled for the last three games of the season, all of which were won. He enlisted in June 1916, but was discharged with tuberculosis two months later, and died shortly afterwards.

TB victim

Fred (TINY) ***FAYERS*** *(1908-1910)*
b Kings Lynn, Norfolk 29/1/1890
d Huddersfield, Yorks 4/2/1954
SL 64 (2), FAC 5 (-), SCC 1 (-)
Watford & District Schools; St Albans City; Watford (am); Huddersfield Town (am 5/10, pro 11/10); Stockport County (1918); Manchester City (8/20); Halifax Town player-coach (5/23 until cs 1924). Guested for Stockport County in WW1.
ENGLAND AMATEUR
He progressed through Watford schools football to become a Southern League player at 18, to represent the county, and at 19 to win the club's first international honour at any level. Altogether he won nine Amateur caps and scored three goals. He was an accomplished centre-half (although under 5′6″ in height) or right-half.

First international cap

W. ***FELLOWS*** *(1899-1901)*
SL 19 (-), BCCL 8 (-)
Watford Wanderers (by 1/95); West Herts (am)
A local player who had a good run as an amateur in the right-half position after the club had adopted professionalism. Never a goalscorer in a first-team shirt, he even failed to score when Maidenhead turned up for a Southern League fixture two men short and were beaten 11-0. All eight forwards and half-backs found the net - except Fellows.

Up-and-down career

John Joseph **FERGUSON** *(1929-1930)*
b Rowlands Gill, Co Durham
FL 4 (-)
North-East junior football; Grimsby Town (10/26); Workington (8/27); Spen Black & White; Wolverhampton Wanderers (12/28); Watford (free 10/29); Burton Town (free 7/30); Manchester Utd (5/31); Derry City (12/31)
He had a strangely up-and-down career so far as the stature of his various clubs was concerned, and played League football for four of them. His Watford appearances were all at outside-right, but he had little chance of dislodging Billy Chapman on a permanent basis, and left on a free transfer after less than a season with the club.

George Edward **FERNE** *(1900)*
b Burton-on-Trent, Staffs 1874
d Coventry, Warwicks 19/5/1955
SL 4 (1)
Hinckley Town; Lincoln City (6/98); Millwall (5/99); Watford (7/00 until 10/00); Fulham (12/00); Coventry City (7/02)
He started the 1900/1 season as the first-team left-winger, but soon lost his place, and in October he left the club, terms having been agreed for the conclusion of his engagement. His first Watford appearance was subsequently chalked off, after the opposition (Chatham) had resigned from the Southern League in mid-season.

Sidney **FIELD** *(1905)*
SEL 1 (-)
Callow Land Old Boys; Watford (am); Rickmansworth (by 9/10); Watford Orient (cs 1912)
Prominent in local football, he turned out for Watford as an amateur, appearing in one first-team friendly and also in a 6-0 South-Eastern League win over Hastings & St Leonards United. Although playing at centre-forward, he didn't score. Like Jimmy Carr and Albert Green, he played for Watford Orient from that club's formation in 1912.

*William (**BILL**)* **FINDLAY** *(1932-1936)* - SEE PART FIVE

Solid defender

KENneth Douglas Walter **FISHER** *(1947-1951)*
b Bitterne, Hants 30/9/1921
d Watford, Herts 29/4/1989
FL 106 (2), FAC 4 (-)
Bitterne Nomads; Southampton (am 8/40, pro 9/46); Watford (6/47); Bedford Town (8/51); Biggleswade Town. Guested for Bristol City in WW2.
After a post-war season at The Dell in which he failed to make the first-team, he had four years at Vicarage Road as a big, solid defender who played in all three half-back positions. It was at left-half that he played throughout the club-record sequence of eight clean sheets in League games. Both his first-team goals came in his final season.

<u>PETER</u> <u>**FISHER**</u> *(1936)*
b Glasgow
FL 3 (1)
St Anthony's (8/32); Clyde (8/34); Stenhousemuir (8/35); Watford (free 7/36); Burnley (undisclosed fee 1/37); Dunfermline Athletic (8/39 until cs 1946)
Under 5'6" in height, he'd experienced regular Scottish League football before joining Watford after a month's trial. Playing at inside-left in the opening match of the season, he scored in a 3-1 win at Newport, but missed the next three games, and then appeared only twice more. A few months later he was playing in the Second Division.

Sold to Divison 2

<u>GARY</u> *Michael* <u>**FITZGERALD**</u> *(1994)*
b Hampstead, London 27/10/1976
FL 1 (-)
Watford (sch 1/92, tr 7/93, pro 11/94 until 8/95); Yeading (briefly 12/95); Enfield (2/96)
Injuries to senior central defenders led to his premature elevation to first-team status as a trainee. The tension of a local derby, and three first-half Luton goals, led to his replacement at the interval. As a youth-team player he was sent off for punching his own goalkeeper, and he was eventually sacked by the club for misconduct unconnected with football.

In at the deep end

<u>GEORGE</u> *Keith* <u>**FLEMING**</u> *(1958-1959)*
b Gourock, Renfrewshire 25/2/1935
FL 27 (10), FAC 4 (-), SFC 1 (-)
Gourock Juniors (1952); Morton (7/52); Watford (6/58); Carlisle Utd (4-figure fee 6/60); Barrow (9/60); Dartford (free, cs 1961); Sittingbourne (briefly); Dunstable Town (until 1964)
A forward with spectacularly fierce shooting ability whose career was ended in 1964 by an ankle injury which had been sustained years before at Vicarage Road. He settled in the Watford area and became a shopkeeper. His sporting prowess extended to the golf course, and he was good enough to be elected captain of the West Herts club in 1988.

Fierce shooting

<u>ELI</u> <u>**FLETCHER**</u> *(1926-1927)*
b Tunstall, Staffs 15/12/1887
d Manchester, Lancs 6/8/1954
FL 23 (-), FAC 2 (1)
Elder Road Juniors (4 seasons); Goldenhill Wanderers; Hanley Swifts; Crewe Alexandra; Manchester City (£300 5/11); Watford (free 6/26); Sandbach Ramblers (free 8/27); Ards (7/28); Manchester City trainer (8/28)
FOOTBALL LEAGUE
His transfer to Watford at the age of 38 ended 15 years' service with Manchester City, during most of which he was the first-team left-back. He was responsible for two of City's three penalty-kick failures in a single First Division match in 1912. His only Watford goal (a freak free-kick) was one of ten against Lowestoft Town in an FA Cup tie.

15 years at Maine Road

1st Division début at 17

Leonard (LEN) **FLETCHER** *(1935-1938)*
b Overton, Cheshire
FL 36 (22), FAC 6 (3), 3SC 3 (1)
Mersey Power; Frodsham; Helsby Athletic; Warrington; Manchester City (11/32); Watford (undisclosed fee 5/35); Runcorn (free 7/38)
A livewire centre-forward who lacked finesse but found the net consistently when in the first-team, and hit League hat-tricks against Swindon Town (away) and Crystal Palace. He'd been a First Division player at 17, but had to wait a couple of seasons for his second game. He married a professional singer named Annie Bate.

80% off list price

William **FLINT** *(1910-1911)*
SL 17 (4), FAC 3 (3), SCC 3 (3)
Scotswood (8/08); Hebburn Argyle (9/08); Middlesbrough (11/08); Watford (£50 5/10); Gateshead (cs 1911); Ashington (8/12)
He was transfer-listed by Middlesbrough with a fee of £250 on his head, but the Football League reduced this to £50, which brought him within Watford's range. He became a regular member of the forward line, finding cup ties particularly to his liking, but faded from the scene after half a season, and returned to the North-East in the summer.

Brought sudden stability

COLIN John **FOSTER** *(1994-1996)*
b Chislehurst, Kent 16/7/1964
FL 66 (7), FAC 6 (-), FLC 6 (1)
Elmstead; Oxford, Kent; Orient (sch 9/78, appr 7/80, pro 2/82); Nottingham Forest (£50,000 2/87); West Ham Utd (£750,000 9/89); Notts County (loan 1/94); Watford (£80,000 3/94)
A 6'4" central defender who, with over four hundred League and cup games under his belt, was signed to bolster a Watford team which was unable to keep a clean sheet and in danger of relegation. So effective was he that, although goals continued to be leaked when he was out injured, only one was conceded in the six games in which he did play that season.

Vigorous attacker

CYRIL James **FOSTER** *(1925-1928)*
b Aylesbury, Bucks 1903
FL 70 (24), FAC 1 (-)
Aylesbury; Wycombe Wanderers; Watford (am 7/25, pro 9/25); Queens Park Rangers (free 6/28 until cs 1930)
Making his first three League appearances before turning professional, he scored in the second and third of them - his first two home games. An inside-forward with a vigorous style, he enjoyed himself with two Christmas Day goals in 1925. He scored again eight days later - but it was Watford's sole reply to Aberdare Athletic's eight.

John (JACK) **FOSTER** *(1905-1907)*
SL 57 (29 inc 1p), FAC 2 (1), SEL 3 (2), UL 17 (7)
Rotherham Church Institute; Thornhill Utd (5/00); Blackpool (5/01); Rotherham Town (free, cs 1902); Watford (5/05); Sunderland (£800 12/07); West Ham Utd (5/08); Southampton (3/09); Huddersfield Town (cs 1909, assistant-trainer cs 1912); Blackpool; Huddersfield Town assistant-manager; Bradford City assistant-manager (8/26); Portsmouth scout (by 9/38)
Signed after scoring heavily in the Midland League, he led the attack for most of his two-and-a-half seasons at Cassio Road. The sum paid by Sunderland was an astronomical one for Watford (three years earlier it would have been a world record), but he proved a poor investment. In his second Huddersfield spell he was Herbert Chapman's assistant.

Massive fee

ARTHUR Thomas **FOXALL** *(1923-1924)*
b Halesowen, Worcs 27/5/1897
d Birmingham, West Midlands 6/5/1980
FL 3 (1)
Pontypridd; Merthyr Town (5/21 until cs 1923); Watford (9/23); Portsmouth (free 5/24); Kidderminster Harriers (cs 1925 until at least 1927/8)
One of three West Midlands brothers who played League football, he was picked twice at left-half (with brother Fred at outside-left) and then later, for his third and final appearance, he actually replaced the ill-fated Fred on the wing. At both Merthyr and Portsmouth Arthur was a team-mate of the third brother, Harry.

Replaced his brother

FREDerick Howard **FOXALL** *(1923-1924)*
b Blackheath, Staffs 2/4/1898
d Smethwick, Staffs 17/6/1926
FL 32 (2), FAC 3 (-)
Saltwells; Aston Villa (am 4/15); Blackheath Town (9/16); Southampton (5/19); Birmingham (player-exchange involving A.J.Elkes and others 3/22); Watford (£300 6/23 until cs 1924)
As the regular first-team outside-left he had much more impact than his brother, but became the first Watford player to break a leg in a Football League match. He broke it again a few months later in his garden, following a walk in Cassiobury Park. This ended his football career, and only two years later he died at 28.

Leg broken twice

ALBERT **FRANCIS** *(1924)*
*(formerly Albert Francis **ALBON**)*
b Arlesey, Beds 21/7/1901
d Stamford, Lincs 17/3/1961
FL 1 (-)
Spalding Utd; Sheffield Utd (5/23); Watford (free 8/24 until cs 1925)
He represented Lincolnshire before making the big leap in status from Spalding to Bramall Lane, where he was unable to make the first team. He did so once after moving to Watford - at outside-right early in 1924/5.

Ashes scattered on pitch

After retiring he refereed in the Stamford area, and his ashes were scattered on the centre-spot at Stamford Town's ground.

Played three, lost three

John Joseph **FRANKISH** *(1913)*
b Darlington, Co Durham 1888
d Northumberland 1954
SL 2 (-), SCC 1 (-)
Chester-le-Street; Wallsend; Watford (5/13 until 11/13)
After playing at centre-half in the first two Southern League games of 1913/4, and later in a Southern Charity Cup tie against Luton Town (all three matches were lost), he was released from his engagement in November and returned to native parts, where he had earlier played for The Rest v The Champions of the North-Eastern League.

Youth Cup ever-present

PAUL Leslie **FRANKLIN** *(1981-1986)*
b Hainault, Essex 5/10/1963
FL 32 (-), FAC 5 (-), FLC 1 (-), FLT 0+1 (-), UEFA 4 (-)
Loughton Boys; Waltham New Town; Watford (sch 1/79, appr 4/80, pro 8/81); Shrewsbury Town (loan 10/86); Swindon Town (loan 11/86); Reading (free 7/87); Wycombe Wanderers (free, cs 1989, later coach); Norwich City assistant-manager (7/95); Leicester City assistant-manager (12/95)
A six-foot defender who spent some time with Birmingham City before committing himself to Watford at 15. He was ever-present in the FA Youth Cup-winning run in 1981/2, and his first-team experience included the remarkable UEFA Cup victory in Bulgaria. He served as assistant to Martin O'Neill at three different clubs in 1995.

Piledriver past Banks

COLIN James **FRANKS** *(1969-1973)*
b Wembley, Middx 16/4/1951
FL 99+13 (8), FAC 7 (1), FLC 3+2 (-)
Boreham Wood; Uxbridge; Wealdstone (mid-1967/8 until cs 1969); Watford (am 3/68, pro 6/69); Sheffield Utd (£60,000 6/73); Toronto Blizzard, Canada (3/79); Edmonton Drillers, Canada (6/82 until 8/82)
A utility player best remembered for the spectacular shot which beat Gordon Banks and took the club closer to its first FA Cup semi-final. He also scored five second-half goals for the Reserves in a Combination match against Orient. After a good career at Bramall Lane he sampled North American soccer, and settled permanently in Canada.

JOHN Watson **FRASER** *(1962-1964)*
b Belfast 15/9/1938
FL 24 (3), FAC 4 (-), FLC 1 (1)
Glentoran; Sunderland (3/59); Portsmouth (6/60 until cs 1961); Margate; Watford (free 7/62); Durban City, South Africa (free 3/64); Port Elizabeth, South Africa; two Transvaal, South Africa clubs including Corinthians; Durban City, South Africa trainer-coach; manager of a coloured club in South Africa

NORTHERN IRELAND SCHOOLS and 'B'
Although they obtained his signature free, Watford later made an *ex gratia* three-figure payment to Margate, after he'd scored on his club début (in a League Cup game), and also in his first home League appearance. An inside-forward or winger, he stayed in South Africa after moving to Durban City, whom he helped to win the national cup competition.

Cup-winner in Africa

GRAHAM *Edward* **FRENCH** *(1964)*
b Wolverhampton, Staffs 6/4/1945
FL 4 (-)
Huddersfield Town (am 5/60); Shrewsbury Town (appr 5/61, pro 11/62); Swindon Town (£11,500 8/63); Watford (£1,250 8/64); Wellington Town (free 11/64); Luton Town (10/65 until 12/70, and 9/72 until 1/74); Reading (loan 11/73); Boston Minutemen, USA (6/74 until 8/74); Southport (3/76 until 4/76)
ENGLAND YOUTH
A talented right-winger of great potential whose career was beset by disciplinary problems which culminated in imprisonment following a shooting incident in Luton. He subsequently changed his surname by deed poll to Lafite. (Could this have been an excruciating play on words, based on his original name and his profession?)

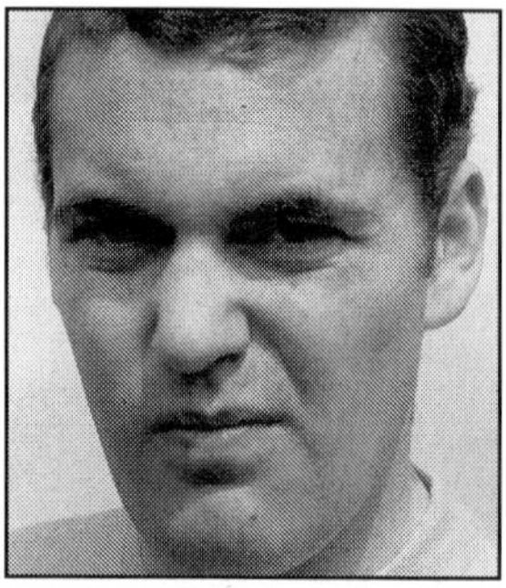

Squandered talent

Edward William ***(EDDIE)*** **FULLER** *(1927-1929)*
b Staines, Middx 1900
FL 55 (-), FAC 4 (-)
London Caledonians; Brighton & Hove Albion (am 2/21, pro 3/21); Watford (free 5/27 until cs 1929); Brighton & Hove Albion (9/29 until cs 1931, and 8/32 until cs 1933); Worthing (permit player 1/34, for several seasons)
Neat and quick, he was a versatile player whose talents were utilised by Watford solely in a defensive half-back role. After returning to the Goldstone he was out of the game for a season, but then joined Brighton yet again, and subsequently enjoyed a successful spell at Worthing, having been granted permission to play as an amateur.

Returned to Brighton

JOHN *Patrick* **FURIE** *(1967)*
b Hammersmith, London 13/5/1948
FL 0+1 (-)
Watford (am 1/65, appr 5/65, pro 5/66); Gillingham (free 6/67); Chelmsford City (cs 1968); Oxhey Jets; Sun Sports manager (until 2/83); Oxhey Jets manager (2/86 until 8/87)
In one of the shortest of all Watford careers in terms of Football League action, he replaced Jimmy Lawton for the final 33 minutes of a home game against Leyton Orient, which ended in a 3-1 defeat. After being released, he had more League opportunities the following season, making 17 appearances in Gillingham's defence.

A first-teamer - just

Brought goals and cash

PAUL Anthony **FURLONG** *(1992-1994)*
b Wood Green, London 1/10/1968
FL 79 (37 inc 1p), FAC 2 (-), FLC 7 (4), AIC 3 (-)
Middlesex Schools; Fox's; Enfield; Coventry City (£130,000 7/91); Watford (£250,000 7/92); Chelsea (£2.3 million 5/94)
ENGLAND SEMI-PROFESSIONAL
His success as an athletic striker in the non-League game brought him what proved an undistinguished season in the Premier League at Coventry. He then spent two seasons as leading scorer at Vicarage Road, before Chelsea took him back into the top flight by means of a fee which Watford found unable to refuse, and which brought them a handsome profit.

KENneth **FURPHY** *(1964-1968)* - SEE PART FIVE

Football in the blood

GEORGE Melville **FURR** *(1906-1909)*
b Barnet, Herts 1885
d Letchworth, Herts 2/1/1967
SL 37 (3), FAC 4 (-), SEL 2 (-), UL 3 (3)
St John's, Hitchin; Hitchin Town (by 8/04); Biggleswade (8/06); Watford (am 1906/7, pro 7/07); Manchester City (5/09 until cs 1910); Croydon Common (cs 1911); Watford (reinstated am, cs 1912)
One of Vic Furr's footballing brothers, George was a forward who returned south whilst on Manchester City's transfer list and temporarily left the game when his first application for reinstatement as an amateur was refused. He later had a butcher's business and also bred greyhounds. (As far as is known, the two activities were not connected.)

VICtor Reginald **FURR** *(1925)*
b Hitchin, Herts 26/4/1897
d Winterton-on-Sea, Norfolk 16/10/1976
FL 1 (-)
Hitchin Town; Watford (am)
One of a family which included George, two other brothers who were professionals, and another who played for Watford Reserves - and their sister married Billy Grimes. Later, a son of George signed amateur forms at Vicarage Road. Vic, who was known as 'The Midget', made his League appearance, on the right wing, 16 years after George left the club.

Stayed for five years

GEORGE **FYFE** *(1905-1919)*
b Govan, Lanarks
SL 119 (7 inc 2p), FAC 9 (-), SEL 4 (-), UL 23 (4), SCC 2 (-), WW1 1 (-)
Neilston Victoria; Hibernian (5/04); Watford (8/05 until 3/10); Dundee Hibernian (8/10); Dumbarton (8/11); Dundee Hibernian (12/11); Halifax Town (1/12); Abercorn (1916/7). Guested for Watford in WW1.
A wing-half or forward who gave the club excellent service for nearly five years before leaving in March 1910, "on the best of terms", to return to Scotland, where he subsequently resumed his career. He turned out for Watford again in a friendly match in April 1919. Before his move to Cassio Road he'd played in the Scottish First Division.

Arthur Edward **(BERT)** ***GALE*** *(1901-1910)*
b Watford, Herts 1882
d Watford, Herts 3/12/1945
SL 4 (-), FAC 1 (-), SCC 1 (-)
Watford Rovers (not the original club of that name); Watford (am); also Melrose (by early 1901/2); also Shepherds Bush (am by 2/06)
A local wing-half whose first two senior competitive appearances were separated by nine-and-a-half years. He captained the Reserves, represented both Herts and Middlesex, was successful on the running track, and became secretary of Watford Amateur Boxing Club. He suffered a broken leg in the 1910 Willesden train crash which caused five deaths.

Leonard **(LEN)** ***GALLIMORE*** *(1937-1946)*
b Northwich, Cheshire 14/9/1912
d Stockport, Cheshire 1968
FL 64 (-), FAC 11 (-), 3SC 5 (-), WW2 19 (-)
Liverpool (am); Huddersfield Town (am 9/30); Dick, Kerr's; Bainton Victoria; Preston North End (am 9/31, pro 1/32); Watford (undisclosed fee 5/37 until 1/47). Guested for Arsenal, Blackpool and Burnley in WW2.
This well-built left-back was sacked by the club, and whilst still living in Watford was convicted several times of criminal offences, and twice jailed. When loaned to Arsenal at Vicarage Road in 1945 (they turned up two men short) he uncharacteristically scored twice, but Watford won 3-2. His brother was in Preston's FA Cup-winning team in 1938.

Only goals were against

Charles **(CHARLIE)** ***GALLOGLY*** *(1952-1954)*
b Gilford, Co Down 16/6/1925
FL 47 (-)
Shelbourne; Belfast Celtic; Waterford (1945/6); football in USA (briefly); Glenavon; Huddersfield Town (12/49); Watford (less than £1,000 7/52); Bournemouth & Boscombe Athletic ("small fee" 7/54 until 9/55)
NORTHERN IRELAND FULL
He didn't enter English football until he was 24, but reached Vicarage Road with 76 First Division games under his belt, as well as international appearances against England and Scotland. The Irish were heavily beaten on both occasions, and he wasn't capped again. Normally a full-back, he played occasionally at right-half for Watford.

Made it in England

TERRY *Graham* ***GARBETT*** *(1966-1971)*
b Lanchester, Co Durham 9/9/1945
FL 196+4 (46), FAC 21 (4), FLC 10 (-)
Pelton Fell; Middlesbrough (youth team, pro 8/63); Watford (£7,000 8/66); Blackburn Rovers (£20,000 9/71); Sheffield Utd (£35,000 2/74 until 2/76); New York Cosmos, USA (4/76 until 9/79); University of South Carolina, USA coach (by 3/94)
He joined Ken Furphy three times in England, and then in America, where Garbett stayed after his career was over. A forward or attacking midfielder with an impressive capacity and willingness for hard work, he missed very few first-team games whilst at Vicarage Road, and scored the club's consolation goal in their first FA Cup semi-final.

Semi-final scorer

Centre-forwards swapped

RAYmond Hardiman **GARBUTT** *(1950-1951)*
b Middlesbrough, Yorks 9/5/1925
d Middlestone Moor, Co Durham 2/11/1994
FL 22 (8), FAC 1 (-)
South Bank East End; Manchester City (9/47); Spennymoor Utd; Watford (5/50); Brighton & Hove Albion (exchange for C.A.Thompson 3/51); Workington (10/52 until cs 1953, but registration retained until cs 1960)
The move to Maine Road constituted a big step up, and he was unable to make the first team before returning to lower levels in the North-East. Watford introduced him to League football, but then used him in an unusual straight swap for Cyril Thompson - centre-forward for centre-forward. He later became a working-men's-club steward in Spennymoor.

Rarely absent

ALAN Henry **GARNER** *(1975-1979)*
b Walworth, London 2/2/1951
FL 200 (15), FAC 10 (1), FLC 22 (-)
South London Schools; Millwall (am 3/67, appr 4/67, pro 2/69); Luton Town (free 7/71); Watford (£22,000 2/75); Portsmouth (£80,000 2/80); Barnet (by 11/82); Chesham Utd (by 1/83); Barton Rovers player/assistant-manager (10/84)
Powerful and solid as a central defender, he was ever-present (as he had been the previous season) when Watford took the Fourth Division championship, and then missed only four games in the second successive promotion season. And at the end of five good years the club was still able to get nearly four times what they'd paid for him.

Success down under

BRIAN **GARVEY** *(1965-1970)*
b Hull, Yorks 3/7/1937
FL 179+1 (2), FAC 11+1 (-), FLC 9 (-)
Hull City (am 8/53, pro 1/58); Watford (free 6/65); also coached in Zambia (cs 1968); Colchester Utd (free 6/70); Bedford Town player-manager (free 7/72); Wolverhampton Wanderers (youth-team coach cs 1974, reserve-team trainer by 8/77); Arsenal reserve-team coach (7/81 until cs 1982); FA summer soccer-camps organiser; Heidelberg Alexander Utd, Australia coach (by 4/84); Hellas, Australia, coach
A sturdy defensive half-back who helped Watford to reach the Second Division for the first time and made a substitute appearance in the 1970 FA Cup semi-final. He later played in Colchester's historic FA Cup win over Leeds United, and later still, in Australia, he won both the Victoria and national coach-of-the-year awards for 1988.

Norwich City record

John Thomas (JOHNNY) **GAVIN** *(1958-1959)*
b Limerick 20/4/1928
FL 43 (12), FAC 3 (1), SFC 2 (-)
Jamesborough Utd; Limerick; Norwich City (£1,500 8/48); Tottenham Hotspur (5-figure fee 10/54); Norwich City (valued at £10,500 in player-exchange 11/55); Watford (7/58); Crystal Palace (4-figure fee 5/59); Cambridge City (free 7/61); Newmarket Town player-coach (8/62); Fulbourn (11/67)
REPUBLIC OF IRELAND FULL
Capped seven times, he was a nimble outside-right with a

quite admirable goalscoring return, which included 15 in only 32 First Division games for Tottenham. His League total of 122 in two spells at Norwich set a club record which still stands. Soon after leaving Watford he scored against them in Crystal Palace's freak 8-1 win.

Little impact at Watford

MARK Wilson **GAVIN** *(1990-1991)*
b Baillieston, Lanarks 10/12/1963
FL 8+5 (-)
Leeds Utd (sch 5/79, appr 5/80, pro 12/81); Hartlepool Utd (loan 3/85); Carlisle Utd (free 7/85); Bolton Wanderers (£10,000 3/86); Rochdale (£20,000 8/87); Heart of Midlothian (£35,000 1/88); Bristol City (£25,000 9/88); Watford (£250,000, including W.A.Allison in part-exchange, 7/90); Bristol City (£65,000 12/91); Exeter City ("nominal fee" 2/94 until 5/96)
In just over five years in his mid-twenties he played for eight different clubs, which did nothing to stabilise or advance a career which was possibly one of under-achievement, although he did contribute substantially to Bristol City's promotion from the Third Division. An introspective winger, he was seldom fit or available at Watford.

Started with big wins

James McLean (JIMMY) **GAY** *(1930)*
b Stanley, Perthshire 17/3/1897
d Blairgowrie, Perthshire 31/8/1967
FL 4 (-), FAC 1 (-)
Perth Celtic; Clydebank (9/20); St Bernards (11/20); Lochgelly Utd (5/21); Dunfermline Athletic (free 5/24); East Fife (free 6/24); St Bernards (11/24); Rhyl Athletic (8/25); Coventry City (free 6/26); Clapton Orient (5/28); Watford (free 5/30); Raith Rovers (free 6/31 until cs 1932)
His brief first-team career at Vicarage Road - all five games were in the left-back position in November/December 1930 - began spectacularly with wins by 6-0 against Torquay United in the League and 5-1 away to Walthamstow Avenue in the Cup. For his other two English clubs he made a total of 73 League appearances in four years.

League début at 15

Anthony Joseph (TONY) **GEIDMINTIS** *(1976-1978)*
b Stepney, London 30/7/1949
d Halifax, W Yorks 16/4/1993
FL 48+1 (-), FAC 5 (-), FLC 7 (-)
Workington (am 8/64, appr 4/65, pro 8/66); Watford (free 6/76); Northampton Town (£6,000 2/78); Halifax Town (7/79 until 4/80); Workington (briefly 1980/1); Watford scout (by 10/92)
An East-Ender whose family moved to Workington when he was nine, where his father (a Lithuanian refugee) took a job in the fur trade. That long career at Borough Park began with a League début at 15. A right-back, he was sent off twice in three weeks as a Watford player. A heart condition ended his career and eventually killed him.

GEORGE **GEMMELL** *(1912-1915)*
b King's Lynn, Norfolk 1889
d Langham, Rutland 25/1/1965

Cricket for Rhodesia

SL 6 (1), WW1 1 (-)
Queens' College, Cambridge; Watford (am 10/11); Ilford (by 11/12); Tottenham Hotspur (am 1913/4). Guested for Watford in WW1.
ENGLAND AMATEUR
An all-round sportsman whose Watford connection arose from his appointment as games master at the Royal Masonic School, Bushey. He was a centre-forward who played for both Norfolk and Herts, and won two Amateur international caps. He also represented Norfolk CCC and played First Class cricket for Rhodesia, where he lived for 13 years.

Let in six in only defeat

FRANK Richard **GEORGE** *(1964-1965)*
b Stepney, London 20/11/1933
FL 10 (-)
Carshalton Athletic; Leyton Orient (7/54); Watford (7/63); Worcester City (free 7/65)
He kept goal in over a hundred League games in his nine years at Brisbane Road, but spent the whole of his first season at Watford as understudy to the ever-present Pat Jennings. Of the first-team appearances which he did eventually make, only one ended in defeat - but it was no ordinary defeat, Reading putting six goals past him.

Famous FA Cup goal

Richard Stuart (RICKY) **GEORGE** *(1964-1965)*
b Barnet, Herts 28/6/1946
FL 4 (-), FAC 1 (-)
Tottenham Hotspur (am 8/61, appr 1/62, pro 10/63); Watford (free 8/64); Bournemouth & Boscombe Athletic (free 5/65); Oxford Utd (7/66); Hastings Utd (cs 1967); Barnet (8/68); Hereford Utd (3/71); Stevenage Athletic (cs 1973); Barnet (11/73); Cambridge City (cs 1975); Boreham Wood; Barnet (1976/7); Corinthian Casuals; Barnet vice-chairman (cs 1993 until 1994)
He failed to make the grade at White Hart Lane and his career total of League appearances as an outside-right was only 13, but he later scored a famous goal for non-League Hereford which knocked Newcastle United out of the FA Cup. As proprietor of a sports-goods business he became involved in the post-Flashman affairs of one of his old clubs, Barnet.

Unchallenged No 2

NIGEL James **GIBBS** *(1983-1996)*
b St Albans, Herts 20/11/1965
FL 287+6 (3), FAC 30+1 (-), FLC 15 (2), UEFA 2 (-), FMC 8 (-), AIC 1 (-)
Herts Schools; St Albans City youth team; Abbots Langley Rovers; Watford (sch 5/81, appr 7/82, pro 11/83 until cs 1996)
ENGLAND YOUTH and UNDER-21
A knee injury shortly after his appointment as club captain in 1992 put him out of the game for over two years, and then he got badly hurt again. His senior début was in the UEFA Cup, after only two days as a professional, and he came to monopolise the right-back position. Although rarely among the goals, he once scored in both legs of a League Cup tie.

PETER Leslie ***GIBBS*** *(1976)*
b Chingola, Northern Rhodesia 24/8/1956
FL 4 (-)
Tring Town; Watford (6/75 until 9/76); Tring Town
He was only 20 years old when, in September 1976, he announced his retirement after keeping goal in a 4-0 defeat against Cambridge United, on the grounds that he lacked the required dedication. He'd also played in the final three League games of the previous season, conceding only one goal in each.

Gave up at 20

FRANK Alec ***GIBSON*** *(1946)*
b Croxley Green, Herts 7/6/1914
FL 1 (-)
Rickmansworth Town (1931); Dickinson's, Croxley (1938/9); Rickmansworth Town (1939 until 1949); also Watford (am 5/46 until cs 1948)
Ricky's outside-right for 15 of his 18 seasons as a player, he retired in 1949 and joined the club's committee. His many medals included two won on the same day, and he played for RAF Uxbridge at Wembley Stadium in the 1942 Middlesex Senior Cup Final. He was one of five different No 7s used by Watford in a sequence of six League games.

Two cup finals in a day

PATrick ***GILLESPIE*** *(1945-1947)*
b Renton, Dunbartonshire 26/9/1922
FL 6 (-), FAC 10 (-), WW2 34 (-)
Maryhill (7/43); St Anthony's (9/43); Partick Thistle (8/44); Watford (free 7/45); Northampton Town (free 8/47); Portadown (cs 1948); Alloa (free 5/50 until cs 1951)
Watford's regular first-team right-half throughout the 1945/6 season, he then lost the No 4 shirt to his compatriot, Bobby Ross, for all but a short run the following December and January. He made 13 Scottish League appearances for Partick Thistle, who originally listed him at £100 in 1945, but then released him on a free transfer.

James Martin (JIMMY) ***GILLIGAN*** *(1981-1985)*
b Hammersmith, London 24/1/1964
FL 18+9 (6), FAC 5 (1), FLC 2+1 (2), FLT 1+1 (2), UEFA 3+1 (2)
Longmeadow Athletic; Watford (sch 4/78, appr 7/80, pro 8/81); Lincoln City (loan 10/82); Grimsby Town (£100,000 7/85); Swindon Town (£30,000 6/86); Newport County (loan 2/87); Lincoln City (£10,000 3/87); Cardiff City (7/87); Portsmouth (£215,000 9/89); Swansea City (£125,000 8/90 until 2/93); Boreham Wood (3/93); Watford (community officer 9/93 until 11/95, with occasional reserve-team appearances 1993/4); also Stamco (by 11/93); Watford (youth development officer 11/95, with occasional reserve-team appearances)
ENGLAND YOUTH
Centre-forward in the 1981/2 FA Youth Cup-winning team, he went on to score the club's first UEFA Cup goal, and later also played in Europe for both his Welsh clubs. He set probably a unique record with his First Division career total of six goals, which all came in pairs.

Scored only in pairs

Close to the Double

Charles Edward ***(CHARLIE) GLADWIN*** *(1919-1920)*
b Worksop, Notts 9/12/1887
d Rotherham, Yorks 1952
SL 12 (-)
Donnington Main Colliery (10/07); Blackpool (12/08); Sunderland (over £1,000 10/12); Watford (cs 1919, trainer 1/20 until cs 1920)
A member of the 1912/3 Sunderland team which won the League championship and was beaten in the FA Cup Final, he later joined Watford as an experienced full-back. After serving the club as a player until the New Year, he spent the remainder of his one season at Cassio Road as club trainer, when it became clear that the dying Tom Coulson couldn't continue.

Pioneer professional

John ***WALTER GLEW*** *(1897-1898)*
b Derby 1871
SL 11 (-)
Singers (10/90 to cs 1891); Northfleet (cs 1897); West Herts (9/97 until cs 1898); Sutton Town (8/02)
An obscure but nevertheless significant figure - he and Ike Marsh were the club's first two paid players following the adoption of professionalism. He was a full-back who'd been in the Royal Field Artillery prior to joining Northfleet, and had earlier helped Singers (later Coventry City) to win the Birmingham Junior Cup in 1891.

Two-year wait in Reserves

James Arthur George ***(JIMMY) GOOCH*** *(1956-1957)*
b Canning Town, Essex 11/7/1921
FL 43 (-), FAC 1 (-), SFC 1 (-)
Becontree; Preston North End (am 3/42, pro 5/42); Bradford City (7/53); Watford ("small fee" 7/54); Bath City (free 7/57); Yiewsley (two seasons); Sandown coach; Preston North End administrative staff (until 1991)
Formerly a London bobby, he kept goal 27 times as Preston took the Second Division championship in 1950/1. At Watford he waited nearly two seasons for a League game, at first being unable to dislodge Ted Bennett, and then, when Bennett was injured, finding Tommy King the next choice. But Gooch outlasted King, and his patience was eventually rewarded.

Seaside publican

Michael ***(MICKY) GOOD*** *(1899-1901)*
d Luton, Beds 1959 (aged 85)
SL 42 (6), FAC 7 (1), BCCL 5 (4)
Airdrie Hill; Airdrieonians (8/95); Small Heath (£70 11/96); Watford (8/99); Preston North End (6/01); Bristol City (5/02); Reading (cs 1903); Brighton & Hove Albion (5/04); Southern Utd (5/05)
Centre-half and captain in 1900/1, when only one away point was gained in the Southern League, and relegation was avoided only after a Test Match. In 1906 Southern United were briefly suspended by the FA until they paid what was due to him under his contract. He became the licensee of a Brighton pub, the *Flowing Tide*, and later went blind.

JOHN ***GOODALL*** *(1903-1907)* - SEE PART FIVE

KENneth George Alfred ***GOODEVE*** *(1974-1976)*
b Manchester, Lancs 3/9/1950
FL 67 (4), FAC 1 (-), FLC 5 (1)
Manchester Utd (sch 10/65, appr 9/66, pro 9/67); Luton Town (one of four players signed for £35,000 4/70); Brighton & Hove Albion (£20,000 12/73); Watford (£10,000 6/74 until cs 1976); Hitchin Town; Bedford Town (8/77 until at least 1981); Buckingham Town (by 3/84); Wootton Blue Cross (by 9/91)
Brought to Vicarage Road by a former Luton colleague, Mike Keen, he was an ever-present defender in 69 senior competitive games from the time of his signing. A groin strain ended his full-time career, but he was still playing in non-League football in his forties. He began at Old Trafford during its most glamorous period, but didn't make the first team.

Signed by ex-colleague

Edward (TED) ***GOODIER*** *(1935)*
b Farnworth, Lancs 15/10/1902
d Farnworth, Lancs 4/11/1967
FL 1 (-)
Brockhouse Utd; Bolton Wanderers (5/23); Lancaster Town (1924/5); Oldham Athletic (5/25); Queens Park Rangers (11/31); Watford (a fee plus H.P. Lowe 6/35); Crewe Alexandra (6/36); Rochdale (6/37, manager 9/38); Wigan Athletic manager (6/52 until 1954); Oldham Athletic manager (5/56 until 6/58). Birmingham caretaker-manager in WW2 (11/44 until 5/45)
A well-built veteran half-back, he was picked at centre-half for the opening game of the 1935/6 season, but didn't appear again in a first-team shirt. During his 14 years in charge at Rochdale he led that club to victory in the Lancs Senior Cup (in 1949), and later managed non-League Wigan when they drew at Newcastle in the FA Cup.

Rochdale boss 14 years

PETER *John* ***GORDON*** *(1958-1960)*
b Northampton 21/5/1932
d Claydon, Suffolk 22/5/1990
FL 43 (13), FAC 3 (-), SFC 3 (-)
Northampton Amateurs; Norwich City (pro 12/49); Watford (7/58); Exeter City (6/60); Newport County (7/62); Poole Town (free 7/63); Hartlepools Utd coach; Southend Utd trainer-coach (10/65 until at least 1/68); Northampton Town coach (until 1969)
After a longish career at Carrow Road he was half of a right-wing pairing which moved to Watford, Johnny Gavin being the partner. A hard-working inside-forward, Gordon had one whole winter in the first-team, but then played only five times in the Holton promotion season. He nevertheless made a good contribution to the Reserves' simultaneous title win.

Came with wing partner

Precocious 13-year-old

PETER John **GOY** *(1964-1965)*
b Beverley, Yorks 8/6/1938
FL 27 (-), FAC 1 (-), FLC 2 (-)
Arsenal (am 8/53, pro 6/55); Southend Utd (10/60); Watford (£1,000 7/64); Huddersfield Town (free 7/65 until 4/67); Hellenic, South Africa; Colchester Utd (free 8/69); Cambridge Utd (free 9/69)
He shared the goalkeeping duties with Frank George and, later, John Cowen, in his one season at Vicarage Road, in which he played in over half the first-team games. Before becoming an Arsenal junior, he'd played in under-18 football in Scunthorpe at the age of 13. In 1992 he was captain of Thorpe Hall Golf Club, Southend.

Scored from corners

LESlie **GRAHAM** *(1955-1957)*
b Barton-on-Irwell, Lancs 14/5/1924
FL 90 (26 inc 2p), FAC 4 (6), SFC 2 (1)
Flixton; Blackburn Rovers (4/47); Newport County (£2,500 2/53); Watford (nearly £3,000 6/55); Newport County (£1,250 9/57); Cambridge Utd (7/59); Merthyr Tydfil player-manager (1959/60 until at least 12/63); Cwmbran manager; Tottenham Hotspur scout; Newport County (coach, manager 2/67 until 5/69)
A crafty inside-forward with a good scoring record, he made 151 League appearances for Blackburn, who signed him when he was playing for the army in India. Among his goals for Watford were two scored direct from corners on successive Saturdays, and his FA Cup total accrued mainly from his five in two games against non-League opposition.

John Joseph (JACK) **GRAN** *(1900)*
b Mile End, London 1875
d Uxbridge, Middx 18/10/1939
BCCL 1 (-)
West Herts (am by 11/95); also Watford St Mary's (4/98); Watford (pro 1900/1)
Although he appeared in a few first-team friendlies from 1895, he played only once in a competitive game - at left-half in an 8-3 away win against Aylesbury United in the Bucks & Contiguous Counties League. He spent 30 years on the stage as 'Jack Cardiff', under which name his son became a renowned Hollywood cinematographer.

Two-goal début

Michael (MICKY) **GRAY** *(1947)*
b Ireland
FL 10 (3)
Glenavon; Aldershot (9/46); Watford (6/47); Worcester City (free, cs 1948)
He was brought to Watford by Jack Bray, in whose RAF station team he had played before he joined Aldershot. He wore the 9, 10 and 11 shirts in a brief first-team career which began with two goals in the opening game of the season, a 3-2 away win for Brighton & Hove Albion. His only other goal came in his tenth and last appearance.

Roland (RON) **GRAY** *(1942-1946)* - SEE PART FIVE

Albert **GREEN** *(1913-1916)*
b Rickmansworth, Herts 7/10/1892
SL 48 (13), FAC 2 (-), SCC 2 (-), WW1 10 (1)
Rickmansworth (by 1908); Watford Orient (cs 1912); Watford (am 8/12, pro 1914); Crystal Palace (1919); Millwall (5/22)
Captain of Rickmansworth, a Watford Orient player from its formation, and a Southern League forward even before turning professional, he took part, with George Edmonds and Ernie Grimsdell, in an England Amateur trial match. Deputising at inside-left for appendicitis victim Charlie White, he shared in the 1914/5 Southern League championship win.

Championship stand-in

F. **GREEN** *(1896)*
SL 1 (-)
West Herts (am)
Very briefly in evidence at the start of the club's first foray into Southern League football, he was part of a remarkable sequence in his sole competitive game, being one of six different centre-forwards tried in successive matches. It was reported that he "was not smart and quick enough, but passed neatly to the inside men lots of times".

George Earl **GREEN** *(1894-1896)*
b Watford, Herts 10/5/1875
d Watford, Herts 30/12/1905
SL 3 (-), FAC 3 (-), FAAC 3 (-), HSC 4 (-)
West Herts (1/92 until 10/96)
A prominent member of the Aldenham School cricket (he was said to be on the verge of county selection) and football XIs, he played for Watford's first team at 16 and became a regular wing-half in 1895/6. Although appointed reserve-team captain, he played in the first three Southern League games, but then an internal strain forced his retirement.

Harry **RODNEY GREEN** *(1968-1970)*
b Halifax, Yorks 24/6/1939
FL 19+11 (8), FAC 1+1 (-), FLC 0+1 (-)
Local football in Halifax; Halifax Town (am 9/58, pro 8/60); Bradford Park Avenue (6/62); Bradford City (£250 1/63); Gillingham (£9,000 7/64); Grimsby Town (8/65); Charlton Athletic (valued at £25,000 in player-exchange 2/67); Luton Town (£7,000 8/67); Watford (£3,000 8/68); Durban Spurs, South Africa (2/70)
Never spending as long as two years with any of his clubs, he was the big, buccaneering variety of centre-forward. Originally signed as a part-time player (he worked as an insurance agent), he went full-time in February 1969. Watford won every one of the seven League games in which he scored, including five *en route* to the Third Division championship.

Not one for long service

Striker's nightmare

***BRIAN Arthur* GREENHALGH** *(1975)*
b Chesterfield, Derbys 20/2/1947
FL 17+1 (1), FAC 0+1 (-), FLC 2 (1)
Preston North End (appr 7/62, pro 2/65); Aston Villa (9/67); Leicester City (2/69); Huddersfield Town (6/69); Cambridge Utd (7/71); AFC Bournemouth (£38,000 2/74); Torquay Utd (loan 8/74); Watford (£5,000 3/75); Dartford (free 7/76); Bedford Town (£1,000 9/77); Staines Town; Carshalton Athletic (by 10/80, manager cs 1981); Maidenhead Utd coach (late-1981); Chesham Utd (by 1/83); Everton chief scout (11/90)
Signed to produce goals to ensure Third Division survival, he suffered a striker's nightmare of eleven barren games before scoring in the final fixture. But Watford lost anyway, and went down. After a wandering League career, he played alongside Vic Akers and Laurie Craker in Dartford's Southern League Cup win in 1977.

Eight-goal defeat

Robert Patrick **GREENSLADE** *(1901-1903)*
b Liverpool, Lancs 1881
d Liverpool, Lancs 1957
SL 31 (-), SEL 1 (-)
Watford (7/01 until cs 1903); St Helens Town (9/07)
Brought down from Liverpool at the age of 19, he was ever-present at left-half from his Southern League début until an 8-0 defeat at Millwall ten months later. The decision not to offer him terms for 1903/4 was delayed until the eve of the season, and he was not registered again with the FA until his re-emergence in Lancashire more than four years later.

FA Cup Final with Luton

Anthony Charles (TONY) **GREGORY** *(1960-1963)*
b Luton, Beds 16/5/1937
FL 107 (14 inc 1p), FAC 8 (3), FLC 4 (-)
Vauxhall Motors; Luton Town (5/55); Watford (£6,000 3/60); Bexley Utd ("small fee" 7/64); Toronto Steelers, Canada, player-coach; Bedford Town (5/66); Hastings Utd (1966/7); Dover (by 10/67); Barnet player-coach; Stevenage Town player-manager; Wolverton player/general manager (until 1976)
ENGLAND YOUTH
Signed whilst on National Service, he filled the outside-left position in the 1959/60 promotion run-in. He subsequently adapted to a wing-half role, but it was on the wing that he'd been capped whilst with Vauxhall Motors and played in Luton's 1959 FA Cup Final side. Later he became managing director of a leading aerosol-manufacturing company.

His goal won the title

***FREDerick James* GREGORY** *(1911-1926)*
b Pinner, Middx 21/10/1886
d Harefield, Middx 24/5/1937
SL 143 (12), FL 168 (1), FAC 22 (4), SCC 3 (-), WW1 53 (3)
Pinner; Watford (am 9/11, pro 11/11 until cs 1927)
One of four brothers on Watford's books, three of them professionals, he was versatile and highly respected, latterly as a left-back. After his 16 seasons on the staff, including three as captain, he played occasionally for the Reserves and ran a pub at Pinner - the *Victory* - until his death. He scored the goal which clinched the Southern League title.

VALentine Francis **GREGORY** *(1911-1920)*
b Pinner, Middx 14/2/1888
d Wolverhampton, Staffs, March 1940
SL 155 (13 inc 1p), FAC 6 (3), SCC 2 (-), WW1 43 (2)
Pinner; Watford (12/11); Wolverhampton Wanderers (£1,500 5/20, player-coach 9/24); Butler Sports, Wolverhampton (permit player 10/27). Guested for Arsenal in WW1.
A Pinner farmer's son, and Fred's brother, he served Watford mostly as a strong, hard right-half, and was selected five times to represent the Southern League. His transfer fee was easily a club record, and George Edmonds went to Molineux with him for a similar amount. They both played for Wolves in the 1921 FA Cup Final, in which Gregory and Arthur Grimsdell were the opposing captains.

Sold for record fee

John (JOCK) **GRIEVE** *(1909-1911)*
b Scotland circa 1885
SL 62 (1), FAC 6 (-), SCC 5 (-)
Belfast Distillery (1904/5); Hibernian (5/05); Watford (7/09); Stoke (£100 to Hibernian and £100 to Watford, 4/11)
Having captained Hibs in 1908/9, he became Watford's regular left-half for two seasons. Together with Fred Cotterill and Peter Kyle he was suspended *sine die* by the club in February 1910, but unlike the others he was reinstated a week later. He was described, on his subsequent departure, as "probably the best wing-half the club has ever had".

Hibs skipper

Thomas (TOM) **GRIEVE** *(1904)*
b Leith, Midlothian 7/7/1875
d Wishaw, Lanarks 28/11/1948
SL 1 (-)
Northfleet Utd (am, cs 1895, pro 2/96); New Brompton (5/98); Gravesend (5/99); Woolwich Arsenal (5/00); Brentford (11/01 until cs 1902); Watford (a month's trial 10/04); Brighton & Hove Albion (11/04); Northfleet Utd (10/05)
As a trialist at Cassio Road he played on the right wing in a 2-1 Southern League win over Fulham, but he wasn't offered an engagement. He was serving in The Royal Scots and stationed at Chatham and Gravesend when he played for Northfleet as an amateur, and turned professional on being discharged by purchase. A clever, energetic little footballer.

William John (BILLY) **GRIMES** *(1906-1907)*
b Ickleford, Herts 27/3/1886
d Arlesey, Beds 6/1/1936
SL 15 (3), FAC 1 (1), UL 6 (-)
St John's, Hitchin; Hitchin Town (by 1904); Watford (5/06); Glossop (5/07); Bradford City (12/08); Derby County (3/10 - Watford received £25); Luton Town (7/19 until cs 1920). Guested for Tottenham Hotspur in WW1.
A Herts player in his amateur days, he scored on his Southern League and FA Cup débuts for Watford, for whom he turned out in all five forward positions. The club received £25 when he later joined Derby, whom he twice helped to win the Second Division, on the first occasion partnering the legendary Steve Bloomer. He married the Furrs' sister.

Partnered a legend

Watford's top sportsman

ARTHUR **GRIMSDELL** *(1911-1915)*
b Watford, Herts 23/3/1894
d Watford, Herts 12/3/1963
SL 36 (3), FAC 5 (1), SCC 1 (-), WW1 1 (-)
St Stephens (4/09); Watford (am, pro 10/11); Tottenham Hotspur (£500 for Grimsdell and W.S.Tattersall 4/12); Clapton Orient player-manager (free 8/29 until 6/30); Watford director (1945 until 8/51). Guested for Watford in WW1.
ENGLAND SCHOOLS and FULL; FOOTBALL LEAGUE
Capped when at Watford Field School, he went on to captain his country at senior level, and led Spurs to FA Cup victory. A great wing-half, he was in Watford's first team just after his 17th birthday, and his transfer was forced by economic crisis. He also played First Class cricket, and his Herts CCC career spanned 26 years.

More caps for the family

Ernest Frederick (ERNIE) **GRIMSDELL** *(1913-1920)*
b Watford, Herts 1892
d Bushey, Herts 20/9/1947
SL 15 (-), WW1 31 (-)
St Stephens (by 4/09); Watford (am 9/09);Watford Orient; St Albans City; Reading (am 2/13); Watford (am 1913/4); Queens Park Rangers (pro 8/20); Guildford Utd (8/21); Queens Park Rangers (6/22); Chatham (8/23); Dartford (by 3/27). Guested for Fulham in WW1.
ENGLAND AMATEUR
Arthur's brother, and an accomplished full-back in his own right, as his two Amateur caps testify. In 1917 he represented the Army against the Royal Navy at Fulham, for whom he went on to guest frequently for two seasons. After a late entry to the professional ranks in 1920, he subsequently took up refereeing and became a Football League linesman.

Scored freely in vain

Joseph Phoenix George (JOE) **GROOME** *(1927-1928)*
b Apsley, Herts 1/9/1901
d Beckenham, Kent 20/8/1956
FL 17 (14)
Apsley; Northampton Town (am 2/27); Watford (pro 7/27); Queens Park Rangers (free 5/29 until 2/30); Apsley manager (by 1933/4 until 10/35)
Even that formidable goalscoring record didn't establish him in the first team. He never played in more than four consecutive games, and was released after only one appearance in 1928/9. A competitive sprinter, he used his pace to good effect as a direct, dashing centre-forward, and scored twice on his League débuts for both Northampton and Watford.

GORDON HAIGH (1951-1952)
b Barnsley, Yorks 18/8/1921
FL 29 (5), FAC 2 (2)
Ransom & Marles; Burnley (11/45); Bournemouth & Boscombe Athletic (4/50); Watford (8/51); Rossendale Utd (cs 1952); Nelson (until 1953)
He wore the first-team No 8 shirt for most of his Vicarage Road season, after which he returned to the area where he had first emerged as a professional footballer immediately after the war, when already in his mid-twenties. Five of his Watford goals, including two against Aylesbury in the FA Cup, came in a mid-season spell of six games.

Returned to East Lancs

Richard (DIXIE) HALE (1967-1970)
b Waterford 29/5/1935
FL 95+3 (7), FAC 8+1 (3), FLC 6 (-)
Waterford; Shamrock Rovers; Swansea Town (10/59); Barrow (7/61); Workington (8/64); Watford (£3,500 7/67); King's Lynn (free 9/70); Wealdstone (cs 1971); Pembroke Borough; Pontardawe manager (1981/2); Pembroke Borough manager; Milford Utd player-manager (by 4/88); resumed club management in the Swansea area (1992/3)
LEAGUE OF IRELAND
An exceptionally busy little Irish midfield player who, at the age of 33, was an influential member of Ken Furphy's promotion team. He'd once played in the League of Ireland for Waterford alongside his three brothers, of whom Alfie became a Full international. Dixie retired from full-time football in 1970 and took a job with AEC at Aldenham.

Four brothers together

H.A. (HARRY) HALL (1897)
SL 2 (-), FAC 1 (-)
Watford St Mary's; West Herts (9/97)
Like many other locals in the mid-1890s, he turned out for both of Watford's major clubs, and he switched his allegiance to Cassio Road just before professionalism was adopted. He started the 1897/8 season as the first-team outside-right, but after three games (7-4, 2-0 and 8-0 defeats) he was muscled out by the influx of the paid men.

Superseded by the pros

Andrew HAMILTON (1900-1901)
b Scotland circa 1874
SL 6 (1)
Falkirk (5/94); Sunderland (5/96); New Brighton Tower (8/97); Warmley (5/98); Ryde (9/00); Watford (10/00 until cs 1901)
He arrived at Cassio Road a few weeks into the 1900/1 season but was unable to turn the club's fortunes in a dismal campaign. In fact, not a single point was gained from the six matches in which he played on the left wing. He'd earlier made the same number of First Division appearances for Sunderland and scored twice in a 4-2 win against Liverpool.

Ever-present captain

*John (**JOCK**)* ***HAMILTON*** *(1901-1902)*
b Ayr circa 1872
SL 30 (3), FAC 2 (-)
Ayr (1891); Wolverhampton Wanderers (6/94); Loughborough Town (8/95); Bristol South End (5/97); Leicester Fosse (9/00); Watford (5/01); Wellingborough Town (5/02); Fulham (cs 1903, assistant-trainer 1904, trainer 10/08); Bristol City reserve-team trainer 1910, manager 5/15 until 8/19)
Reaching Watford with a fair amount of experience under his belt, he was appointed captain and was ever-present in his only season, firstly at left-half and then as the defensive pivot. In 1911, six years after retiring, he was refused permission to play as an amateur. At the start of his career he had taken part in three Ayr Charity Cup wins.

Scottish club honours

JOHN HAMILTON *(1967)*
b Larkhall, Lanarks 22/1/1935
FL 7+1 (2), FLC 3 (-)
Lesmahagow (9/54); Heart of Midlothian (4/55); Watford (free 5/67 until 5/68)
SCOTLAND UNDER-23; SCOTTISH LEAGUE
A forward whose 12 seasons at Tynecastle included the best years in Hearts' history. He scored in two of his four Scottish League Cup Finals, gaining winners' medals in three of them, and contributed to two Scottish League championship wins, making four appearances (four goals) and 27 (7) respectively. His Watford contract was cancelled by mutual consent.

Did well on trial

*John Eley (**JACK**)* ***HAMILTON*** *(1921)*
b Nottingham 23/1/1902
d Nottingham 16/1/1980
FL 2 (-)
Heanor Athletic; Welbeck Colliery (mid-1920/1); Watford (6/21); Sutton Town (free 7/22); Blackpool (5/24); Queens Park Rangers (6/26); Sutton Town (4/27); Loughborough Corinthians (8/29)
After playing under a pseudonym and scoring twice in a benefit match in March 1921, he joined the club in the summer. He was seen as a promising forward with good ball control, but played only two League games before returning to the East Midlands. In a further foray into League football, he played a few first-team games for Blackpool and QPR.

Army medical suspicions

Richard Whitecross ***HAMMETT*** *(1900-1901)*
b East Stonehouse, Devon 1869
d St Martin-in-the-Fields, London 4/9/1925
SL 33 (-), FAC 3 (-)
Royal Engineers (1894 until 4/96); Ryde (pro 5/97); Watford (7/00 until 9/01)
The son of a senior warder at Dartmoor, he was ever-present in goal whilst on Watford's books, and released to become caretaker at the newly-opened Callowland Schools, a job for which there were 60 applicants. He'd been invalided out of the army with varicose veins and a leg ulcer which it was officially suspected had been deliberately self-inflicted.

Edris Anthony (**TONY**) **HAPGOOD** *(1953)*
b Kettering, Northants 13/6/1930
FL 1 (-)
Burnley (2/48); Watford ("small fee" 7/53); Ashford Town (8/54); Chatham (one season); Bushey Utd (11/57)
His father was the Arsenal and England captain who became Watford's manager, but Tony's employment at Vicarage Road owed nothing to nepotism, as his father had departed more than three years earlier. A right-winger, he played at Millwall in the League early in the season, but thereafter his first-team experience was limited to three friendly games.

No nepotism

A. **HARDING** *(1901-1903)*
SL 12 (-), FAC 3 (-), SEL 1 (-)
Chesham Town (am by 9/98, pro 8/00); Watford (8/01 until cs 1904); Leyton (11/04)
A professional with Chesham when that club decided to revert to amateur status, he was thereupon given an engagement at Cassio Road, where he was used as a centre-half and full-back, and once at centre-forward. His first match was a five-goal defeat at Southampton, and he also played in the corresponding game the following season. Watford lost 11-0.

Grim Southampton trips

PAUL *John* **HARDING** *(1993)*
b Mitcham, Surrey 6/3/1964
FL 1+1 (-)
Sutton Utd; Whyteleafe; Epsom & Ewell; Carshalton Athletic; Dulwich Hamlet; Enfield; Barnet (2/90); Notts County (£60,000 9/90); Southend Utd (loan 8/93); Watford (loan 11/93); Birmingham City (loan 12/93, £50,000 1/94); Cardiff City (free 8/95)
A midfielder who didn't play League football until he was 26, and became one of many players signed more than once by Barry Fry. He was involved in probably a unique coincidence when, within a few weeks, he played at Roots Hall both as a substitute against Watford whilst on loan to Southend and as a substitute against Southend whilst on loan to Watford.

Roots Hall coincidence

Charles Boyd (**CHARLIE**) **HARE** *(1898-1900)*
b Yardley, Worcs 1870
d Birmingham, Warwicks 1947
SL 43 (23 inc 1p), FAC 12 (12), BCCL 16 (24 inc 1p)
Warwick County; Birmingham Utd; Aston Villa (3/91); Woolwich Arsenal (2/95); Small Heath (11/96); Watford (6/98 until cs 1901); Argyle (10/02); Green Waves player-coach (9/04 until cs 1905); reinstated am (1906)
Good enough to have scored seven times in ten appearances when Villa won the League in 1893/4, he was a centre-forward who started with six goals in a friendly and continued to score freely. He served with the Herts Yeomanry in the Boer War, was discharged in April 1902 as being medically unfit, and resumed his career in Devon.

Boer War volunteer

ABOVE *George Furr challenges the Swindon Town goalkeeper at Cassio Road in December 1907. Furr's brother Vic made a Football League appearance for Watford - but not until 18 years later.*

ABOVE *Watford's first manager,* ***John Goodall****, in his 19th-century prime as England's greatest inside-forward.*

RIGHT *Watford 0 Luton Town 3, on Good Friday 1909, in front of a record home attendance.* ***Billy Biggar*** *punches clear, with England cap* ***Arthur Lockett*** *behind him. Biggar played in more Southern League games for the club than anyone else.*

BELOW *The 1921 FA Cup Final captains at Stamford Bridge were former Watford colleagues. Val Gregory's Wolves team lost 1-0, and* ***Arthur Grimsdell*** *of Spurs collected the trophy from King George V.*

*__ABOVE__ **Taffy Davies** (on the left) served Watford as a winger or inside-forward, and was one of very few players who have ever spent 20 years with one Football League club. Never-say-die wing-half **Arthur Woodward** broke the club's appearances record, but it was soon taken from him by......*

*__RIGHT__ .....the gifted **Tommy Barnett**, who retained it for 36 years - as well as setting a career goalscoring record which lasted even longer.*

*The photographer got his angles all wrong, but the leaping figure in the dark shirt is the prolific **George James**, heading one of his two FA Cup 4th Round goals against Brighton & Hove Albion at Vicarage Road in 1931. The background view of houses and main stand is unchanged to this day.*

*An illustrious Arsenal trio of the 1930s - **Eddie Hapgood**, Frank Moss and Alex James - allow their attention to wander, but young **Tony Hapgood** keeps his eye on the ball. Both Hapgoods were destined for Vicarage Road after the war - Eddie as manager and his son as a player.*

*Until his transfer to Fulham, **Maurice Cook**'s vigorous forward play was the club's best asset in the mid-1950s.*

*The majestic **Cliff Holton** is followed onto the field by **Dennis Uphill**. Their combined goals total in 1959/60 was 84.*

One of Vicarage Road's great moments. **Barry Endean** launches himself against Liverpool to head Watford into their first FA Cup semi-final.

In 1973 the tigerish **Duncan Welbourne** broke Tommy Barnett's long-standing appearances record. No fewer than 280 of his League games were consecutive.

John Barnes touches the ball past **Tony Coton** during Watford's 3-1 win at St Andrews in the 6th Round of the FA Cup in 1984. Three years later there was another quarter-final away win - at Highbury. Again it was 3-1, and again Barnes was a scorer, but this time Coton was in the Watford goal.

Tiny genius

*Thomas Charles (**TOMMY**)* ***HARMER*** *(1960-1962)*
b Hackney 2/2/1928
FL 63 (6), FAC 7 (1p), FLC 4 (-)
Finchley; Tottenham Hotspur (am 8/45, pro 8/48); Watford (£6,000 10/60); Chelsea (£3,500 9/62 until cs 1965); Hastings Utd (8/67 until cs 1968)
ENGLAND 'B'
A tiny figure who looked anything but athletic. He couldn't head a ball and had no pace, but there was footballing genius in his brains and feet, and in spite of his physical disadvantages he won England 'B' caps as a creative inside-forward. In 1963 he scored the goal which, in particularly dramatic circumstances, took Chelsea back to Division One.

*- **HARPER*** *(1906)*
SEL 1 (-)
Watford (1906)
Playing at inside-left in a goalless draw against Leyton at Cassio Road, he had his only experience of senior football. In the South-Eastern League the club often fielded almost a full first team, and gave one or two reserves or amateurs a taste of action. On this occasion player-manager John Goodall stood down to accommodate Harper.

Local schools product

IVOR** Roy* ***HARPER *(1952)*
b Watford, Herts 23/6/1933
FL 3 (-)
Whippendell Road Guild; Watford (am 2/49); Bushey Utd; Leyton Orient youth team (8/49); Chelsea youth team (12/49); Watford Boys Club 'B' XI (early 1950/1); Hemel Hempstead Town (1/51); Watford (am 12/51); Wolverhampton Wanderers (am 5/52); also Knutsford (9/52); Wealdstone; Aylesbury Utd (11/53); Berkhamsted Town (by 9/62)
Prolific as a goalscorer when he was a colleague of Peter Walker in schools and youth football locally, he served many clubs as an amateur, and had several months in Wolves' reserve team when he was doing his National Service. He also represented Herts, Middlesex, and Berks & Bucks, and had three League games for Watford at inside-right.

Hampden penalties

*Joseph John (**JOE**)* ***HARPER*** *(1946-1952)*
b Garnkirk, Lanarks 12/1/1920
d Watford, Herts 5/3/1987
FL 159 (1), FAC 11 (-)
Heathfield Rovers; Twechar United (8/36); Watford (5/37); Snowdown Colliery (8/52); Biggleswade Town. Guested for Darlington and Kirkintilloch Rob Roy in WW2.
He made his League début in his tenth season with the club, but then had a good run at wing-half and full-back. He scored two penalties at Hampden Park in helping Kirkintilloch Rob Roy to win the 1943 Scottish Junior Cup Final, and after retiring from football represented Herts at bowls. His son Bobby was an England Youth international.

GEORGE *Alfred* **HARRIS** *(1962-1966)*
b Lambeth, London 10/6/1940
FL 162+1 (55 inc 4p), FAC 10 (3), FLC 5 (2 inc 1p)
Tottenham Hotspur (am 5/57); Woking; Chelsea (am 4/61); Newport County (7/61); Watford (4/62); Reading (£4,500 7/66); Cambridge Utd (£3,000 10/69); Hillingdon Borough (free 7/72); Wokingham Town (player-coach 6/74, manager); Maidenhead manager (6/75 until cs 1977)
He ran well and could deliver a good cross, his heading ability was outstanding, and his goalscoring consistency was far greater than could reasonably be expected from an outside-left. He played in every game of the near-promotion season under Bill McGarry, and later at Reading continued - and indeed improved - his excellent scoring record.

Wing-play plus goals

John **HARRIS** *(1925-1926)*
b Redcar, Yorks, circa 1903
FL 29 (5), FAC 3 (-)
Middlesbrough (am 2/21 until 8/23); Wolverhampton Wanderers (pro 11/23); Watford (£100 7/25 until cs 1926); Darlington (8/27); Hartlepools Utd (10/27 until 11/27); Barrow (2/29); Spennymoor Utd (8/31)
After two seasons at Molineux he was recommended to Watford by Val Gregory. A bustling forward, he was tried at inside-left and centre-forward before being given the left-wing role and keeping it to the end of the season. He was transfer-listed and his registration retained, but he didn't re-sign, and he also later spent the whole of 1928 out of the game.

Val Gregory referral

*William Thomas (***TOMMY***)* **HARRIS** *(1936-1948)*
b Aberbargoed, Mon 30/6/1913
FL 94 (6), FAC 8 (-), WW2 73 (-)
New Tredegar; Watford (am 3/33, pro 4/33 until cs 1950); De Havilland, Leavesden (8/51 until at least 10/52); Biggleswade Town. Guested for Ipswich Town and Leeds Utd in WW2.
After becoming one of the strong Vicarage Road representation from the Valleys, he played in three League games in 1936 and then had to wait over ten years for his fourth peacetime appearance. He could perform both on the wing (his original role) and at full-back, in which position he had most of his League experience and also had a spell as captain.

Ten-year wait

GERALD *Randall* **HARRISON** *(1990)*
b Lambeth, London 15/4/1972
FL 6+3 (-), FMC 1 (-)
West Norwood; Watford (sch 2/87, tr 7/89, pro 12/89); Bristol City (free 6/91); Cardiff City (loan 1/92); Hereford Utd (loan 11/93); Bath City (loan 2/94); Huddersfield Town (3/94); Burnley (free 8/94)
ENGLAND SCHOOLS
A League player at 17, he was nevertheless released just over a year later, and his career became a bitty affair, except for one good season at Ashton Gate, until he reached Burnley. Although a midfielder, he played twice in goal for London Schools, filling in on the first occasion when he was present as an outfield reserve and the selected 'keeper didn't turn up.

Midfielder in goal

Came back to lose 10-0

H. (DABBER) **HARRISON** *(1896-1897)*
SL 8 (1), HSC 2 (1)
West Herts; Leighton Cee Springs (cs 1897 until at least 11/00)
He turned out in a variety of half-back and forward positions in 1896/7, and was later on the receiving end of ten Watford FA Cup goals against Leighton Cee Springs. In March 1897 he and Busby both incurred the Committee's censure for the frequency with which they strayed offside.

STEVEn John **HARRISON** *(1978-1981)* - SEE PART FIVE

Last six games all lost

John (JACK) **HARROP** *(1956-1960)*
b Manchester, Lancs 25/6/1929
d Hemel Hempstead, Herts 18/2/1977
FL 111 (-), FAC 6 (-), SFC 7 (-)
Charlton Athletic (am 9/49); Swansea Town (8/52); Watford (undisclosed fee 7/56); Hastings Utd (7/60); Tunbridge Wells (cs 1961)
His last six first-team games for Watford all ended in defeat, but by then he'd given three seasons of good service at left-back. (Like his immediate alphabetical predecessor, he played over a hundred games in that position without scoring.) He succeeded Frank Mitchell as cricket coach at Dulwich College, and in 1960 was appointed captain of Watford Town CC.

Known around Div 3(S)

John (JOHNNY) **HARTBURN** *(1949-1951)*
b Houghton-le-Spring, Co Durham 20/12/1920
FL 66 (19 inc 4p), FAC 5 (2)
Yeovil Town; Queens Park Rangers (3/47); Watford (£1,000 9/49); Millwall (£2,500 3/51); Leyton Orient (6/54); Guildford City (7/58); Leyton Orient programme editor, commercial manager (4 years); Fulham commercial manager (9 years); Watford commercial manager (7/76 until 3/81); Barnet commercial manager, hon secretary (circa 1982-1987)
Despite his Geordie birth, he was a player very much of the south of England, and a familiar figure on the Division 3 (South) circuit. A small winger with a good scoring record, he hit one of the fastest hat-tricks in League history in his first season with Leyton Orient. Shrewsbury Town were beaten 5-0 and the treble was timed at three minutes.

Creative influence

BARRY **HARTLE** *(1958-1960)*
b Salford, Lancs 8/8/1939
FL 39 (7), FAC 6 (1)
Salford Boys' Club; Watford (am 8/56, pro 8/56); Sheffield Utd (just under £3,000 6/60); Carlisle Utd (7/66); Stockport County (9/67); Oldham Athletic (6/70); Southport (free 7/71 until cs 1972); Macclesfield Town (by 10/73)
Possessing far more skill than power, he was the creative component, at inside-left, of the Holton-inspired 1959/60 promotion team. He returned north at the end of that season, spent the rest of his career there, and later became a self-employed taxi-driver in Stockport. He was more familiar as a left-winger after leaving Vicarage Road.

Thomas William (TOM) **HARTLEY** *(1948)*
b Gateshead, Co Durham 7/5/1917
d Chesterfield, Derbys, January 1984
FL 6 (1)
Birtley Boys' Club; Gateshead (am 2/36 until cs 1937); Bury (pro 5/38); Chesterfield (5/39); Stockton (9/47); North Shields (12/47); Leicester City (12/47); Watford (one of four players signed for combined fee of £4,750 1/48 until cs 1948). Guested for Doncaster Rovers and Mansfield Town in WW2.
His six appearances at inside-forward brought only one win, his goal at Torquay being the only one of the game. Accompanying Calvert, Cheney (on loan), Eggleston and Osborne from Filbert Street, he joined his fifth club in five months, and his Watford début (on 31st January 1948) was his first Football League game since 1936/7.

Five months, five clubs

HOWARD **HARVEY** *(1901-1903)*
b Birmingham, Warwicks circa 1877
SL 39 (4), FAC 3 (-), SEL 1 (-)
Aston Villa (11/94); Burslem Port Vale (6/98); Manchester City ("big fee" 1/00); Watford (8/01 until 2/03); Glentoran (8/03)
Making the first team in his fourth season at Villa Park, he scored twice in ten First Division games for the reigning League champions. He was suspended twice by Watford, on the second occasion permanently, for "a breach of training regulations", after serving the club at both centre-forward and inside-right.

Suspended, then sacked

William **HASTINGS** *(1914-1917)*
b West Hartlepool, Co Durham, circa 1888
SL 34 (6), FAC 1 (-), SCC 1 (-), WW1 24 (1)
West Hartlepool Expansion; Brighton & Hove Albion (4/10); Birmingham (£100 2/12); Watford (7/14); Hartlepools Utd (1919/20)
A missed penalty in his first game for Watford was soon forgotten, as the game was won and he went on to appear regularly on the wing as the club proceeded to take the Southern League championship. Five years earlier he'd enjoyed similar success with Brighton. Whilst serving in the Royal Flying Corps he turned out for Watford frequently in 1916/7.

Two Southern Lge titles

SAMuel Thomas **HATTON** *(1914-1917)*
b Watford, Herts 18/5/1892
d Watford, Herts 9/10/1955
SCC 1 (-), WW1 2 (-)
Callow Land Juniors (by 3/10); St Albans City; Watford (am, cs 1913, pro 9/14)
His only senior competitive game under peacetime conditions was actually a few months after war had been declared. when he stood in at left-back for rested skipper Alex Stewart, in a Southern Charity Cup tie at Luton. He made one further appearance in each of the next two seasons. In common with many of the early amateurs, he played for the county.

County player

50 goals not enough

HARRY **HAWKINS** *(1937-1938)*
b Middlesbrough, Yorks 24/11/1915
d Middlesbrough, Cleveland 14/3/1992
FL 5 (-), 3SC 4 (-)
South Bank East End; Middlesbrough (am 7/34, pro 2/35); Watford (6/37); Southport ("small fee" 7/38); Gateshead (6/47); Hartlepools Utd (3/48 until cs 1949). Guested for York City in WW2.
Fifty goals in 53 North-Eastern League appearances were not enough to win him much of a first-team career at Middlesbrough, for whom he played only once in the First Division. He represented Watford at both inside-forward and wing-half, and after leaving Vicarage Road played in nearly a hundred games in Division 3 (North).

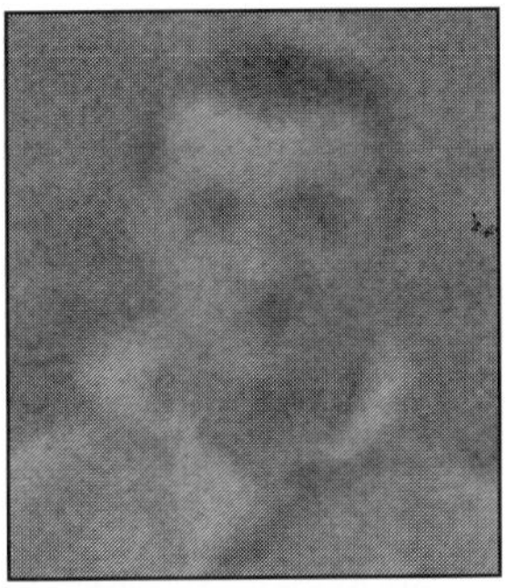
Kirkcaldy record-holder

Norman Scott Carmichael (NORRIE) **HAYWOOD** *(1933)*
b Portobello, Midlothian 7/9/1910
d Edinburgh 30/7/1979
FL 1 (-)
Peebles Rovers (am 6/33); Watford (7/33); Peebles Rovers (free 9/34); Queen of the South (12/35); Raith Rovers (free 5/37 until cs 1938); Leith Athletic (8/41); Raith Rovers (4/45 until 2/46); Peebles Rovers (8/46)
He came a long way for his one Football League appearance, but back in Scotland enjoyed success as a goalscoring centre-forward. In his first reserve game on trial for Queen of the South he hit six against Hibernian, and in 1937/8 he scored 55 goals in first-team competitions (still a club record) as Raith Rovers walked the Second Division championship.

Derby spoiled his début

DAVID Mark **HEARD** *(1960)*
b Edmonton, Middx 25/1/1942
FLC 1 (-)
Arsenal (am 8/58); Canterbury City (am 10/59); Watford (am 11/59, pro 1/60); Bexleyheath & Welling (free 7/61); Canterbury City (by 1964/5)
ENGLAND YOUTH
Although capped when playing for Arsenal's youth team, he drifted into non-League football before turning professional with Watford after two months' trial. His one senior game was at outside-left in the club's first Football League Cup tie, a 5-2 home defeat against Derby County. He later became proprietor of a horticultural nursery in Aldenham.

Made way for Rice

Michael Robert (MICK) **HENDERSON** *(1979-1982)*
b Gosforth, Northumberland 31/3/1956
FL 50+1 (-), FAC 4 (-), FLC 8+1 (-), FLT 3 (-)
Sunderland (sch 5/72, app 7/72, pro 4/74); Watford (£120,000 11/79); Cardiff City (free 3/82); Sheffield Utd (free 8/82); Chesterfield (1/85, player-coach cs 1987, briefly caretaker-manager 10/88); Matlock Town (9/89)
Ever-present at right-back from the time of his signing until the arrival of Pat Rice, he played only a handful of games in his remaining 15 months at Vicarage Road. He made over two hundred more League appearances after leaving, and later joined the Sheffield Police.

William (BILLY) **HENDRY** *(1898)*
b Newport-on-Tay, Fife
d Shrewsbury, Salop 4/5/1901 (aged 31)
SL 5 (-)
Dunblane Thistle; Dundee Wanderers (1885); West Bromwich Albion (5/88); Kidderminster Harriers (3/89); Stoke (8/89); Preston North End (8/90); Sheffield Utd (2/91); Dundee (5/95); Bury (5/96); West Herts (3/98); Brighton Utd (5/98); Shrewsbury Town (7/99 until death)
An immensely influential centre-half and captain in Sheffield United's early history (the great Ernest Needham acknowledged how much he learned from him), Hendry spent his brief Cassio Road career as a full-back before joining the newly-formed Brighton United. He died of heart disease at the end of his second season with Shrewsbury.

Major Bramall Lane figure

LIBURD Algernon **HENRY** *(1989-1990)*
b Dominica 29/8/1967
FL 8+2 (1), FAC 3 (-), FLC 1 (-), FMC 1 (-)
Essex Schools; Colchester Utd (non-contract 4/86); Rainham Town; Millwall Reserves; Leytonstone & Ilford; Watford (£20,000 11/87); Halifax Town (loan 9/88); Maidstone Utd (£40,000 6/90); Gillingham (6/92); Peterborough Utd (free 8/94); Woking (free 8/95); Dagenham & Redbridge (9/95); Welling Utd (10/95); Bromley (by 4/96)
A forward who had links with League clubs, but didn't get a contract until he reached Watford. His few first-team games en-compassed four competitions, and his goal was one of seven against Bradford City. He was among the players who left the ill-fated Maidstone United with wages still owed to them.

Wages owed at Maidstone

James (JIMMY) **HERNON** *(1954-1956)*
b Cleland, Lanarks 6/12/1924
FL 43 (10), FAC 2 (1), SFC 1 (-)
Clydesdale Juniors; Mossvale Strollers; Leicester City (4/42); Bolton Wanderers (£14,750 9/48); Grimsby Town (£2,500 8/51); Watford (4-figure fee 7/54); Hastings Utd (7/56). Guested for Partick Thistle in WW2.
A slightly-built, creative inside-forward who had been the subject of what was, in 1948, a big-money transfer to First Division Bolton. Although by no means robust, he later adapted to the rigours of Third Division football sufficiently well to accumulate a total of 34 goals in his 134 League appearances for Grimsby and Watford.

Big-money transfer

Andrew (ANDY) **HESSENTHALER** *(1991-1996)*
b Gravesend, Kent 17/8/1965
FL 195 (12), FAC 5 (2), FLC 13 (1), FMC 1 (-), AIC 3 (-)
Kent Schools; Dartford; Charlton Athletic Reserves (March 1984 until cs 1986); also Corinthian (1984 until 1986); Dartford (10/86); Redbridge Forest (7/90); Watford (£85,000 9/91)
ENGLAND SEMI-PROFESSIONAL
Formerly well-known to assistant-manager Peter Taylor in senior non-League football, he joined Watford at 26 as a

Relished belated chance

short, muscular midfield player with prodigious reserves of energy and stamina. To these he added other qualities as he took full advantage of his belated chance of a full-time career and an automatic first-team place.

Early injury

John **ARTHUR HETHERINGTON** *(1938)*
b Rotherham, Yorks 7/8/1906
d Rotherham, Yorks 1977
FL 8 (1)
Denaby Utd (pro); Dalton & Eastwoods, Rotherham (permit player 9/28); Wolverhampton Wanderers (2/29); Preston North End ("substantial fee" 1/35); Swindon Town (£550 6/36); Watford (about £500 2/38 until cs 1939)
A late-season signing whom it was hoped would provide the answer to a left-wing weakness, he was injured in his third game and never held a regular place. Fast and tricky, he'd scored 27 goals in 110 appearances in the top two divisions for Wolves and Preston, after which he was in Swindon's first team for nearly two seasons.

Twice a Bassett signing

PETER HETHERSTON *(1987-1988)*
b Bellshill, Lanarks 6/11/1964
FL 2+3 (-). FAC 1 (-), FLC 1+1 (2), FMC 1 (-)
Bargeddie Utd; Falkirk (12/84); Watford (£63,000 7/87); Sheffield Utd (£50,000 2/88); Falkirk (7/88); Raith Rovers (£20,000 cs 1991); Aberdeen (over £200,000 6/94); Airdrieonians (3/96)
His brief flurry in English football involved two clubs and a total of only 12 months' service. It was the same manager, Dave Bassett, who signed him on both occasions. A right-sided attacking player, he scored twice in his first 90-minute appearance for Watford, an 8-0 win against Darlington. He appeared in the 1995/6 Scottish League Cup Final.

A rare century

Joseph Thomas (**JOE**) **HEWITT** *(1927-1931)*
b Coventry, Warwicks 1902
FL 104 (-), FAC 6 (-)
Coventry Sundries; Watford (9/27); Coventry City (free 8/31 until cs 1932)
Spotted whilst keeping goal for a Coventry works team, he was invited to Vicarage Road for a trial period, as a result of which he was given an engagement. He took his chance well when Bill Yates was injured, and accumulated over a hundred League appearances, being the only one of a sequence of 15 Watford goalkeepers to do so.

Unusual scoring feat

Albert William (**BILL**) **HICKLIN** *(1947-1948)*
b Dudley, Worcs 20/9/1924
FL 21 (5 inc 1p), FAC 2 (-)
Birmingham (3/45); Watford (6/47); West Bromwich Albion (free 6/48)
He was serving with RAF Coastal Command when transferred to Watford, and performed the probably unique feat of scoring from wing-half in each of his first three League appearances. After three wins and a draw in his first four games, he was brought sharply down to earth by a seven-goal beating at Northampton in his fifth.

<u>Her**BERT** Wilson **HIGGINS**</u> *(1902-1910)*
b Leeds, Yorks 1877
d Abergrave, Brecknockshire 3/2/1952
SL 45 (-), FAC 2 (-), SEL 18 (-), UL 3 (-)
Oulton St John's; <u>Watford</u> (am, pro 5/03 until cs 1908, and 7/09 until cs 1910)
A goalkeeper who survived the trauma of conceding eleven goals on his first-term début, and later scored from open play when up in support of his forwards during another Southern League match - only for it to be abandoned. He owned a thriving cycle business in Rickmansworth, and became a Watford Town Councillor and President of the Supporters Club.

Survived traumatic start

<u>**SID**ney William **HIGH**</u> *(1948-1949)*
b Waterbeach, Cambs 30/9/1922
FL 7 (3)
Cambridge Utd; Luton Town (10/46); <u>Watford</u> (8/48 until cs 1949); King's Lynn (9/49); Aldershot (a month's trial 8/51)
A right-winger who made no lasting impact at Vicarage Road, despite scoring all of the club's three goals in his first two League games, a 1-1 draw at Northampton and then, eight weeks later, a 2-0 win against Crystal Palace. These were his only goals in League football, his two seasons at Luton having been spent in the Reserves.

Bright start petered out

<u>Daniel Ronald Louis (**DANNY**) **HILL**</u> *(1996)*
b Enfield, London 1/10/1974
FL 1 (-)
Tottenham Hotspur (sch 11/88, tr 8/91, pro 9/92); Birmingham City (loan 11/95); <u>Watford</u> (loan 2/96)
ENGLAND SCHOOLS and UNDER-21
As a developing midfield player with an excellent pedigree, he had an undistinguished spell with Watford. His only game was a four-goal defeat at Crystal Palace which was Glenn Roeder's swansong. Hill was unwanted by the incoming regime, and spent the rest of his loan period back with his regular employers, rather than in Watford's Reserves.

Ill-fated loan deal

<u>John (**JOHNNY**) **HILL**</u> *(1897-1900)*
b Kirkcaldy, Fife, circa 1871
SL 65 (25 inc 1p), FAC 10 (1), BCCL 18 (11)
Leith Rangers; Leith Athletic; Middlesbrough Ironopolis (1892); Leicester Fosse (cs 1893); Glossop North End (7/95); <u>West Herts</u> (10/97 until cs 1901, director 6/09 until 1914)
SCOTLAND JUNIOR
Among the best of the early professionals, he played mostly at outside-left. He shares with Arthur Grimsdell the distinction of having served the club as both player and director, and he also owned the Watford High Street newsagent/tobacconist business which later became Grimsdell's. In 1891 he scored in a Junior international in Belfast - a 1-1 draw.

Player, then director

M. **HILL** *(1897)*
SL 1 (-), HSC 1 (-)
West Herts (1896/7)
He had only a brief connection with the club as a player, but did appear in the senior team at centre-half in three successive games, including a friendly. On the first occasion he was brought in to replace George Davenport, who was "still feeling the effects" of the previous week's game. The club won both of the competitive games in which Hill played.

Big fee soon recouped

RICHARD *Wilfred* **HILL** *(1987)*
b Hinckley, Leics 20/9/1963
FL 2+2 (-)
Leicester City (sch 11/77, pro 11/81); Christchurch Utd, New Zealand (free 1982); Grankulla, Finland; Nuneaton Borough (1983); Northampton Town (one of two players signed for £25,000 6/85); Watford (loan 5/87, £258,000 7/87); Oxford Utd (£260,000 9/87); Kettering Town (free, cs 1991 to 9/92); Reading community officer (late 1992/3 until 1994); Worcester City (cs 1993); Racing Club Warwick; Witney Town player-coach (2/94); Nuneaton Borough (10/94); Hinckley Athletic (8/95); Reading youth-team coach (11/95)
Given a second chance to make a Football League career, he scored prolifically from midfield (32 League and cup goals) when Northampton won the Fourth Division championship. Watford paid record money for a player at that level, but a change of manager led to his departure within weeks. His full-time career was ended by injury at Oxford.

Served Southport well

William **RALPH HILLS** *(1927-1929)*
b Ely, Cambs 16/12/1904
d Walney, Lancs 3/4/1970
FL 30 (3), FAC 1 (-)
Northumberland Schools; St Peter's Albion; Middlesbrough (am 1/25 until 5/25); St Peter's Albion; Huddersfield Town (am 1925, pro 2/27); Watford (free 5/27); Southport (free (6/29); Barrow (6/32); Crewe Alexandra (7/34 until cs 1936)
Ever-present at outside-right for two thirds of his first season before being injured, he reappeared after 14 months, for the last two games of 1928/9, but was then released. He then made over a hundred League appearances in his three years with Southport, whom he captained. Although born in East Anglia, he was a product of North-East schools foootball.

Long-term Newport boss

James Lyons **(JIMMY) HINDMARSH** *(1907-1908)*
b Whitburn, Co Durham 1885
d Luton, Beds 16/3/1959
SL 10 (4)
Whitburn Colliery; Sunderland (3/05); Fulham (£20 5/06); Watford (12/07); Plymouth Argyle (5/08); Stockport County (£100 6/10); Manchester City (11/12); Newport County (reserve-team player-coach 9/19, first-team coach 1920, manager 5/22 until 5/35)
Signed as Jack Foster's mid-winter replacement at centre-forward, he was not a success, but later became a major figure in the history of Newport County. During his 13 years of management the club was voted out of the Football League and back in again.

England trialist

ALFred **HITCH** *(1906-1908)*
b Walsall, Staffs 1876
d Uxbridge, Middx 1962
SL 69 (2 inc 1p), FAC 3 (-), SEL 1 (-), UL 7 (1)
Walsall Unity; Walsall (10/97); Wellington Town (1/98); Thames Ironworks (9/98); Grays Utd (12/98); Queens Park Rangers (5/99); Nottingham Forest (5/01); Queens Park Rangers (5/02); Watford (5/06 until cs 1908)
He excelled in the air at centre-half and was given the club captaincy in 1907, having been good enough to play for the South in a Full England trial match during his first QPR spell, early in 1901. Soon after scoring in a 1-1 draw against Tottenham Hotspur in his first home match for Watford, he opened a tobacconist shop in St Albans Road.

Captaincy disappointment

Sydney George **HOBBS** *(1894-1897)*
b Edmonton, Middx 29/9/1876
SL 18 (8), FAC 3 (1), FAAC 7 (6)
Tottenham Hotspur; Woodville (1892/3); Crouch End (by 1895/6); West Herts (1894 until 9/97)); also Crouch End (briefly 1895/6)
First associated with the town as a pupil at the London Orphan School, he was the club's main goalscorer for two seasons before it entered the Southern League. After sustaining a knee injury in April 1897 he was was appointed captain for the following season, but broke down in the first game and didn't play again.

Two club records

Francis (FRANK) **HODDINOTT** *(1919-1921)*
b Brecon, Brecknockshire 29/11/1894
d Southend, Essex, November 1980
SL 13 (7), FL 39 (22 inc 6p), FAC 2 (3)
Aberdare (1913); Watford (7/19); Chelsea (£3,500 6/21); Crystal Palace (5/23); Rhyl (7/26); New Brighton (5/27); Newark Town (8/28, player-manager cs 1929); Grantham player-manager (cs 1930); Chelmsford trainer (by 9/33)
WALES FULL
A centre-forward whose goalscoring in Watford's first Football League season brought the club's first Full international honour and a club-record fee from Chelsea. The goals dried up, however, at Stamford Bridge, where in two seasons he totalled only four in 31 League games. He boxed professionally during his football career, and after turning his back on the game he took to plying pleasure-boats at Southend.

Life at the top

Stephen Brian (STEVE) **HODGE** *(1995)*
b Nottingham 25/10/1962
FL 2 (-)
Nottingham Forest (sch 10/77, appr 7/79, pro 10/80); Aston Villa (£450,000 8/85); Tottenham Hotspur (£650,000 12/86); Nottingham Forest (£550,000 8/88); Leeds Utd (£900,000 7/91); Derby County (loan 8/94); Queens Park Rangers (£300,000 10/94); Watford (free 12/95 until 1/96)
ENGLAND UNDER-21, 'B' and FULL

Twenty-four Full caps bear testimony to his midfield talent in a career which included three Wembley wins with Nottingham Forest in two seasons - two in the Football League Cup and one in the Full Members Cup. He'd previously been a beaten FA Cup finalist with Tottenham Hotspur, having scored twice in the semi-final against Watford.

Through the divisions

GLYN Peter **HODGES** *(1987-1990)*
b Streatham, London 30/4/1963
FL 82+4 (15 inc 3p), FAC 8 (1), FLC 5 (2), FMC 2+1 (1)
Wimbledon (sch 2/79, appr 7/79, pro 2/81); Newcastle Utd (£300,000 7/87); Watford (£320,000 9/87); Crystal Palace (£410,000 6/90); Sheffield Utd (loan 1/91, £400,000 4/91); Derby County (free 2/86)
WALES UNDER-21, 'B' and FULL
Although lacking John Barnes's pace and athleticism, and sometimes criticised for his temperament and commitment, he brought to the left side of Watford's attack a level of skill and vision equal to that of his illustrious predecessor. A magnificent striker of the ball with his left foot, he went from the Fourth Division to the First with Wimbledon.

Military background

Cornelius **HOGAN** *(1901)*
b Malta 1878
d Preston, Lancs 14/3/1909
SL 2 (-)
Aston Villa (11/97); Millwall (5/98); New Brighton Tower (5/99); Watford (7/01); Burnley (11/01); Fulham (6/03); Swindon Town (by 3/04); St Helen's Recreation (7/04); Nelson (11/05); Rossendale Utd (1/06)
The son of an army sergeant, he himself enlisted in the Royal Munster Fusiliers as a boy soldier, and was bought out by Aston Villa in February 1898, three months after he'd signed for the club. He began his Watford spell by playing centre-half in the first two Southern League games of the season, but didn't appear in the first team again.

Extrovert academic

Richard William (**RICK**) **HOLDEN** *(1988-1989)*
b Dewsbury, Yorks 9/9/1964
FL 42 (8), FAC 6 (1), FLC 2 (-), FMC 3+1 (1)
Harrogate Railway; Carnegie College, Leeds; Burnley (non-contract 3/86); Halifax Town (9/86); Watford (£150,000 3/88); Oldham Athletic (£165,000 8/89); Manchester City (valued at £900,000 in part-exchange 8/92); Oldham Athletic (£450,000 10/93); Blackpool (free 9/95)
University graduate, popular extrovert, ungainly but effective left-winger, and a very fine crosser of the ball, especially from awkward positions. He was one of a number of good signings by Steve Harrison who were then, to the surprise of many, discarded by the same manager. He enjoyed a good run in the top flight after leaving Vicarage Road.

Made his mark elsewhere

DEAN *Christopher* **HOLDSWORTH** *(1987-1989)*
b Walthamstow, London 8/11/1968
FL 2+16 (3), FMC 0+2 (-)
Watford (sch 5/84, appr 4/85, pro 11/86); Carlisle Utd (loan 2/88); Port Vale (loan 3/88); Swansea City (loan 8/88); Brentford (loan 10/88, £285,000 9/89); Wimbledon (loan 7/92, £720,000 8/92)
ENGLAND 'B'
David's twin brother. His rise to prominence as a free-scoring striker suggests that Watford might have benefited by giving him more opportunities at the start of his career. The fee received includes £160,000 of Brentford's subsequent 'sell-on' profit. His first six League goals were all scored in 1988, for five different clubs and in all four divisions.

The twin who stayed

DAVID *Gary* **HOLDSWORTH** *(1988-1996)*
b Walthamstow, London 8/11/1968
FL 249+11 (11), FAC 14+1 (1), FLC 20 (2), FMC 6 (-), AIC 2 (-)
Redbridge Schools (Under-12); Watford (sch 5/84, appr 4/85, pro 11/86)
ENGLAND YOUTH and UNDER-21
Forty minutes older than Dean, with whom he played in the 1985 FA Youth Cup Final, David captained the England Under-17 team and was an Under-21 international at centre-half, his pace being a major asset. After a serious knee injury had left him looking less than his old self, he recovered his best form in 1994/5 alongside Colin Foster.

Record fee, then released

PETER *Byrom* **HOLLAND** *(1928-1930)*
b Hindley, Lancs 5/10/1898
d Co Durham 1963
FL 21 (3), FAC 1 (-)
New Herrington Swifts; Houghton Rovers; Blackburn Rovers (3/19); Watford (£1,250 9/28); West Ham Utd (free 10/30); Tunbridge Wells Rangers (cs 1931)
ENGLAND SCHOOLS
He arrived at Vicarage Road for a club-record fee, having played in over a hundred First Division games, and in an FA Cup semi-final only a few months earlier. The club nevertheless got little return for its money, as he made only spasmodic appearances in various forward positions before having his engagement cancelled.

Opponent who impressed

Thomas (TOM) **HOLLAND** *(1930-1932)*
b Sheffield, Yorks 16/7/1902
d Weymouth, Dorset, July 1987
FL 62 (-), FAC 11 (-)
Rotherham Town; Manchester Utd (am 5/24); Doncaster Rovers (8/25 until 11/25); Weymouth (5/26); Exeter City (6/27); Watford (free 5/30); Gillingham (free 6/32); Weymouth player-coach (free 8/36, trainer until 12/62)
A six-feet-tall goalkeeper who appeared only twice in the Football League (during his brief period with Doncaster) before he was 25. It was whilst in opposition, in an Easter fixture in 1930, that he took the eye of the Watford

management, who signed him in the summer. His marathon service at Weymouth was ended by ill-health.

H. **HOLLINGSHEAD** *(1896)*
SL 4 (-), FAC 1 (-), FAAC 2 (-)
Ilford; West Herts (10/96); Dartford (2/97)
He made his West Herts début in an FA Cup tie and his final appearance in a Boxing Day friendly against Watford St Mary's, which attracted a record Cassio Road crowd of more than two thousand. A full-back, he soon afterwards became captain of Dartford, who had beaten West Herts 6-1 in his last competitive game for the club.

Commanding figure

CLIFFord Charles **HOLTON** *(1958-1966)*
b Headington, Oxon 29/4/1929
d Almeria, Spain 30/5/1996
FL 144 (96 inc 16p), FAC 17 (7 inc 1p), SFC 3 (1), FLC 2 (1)
Oxford City; Arsenal (11/47); Watford (£10,000 10/58); Northampton Town (£7,000 9/61); Crystal Palace (undisclosed fee 12/62); Watford (£5,000 5/65); Charlton Athletic (exchange for S.M.A.Scullion and £4,000 2/66); Leyton Orient (7/66 until 11/67)
Dominating the club to a unique extent as a commanding player and personality, he was at home in the half-back line, but achieved his glory as a powerful, hard-shooting forward who hit 48 goals in 1959/60. His sale in 1961 caused bitter and lasting controversy. In 1952/3 he contributed 19 goals in 21 games to Arsenal's League-championship win.

Goalkeeping winger

STANley **HOPKINSON** *(1947)*
b Kiveton Park, Yorks 15/3/1922
FL 1 (-)
Apsley; Watford (am 5/46); Berkhamsted Town (by 9/55 until at least 9/58)
He was registered with the Football League on amateur forms in time to make his one appearance - in goal at Vicarage Road in the final game of 1946/7, in which he conceded four goals to Brighton & Hove Albion. A few months later he showed his versatility by lining up at outside-left - and scoring - in a pre-season public practice match.

OSCAR Alfred **HORNE** *(1909)*
b Winslow, Bucks 1889
d Arlesey, Beds 17/11/1946
SL 5 (-), SCC 2 (-)
Leighton Town (by 11/08); Watford (am 1909/10)); Aylesbury Utd (by 10/11 until at least 10/13); Leighton Utd (by 1/30)
His first-team appearances were all on the left wing, in a single run early in the 1909/10 season, starting with a Southern Charity Cup win against his local professional club, Luton Town. He was turning out as late as the 1930s for Leighton United, when past his 40th birthday, and earlier in his career had been picked for the combined Berks & Bucks XI.

<u>*FRED*</u>*erick Young* **HORNER** *(1902)*
b Cheshunt, Herts 1882
SL 27 (-), FAC 2 (-), SEL 1 (-)
Oxford City; Watford (am 1/02 until 1903); Oxford City (12/02); Cheshunt (by 3/03); Reading (am 9/03); Ilford (10/04); Cheshunt (by 10/06); Oxford City (by 10/07)
Not the first young player, nor the last, to be given a rough time by the Cassio Road crowd, he was eventually replaced after a year-long stint in goal - but in the first game without him the team conceded eleven goals at Southampton. He went on to a good career in amateur football, playing for Oxfordshire, and on many occasions for Herts.

They soon missed him

ARTHUR **HORSFIELD** *(1975-1977)*
b Newcastle-upon-Tyne, Northumberland 5/7/1946
FL 78 (16), FAC 4 (-), FLC 1 (-)
Montague & North Fenham Boys' Club; Middlesbrough (am 6/62, appr 8/62, pro 7/63); Newcastle Utd (£17,500 1/69); Swindon Town (£17,000 5/69); Charlton Athletic (valued at £35,000 in exchange deal 6/72); Watford (£17,000 9/75); Dartford (loan 8/77, free 10/77, youth-team coach 1979/80)
ENGLAND YOUTH
He came to Vicarage Road, for a fee not far short of the club record, as an experienced centre-forward with nearly 150 League goals to his name. But by the time he left he'd become Watford's regular first-team centre-half whilst Keith Mercer took the No 9 shirt and enjoyed his most productive spell. Horsfield played once for the England Youth team.

Converted to centre-half

*FRED*erick **HORSMAN** *(1919-1924)*
b Leeds, Yorks 12/12/1889
d Watford, Herts 15/5/1959
SL 32 (-), FL 100 (-), FAC 6 (-)
Grantham; Mansfield Town (1910 until 1912); Watford (6/19); Doncaster Rovers (free 6/24); Peterborough (cs 1925); Luton Town (free 10/25 until 12/25); Ashford (by 3/26); Chatham (8/27 until cs 1928)
A beefy, hard-tackling full-back who, like a number of his contemporaries, was known to enjoy a glass of beer. He arrived at Vicarage Road without much sophistication to his game, but settled down to give good service, and during his five seasons with the club was picked to represent the FA against Cambridge University.

No frills

Leslie George **HOSIER** *(1906)*
b St Albans, Herts 25/3/1888
d Eastbourne, Sussex 1970
UL 2 (2)
St Albans Abbey; Watford (am 1906/7); St Albans City (by 5/09 until at least 3/11)
He was given only two chances in Watford's first team, and scored the club's only goal in both games. Aged 18, he played on the right wing in United League games against Norwich City at home (1-1) and Crystal Palace away (1-6). Educated at St Albans Grammar School, he represented Hertfordshire at both football and cricket.

Medal at Ipswich

William Gascoigne (**BILLY**) **HOUGHTON** *(1964-1966)*
b Hemsworth, Yorks 20/2/1939
FL 48 (2), FAC 3 (1)
Yorkshire Schools; Barnsley (8/57); Watford (nearly £10,000 6/64); Ipswich Town (free 6/66); Leicester City (7/69); Rotherham Utd ("small fee" 1/70 until 6/74)
ENGLAND YOUTH
He made the first of more than two hundred League appearances for Barnsley after only four reserve games. A physically strong left-half, he was signed by Bill McGarry for both Watford and Ipswich, where he won a Second Division Championship medal. He played in over five hundred League games altogether before returning to the joinery trade.

Father a top sportsman

TREVOR Anthony **HOW** *(1975-1979)*
b Amersham, Bucks 8/8/1957
FL 90+1 (2), FAC 3 (-), FLC 7 (-)
Watford (appr 11/73, pro 3/75); Aylesbury Utd (free 3/81); Wycombe Wanderers (1983); Harrow Borough (cs 1985, player/assistant-manager 11/85); Slough Town (by 2/88, assistant-manager cs 1988); Prestwood player-coach (by 4/92)
Watford's first-team right-back before he'd finished his apprenticeship, he then spent six years in and out of the side as a full professional. His contract was cancelled by mutual consent, and he went on to combine a career in non-League football with that of a publican. His father was one of the top riders in speedway's post-war heyday.

Played in Europe

GEORGE Albert **HOWARD** *(1906-1907)*
b Stotfold, Beds 1883
SL 1 (-), SEL 3 (-)
Arlesey Asylum (1897); Church Lads Brigade, Arlesey; Borough Polytechnic; Croydon Wanderers (3 seasons); Hitchin Town (3/04); Arlesey Asylum (1905/6); also Shepherd's Bush (1905/6); Stotfold (1906); Watford (am, pro 9/07)
He started in men's football at the age of 14, playing for the Three Counties Asylum team at Arlesey, and toured the Netherlands with Croydon Wanderers at Easter 1902, during his time in London. His four games in Watford's first-team defence included a 1-0 Southern League win against Millwall when he was still an amateur.

Gridiron star

Robert Michael (**BOBBY**) **HOWFIELD** *(1957-1963)*
b Watford, Herts 3/12/1936
FL 92 (22 inc 1p), FAC 5 (2), SFC 2 (1), FLC 2 (-)
Bushey Utd; Millwall (am 5/57); Watford (pro 9/57); Crewe Alexandra (7/59); Aldershot (10/59); Watford ("substantial fee" 7/62); Fulham (£6,000 11/63); New Yorkers, USA (cs 1965); Aldershot (8/65 until cs 1967)
An unpredictable and volatile forward, he had a powerful shot which he adapted for use in American gridiron football after finishing with soccer, enjoying a highly successful career as a kicker. His 23 League goals for Aldershot in 1961/2 were a club record for some years, and he scored three for Fulham in the last ten-goal performance by a top-flight club.

Archibald (**ARCHIE / RANJI**) **HUBBARD** *(1908-1909)*
b Leicester 7/2/1883
d Gloucester 1967
SL 50 (18 inc 1p), FAC 3 (2)
Leicester Imperial; Humberstone Victoria (10/01); St Andrews, Leicester; Leicester Fosse (am 3/04, pro 8/04); Fulham (5/07); Watford (1/08); Norwich City (5/09); Grimsby Town (11/10); Lincoln City (8/12); Leicester Imperial (9/13)
His enthusiastic, dashing style of forward play pleased the home crowds at all his clubs. He missed only a handful of first-team games during his time at Cassio Road, and was the top scorer in 1908/9. In Grimsby Town's one-season absence from the Football League, he helped them to win the championship of the Midland League.

Always a crowd favourite

Arthur Edward (**TED**) **HUFTON** *(1932)*
b Southwell, Notts 25/11/1892
d Swansea, West Glamorgan 2/1/1967
FL 2 (-)
Atlas & Norfolk; Sheffield Utd (£20 5/12); West Ham Utd (5/19); Watford (free 6/32 until cs 1933); West Ham Utd press-room steward after WW2.
ENGLAND FULL
The only man to have kept goal for both England and Watford. Spectacular and courageous in his prime, he played in the first Wembley Cup Final. He was often injured, and also received wounds whilst serving with the Coldstream Guards. Only nine older men have played for England, and only two older for Watford in the Football League.

The only England 'keeper

ROGER Victor **HUGO** *(1965-1966)*
b Woking, Surrey 6/9/1942
FL 24+1 (6), FLC 1 (-)
South London Schools; Surrey Schools; West Ham Utd (am 10/58, pro 10/60); Watford (£2,500 6/65); Port Elizabeth, South Africa (free 6/66)
After coming through West Ham's productive youth scheme, he scored twice in his three First Division games, but found it difficult to hold a first-team place. His career as a forward at Vicarage Road was a modest one, but he did make a bit of club history by becoming its first League substitute - and he celebrated with a goal.

Made club history

GEORGE Harold **HUNT** *(1941-1949)*
b Bethnal Green, London 5/3/1917
d Barnstaple, Devon, August 1990
FL 35 (-), WW2 2 (-)
Hackney Schools; Bexleyheath; Charlton Athletic (am 5/35, pro 5/37); Barnsley (5/38); Watford (6/46 until cs 1950); St Helens, Watford, coach (8/50); Rickmansworth Town coach (cs 1954). Guested for Luton Town and Watford in WW2.
In and out of the first team during his last three seasons at Vicarage Road, he was then forced into retirement by injury. A strong and wholehearted centre-half, he spent all the 1946/7 season as captain of the Reserves, before getting into the League side.

Led the stiffs

Winger who scored goals

STANley Charles **HURST** *(1936-1937)*
b Newton St Cyres, Devon 21/6/1911
d Crediton, Devon 28/5/1993
FL 29 (12), FAC 1 (-), 3SC 2 (2)
Jackson's Utd, Crediton; Newton Poppleford; Tipton St John; Exeter City (am 2/32, pro 12/32); Watford (undisclosed fee 6/36); Brighton & Hove Albion (£125 6/37); Aldershot (6/39); Crediton Utd
He took his League chance impressively at Watford, with four goals in his first three games, and maintained a healthy strike-rate for a left-winger. In his Exeter days he enjoyed two goalscoring jaunts for the Reserves, with five against Taunton Town, and seven in a Southern League game against Swindon Reserves. He collapsed and died playing golf.

John Hyde **ILES** *(1897)*
b Watford, Herts 19/11/1878
d Starcross, Devon 12/12/1954
SL 1 (-)
West Herts (1/96)
His father was a doctor who lived in Watford High Street and was very prominent in public life and in freemasonry. Only 18 when he made his Southern League appearance, Iles played on the right wing in a 3-0 defeat away to the 1st Scots Guards. He studied at Cambridge and followed his father into the medical profession.

Never short of goals

ALEXander Matthew **INGLETHORPE** *(1990-1994)*
b Epsom, Surrey 14/11/1971
FL 2+10 (2), FLC 1+2 (-), AIC 1+1 (1)
Watford (sch 6/88, pro 7/90); Barnet (loan 3/95); Leyton Orient (£15,000 and possible further payments 5/95)
Registered by the club as a schoolboy, he by-passed the apprenticeship stage in order to continue with his A-Level studies, on completion of which he signed as a full professional. A striker with a good scoring rate for the Reserves, he was never deemed worthy of a decent first-team run. He scored all his three senior goals as a substitute in 1993/4.

Promotion with Reading

William John **INGLIS** *(1932-1933)*
b Newcastle-upon-Tyne, Northumberland 4/9/1899
FL 12 (-)
Hebburn Colliery; Derby County (6/21); Brentford (free 5/22); Reading (5/25); Exeter City (6/30); Stockport County (8/31); Watford (7/32); Dartford (free 8/33); Cray Wanderers (permit player 8/34)
Despite his origins, he played most of his football in the South, and helped Reading into the Second Division for the first and, until recent years, only time. A strongly-built half-back, he spent just one winter with Watford, his last League club, and although he ended the season with a first-team place, was released on a free transfer.

DEREK Vincent **IRVIN** *(1968)*
b Stockton-on-Tees, Co Durham 23/8/1943
FL 0+2 (1)
Middlesbrough (9/61); Falkirk (free 7/63); St Johnstone (4/64); Brechin City (11/64); Watford (free 6/67); Corby Town (free, cs 1968)
A forward who is very probably the only Englishman to have joined a Football League club from Brechin City, and is certainly the only Watford player to have scored a League goal without ever starting a first-team game. The goal came at Shrewsbury, in a 3-1 defeat. He'd been Brechin's top scorer in his final season at Glebe Park.

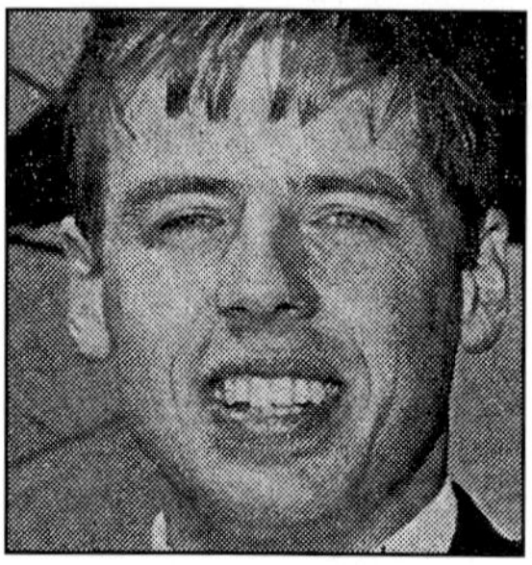

Unmatched record

Robert (BOB) **IRVINE** *(1933-1934)*
b Lisburn, Co Antrim 29/4/1900
d Leicester 1979
FL 22 (2), FAC 1 (-), 3SC 1 (1)
Dunmurry; Everton (9/21); Portsmouth (3/28); Connah's Quay (free 8/30); Chester (12/30); Derry City (8/31); Watford (free 6/33 until cs 1934)
IRELAND JUNIOR and FULL; IRISH LEAGUE
He arrived at Vicarage Road as a highly-experienced forward, having spent a total of nine years in First Division football with Everton and Portsmouth, and won 15 Full international caps. Before announcing his retirement after being released in the summer of 1934, he had two runs in the first team - one at inside-left and the other at centre-forward.

Nine years at the top

Ernest (ERNIE) **ISON** *(1932)*
b Coton, Warwicks 12/6/1903
d Burntwood, Staffs 26/10/1983
FL 3 (1)
Nuneaton Town; Brighton & Hove Albion (8/24); Southport (6/31); Watford (free 8/32); Ramsgate Athletic (free cs 1933)
After, for some reason, playing under the corny pseudonym 'Newman' in the 1932 pre-season public trial match, he was signed on and went straight into the first-team at outside-left. He scored on his début, against Norwich City, but Jack Barnes was recalled after three games and Ison was not seen again at senior level.

Quickly discarded

FRANK **JACKETT** *(1949-1953)*
b Ystalfera, Glam 5/7/1927
FL 14 (-)
Glanrhyd; Pontardawe Athletic; Swansea Town (am 1948/9); Watford (pro 11/49); Leyton Orient (free 7/53); Ramsgate Athletic (cs 1954); Margate (1958); Adeyfield Athletic player-coach (permit player 1/60 until 1962)
The senior half of the only father-and-son pair to represent Watford in first-team competitions during peacetime - and his elder son was a Luton Town apprentice. Frank played for South Wales as a youth player and for Swansea Town youth team and Reserves, before joining Watford, who converted him from an inside-forward to a strong-tackling wing-half.

Two generations

Capped 31 times

Kenneth Francis (**KENNY**) ***JACKETT*** *(1980-1990)*
b Watford, Herts 5/1/1962
FL 330+7 (25 inc 7p), FAC 38+1 (5 inc 3p), FLC 34+1 (4 inc 1p), FLT 7 (-), UEFA 5 (-), FMC 5 (-)
Watford (sch 10/76, appr 6/78, pro 1/80, part-time coach 9/90, youth-team coach 1/91, youth-team manager 11/91, assistant-manager 7/93, youth-team manager 7/94, joint-coach 2/94, team manager 5/96)
WALES YOUTH, UNDER-21 and FULL
Bringing a cultured, thoughtful influence to the left side of defence or midfield, he was within sight of the club's appearance record at 28 when injury ended his playing days. He won 31 senior caps for Wales, his Welsh father having remained in the town after his own Vicarage Road career.

Knew the reserve scene

William (**BILLY**) ***JACKSON*** *(1935)*
b Farnworth, Lancs 15/7/1902
d Blackpool, Lancs 1974
FL 4 (1)
Leyland; Altrincham (1921); Darwen (cs 1922); Sunderland (5/24); Leeds Utd (9/25); West Ham Utd (5/27); Chelsea (2/28); Leicester City (5/31); Ashford Town (1931); Bristol Rovers (5/32); Cardiff City (6/34); Watford (1/35 until cs 1935)
By the time he got to Watford he'd accumulated more than a fair share of employers during his football career, but had spent most of the time in their reserve teams. A two-footed winger, he scored in his first Vicarage Road appearance, but didn't last long in the senior side and wasn't in the club's retained list at the end of the season.

Seized his chance

DAVID Benjamin ***JAMES*** *(1990-1992)*
b Welwyn Garden City, Herts 1/8/1970
FL 89 (-), FAC 2 (-), FLC 6 (-), FMC 1 (-)
Panshanger Yellows; Watford (sch 11/84, tr 7/86, pro 7/88); Liverpool (£1.25 million 6/92)
ENGLAND UNDER-21 and 'B'
Suddenly promoted at the start of 1990/1, after Mel Rees had kept goal in the pre-season friendlies, he excelled in a struggling team and was clearly destined for higher things. A giant, athletic frame enabled him to command the penalty area, and his shot-stopping was remarkable. He'd helped Watford to to win the FA Youth Cup in 1989.

The most prolific

GEORGE Charles ***JAMES*** *(1930-1933)*
b Rood End, Staffs 14/2/1899
d West Bromwich, West Midlands 12/12/1976
FL 83 (67), FAC 11 (9)
Oldbury Schools; Chance's Glass Works; Daimler Repair Works; Bilston Utd; West Bromwich Albion (5/21); Reading (5/29); Watford (part-exchange for F.C.McPherson 2/30 until cs 1933)
An England trialist in 1925, he became the most prolific of all of Watford's major goalscorers, and the club did well out of the deal under which they lost that other free-scoring centre-forward, Frank McPherson. James retired after three seasons at Vicarage Road and took a pub back in the West Midlands.

William H. **JANES** *(1899)*
SL 2 (1), BCCL 2 (-)
Barnet Alston; Watford (am 1/99); Thames Ironworks (pro 5/99); Grays Utd (by 4/01); Clapton Orient; reinstated am (1906)
He made his Watford appearances at outside-right at a time when the position had no regular occupant, and scored in a 5-1 win at Maidenhead. He turned professional at Upton Park shortly afterwards, having been a Middlesex player as an amateur, and having helped the Middlesex FA to beat a Derby County side containing the immortal Steve Bloomer.

ALFred **JEBB** *(1912-1913)*
b Nottingham circa 1887
SL 38 (-), FAC 3 (-), SCC 2 (-)
Ilkeston Utd (pro 5/08); Barnsley (3/10); Watford ("small fee" 5/12 until cs 1914)
His transfer to Watford reunited him with former Ilkeston colleagues Alex Stewart and Joe Webster. A wholehearted player, he was ever-present in competitive matches in 1912/3, turning out in all the half-back positions and at outside-left, but then had the misfortune to miss the whole of the following season through injury.

Change of fortune

Alec **JEFFREY** *(1900-1901)*
b circa 1877
SL 18 (-), FAC 3 (-)
Bacup (until 1/97); Madeley Institute (3/97); Wrockwardine Wood (10/97); Wellington Town (9/98); Ashford Utd (1/99); Watford (7/00); Stockport County (6/01 until cs 1903); Dudley (1/04); Heckmondwike (10/06 until at least cs 1909)
He played in the half-back line in more than half the first-team games in his only season at Cassio Road, ending with a Southern League Test Match from which the club emerged with a goalless draw to secure First Division survival. Not a single Watford goal was scored in his last five games, one of which was a seven-goal beating at Tottenham.

NIGEL Bradley **JEMSON** *(1995)*
b Hutton, Lancs 10/8/1969
FL 3+1 (-)
Preston North End (sch 8/84, tr 8/86, pro 7/87); Nottingham Forest (£150,000 3/88); Bolton Wanderers (loan 12/88); Preston North End (loan 3/89); Sheffield Wednesday (£800,000 9/91); Grimsby Town (loan 9/93); Notts County (£300,000 9/94); Watford (loan 1/95); Coventry City (loan 3/95); Rotherham Utd (loan 2/96)
ENGLAND UNDER-21
An unsuccessful loan signing as a striker at Watford, but at the age of 20 he'd scored the goal which won Forest the Football League Cup. He later performed the unusual feat of scoring a penalty in a club début - for Grimsby, against Watford - and further personal Wembley glory came his way with Rotherham, his two goals winning the Associate Members Cup.

Three Wembley goals

Ugly duckling to swan

ROSS Anthony **JENKINS** *(1972-1983)*
b Kensington, London 4/11/1951
FL 312+27 (118), FAC 18+1 (5), FLC 33+4 (16), FLT 3 (3)
Crystal Palace (appr 7/68, pro 11/69); Watford (£35,000 11/72); Washington Diplomats, USA (£7,500 3/81); Watford (£7,500 9/81); Eastern Athletic, Hong Kong (free 7/83); Apollon, Cyprus (7/84 until early 1985); Watford part-time coach (9/87 until 10/87)
Rarely can a player have won over a hostile crowd so completely as did this gangling centre-forward, who eventually blossomed to become a key component in Watford's rise to prominence. He played for the club when it was in both 92nd and 1st position in the Football League, and along the way became the competition's top scorer in 1978/9.

Went out in style

PATrick Anthony **JENNINGS** *(1963-1964)*
b Newry, Co Down 12/6/1945
FL 48 (-), FAC 3 (-), FLC 1 (-)
Newry Utd; Newry Town; Watford (£6,500 5/63); Tottenham Hotspur (£27,000 6/64); Arsenal (£45,000 8/77); Tottenham Hotspur (non-contract 8/85); Everton (non-contract 3/86); Tottenham Hotspur (non-contract 5/86 until 6/86, goalkeeping coach 7/93)
NORTHERN IRELAND YOUTH, UNDER-23 and FULL
One of the game's greatest goalkeepers. An honour-strewn career ended on his 41st birthday with his 119th international appearance - against Brazil in the World Cup Finals. Undemonstrative, and the essence of composure, he was an FA Cup winner with both the big London clubs. His Watford appearances were all consecutive.

Record fee sent soaring

William John (BILLY) **JENNINGS** *(1970-1974)*
b Hackney, London 20/2/1952
FL 80+13 (33), FAC 3 (-), FLC 4 (4)
Watford (am 3/69, pro 4/70); West Ham Utd (£110,000 9/74); Chicago Sting, USA (loan 5/77 until 8/77); Orient (£100,000 8/79); Luton Town (3/82 until cs 1982); Dagenham (3/83); Bishops Stortford (cs 1983); Heybridge Swifts (briefly, early 1984/5)
ENGLAND YOUTH
A striker who had little interest in any aspect of the game except goalscoring, he was especially capable in the air for one who was not tall. His 26 League goals in 1973/4 (the Third Division's best tally) prompted West Ham nearly to double Watford's record incoming transfer fee. He got a winner's medal in the 1975 FA Cup, despite scoring a semi-final own goal.

Injury setback

GEORGE **JEWETT** *(1927-1928)*
b Bitterne, Hants 2/5/1906
FL 29 (-)
Thornycrofts, Southampton; Cowes (pro, cs 1926); Watford (5/27); Southampton (free 7/29); Crystal Palace (5/31 until cs 1932); Basingstoke Town player-coach (cs 1934); Cowes (cs 1935 until cs 1937); Lymington (reinstated amateur, manager 1948/9)

Whilst a shipyard apprentice he attracted interest from Arsenal and West Ham, and the latter offered him a contract, but it was eventually with Watford that he began his full-time career. A tall defender, skilful on the ground, he ran into injury problems at Vicarage Road and was never fully fit again. His brother Alf played for Arsenal.

BEDFORD *Alfred George* **JEZZARD** *(1945)*
b Clerkenwell, London 19/10/1927
FAC 3 (1), WW2 18 (6)
Watford Schools; Croxley Boys Club; Watford (am 12/44); Fulham (am 7/48, pro 10/48, youth-team coach 8/57, manager 6/58, general manager 10/64 until 12/64)
ENGLAND 'B' and FULL; FOOTBALL LEAGUE
With Bobby Robson and Johnny Haynes he was to form an illustrious Craven Cottage inside-forward trio of England internationals, but much less well-known is that he began his senior career with Watford. It's a strange fact that this dashing, free-scoring centre-forward scored an FA Cup goal for Watford - as an 18-year-old amateur winger - but never for Fulham.

FA Cup oddity

RICHARD *Ian* **JOBSON** *(1982-1984)*
b Cottingham, Yorks 9/5/1963
FL 26+2 (4), FAC 0+1 (-), FLC 2 (-), FLT 1 (-), UEFA 5+1 (-)
Rolleston Evening Institute; Vadis, Burton-upon-Trent; Nottingham Forest youth team; Aston Villa youth team; Nottingham University; Burton Albion (cs 1982); Watford (£27,500 10/82); Hull City (£40,000 2/85); Oldham Athletic (£460,000 8/90); Leeds Utd (£1 million 10/95)
ENGLAND 'B'
Tall, elegant, athletic and versatile, he received belated international recognition as a centre-half and came close to a Full cap under Graham Taylor, who much earlier had signed him for Watford but then rejected him. As a teenager he represented the English Universities and had unsuccessful trials with several League clubs in the Midlands.

Belated recognition

DAVID *Nicholas Conrad* **JOHNSON** *(1981-1983)*
b Gloucester 26/12/1962
FL 4+3 (-), FLC 1+1 (-), FLT 1+2 (-), UEFA 1+1 (-)
Redhill; Watford (9/81); Peterborough Utd (free 6/84); Bishops Stortford (free, cs 1986); Bourn; King's Lynn; Dover Athletic (1989/90); Heybridge Swifts (1990/1); Whyteleafe (9/94)
Given an extended trial after opposing the club in a youth fixture, he earned a contract, but found himself behind Barnes, Callaghan and Sterling in the queue for the first-team wing positions. In 1981/2 he somehow was allowed to play a season of South-East Counties League football, and win an FA Youth Cup medal, despite being over-age for both competitions.

Competition for places

Flying start for Reading

GEORGE *Alfred* **JOHNSON** *(1937-1938)*
b Ashington, Northumberland 20/7/1904
d Reading, Berks 26/5/1985
FL 23 (8), FAC 2 (1)
Ashington (by 10/24); Sheffield Wednesday (7/29); Reading (6/32); Watford (free 5/37 until cs 1939) Krooger, Netherlands, coach (by 6/46); Gauda, Netherlands, coach (3 years to 11/49); Oxford City coach and groundsman (12/49)
Signed by Reading as a centre-forward, he responded with an away hat-trick on his début, but almost immediately was switched to a more defensive role, which he retained for five seasons of League football. Recruited by Watford to captain the Reserves from wing-half at the age of 33, he nevertheless enjoyed a decent first-team run at inside-left.

Waterford to Watford

GEORGE *Edward* **JOHNSON** *(1938)*
b Sheffield, Yorks 15/7/1913
d Paignton, Devon 6/1/1989
FL 1 (-)
Torquay Utd (am 12/35, pro 1/36); Waterford (1937/8); Watford (8/38 to cs 1947, 'A'-team coach 1947/8); Tring Town coach (cs 1950). Guested for Lincoln City, Rotherham Utd and Torquay Utd in WW2.
One of two George Johnsons on the books in 1938/9, he was a quick and enthusiastic centre-half who turned up for a trial after spending a season in Irish football. He got only one first-team chance as Jimmy Armstrong's deputy, featuring in a goalless draw against Ipswich Town, who were making their first League visit to Vicarage Road.

Compensated for injury

Joseph (JOE) **JOHNSON** *(1920-1924)*
b Lincs
d by July 1948
FL 94 (1), FAC 8 (-)
Stamford Town; Mansfield Mechanics; Notts County (cs 1918); Watford (5/20); Luton Town (£75 6/24 until cs 1925)
Classier than the average Third Division full-back, he sustained a leg injury in a reserve-team match six months after moving to Kenilworth Road. It ended his career, and he received £300 compensation, which had apparently disappeared by January 1927, when he was sued for rent arrears in respect of his home on the Harebreaks estate.

Long journey rewarded

RICHARD *Mark* **JOHNSON** *(1991-1996)*
b Kurri Kurri, Australia 27/4/1974
FL 67+18 (4), FAC 4 (-), FLC 6+1 (1), AIC 0+1 (-)
Newcastle Astrals, Australia; Tottenham Hotspur youth team; Watford (tr 3/91, pro 5/92)
The son of a former Preston North End apprentice who emigrated, he came to England aged 16 in search of a football career. After a period with Tottenham, he was fixed up at Vicarage Road, with the help of former Watford defender Bill Shipwright. A strong, determined midfield player with a fierce shot, he made his League début whilst still a trainee.

<u>*MAURICE*</u> *John Giblin* **<u>JOHNSTON</u>** *(1983-1984)*
b Glasgow 13/4/1963
FL 37+1 (23), FAC 7 (4 inc 1p), FLC 1 (-)
Milton Battlefield; Partick Thistle (8/80); <u>Watford</u> (£200,000 11/83); Celtic (£400,000 10/84); Nantes, France (£350,000 6/87); Rangers (£1.5 million 7/89); Everton (£1.5 million 11/91); Heart of Midlothian (free 10/93); Falkirk (free 3/95); Kansas City Wiz, USA (5/96)
SCOTLAND UNDER-21 and FULL
An exceptional goalscorer in any company (14 in 38 Full internationals), and at the age of 20 an astute signing by Graham Taylor. Nimble and predatory, he was an ideal foil at Watford for the lofty George Reilly. A high-profile player, never far from controversy off the field, he won a string of domestic honours with the big Glasgow clubs.

High-profile

<u>*BRYN*</u> *Edward* **<u>JONES</u>** *(1963)*
b Bagillt, Flints 26/5/1939
FL 2 (-)
Bangor City (am); Holywell (am); <u>Watford</u> (pro 1/63); Chester (free 8/64 until 1967)
WALES AMATEUR
A full-back who was well into his 24th year when he turned professional after winning international honours as an amateur in North Wales. He made the first team for the last two games of 1962/3, but spent the following season in the shadows and then returned to familiar territory on a free transfer. He suffered a broken leg soon afterwards.

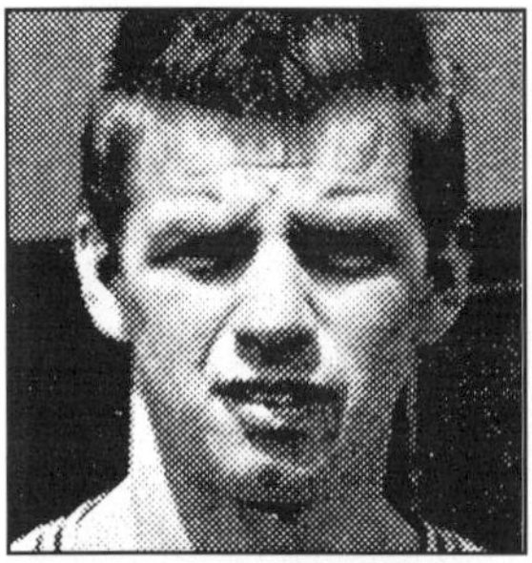
An amateur until 23

<u>*Benjamin James* **(JIMMY)** **JONES**</u> *(1947-1954)*
b Tonypandy, Glam 16/11/1919
d Watford, Herts 1976
FL 158 (-), FAC 9 (-)
Rhondda Working Men's FC; Slough Utd; <u>Watford</u> (9/47); Chelmsford City (free 7/55 until at least 1958); <u>Watford</u> youth-team coach (5/60); Oldham Old Boys Reserves, Watford (permit player, by 2/68)
WALES AMATEUR
He signed for Watford from Slough as a hard-as-nails full-back, for a £25 donation to the Welsh club with whom he was still registered. After joining Slough he'd been ordered down the mines as a Bevin boy, but fell ill and spent six months in hospital, Although told he might never play football again, he was soon to win Amateur international recognition.

Bevin boy

<u>*Brinley Roy* **(BRYN)** **JONES**</u> *(1963-1966)*
b Swansea, Glam 20/5/1931
d Camden, London 5/10/1990
FL 90+1 (1), FAC 3 (-), FLC 5 (-)
Swansea Team (youth team, pro 9/51); Newport County (6/58); Bournemouth & Boscombe Athletic (2/60); Northampton Town (£7,000 10/63); <u>Watford</u> (exchange

Unorthodox transfer

for R.H.Brown plus cash 11/63); Chelmsford City (10/66); Folkestone (player-manager until 12/67)

A member of an immensely distinguished Welsh footballing family, and a strong-tackling full-back who became Watford's captain. He reached the club, with the connivance of Northampton Town, under a bizarre arrangement arising from Bournemouth's resentment of manager McGarry's move to Watford, and their consequent refusal to do business with the club.

Only briefly in the south

David ***OSWALD*** *Edwards* ***JONES*** *(1938)*
b Ruabon, Denbighs 15/7/1909
FL 2 (-)
Connah's Quay & Shotton; Nottingham Forest (10/31); Wrexham (7/32); Oswestry Town; Macclesfield Town (7/34); Tranmere Rovers (5/36); Watford (5/38); Southport (free 11/38); Crewe Alexandra (cs 1939)

He joined Watford at the end of a season in which he had made 17 appearances during Tranmere's progress to the championship of the Third Division (North). A strongly-built inside forward, he was picked only twice for the first team during his short spell at Vicarage Road, before heading back to the North-West.

Confusion of identity

J. (JIMMY) ***JONES*** *(1904-1905)*
b Wales
SL 7 (-), SEL 4 (-)
Tottenham Hotspur; Watford (5/04 until cs 1905)

The least-known of three J.Joneses simultaneously on Tottenham Hotspur's books, this being a source of much confusion which has led to his transfer to Watford being wrongly ascribed to one - and even both - of his namesakes. Never a first-team player at White Hart Lane, he began and ended the 1904/5 season as Watford's first-team left-half.

Astonishing start

ORMOND *Henry* ***JONES*** *(1936)*
b Towyn, Merionethshire 24/8/1910
d Bilston, Staffs 10/4/1972
FL 8 (-)
Hickman's Town; Towyn; Bilston Utd; Wednesbury Town; Blackpool (3/32 until cs 1932); Yeovil & Petters Utd; Port Vale (5/33); Norwich City (5/34); Watford (1/36); Mansfield Town (free 8/36 until cs 1937); Norwich City Reserves (briefly 9/37); Yarmouth Town (10/38 until 5/39)
WALES SCHOOLS

Making probably the best start that any player has ever done with a new club, he had wins of 6-1 (away), 5-0 (home) and 5-0 (away) in his first three Watford games. He'd been signed to meet a goalkeeping crisis, both McLaren and McHugh having been injured whilst on first-team duty, and was soon discarded once the emergency was over.

One of eight wingers

TREVOR JONES *(1949-1950)*
b Aberdare, Glamorgan 27/1/1923
d Merthyr Tydfil, Mid Glamorgan, March 1983
FL 15 (2), FAC 1 (1)
Aberaman; Plymouth Argyle (am, pro 5/48); Watford (8/49 until cs 1950); Leyton Orient (a month's trial 4/52)
An enthusiastic winger with a fine turn of speed, he had a trial period before being taken on, and was one of eight players used in the flank positions during 1949/50. That was the only season in which he had Football League experience, and it also included his sole FA Cup appearance, in which he scored - in a 2-1 win at Bromley.

Set a wartime record

Thomas John (TOM) JONES *(1935-1946)*
b Tonypandy, Glam, circa 1908
d circa 1980
FL 118 (23), FAC 13 (3), 3SC 6 (1), WW2 241 (29 inc 1p)
Mid Rhondda; Tranmere Rovers (2/26); Sheffield Wednesday ("substantial fee" 6/29); Manchester Utd (6/34); Watford (nearly £1,500 5/35); Guildford City (free 6/46); Tranmere Rovers trainer-coach (8/46); Workington trainer-coach (circa 1953, briefly caretaker-manager 9/53); Birmingham City assistant-trainer (8/58); West Bromwich Albion assistant-physiotherapist (1966 until 1968). Guested for Arsenal in WW2.
WALES FULL
Capped once in his Hillsborough days (Wales lost 4-0 in Belfast), he had a long Watford career, most of it absorbed by the war, during which he played more games for the club than anyone else. Primarily a right-winger, he later turned out in a variety of other positions. He scored five of Tranmere's 19 goals in his first four League appearances.

Had scored goals

William MORRIS JONES *(1951-1952)*
b Liverpool, Lancs 30/11/1919
d Liverpool, Merseyside, July 1993
FL 27 (7 inc 1p), FAC 1 (-)
South Liverpool; Port Vale (6/46); Swindon Town (£2,500 11/47); Crystal Palace (£4,000 5/50); Watford (four-figure fee 3/51 until 2/52); Leyton Orient (3/52); Bangor City (6/52). Guested for Celtic in WW2.
An inside-forward with an excellent scoring record (77 goals in 164 League appearances) before his transfer to Watford, he was with the club when its fortunes were at a low ebb. He took part in a 7-1 home defeat by his former employers, Swindon Town, but before leaving he did score twice in his penultimate game, helping to beat Shrewsbury 4-1.

H. (HARRY) JORDAN *(1898-1899)*
SL 1 (-), BCCL 2 (-)
Watford St Mary's; Watford (am); Queens Park Rangers (am, pro 6/99 until cs 1901); Watford (10/01)
A centre-half who knew nothing but victory in his spasmodic first-team career, which (including two friendlies) amounted to five games. The three competitive appearances brought three away wins during his first period at Cassio Road, before he turned professional with QPR, for whom he played once in the Southern League.

500-game career

ROGER *Douglas William* **JOSLYN** *(1974-1979)*
b Colchester, Essex 7/5/1950
FL 178+4 (17), FAC 9+1 (-), FLC 21+1 (4)
Colchester Utd (am 8/67, pro 5/68); Aldershot (£8,000 10/70); Watford (valued at £20,000 in exchange for P.J.Morrissey and £10,000 11/74); Reading (£40,000 11/79 until 1/82)
He contributed energy and drive to the midfield effort as a regular member of the side which won successive promotions between 1977 and 1979. His total League experience amounted to over five hundred games, all but eleven of them in the lower divisions. An arthritic hip forced his retirement and later severely restricted his mobility.

Physician and biologist

Norman Humbert **JOY** *(1896)*
b Barrow-in-Furness, Lancs 7/7/1874
d Chichester, Sussex 20/1/1953
SL 1 (-)
St Bartholomew's Hospital; United Hospitals; West Herts (1896/7)
One of three brothers who were boarders at Aldenham School and also represented West Herts. He played at right-half in the club's second Southern League game, but made only one other first-team appearance - in a friendly. Subsequently the medical officer at Bradfield College for 17 years, he was also a noted ornithologist and coleoptorist.

Michael Thomas (MIKE) **KEEN** *(1972-1975)* - *SEE PART FIVE*

Two Watford spells

Francis (FRANK) **KELLY** *(1905-1909)*
b Ireland, circa 1883
SL 46 (5), FAC 4 (3), SEL 4 (1), UL 15 (5 inc 1p)
Chester (9/02); Barnsley (5/03); Chesterfield Town (6/04); Watford (5/05); Leyton (6/06); Watford (5/08); Stockport County (5/09); Nelson (cs 1911)
By no means the only man to be hauled before the Committee in the club's early days of professionalism, he was in trouble in both his seasons as the club's principal outside-left. Before returning for the second spell, he had two years' service with Southern League rivals Leyton.

Life after football

James (JIMMY) **KELLY** *(1950-1954)*
b Linton, Northumberland 11/8/1931
FL 119 (4), FAC 4 (-)
Blyth Spartans; Watford Amateurs; Watford (groundstaff 1/49, pro 3/49); Blackpool (£15,000 10/54); South Coast Utd, Australia, player-coach (4/61)
His progress as a talented young wing-half in nearly six years at Vicarage Road made him a crowd favourite and eventually attracted a club-record fee. He made nearly two hundred First Division appearances and then became a leading player and coach in Australia, before returning to Blackpool to begin an extremely successful business career.

William Bainbridge **KELLY** *(1910-1911)*
b Newcastle-upon-Tyne, Northumberland 1890
SL 29 (8), FAC 2 (-), SCC 3 (1)
Benwell Adelaide; Newcastle Balmoral; Blaydon; North Shields Athletic; Watford (8/10); Newcastle Utd (£200 5/11); Manchester City (£400 11/11); Blyth Spartans (8/13); Rochdale (cs 1914)
Venturing further south than Manchester for employment just once in his career, he spent most of his one season at Cassio Road as the first-team inside-right. He then acquired what for a Geordie was the perfect transfer - and at a time when Newcastle were enjoying a golden era. Watford, for their part, were glad of the money.

Went home for £200

Andrew John **(ANDY) KENNEDY** *(1990-1991)*
b Stirling 8/10/1964
FL 17+8 (4), FAC 0+1 (-), FLC 2 (1), FMC 1 (-)
Sauchie Athletic; Rangers (7/82 until 2/85); Everton Reserves (briefly 1985); Seiko, Hong Kong; Birmingham City (£50,000 3/85); Sheffield Utd (loan 3/87); Blackburn Rovers (£50,000 6/88); Watford (valued at £190,000 in exchange for L.J.Richardson and £60,000 7/90); Bolton Wanderers (loan 10/91); Brighton & Hove Albion (£30,000 9/92 until cs 1994); Gillingham (9/94 until 10/94); Hong Kong football (1994 until 2/95); Witton Albion (11/95); Hastings Town; Hendon (3/96)
SCOTLAND YOUTH
Signed by Colin Lee, but out of favour after Steve Perryman took over less than six months later, he was available for transfer for some time before a buyer was found. An athletically-built striker, he went for a basic £10,000. Although this was boosted by further payments based on appearances for Brighton, Watford's net loss was still substantial.

Fell out of favour

James John **(JIM) KENNEDY** *(1913-1915)*
b Dundee, Angus 8/5/1883
d Glasgow 20/7/1947
SL 51 (3 inc 2p), FAC 1 (-), SCC 1 (-)
Celtic (12/03); Brighton & Hove Albion (5/05); Leeds City (5/06); Stockport County (8/09); Tottenham Hotspur (3/10); Swindon Town (4/12); Norwich City (7/13); Watford (£75 12/13); Gillingham (£25 12/19, trainer cs 1920); Partick Thistle trainer at time of death
Having made his Watford début on Christmas Day 1913, he settled into the centre-half position, impressing with intelligence and good distribution, and then led the club to the 1914/5 Southern League championship after skipper Alex Stewart (who continued in the side, but not as captain) had enlisted in mid-season. Kennedy broke a shoulder blade in a Tottenham Hotspur reserve game in 1910.

Led the title charge

Manager in South Africa

Michael John (**MIKE**) **KENNING** *(1972-1973)*
b Birmingham, Warwicks 18/8/1940
FL 35+6 (2), FAC 3 (1p)
Birmingham District Schools; Brookhill; Aston Villa (am 1/57, pro 10/59); Shrewsbury Town (5/61); Charlton Athletic (£10,000 11/62); Norwich City (£25,000 12/66); Wolverhampton Wanderers (£35,000 1/68); Charlton Athletic (£20,000 3/69); Watford (£7,000 12/71); Germiston Callies, South Africa, player-manager (free, cs 1973 until 1977); also Nuneaton Borough (9/73); also Atherstone Town; also Malvern Town; Durban Utd, South Africa, manager (1979); Wits University, South Africa, manager
This galloping, hard-shooting winger's entire Watford career coincided with a dire sequence of results which brought the club within a whisker of successive relegations. The experience may have taken its toll, for he promptly left for South Africa, and is still there. His total of League appearances exceeded four hundred, over half of them being for Charlton.

Henry (**HARRY**) **KENT** *(1909-1913)* - *SEE PART FIVE*

Soon lost his place

E. **KILNER** *(1912-1913)*
b circa 1890
SL 5 (-)
Sutton Junction; Watford (5/12 until cs 1913)
A product of one of Harry Kent's many raids on the minor clubs of the East Midlands, he was a pacy winger signed around the same time as Tommy Mitchell, following Wally Tattersall's departure. Kilner began as the first-choice outside-right, but Mitchell soon claimed the position, and kept it. Kilner was released at the end of the season.

F. **KING** *(1896)*
SL 1 (-)
West Herts (1896)
No fewer than 35 players were used in the club's 24-match inaugural season of Southern League football - professionalism had not yet been adopted - and King was one of ten of them who played just once. He was at inside-left in a 1-0 home defeat against Uxbridge, which was the second of five consecutive Southern League defeats.

First Southern Lge goalie

SIDney **KING** *(1893-1897)*
b Watford, Herts 15/12/1870
d Watford, Herts 27/10/1943
SL 24 (-), FAC 5 (-), FAAC 8 (-), HSC 8 (-)
Watford Gymnasium (1887); Watford Church Institute (1890/1); Watford St Mary's (1891/2); West Herts (1892 until 1898)
He'd represented the county and was well-established as the first-choice goalie for West Herts by the time they entered the Southern League, in which he was ever-present in 1896/7. Four seasons earlier he'd been sent off whilst playing for the Reserves v St Mary's in the West Herts League, for striking a former colleague, Bangy Harrison.

*Thomas Henderson (**TOMMY**) **KING** (1955-1956)*
b Leith, Edinburgh 18/7/1933
FL 20 (-), FAC 1 (-), SFC 1 (-)
Ormiston Primrose (4/51); Watford ("small fee" 3/54 until cs 1956); Ormiston Primrose (7/57); Linlithgow Rose (8/61 until cs 1963)
He had an 18-month wait for first-team action after crossing the border, but eventually got his chance in goal when Ted Bennett's long continuous tenancy was ended by a broken finger. King was on the winning side only five times in the senior side. He declined renewed terms for 1956/7 and returned home, where he later resumed his career at Scottish Junior level.

Declined renewed terms

*W. **KINGHAM** (1913)*
SCC 1 (-)
Apsley; Watford (am 1913)
For ties in the Southern Charity Cup, a knockout competition for Southern League clubs which ran for several seasons up to the First World War, Watford occasionally brought in a player who would not normally claim a first-team place. It was in such circumstances that Kingham led the forward line at Luton, in a game won 3-0 by the home team.

*Reginald John Stanley (**BADGER**) **KIRBY** (1922)*
b Hendon, Middx 13/8/1893
d Colindale, Middx 8/7/1960
FL 1 (-)
Wealdstone; Hampstead Town (early 1921/2); Arsenal (am 1921/2); Watford (am 9/22)
A free-scoring Hampstead Town forward who had represented Middlesex, he was registered by Watford as an amateur and played once in the League, at outside-left. He was a brother-in-law of Wilfred Minter, who was immortalised by his feat of being on the losing side in an FA Cup game in which he scored seven times for St Albans City.

*James (**JIM**) **KIRKPATRICK** (1927)*
b Annan, Dumfriesshire
FL 9 (-)
Solway Star (9/21); Workington (by cs 1922); Leeds Utd (£150 5/24); Watford (free 6/27); Solway Star (8/28 until cs 1929)
One of two brothers who both had a crack at English football before returning to Dumfriesshire, he was a left-back who had ten First Division games during his three seasons at Elland Road. Leeds retained his registration but made him available for transfer in the summer of 1927, and Fred Pagnam managed to recruit him without paying a fee.

Transfer fee waived

***MARTIN KUHL** (1988)*
b Frimley, Surrey 10/1/1965
FL 4 (-)
Chelsea (sch 5/79); Birmingham City (appr 6/81, pro 1/83); Sheffield Utd (3/87); Watford (valued at £125,000 in exchange for P.A.O.Agana, P.Hetherston and £40,000 2/88); Portsmouth (£125,000 9/88); Derby County (£650,000 9/92); Notts County (loan 9/94); Bristol City (£330,000 12/94)
Conspicuous as an aggressive midfield opponent both before and after his brief stint at Vicarage Road, where his impact was minimal. He nevertheless went on to captain both Portsmouth and Derby. His combative approach was

Aggressive opponent

never more apparent than in the rugged Birmingham side beaten at home by Watford in the 1984 FA Cup quarter-final.

Indiscipline

*PETER **KYLE** (1909-1910)*
b Cadder, Lanarks 21/12/1878
d Glasgow 19/1/1957
SL 12 (4), FAC 1 (-)
Glasgow & District Schools; Parkhead; Clyde (10/98); Liverpool (5/99); Leicester Fosse (5/00 until cs 1901); West Ham Utd (9/01); Kettering (12/01); Wellingborough; Aberdeen (9/02); Cowdenbeath (1/03); Heart of Midlothian (8/03); Leicester Fosse (10/03); Port Glasgow Athletic (4/04); Royal Albert (cs 1904); Partick Thistle (4/05); Royal Albert (5/05); Tottenham Hotspur (5/05); Arsenal ("a few pounds" 4/06); Aston Villa (3/08); Sheffield Utd (one of two players signed for £1,100 10/08); Royal Albert (cs 1909); Watford (11/09 until 2/10); Royal Albert (cs 1910)
Those many moves, featuring a magnificent array of clubs, may be at least partly attributable to the disciplinary problems to which he was prone. Sheffield United and Spurs both suspended him and his brief reign as Watford's centre-forward ended when the club kicked him out after shenanigans which also involved Frank Cotterill and Jock Grieve.

Man of few words

*Reginald William James (**DICK**) **LACEY** (1923)*
b Chesham, Bucks 18/9/1901
d Chesham, Bucks 7/12/1970
FL 3 (1)
Chesham Utd (until at least 1932/3); Watford (am 8/22)
A solitary man who kept his own counsel, he was a Chesham resident from cradle to grave. He enjoyed a lengthy career as a forward with Chesham United, where he was a colleague of George Barnes, in whose family boot-manufacturing business he earned his living until retirement. He scored on his Football League début, in a 4-0 win over Merthyr Town.

A pro in three countries

*David Buick Peter **LAING** (1937-1938)*
b Dundee, Angus 14/11/1913
d Dundee, Tayside 24/4/1981
FL 15 (5), FAC 2 (-), 3SC 2 (1)
East Craigie (8/32); Dundee Utd (12/32); East Craigie (7/34); Portadown (cs 1935); Forfar Athletic (1/36 until 6/36); Liverpool (11/36); Watford (11/37); Yeovil & Petters Utd (cs 1938). Guested for Torquay Utd in WW2.
After playing professionally in both Scotland and Northern Ireland, he had 12 months at Anfield, but was unable to break into the first team. His only League experience was therefore the few months which he spent as Watford's left-winger. The club held onto his Football League registration until as late as the summer of 1946.

Robert Smith (**BOBBY**) **LAING** *(1950-1952)*
b Glasgow 1/2/1925
d Birmingham, West Midlands, September 1985
FL 60 (8)
Falkirk (1/45); Birmingham City (3/46); Watford (4-figure fee 6/50); Kettering Town (7/52); Worcester City (8/54); Halesowen Town (1956); Brierley Hill; Brush Sports. Guested for Manchester City in WW2.
Signed as an outside-right, a problem position for Watford during the previous season, he started with six goals in his first eight games in that berth, but later showed his versatility by playing everywhere in the forward-line except in the centre. As a National Serviceman he'd represented the Royal Navy against the Netherlands.

Played for the Royal Navy

William Harry Charles (**BILLY**) **LANE** *(1932-1942)*
(formerly William Harry Charles **LOHN***)*
b Tottenham, Middx 28/10/1903
d Chelmsford, Essex 10/11/1985
FL 124 (68), FAC 3 (-), 3SC 9 (9), WW2 1 (-)
London City Mission; Gnome Athletic; Park Avondale; Summerstown (11/23); Barnet (1/24); Tottenham Hotspur (am 9/23, pro 5/24); Northfleet (loan 1924); Leicester City (£2,250 11/26); Reading (£490 5/28); Brentford (5/29); Watford (under £1,000 5/32); Bristol City (£200 1/36); Clapton Orient (7/37); Gravesend (cs 1938); Brentford assistant-manager (1938); Guildford City manager (6/47); Brighton & Hove Albion (assistant-manager 4/50, manager 3/51 until 5/61); Gravesend & Northfleet manager (12/61 until 1963); Arsenal scout (1963); Queens Park Rangers scout (1/68); Arsenal scout; Brighton & Hove Albion scout (9/78). Guested for Brighton & Hove Albion and Watford in WW2.
He didn't enjoy regular League football until he got to Brentford, but then had several seasons as a prolific scorer in any of the three inside-forward positions. His Watford tally included a three-minute hat-trick against Clapton Orient. During his decade in the manager's chair at Brighton the club was promoted to the Second Division for the first time.

Quick-fire hat-trick

Bernard Patrick (**BUNNY**) **LARKIN** *(1962-1964)*
b Digbeth, Warwicks 11/1/1936
FL 49 (3), FAC 5 (-), FLC 3 (-)
Saltley Boys; Lea Hall Youth Club; Birmingham City (am 7/51); Rockwood Albion; Birmingham City (pro 7/54); Norwich City (3/60); Doncaster Rovers (10/61); Watford (£4,000 5/62); Lincoln City ("small fee" 10/64); Wisbech Town (free 8/66); Nuneaton Borough (6/68); King's Lynn (7/69); Stevenage Athletic (6/70); Attleborough coach (1975 until 1977)
Originally a First Division player at St Andrews (23 goals in 79 appearances), he served Watford as a useful all-round wing-half or inside-forward. After a season of regular first-team football, his opportunities were fewer following the arrival as manager of Bill McGarry. He later settled in Norwich and had a long career selling cakes for Lyons.

Scored top-flight goals

Four penalties

GERARD LAVIN *(1992-1995)*
b Corby, Northants 5/2/1974
FL 121+5 (2), FAC 6 (-), FLC 11 (1), AIC 3+1 (-)
Watford (sch 6/88, tr 7/90, pro 5/92); Millwall (£400,000 plus 20% of any 'sell-on' profit 11/95)
SCOTLAND YOUTH and UNDER-21
Equally at home in midfield or at full-back, he made his League début as a trainee. During Nigel Gibbs's long absence he became a fixture at right-back and was ever-present in 1993/4, as well as establishing himself in the Scotland Under-21 team, qualifying through his father's nationality. He once scored four penalties in a match for Watford Under-16s.

Unbeaten at West Brom

William **(BILLY) LAW** *(1906-1908)*
b Walsall, Staffs 1882
SL 63 (7), FAC 3 (-), SEL 3 (-), UL 14 (1)
Rushall Olympic; Walsall; Scarborough; Doncaster Rovers (6/04); West Bromwich Albion (5/05); Watford (6/06); Queens Park Rangers (5/08); Glossop (1909 until at least 1913)
The automatic choice at outside-left for most of his two years at Cassio Road, he was fast and clever, got the ball across well, and had a good shot. He'd earlier joined West Bromwich when Doncaster Rovers dropped out of the League, and had eleven games in the first-team at The Hawthorns. Although none of them was lost, he didn't get picked again.

Played in new competition

NORMAN LAWSON *(1960)*
b Hetton-le-Hole, Co Durham 6/4/1935
FLC 1 (-)
England Grammar & Public Schools; Hednesford; Bury (9/55); Swansea Town (7/58); Watford (4-figure fee 6/60); Kettering Town (free 7/61)
It's not often that the club pays a fee for a player who doesn't get a League game, but Lawson's only Watford first-team appearance (at left-back) was, like David Heard's, in the club's first League Cup tie, which Derby County won 5-2 at Vicarage Road. He did, however, turn out in 80 League games for Bury and Swansea Town.

Good and bad at Swindon

James Michael **(JIMMY) LAWTON** *(1967-1968)*
b Middlesbrough, Yorks 6/7/1942
FL 10+3 (1), FAC 1 (-), FLC 1+1 (2)
Middlesbrough (am 10/60); Darlington (pro 10/61); Swindon Town (9/65); Watford (£4,000 3/67); Darlington (£1,500 3/68 until cs 1969)
Boasting a record of 60 goals in 120 League games in his first Darlington spell, this hefty centre-forward was crocked at Swindon and was clearly not his old self after being brought to Watford by his former Feethams colleague, Ken Furphy. It was on Swindon's ground that he enjoyed his best Watford moment, with two League Cup goals against Bournemouth.

*James (JIMMY) **LEAVER** (1926-1927)*
b Blackburn, Lancs 26/12/1897
d Blackburn, Lancs 1959
FL 35 (3)
Blackburn Rovers (12/19); Blackpool (5/20); Watford (7/26); Mossley (free 8/28); Stalybridge Celtic (8/32)
After failing to make the grade with his home-town club, he got plenty of Second Division experience during his six years at Bloomfield Road. A big and powerful defender, he made most of his Watford appearances in the position for which he was best equipped, centre-half, and captained the side for a time towards the end of his first season.

Strapping pivot

*John (JACK) **LEE** (1924-1925)*
b Sheffield, Yorks 1890
d Hull, Yorks 10/8/1955
FL 8 (-)
Bird in Hand, Sheffield; Hull City (3/13); Chelsea (£1,500 2/20); Watford (free 7/24); Rotherham Utd (6/25 until cs 1926)
Discovered in local football in Sheffield, he was brought into the professional game by Hull City. His progress there induced Chelsea to part with a useful fee, but he made only seven League appearances in more than four years at Stamford Bridge, and was then released. He began at Watford as the first-team outside-left, but soon lost his place.

Cost Chelsea £1,500

*William (DON) **LEES** (1904-1905)*
b Cronberry, Ayrshire, circa 1873
SL 6 (2), FAC 1 (-), SEL 7 (5)
Cronberry Eglinton; Celtic (9/92); Lincoln City (7/93); Celtic (6/94); Lincoln City (10/94); Barnsley St Peter's (5/95); Darwen (5/96); Barnsley (5/97); Watford (5/04 until 2/05); Barnsley (3/05); Denaby Utd (5/05)
Falling well short of the club's requirements in the matter of personal conduct, he was twice sacked for repeated transgressions, mostly booze-related. On the second occasion the club presented him with a single ticket from Watford Junction to his home in Barnsley, where he'd been a major figure with the local club. He was a versatile half-back or forward.

Problems, problems

***WALTER** Joseph **LEES** (1968-1976)*
b Glasgow 2/2/1947
FL 220+6 (10), FAC 17 (1), FLC 10 (-)
St Roch's (am 6/64); Celtic (pro 8/64); St Roch's (6/65); Kilsyth Rangers; Watford (£500 6/68); Barnet (free 7/76 until at least 2/78); Hayes (by 11/79)
SCOTLAND JUNIOR
This unspectacular but consistent performer at centre-half played in Watford's first FA Cup semi-final, and was the club's longest-serving player by the time he was released. Before crossing the border he captained the Scotland Junior XI. He had also completed a five-year glazing apprenticeship, and he resumed his connections with the trade in Watford.

Long service

The shortest ever

FREDerick John Sidney **LE MAY** *(1932)*
b Bethnal Green, London 2/2/1907
d Suffolk, September 1988
FL 4 (-)
Bulpham; Laindon Hills; Tilbury; Southend Utd Reserves (half a season); Grays Thurrock; Grays Athletic; Woking; Thames (am 7/30, pro 5/31); Watford ("small fee" 7/31); Clapton Orient (8/32); Margate (8/33); Chelmsford (permit player 8/36)
He's reputed to have been - and probably was - the shortest player (at just 5ft) in Football League history. He was one of a succession of right-wingers whose first-team aspirations were thwarted by Billy Chapman's consistency. It was as an amateur that he'd made his League début - against Watford. His brother signed amateur forms for Watford for 1931/2.

Scored in only Cup game

KENneth Gordon **LESSLIE** *(1948)*
b West Ham, Essex 4/1/1923
d Leigh-on-Sea, Essex 12/12/1991
FL 7 (1), FAC 1 (1)
Ipswich Town (8/47); Watford (7/48 until cs 1949)
At the end of the 1947/8 season, which he'd spent in the Reserves at Portman Road, he played for Watford as a trialist in a charity match against Edgware Town. He was taken on for the following season, and although he scored on his first appearances in both League and Cup, his career as the first-team right-winger was a brief one.

Two first-kick goals

Bernard **(BERNIE) LEWIS** *(1967-1970)*
b Aberfan, Glam 12/3/1945
FL 41+10 (9), FAC 3 (-), FLC 3 (-)
Cardiff City (am 5/61, pro 4/64); Watford (£8,000 11/67); Southend Utd (free 9/70); Chelmsford City (free 7/72)
WALES UNDER-23
After making his Watford début in a 7-1 beating of Grimsby Town, this winger had frequent bursts of first-team action without ever getting himself established. His final senior run, the longest he'd had, lasted nine games. On 8th April 1969 he scored with his first kick as a substitute - and did exactly the same thing six months to the day later.

Led the way from Wales

Daniel James ***(JIM)*** **LEWIS** *(1931-1944)*
b Troedrhiwfuwch, Glam 21/6/1909
d Tipton St John, Devon 7/10/1980
FL 111 (-), FAC 5 (-), 3SC 8 (-), WW2 72 (-)
New Tredegar; Watford (3/30 until 1944/5)
The first of the substantial influx from South Wales in the Thirties, which included his brother George, he gave long service as a non-scoring full-back. He continued to play regular first-team football in wartime, until December 1941, and helped the Reserves in 1944/5. He became the proprietor of a shoe-mending business in Durban Road.

Thomas **LEWIS** *(1920)*
SL 1 (-)
Watford (am 1919/20 until cs 1922)
He played outside-left in a benefit match, and also in a 3-0 win at Brentford, Watford's biggest away victory in any game for five years. The club was well served on the wings at this time, and he didn't play in the first team again, although his Southern League amateur registration was carried forward to the Football League, and retained for two seasons.

Thomas **GEORGE LEWIS** *(1936-1946)*
b Troedrhiwfuwch, Glam 20/10/1913
d Hemel Hempstead, Herts 6/8/1981
FL 25 (11), FAC 9 (4), 3SC 8 (3), WW2 143 (114)
New Tredegar; Watford (am 8/33, pro 12/33); Southampton (7/46); Brighton & Hove Albion (6/48); Dartford (8/49 until at least 10/52, when he was also groundsman). Guested for Chester in WW2.
He followed his brother Jim from the Valleys and, as the figures show, became a classic example of a player whose best years were lost to the war. Converted from full-back to centre-forward, he scored freely in wartime, and twice hit eleven goals in the space of four games. In 1936 he played in goal for the Reserves in an emergency. They won 5-1.

Best years were wartime

James Young **(JIMMY) LINDSAY** *(1971-1973)*
b Hamilton, Lanarks 12/7/1949
FL 64+1 (12 inc 1p), FAC 1 (-), FLC 7 (1)
West Ham Utd (youth team, pro 8/66); Watford (£20,000 5/71); Colchester Utd (free 7/74); Hereford Utd (8/75); Shrewsbury Town (8/77 until cs 1981)
His pedigree as a First Division player alongside Moore, Peters and Hurst induced Ken Furphy to lay out a club-record fee shortly before his own resignation. The club fell into steep decline, and this scheming midfielder soon became a lower-divisions player, which he remained. He later ran a pub in Shrewsbury, where his League career ended.

First £20,000 outlay

Thomas **(JOCK) LINDSAY** *(1930)*
b Paisley, Renfrewshire 11/3/1903
d Leyland, Lancs 25/1/1979
FL 7 (-), FAC 2 (1)
Renfrew Juniors (1922/3); Pollok (1923/4); Ardeer Thistle; Kilmarnock (9/24); Alloa (free 6/26); Reading (free 7/27); Wigan Borough (7/28); Rochdale (6/29); Watford (free 9/30); New Brighton (free 7/31); Southport (11/31); Chester (12/31); Prescot Cables (2/32); Wrexham (7/33); Leyland Motors (4/34)
He had nine straight games at outside-left before the ink was dry on his contract, which followed a trial period, but then Bill Pick was signed, and replaced him immediately. Lindsay was never selected for the first team again, and was off on one of his frequent moves at the end of the season. His only goal had been in an FA Cup tie at Walthamstow.

Wandering winger

Skipper at four clubs

*William (**BILLY**) **LINDSAY** (1903-1906)*
b Stockton-on-Tees, Co Durham 10/12/1872
d Luton, Beds 27/2/1933
SL 59 (-), FAC 9 (-), SEL 20 (-), UL 7 (-)
Stockton St John's (1½ seasons); Stockton (4 seasons); Everton (4/93); Grimsby Town (5/94); Newcastle Utd (2/98); Luton Town (free 5/00); Watford (5/03); Luton Town (4/07); Hitchin Town (9/07)
A fast and powerful back who captained Newcastle on their First Division début, and also skippered Grimsby, Luton, and (in 1905/6) Watford. He nevertheless displayed a casual approach to attendance at training, and was also reported for being "spotted at Kempton Park on a Saturday". His brother Jimmy helped Bury to win the FA Cup in 1903.

Promotion goalie

*James (**JIMMY**) **LINTON** (1959-1963)*
b Tollcross, Lanarks 2/12/1930
FL 71 (-), FAC 13 (-), SFC 1 (-), FLC 3 (-)
Beith Juniors; Vale of Clyde (am 7/48); Kirkintilloch Rob Roy (am); Notts County (7/51); Watford (6/59); Poole Town (free 7/63); Ramsgate Athletic (3 seasons); Dunstable Town; Hatfield Town
Watford's last line of defence when the club won its first Football League promotion in 1959/60, he kept goal in 43 of the 46 games, as well as all the cup ties, in that eventful season. He stayed on as a part-time professional, as Dave Underwood's deputy, after losing his first-team place, before eventually spending several seasons in non-League football.

Knighthood

*Frederick Spencer **LISTER** (1897-1899)*
*(later Sir Spencer **LISTER**, MRCS LRCP)*
b Norwell, Notts 8/4/1876
d South Africa 6/9/1939
SL 11 (3), FAC 1 (-)
Newark; West Herts (am 1897); St Bartholomew's Hospital
Before captaining Watford Reserves and Bart's Hospital, this left-winger had shown his dedication by travelling from Nottinghamshire to play in a game at Cassio Road. He emigrated to Transvaal in 1905, became a distinguished figure in medical research in South Africa, and in 1920 was knighted for his pioneering work in the field of bacteriology.

Cavalier

*Charles Edward (**CHARLIE**) **LIVESEY** (1962-1964)*
b West Ham, Essex 6/2/1938
FL 64 (26), FAC 6 (1), FLC 1 (1)
Wolverhampton Wanderers (am 5/55); Southampton (pro 3/56); Chelsea (5/59); Gillingham (8/61); Watford (£6,000 10/62); Northampton Town (£17,000 8/64); Brighton & Hove Albion (£7,000 9/65); Crawley Town (8/69)
An ex-First Division centre-forward (he'd partnered the young Jimmy Greaves at Stamford Bridge) whose career was mostly one of under-achievement. He nevertheless nearly inspired Watford's first advance to the Second Division with a season of cavalier displays and an individual virtuosity comparable with almost anything ever seen at Vicarage Road.

FRANK William **LOCK** *(1955-1957)*
b Whitechapel, London 12/3/1922
d Clacton-on-Sea, Essex 17/3/1985
FL 42 (1), FAC 2 (-), SFC 1 (-)
Finchley; Charlton Athletic (12/45); Liverpool (one of two players transferred for £20,000 12/53); Watford (6/55); Cambridge Utd (free 7/57); Clacton Town (by 1959/60)
ENGLAND 'UNOFFICIAL'
His long service at The Valley incorporated over two hundred First Division appearances as a full-back, and he also played for England in an 'unofficial' international match during the 1951 FA tour to Australia. He was relegated with Liverpool a few months after joining them, and dropped a further division a year later by moving to Watford.

FA tourist

ARTHUR **LOCKETT** *(1908-1912)*
b Alsagers Bank, Staffs 11/3/1877
d Crewe, Cheshire 1957
SL 141 (1p), FAC 13 (-), SCC 5 (-)
Alsagers Bank Friendly (1893 until 1/96); Audley (11/96); Cross Heath (10/98); Audley (10/98); Crewe Alexandra (7/99); Stoke (5/00); Aston Villa (£400 4/03); Preston North End (4/05); Watford (8/08); Mardy (free 10/12, player-manager 4/13)
ENGLAND FULL; FOOTBALL LEAGUE
He was so highly esteemed by the Cassio Road crowd that his release after four seasons prompted a petition urging reconsideration, but the decision stood and he rejoined John Goodall at Mardy, where he subsequently succeeded him as manager. He made his name and got his one England cap as a winger, but came to Watford as a full-back.

Petition failed

Johaanas Hermanus Petrus (JAN) **LOHMAN** *(1981-1986)*
b Dussen, Netherlands 18/2/1959
FL 51+12 (6), FAC 9+2 (3), FLC 2+1 (-), FLT 2+1 (1), UEFA 1 (-)
Sporting Lokeren, Belgium; Vlaardingen, Netherlands (loan); NEC Nijmegen, Netherlands (loan); Watford (£35,000 9/81); Germinal Ekeren, Belgium (free 6/86); SSV, Netherlands (cs 1988); R Cappallen, Belgium (8/90 until cs 1991)
NETHERLANDS YOUTH and UNDER-21
After being capped nine times at Under-21 level, he became the only foreigner ever to be transferred to Watford from an overseas club, having first come to Vicarage Road on a trial basis. He scored on his Football League début and stayed for five seasons as a hard-tackling midfield player. Before returning to Belgium he suffered badly from injury problems.

The only foreign import

Helped to keep it tight

***CLIVE** Ian* **LOMAS** *(1966)*
b Ealing, Middx 18/1/1947
FL 6+1 (-)
Watford (appr 4/63, pro 1/65 until cs 1967)
After breaking through into the first team with a substitute appearance, he had a short run as Brian Garvey's central-defensive partner. A record of four goals conceded in the six games might have been expected to earn him further opportunities, but in fact he then spent more than a year out of the reckoning before being released.

Leggatts Way cap

*Anthony **ROY** LOW* *(1967-1968)*
b Watford, Herts 8/7/1944
FL 25+1 (4)
Tottenham Hotspur (am 8/59, pro 7/61); Watford (free 3/67 until cs 1969); Bedford Town (8/70)
ENGLAND SCHOOLS
He first achieved prominence locally through international recognition whilst at Leggatts Way School, but didn't join his home-town club until eight seasons later, as a makeweight in the deal which took Dennis Bond to White Hart Lane. After occasional appearances in the first-team forward-line, he spent a year out of the game before signing for Bedford.

Wedding-day goal

*Henry Pratt **(HARRY)** LOWE* *(1929-1944)*
b Kettle, Fife 24/2/1907
d Calne, Wilts, October 1988
FL 120 (41 inc 1p), FAC 10 (6), 3SC 7 (-), WW2 4 (-)
St Andrews Utd (8/28); Watford (free 3/29); Queens Park Rangers (part-exchange for E.Goodier 6/35 until circa 1943); Chelsea scout; Guildford City manager (7/45); Bournemouth & Boscombe Athletic manager (5/47 until 2/50); Yeovil Town manager (1951 until 1953); Watford scout (3/54); Cheshunt manager (9/55). Guested for Aldershot, Brighton & Hove Albion, Chelsea, Crystal Palace, Millwall, Tunbridge Wells Rangers and Watford in WW2.
A successful recruit from Junior football in the east of Scotland, he spent over six years on the staff as a direct inside-forward with a powerful long-range shot. He scored, but also failed with a penalty, in a 4-1 win against Swindon Town on his wedding day. QPR got infinitely the better of the exchange deal which brought Ted Goodier to Vicarage Road.

Early goal on début

***DOMINIC** James Robert* **LUDDEN** *(1994-1996)*
b Basildon, Essex 30/3/1974
FL 10+3 (-), FAC 1+1 (-)
Billericay Town; Leyton Orient (sch 7/91, pro 7/92); Watford (£60,000 8/94)
ENGLAND SCHOOLS UNDER-18
Unusual in having joined Orient on schoolboy forms when as old as 17 (when most potential professionals would be taken on as trainees), he was continuing his academic studies and was rewarded with recognition by the English Schools FA. Originally a midfield player who scored eleven minutes into his League career, he came to Watford as a left-back.

Peaked against Liverpool

RAYmond **LUGG** *(1969-1972)*
b Jarrow, Co Durham 18/7/1948
FL 51+8 (3 inc 1p), FAC 5 (2), FLC 3 (1)
Primrose; Middlesbrough (am 6/65, pro 7/65); Watford (£8,000 11/69); Plymouth Argyle (£3,500 7/72); Crewe Alexandra (7/73); Fort Lauderdale Strikers, USA (loan 4/77 until 8/77); Bury (£17,500 7/78); Chorley
Outstanding in midfield when Watford beat Liverpool to reach their first FA Cup semi-final, he was unable to sustain that level of performance as the club's fortunes plummeted. Although listed at £8,000 at the end of 1971/2, he fetched less than half that amount, but later Crewe must have been pleased with their sale after he'd given them five years' service.

GEORGE **LUNN** *(1941-1947)*
b Bolton-upon-Dearne, Yorks 28/6/1915
FL 5 (-), FAC 2 (-), WW2 1 (-)
Frickley Colliery; Aston Villa (5/38); Birmingham City (9/46); Irish football (1947/8); Watford (10/47 until cs 1948); Halifax Town (8/50 until 9/50). Guested for Chester, Clapton Orient, Doncaster Rovers, Fulham, Northampton Town, Rochdale, Southport, Stockport County, Watford and Wrexham in WW2.
A tall centre-half whose association with Football League clubs spanned more than 12 years, but whose only peacetime appearances in the competition were that handful for Watford. His first-team run ended with 1-0 and 5-1 Christmas defeats by Queens Park Rangers on successive days. Nearly seven years earlier he'd made a wartime guest appearance.

Singing goalkeeper

Thomas John **LYNCH** *(1937)*
b Tredegar, Mon 31/8/1907
d Bangor, Gwynedd 1976
FL 2 (-)
Rhymney; Rochdale (am 7/29, pro 8/29); Colwyn Bay Utd (7/31); Barnsley (6/32); Barrow (7/33); Yeovil & Petters Utd (7/34); Brentford (5/35); Watford (unspecified fee 1/37); Guildford City (free, cs 1937)
Bought hurriedly to meet a goalkeeping crisis, both McLaren and McHugh being injured, he was rushed into his first Football League experience since his season at Barrow, but was soon back out of the metaphorical limelight. He was no stranger to the real stuff, however, being a professional tenor whose venues included the Chiswick Empire.

Lavishly praised

FRANK **LYON** *(1902-1903)*
b Crewe, Cheshire 23/9/1879
SL 14 (-)
Stockport County (am); Crewe Alexandra (am); Stoke (am 8/00 until cs 1901, and 1902/3); Watford (am 8/02); Queens Park Rangers (am cs 1903, pro 9/05); Chelsea (3/07); Crewe Alexandra (5/08)
Although playing for professional clubs, he retained his amateur status until his third season with QPR. He was a full-back who established a reputation for his exceptional pace - and indeed was a competitive sprinter - and at Watford was extravagantly praised by a local scribe as "the most brilliant player who has ever worn the club colours".

Kept goal as well

HerBERT LYON (1901-1902)
b Yorks circa 1877
SL 30 (12), FAC 2 (2 inc 1p)
Overseal Town (9/95); Gresley Rovers (5/96); Leicester Fosse (1/98); Gresley Rovers (8/98); Leicester Fosse (1/99); Nelson (6/00); Watford (6/01); Reading (5/02); West Ham Utd (cs 1903); Brighton & Hove Albion (5/04); Swindon Town (5/05); Carlisle Utd (5/06); Swindon Town (cs 1907); Blackpool (5/08 until cs 1909); Walsall
A peripatetic footballer of some versatility, he was ever-present at either inside-right or centre-forward throughout his Cassio Road season, but could also play in the half-back line. Furthermore, he kept goal - and a clean sheet - for Leicester in a First Division game, having prepared for the position with three outings for the Reserves.

Bank holiday hat-trick

James (JIMMY) McANEARNEY (1963-1966)
b Lochee, Angus 20/3/1935
FL 84+2 (19), FAC 1 (-), FLC 1 (-)
St Stephen's Juniors; Sheffield Wednesday (am 10/51, pro 3/52); Plymouth Argyle (1/60); Watford (£10,000 11/63, also assisted with coaching from cs 1965); Bradford City player-coach ("small fee" 9/66); Rotherham Utd (assistant-manager 5/68, caretaker-manager 11/68, manager 12/68 until 5/73); Sheffield Wednesday (coaching staff mid-1973 until 10/75, caretaker-manager briefly 10/75); Leeds Utd coaching staff (3 years); Frickley Athletic coach: Scarborough manager (1981 until 4/82); Hallam manager (1989)
Only Cliff Holton had commanded a five-figure fee from Watford before McAnearney came out of the First Division. The Scot was a hardworking and creative inside-forward, and his goals included a Good Friday hat-trick against Scunthorpe United. At Hillsborough he'd played alongside his brother Tom, later a long-serving manager of Aldershot.

Registration problem

Patrick McARDLE (1910-1911)
b Scotland
SL 11 (-), FAC 1 (-), SCC 2 (-)
Cambuslang Hibs; Falkirk (1/06); Broxburn Shamrock (cs 1906); Bathgate (4/08); Dumbarton Harp (5/08); Bathgate 5/08); Dumbarton Harp (cs 1909); Watford (trial 4/10, then 9/10 after further trial); Dumbarton Harp (cs 1911); Broxburn Shamrock (cs 1912); Pontypridd (9/13)
After playing once in the Southern League as a trialist at the end of 1909/10, he had to return home due to a problem in connection with his registration. He later came back, however, and signed for the following season after a further trial. Before rejoining Dumbarton Harp he made spasmodic first-team appearances on both wings.

Francis (FRANK) McAVOY *(1902-1903)*
b Ayr 16/11/1875
SL 23 (2), FAC 1 (-), SEL 1 (-)
Ayr; Woolwich Arsenal (5/95); Brighton Utd (5/98); Gravesend Utd (8/00); Brighton & Hove Albion (8/01); Watford (9/02 until cs 1903); St Mirren (10/03); Ayr (1/04 until cs 1905)
Owing his chance to Tot Farnall's suspension, he made his first-team début at centre-half in an FA Cup replay against Fulham, and held the position to the end of the season, which ended with relegation. When captain of Brighton & Hove Albion he assaulted his manager, and with a colleague was subsequently convicted of issuing threats against him.

Assaulted his manager

NEIL McBAIN *(1928-1931)* - SEE PART FIVE

ALAN James McCARTHY *(1993-1994)*
b Wandsworth, London 11/1/1972
FL 8+1 (-)
Queens Park Rangers (sch 2/86, tr 1989, pro 1/90); Watford (loan 11/93); Plymouth Argyle (loan 2/94); Leyton Orient (£25,000 8/95)
ENGLAND YOUTH; WALES UNDER-21 and 'B'
QPR were happy to keep him on their senior playing strength whilst giving him only eleven top-flight outings in six seasons. His Watford loan period arose from a difficulty with the left-back position caused mainly by injury to Jason Drysdale, and he's the only Watford player to have represented two countries in international football.

Dual nationality

KEVIN John McCARTHY *(1975-1977)*
b Bethnal Green, London 24/12/1957
FL 35+1 (1), FLC 2 (-)
Watford (sch 1/73, appr 8/74, pro 12/75); Lillehammer, Norway (free 3/78)
A League débutant as an apprentice midfield player in November 1975, he retained his place for the rest of the season - an unusual achievement for one so young. Unable to sustain that rate of progress, he went to Norway with Guy Bristow, where they helped Lillehammer to make rapid advances through the divisions. He weighed only 9st.

Made his mark at 17

David (DAVE) McCARTNEY *(1903-1906)*
b Ayrshire
SL 82 (13 inc 7p), FAC 9 (1), SEL 25 (5), UL 16 (3)
Cronberry; Dalbeattie; Lugar Boswell (8/00); Glossop (10/00); Watford (5/03); Chelsea (5/06); Northampton Town (5/07 until cs 1910)
He was first choice as the defensive pivot throughout his three seasons at Cassio Road after receiving a signing-on fee of £10, twice the club's norm. Dependable and solid, he shared in Southern League championship wins with Watford (Second Division) and Northampton (First). His brother enjoyed managerial success on both sides of the border.

Signing-on fee doubled

Faced Rest of the World

JOHN **McCLELLAND** (1984-1990)
b Belfast 7/12/1955
FL 187 (3), FAC 32 (-), FLC 12 (-), FMC 2+1 (-)
Portadown; Cardiff City (2/74); Bangor City (free, cs 1975); Mansfield Town (£8,000 5/78); Rangers (£90,000 5/81); Watford (£225,000 11/84); Leeds Utd (£100,000 6/89); Watford (loan 1/90); Notts County (loan 2/92); St Johnstone (player-coach free, cs 1992, acting player-manager 12/92, manager 4/93 until 11/93); Carrick Rangers; Wycombe Wanderers (non-contract 3/94); also Yeovil Town (non-contract 3/94); Doncaster Rovers coach (by 1/95 until 6/95); Farsley Celtic (8/95); Bradford City reserve-team manager (3/96)
NORTHERN IRELAND FULL; FOOTBALL LEAGUE
A tall, distinguished international captain (53 caps) and an instant success as a central defender after being signed when goals were being conceded freely. His leadership and coolness influenced those around him, and an ungainly, stiff-shouldered running action belied his exceptional pace. He faced the Rest of the World in the Football League's centenary game.

Returned to Larne

ALBERT **McCLENAGHAN** (1978)
b Londonderry 7/7/1954
FL 2 (-)
Coleraine; Larne; Watford (£2,000 11/77); Larne (free, cs 1979 until cs 1981); local football in Limavady
His engagement at Vicarage Road was preceded by a fortnight's trial, and he spent almost all of what remained of the 1977/8 season gaining experience in the Reserves. A hard tackler of formidable physical proportions, he then had a couple of Fourth Division outings at right-back with the championship already won, but thereafter couldn't break through again.

Brother of Scotland cap

James Clark Fulton (JIMMY) **McCRAE** (1926)
b Bridge of Weir, Renfrewshire 2/9/1894
d Paisley, Renfrewshire 3/9/1974
FL 2 (-)
Clyde (12/12); Rangers (4/16); Clyde (4/16); West Ham Utd (6/19); Bury (12/20 until cs 1923); Wigan Borough (9/23 until cs 1924) New Brighton (11/24); Manchester Utd (8/25); Watford (free 6/26); Clyde (free 8/27 until 1/28). Guested for West Ham Utd in WW1.
Briefly a First Division colleague of Frank Barson and Frank McPherson just before he joined Watford, and (like Ted Hufton) a regular throughout West Ham's first Football League season, in which they used 39 men. A centre-half or left-half, he made little impact at Watford. His younger brother scored prolifically for St Mirren and won two Scottish caps.

Thomas (TOM) **McCREADY** (1963)
b Johnstone, Renfrewshire 19/10/1943
FL 1 (-), FAC 2 (-)
Hibernian (7/61 until 7/63); Watford (9/63); Wimbledon (free,

7/64 until cs 1974)
SCOTLAND SCHOOLS
At Watford this left-back was distinguished mainly, perhaps, for the unusual feat of having played twice as often in the FA Cup as in the League. His long Wimbledon career began as the club was relinquishing its amateur status after three successive Isthmian League titles, and prior to its astounding rise to the upper echelons of English football.

Wimbledon veteran

DENNIS McCRYSTAL *(1950)*
b Welwyn Garden City, Herts 13/1/1932
FL 1 (-)
Watford First Community Centre; Kingsway Youth Club; Rickmansworth Town Reserves; Bushey Utd; Watford (3/50 until cs 1951); Fulham Reserves (11/51); De Havilland, Hatfield (permit player 1955 until 1957); Leavesden Hospital (8/57 until 1969); Leggatts Way Old Boys Reserves (by 12/70); Leggatts Way Old Boys manager (by 8/78); Evergreen (hon secretary by 1986/7, chairman by 3/94)
He kept Watford's goal once, when Geoff Morton was away on an MCC cricket tour. McCrystal was then 18, and he was 56 when he finally hung up his boots after turning out for Evergreen Reserves. But whatever he derived from the game as a player was long ago repaid by his decades of service to Evergreen (formerly Leggatts Way Old Boys).

Decades in local football

Robert Gray ***McCULLOCH*** *(1925)*
b Cathcart, Glasgow 20/4/1900
d Glasgow 24/4/1964
FL 14 (2)
Auchinleck Talbot; Kilmarnock (10/22); Arbroath (2/24); Bournemouth & Boscombe Athletic (5/24); Watford (£50 6/25 until cs 1926)
He was signed with a view to solving an outside-left problem, Watford having been poorly served in that position in 1924/5, but he proved no long-term answer. He did score in his first away game, but his senior appearances were all in the early part of the season. His transfer in May 1924 was among the longest moves possible in British football.

He wasn't the answer

Lawrence (LARRY) ***McGETTIGAN*** *(1971-1974)*
b Hackney, London 25/12/1952
d Watford, Herts 9/1/1994
FL 40+10 (3), FAC 1 (-), FLC 4 (-)
Watford (am 11/68, appr 2/69, pro 11/70); Barnsley (free 7/75 until 8/75); Brentford (non-contract 1/76 until cs 1976); Emeralds (by 10/76 until at least 3/78); Sandridge (3/83); local Post Office teams until 1992/3
After establishing a League career for himself as a winger he threw it all away before he was 23. He walked out on Barnsley within weeks of joining them, and was soon working for the Post Office, although he did later play for Herts County League champions Sandridge. He died of a heart attack, and of post-war Watford players only Mel Rees had a shorter life.

Walked out

Began season on loan

Michael John (MICK) **McGOVERN** *(1972)*
b Hayes, Middx 15/2/1951
FL 4 (-), FLC 1 (-)
Queens Park Rangers (appr 7/66, pro 11/68); Watford (loan 8/72); Swindon Town (2/73); Aldershot (loan 3/75); Hillingdon Borough (free 8/75); Hayes (by 8/77 until at least 11/84); Southall (by 1/86); Chalfont (by 3/87)
A forward who was secured on a temporary transfer at the beginning of the 1972/3 season and had a run of five games, in four of which Watford failed to score. In four-and-a-half years as a QPR professional he made only ten League appearances, and he later had a long career with his local club, in what used to be the Isthmian League.

One of an Ashington pair

Robert **McGUIRE** *(1914-1915)*
b Pelaw, Co Durham
SL 3 (-)
Choppington (early 1912/3); Ashington (1913); Watford (5/14 until cs 1915); Pelaw; Blyth Spartans (12/21 until at least 1922/3)
He helped Ashington to win the Northern Alliance championship and then signed for Watford with team-mate McMorran. McGuire had just completed a shipyard apprenticeship. With relatively few team changes made as the club moved towards the Southern League title, McGuire had only three first-team games - all away from home - at outside-right.

Foiled by the war

John (JOCK) **McHUGH** *(1933-1941)*
b Hamilton, Lanarks 13/8/1909
d Bushey, Herts 9/10/1966
FL 38 (-), FAC 2 (-), 3SC 4 (-), WW2 79 (-)
Strathclyde; Burnbank Athletic; Dundee Utd (2/28); Portsmouth ("big fee" 11/30); Watford (loan 7/33, free cs 1934 until 1941); Southend Utd (loan 4/36); St Helens, Watford coach (cs 1947)
Having waited ages to supersede Jim McLaren as first-choice goalie, he was denied the chance of a good League career by the outbreak of war. His first season at Watford was under a loan arrangement whilst he was on Portsmouth's transfer list at £1,000, but eventually he was freed. He worked for Universal Asbestos Manufacturers for 25 years.

Versatile forward

David **McKINLEY** *(1908-1909)*
b Dumbarton, Dunbartonshire
SL 23 (5), FAC 3 (1)
Dumbarton Harp; Aberdeen (5/06); Watford (8/08); Pontypridd (1909); Aberdare (10/10); Rochdale (cs 1912)
He scored four goals in his first four home games, in a Southern League season in which the Cassio Road record (only one defeat) was nullified by an away return of only six points. His versatility enabled him to play in four of the five forward positions. Aberdeen retained his Scottish League registration (he was listed at £100) until he joined Aberdare.

C.F. (MAC) **MacLACHLAN** *(1895-1896)*
SL 1 (-), FAC 3 (1), FAAC 2 (2)
West Herts (am 1894); Crouch End Vampires (by 2/97)
He'd played frequently as an inside-forward in the last two seasons before the club entered the Southern League, and scored 11 goals in 25 appearances in all matches in 1895/6. His one Southern League game was a 6-1 defeat at the hands of Old St Stephens, and as a Crouch End Vampire he was selected as a reserve for Middlesex.

James (JIMMY) **MacLAINE** *(1908-1911)*
b Govan, Lanarks 11/7/1881
d Glasgow 22/7/1930
SL 99 (27), FAC 8 (8), SCC 5 (-)
Ashfield; Clyde (10/05); Watford (5/08 until cs 1911)
He helped Ashfield to win a succession of knockout competitions, including the Scottish Junior Cup, before becoming a First Division player. Recommended to Watford by George Fyfe, he played regularly in any of the three inside-forward positions for nearly three seasons. Still on Clyde's Scottish League retained list five years after leaving them, he was listed at £100 in 1913.

Recommended by Fyfe

James (JIM) **McLAREN** *(1933-1939)*
b Falkirk, Stirlingshire 12/7/1897
d Leicester 16/11/1975
FL 194 (-), FAC 14 (-), 3SC 18 (-)
Bonnybridge Heatherbell; Stenhousemuir (1919); Bradford City (5/22); Leicester City (5/27); Watford (10/33 until cs 1939).
SCOTLAND SCHOOLS
The son of a cycling champion, this big, fearless goalkeeper saved a late penalty to earn a draw against England in the first-ever schools international. After achieving the extremely unusual distinction of qualifying for a benefit with three different clubs, he became - and remains - Watford's oldest player in both the Football League and the FA Cup.

The club's oldest

Joseph James Simpson **McLAUCHLAN** *(1913-1916)*
(also known - incorrectly - as **McLAUGHLAN***)*
b Edinburgh 5/2/1891
d Leith, Edinburgh 6/1/1971
SL 20 (8), FAC 1 (-), SCC 1 (-), WW1 8 (6 inc 3p)
Linlithgow; Bathgate (cs 1910); Woolwich Arsenal (10/11); Watford (£50 6/13 until 1916)
He arrived at Watford as a centre-forward with First Division experience, but his effectiveness was reduced by injury problems, and he suffered further physical damage in June 1916 - a shrapnel wound in the leg. He was still in a convalescent camp when he travelled to Watford for his wedding six months later. Once he played in goal for the Reserves.

Shrapnel wound

Six seasons at Chelsea

Joseph (**JOE**) **McLAUGHLIN** *(1990-1992)*
b Greenock, Renfrewshire 2/6/1960
FL 46 (2), FAC 1 (-), FLC 5 (-), FMC 1 (-)
Holy Family Boys' Club; Morton (6/77); Chelsea (£95,000 6/83); Charlton Athletic (£600,000 8/89); Watford (£300,000 8/90); Falkirk (£70,000 9/92); Hibernian (free 1/96)
SCOTLAND UNDER-21
When signed by Colin Lee (a former Stamford Bridge colleague), he'd had a wealth of experience in England and Scotland. A well-built centre-half, he was sold for a handsome profit after six years with Chelsea, whom he'd helped to win two Second Division championships and the first Full Members Cup competition. He was Watford's captain in 1991/2.

Rash of hat-tricks

Thomas Pearson (**TOMMY**) **McMILLAN** *(1956-1958)*
b Auchinleck, Ayrshire 16/1/1936
FL 33 (13), SFC 3 (2)
Maybole Juniors (10/54); Watford (8/56); Carlisle Utd (7/58 until cs 1961); Airdrieonians (9/61); Queen of the South (10/61 until 12/61); Dumbarton (1/62 until cs 1962)
An inside-right or outside-right who finished his National Service shortly before joining Watford as the first of a succession of Scottish signings in Neil McBain's second spell as manager. He hit two hat-tricks in the space of six League games during the first half of 1957/8, a period in which he also performed the feat twice for the Reserves.

Came down with McGuire

F.A. **McMORRAN** *(1914-1915)*
b Newcastle-upon-Tyne, Northumberland
SL 6 (-), FAC 1 (-)
Choppington (by end of 1911/2); Ashington (5/13 until 5/14); also Newcastle City (8/13); Watford (5/14 until cs 1915)
Signed with McGuire from Ashington, who'd won the 1913/4 Northern Alliance championship, and with whom he'd simultaneously been registered with Newcastle City on North-Eastern League forms. A busy little wing-half, he understudied the Gregory brothers, established members of the settled Watford team which won the Southern League.

"Purest ray serene"

John (**JACK**) **McNEE** *(1897-1900)*
b Renton, Dunbartonshire, circa 1867
SL 62 (32), FAC 9 (-), BCCL 18 (12)
Renton Wanderers; Renton; Bolton Wanderers (10/89); Kingsland player-coach; Newcastle Utd (9/94); Gateshead NER player-coach (7/95); West Herts (10/97 until cs 1900); Fulham (8/01 for less than a season)
He had easily the best pedigree of the club's first wave of professionals, being a Scottish FA Cup Final scorer and an established Bolton inside-forward. "Poor old McNee!" reminisced an admirer, "Watford should never have allowed him to rough life as he did, but should have retained him as coach and general adviser. He was a gem of purest ray serene."

VINCEnt **McNEICE** *(1957-1964)*
b Cricklewood, Middx 25/10/1938
FL 231 (-), FAC 22 (1), SFC 4 (-), FLC 6 (-)
Middlesex Schools; Brentford (groundstaff and youth team); Watford (youth team, pro 3/57 until 7/64); Montreal Concordia, Canada (summer 1961); Bexley Utd ("small fee" 7/64); also Hamilton Primos, Canada, player-coach (5/65); Hillingdon Borough (5/66 until cs 1969); BK 1903, Denmark manager (12/71); manager of two other Danish clubs; Aarhus, Denmark reserve-team coach (by 7/92)
An England Schools trialist whose stylish centre-half performances, both for Watford and in his many games for the RAF as a National Serviceman, led to early expectations that he would perform at a higher level, but he actually played his last Football League game at the age of 25. He gained engineering qualifications and later settled in Copenhagen.

Stylish

Francis Comber (FRANK) **McPHERSON** *(1928-1936)*
b Barrow-in-Furness, Lancs 14/5/1901
d Davyhulme, Lancs 5/3/1953
FL 94 (67 inc 10p), FAC 8 (8 inc 1p), 3SC 4 (2 inc 1p)
Barrow Shipbuilders; Partick Thistle (am 4/19); Chesterfield Municipal (10/19); Barrow (2/21); Manchester Utd (5/23); Manchester Central (7/28); Watford (£850 9/28); Reading (exchange for G.C.James and £1,500 2/30); Watford (6/33 until cs 1936); Barrow (3/37)
Born to Aberdonian parents, he became a prolific scorer who hit 22 of Watford's first 28 League and Cup goals in 1929/30, having already set the pre-Holton club record for a season. Very quick, he was able to play at outside-left or centre-forward. He scored a hat-trick on each of three successive visits to Leicester City, the last of them for Watford.

Enjoyed Filbert Street

Robert **McWILLIAMS** *(1930-1931)*
b Kirkintilloch, Dunbartonshire 12/9/1907
FL 22 (1)
Denny Hibernians (7/28); Celtic (9/28); Watford (free 6/29); Leith Athletic (free 8/31); Celtic (2/32 until cs 1932, and 3/33 until cs 1933)
Claiming the first-team left-wing position from the experienced Arthur Daniels towards the end of his first season at Vicarage Road, this young Scot remained in favour until the autumn, but then lost his place. After seeing out the remainder of his two-year stint as a reserve, he was released and returned home from his only spell in English football.

Three spells with Celtic

Laurence **MAHON** *(1913)*
b Northwich, Cheshire 1888
SL 10 (-), FAC 1 (-)
Mansfield Town (1911 until 1912); Shirebrook; Watford

10-0 FA Cup win

(5/13); West Hartlepool (cs 1914); Clowne Colliery; Hartlepools NE Railway Institute (permit player 10/22)
Immediately before being recruited to Cassio Road he was a member of the Shirebrook side which won the championship of the Central Alliance. His handful of half-back appearances for Watford included a 10-0 FA Cup win against amateurs Bournemouth. His elder brother Jack gave long service to Gillingham after playing League football for Gainsborough Trinity.

Helped set Arsenal record

*Alexander (**SANDY**)* **MAIN** *(1904-1907)*
b West Calder, Midlothian
SL 67 (1), FAC 8 (-), SEL 12 (-), UL 20 (-)
West Calder (6/98); Rangers (3/99); West Calder (4/99); Hibernian; Woolwich Arsenal (11/99); West Calder Swifts (9/03); Motherwell (9/03); Watford (6/04 until cs 1907)
He joined Watford as a forward, but made nearly all his appearances at right-half, from which position he captained the side in the season which preceded his retirement. His style lacked frills, but was dour and dependable. He was also a professional half-miler, and in his previous spell in England he'd scored twice in Woolwich Arsenal's record 12-0 win.

Crowd liked his style

SAMuel Thomas **MALPASS** *(1943-1949)*
b Consett, Co Durham 12/9/1918
d Cambridge 1983
FL 41 (-), WW2 1 (-)
Huddersfield Town (10/36); Fulham (5/39); Watford (£750 1/47); Great Yarmouth Town (8/49). Guested for Bradford City, Brighton & Hove Albion, Chelsea, Crystal Palace, Halifax Town, Hartlepools Utd, Millwall and Watford in WW2.
He could play at wing-half, but was primarily a full-back whose fast, fearless tackling earned him great popularity with the Vicarage Road spectators. Nevertheless, although he held a first-team place from the time he signed until the end of the season, he was by no means a fixture in the team during the two full seasons which followed.

Success came late

*Terence John (**TERRY**)* **MANCINI** *(1961-1965)*
b Camden Town, London 4/10/1942
FL 66+1 (-), FAC 6 (-), FLC 3 (-)
Watford (am 9/59, pro 7/61); Port Elizabeth, South Africa (free 4/66); Orient (11/67); Queens Park Rangers (£25,000 10/71); Arsenal (£22,500 10/74); Aldershot (free 9/76); Los Angeles Aztecs, USA (free 4/77 until 8/77); Fulham (reserve-team coach 9/78, assistant-manager circa 4/84 until cs 1985); Brentford coaching staff (cs 1986 until 1/87); Luton Town (assistant-manager cs 1989, acting-manager briefly 1/90); Blackburn Rovers scout (by 12/92)
REPUBLIC OF IRELAND FULL
A strong centre-half who was perhaps undervalued at Vicarage Road. Certainly he achieved much in the game late in his career, becoming captain of Arsenal and being capped five times in his thirties. He'd led Port Elizabeth to the South African League championship, and on his return to this country was fixed up with Orient by Cliff Holton.

ReuBEN John **MARDEN** *(1955-1956)*
b Fulham, London 10/2/1927
FL 41 (11), SFC 1 (1)
A Chelmsford works team; Chelmsford City; Arsenal (2/50); Watford (4-figure fee 6/55); Bedford Town (free 3/57); Romford (1957/8, trainer by 11/61)
His First Division record in five years at Highbury (11 goals in 42 games) was almost identical to the totals he ran up during his shorter stay at Vicarage Road as a fast and direct left-winger who could also play at centre-forward. He scored on his début (Watford 4 Millwall 2), and later was the only scorer when the Reserves beat Swindon Town 5-0.

Nap hand for Reserves

LEO Sargent **MARKHAM** *(1972-1975)*
b High Wycombe, Bucks 22/3/1953
FL 22+11 (3), FAC 1+1 (-)
Luton Town (am 7/69 until 3/71); Marlow Town (am); Watford (pro 8/72); Wimbledon (loan 3/75, free cs 1975); Aylesbury Utd (player/acting-manager 7/78, manager until 1982)
Before getting a professional engagement at Vicarage Road, he'd had trials with Chelsea, Luton Town and Derby County. A strapping forward, he soon got a League chance after signing, but was never able to hold a first-team place for long. He made two appearances at Plymouth, both as a substitute, and scored on each occasion to earn a 1-1 draw.

Déja vu at Plymouth

William Arthur **MARKLAND** *(1919-1920)*
b Derby 1887
d Watford, Herts 12/12/1942
SL 13 (-), WW1 4 (-)
Leavesden Mental Hospital (by 10/14); Watford (am 1915, pro 5/19)
After turning out for the Reserves before the Great War, he played in the four friendly games in April 1919 which marked the club's return to playing activity after two barren years, and was then taken on the professional staff as a full-back for one season. At the time of his death he'd been with LPTB, who ran the local bus services, for 15 years.

Helped re-start in 1919

Isaac (IKE) **MARSH** *(1897-1898)*
SL 23 (5), FAC 5 (1), BCCL 1 (1)
Notts Jardines (1893/4); Clifton Colliery (1894/5); Hucknall Portland; Burton Wanderers (1/97); Northfleet (6/97); West Herts (9/97); Gainsborough Trinity (12/98); Hucknall Portland (3/99); Notts County (1899/1900); Newark (1900/1); Doncaster Rovers (£10 to Notts County 6/01); Somercotes Utd (3/03); Chesterfield Town (1903/4); Worksop Town (9/05); Worksop North End (1/06); Dinnington Main Colliery (8/07); Birchwood Colliery (11/08); Denaby Utd (1908/9); Chesterfield Town (1909/10); Denaby Utd (1910/1)
A big man and one of the club's first two paid players, he scored a hat-trick in the historic first game (a friendly), but soon moved from centre-forward to left-half, where he stayed. In November 1898 he applied for his release and left without waiting for a reply, stating that he had no quarrel with the club but couldn't find suitable lodgings.

Historic signing

Two seasons, two games

William ***MARSHALL*** *(1922)*
b Newcastle-upon-Tyne, Northumberland circa 1900
FL 2 (-)
Dunstan Atlas Villa; Watford (5/21); Leadgate Park (free cs 1923, player-manager cs 1924)
On completion of a good season at centre-half for the club which finished second in the Tyneside League and won the Gateshead Charity Cup, he travelled down to Watford and made one League appearance in each of his two seasons. Both games were lost, but in a friendly against Queens Park Rangers he was tried at centre-forward, and scored in a 1-1 draw.

Went home disappointed

DENNIS MASKELL *(1951-1952)*
b Mountain Ash, Glam 16/4/1931
FL 5 (-)
Watford (am 8/51, pro 9/51 until cs 1952)
He played on the left-wing as an amateur in the first four games of 1951/2, having been employed for a few weeks on the groundstaff. This soon led to his engagement as a professional, but he appeared only once more in the first team, at inside-left on Easter Monday. He was released at the end of the season and returned to the Valleys deeply disappointed.

£1 for long journey home

Henry Moram ***(HARRY) MATTHEW*** *(1903)*
b Dundee, Angus 16/4/1870
d Dundee, Angus 19/2/1956
SL 10 (-), SEL 2 (1p)
Darlington; Bolton Wanderers (1892/3); Dundee (10/93); Millwall (cs 1894); Preston North End (5/97); Gravesend Utd (cs 1898); Distillery (9/99); Watford (1/03 until cs 1903)
IRISH LEAGUE
Ever-present at left-half in his brief spell with Watford, which ended with relegation, he was then awarded £1 by the committee to pay his expenses home. He'd been good enough to play for Forfarshire, for the Southern League (twice against London whilst on Millwall's books), and in 1899 against the Football League for its Irish counterpart.

Home wins, away defeats

James F. ***(JIMMY) MAXWELL*** *(1926)*
b Glasgow circa 1904
FL 4 (1)
Neilston Victoria; Stoke City (6/25); Watford (free 8/26 until cs 1927)
SCOTLAND JUNIOR
Introduced to English football by Stoke City, he made ten Second Division appearances (including a 7-3 defeat and a 6-1 victory) before being released after one season. A similar period at Vicarage Road brought him four League games as a left-winger. The results were emphatic - two 4-0 wins at home, followed by 1-4 and 0-3 away.

ALAN Kenneth **MAYES** *(1974-1979)*
b Edmonton, Middx 11/12/1953
FL 110+23 (31), FAC 5+4 (1), FLC 11+4 (4)
Queens Park Rangers (sch 6/69, appr 6/70, pro 7/71); Watford (£8,000 11/74); Northampton Town (loan 1/76); Swindon Town (£72,500 2/79); Chelsea (£175,000 12/80); Swindon Town (free 7/83); Carlisle Utd (free 7/85); Newport County (loan 2/86); Blackpool (loan 9/86, £5,000 10/86); Wycombe Wanderers (free 8/87); Chalfont St Peter (3/88); Harrow Borough manager (10/88 until 2/89)
As his later transfer fees were to emphasize, Watford had good value for their modest outlay for this very fast, elusive forward. His generous contribution to the Fourth Division championship win included a hat-trick in the snow at York City, and he also got an away threesome on his début for Swindon, for whom he scored 65 times in 141 League games.

More than good value

John Alfred (JOHNNY) **MEADOWS** *(1951-1960)*
b Hoxton, London 13/11/1930
FL 222 (42 inc 14p), FAC 14 (4 inc 1p), SFC 8 (3)
Kingsbury Town; Chelsea (am 5/48); Willington; St Albans City; Watford (am 1/51, pro 6/51); Yiewsley (free 6/61)
As a Willington player he missed the 1950 Amateur Cup Final through injury. The merit of a long and worthy Vicarage Road career as a stylish wing-half and inside-forward was subsequently tarnished by his admitted involvement, when Watford's captain, in match-fixing irregularities. His father composed "Oh, My, What a Referee!" and other popular songs.

Missed Amateur Final

JAMES Stephen **MEARA** *(1993)*
b Hammersmith, London 7/10/1972
FL 1+1 (-)
Watford (sch 11/86, tr 7/89, pro 4/91 until cs 1994); Atletico Madrid, Spain (two months' trial 2/92); Doncaster Rovers (free 7/94 until 3/96); Seville, Spain (trial 3/96)
A creative midfield player who represented the Independent Schools. His Aldenham School background was a throwback to the club's Victorian past, but unlike his 1890s predecessors he became a professional. That exotic trial period when he was a 19-year-old on Watford's books, but with no experience of first-team football, was highly unusual.

Victorian throwback

GORDON **MEE** *(1945-1946)*
b Belper, Derbys 13/5/1913
d Hove, Sussex 9/1/1975
FAC 8 (-), WW2 27 (-)
Matlock Town; Brighton & Hove Albion (1/35); Watford (10/45 until cs 1946)
A good all-round sportsman who was a police reservist in the Second World War, he became Watford's goalie in 1945/6. His release the following summer meant that he played no peacetime League football for the club, but his

FA Cup-run goalkeeper

FA Cup appearances included three eventful games with Nottingham Forest, who were ultimately beaten after extra time.

Cambridge Utd's first

COLIN **MELDRUM** *(1960-1962)*
b Glasgow 26/11/1941
FL 32 (-), FAC 3 (-), FLC 5 (-)
Arsenal (am 8/58, pro 12/58); Watford (4-figure fee 11/60); Reading (£1,500 4/63); Cambridge Utd (£4,000 10/69); Hillingdon Borough player-manager (7/71); York City trainer-coach (2/73); Workington player-manager (11/74 until 4/75); Stafford Rangers player-manager (9/75 until 5/76); Workington manager (2/77 until 5/77); Scarborough assistant-manager (1979/80); Frickley Athletic assistant-manager (1980/1); Barnet coach (1981/2); York City assistant-manager (1982/3); Hull City chief scout (1983/4); Swansea City coaching staff (briefly until 12/84); coach in Saudi Arabia (1986); Wealdstone manager (2/87 until 9/87); Workington manager (11/87)
He came to Vicarage Road after failing to get into the first team at Highbury, as also did Ken Nicholas, an erstwhile Arsenal colleague with whom he contested Watford's left-back position. He scored Cambridge United's first Football League goal, and won a Fourth Division Manager of the Month award in the first of his three spells at Workington.

Rumbustious

Terence (TERRY) **MELLING** *(1966-1967)*
b Haverton Hill, Co Durham 24/1/1940
FL 23+1 (5), FAC 4 (2), FLC 2 (-)
Tow Law Town; Newcastle Utd (am 12/65, pro 12/65); Watford (free 5/66); Newport County (£2,000 2/67); Mansfield Town (11/67); Rochdale (9/68); Darlington (3/69); Scarborough (10/69); Tow Law Town
A rumbustious striker who'd been in the army before taking the route to St James's Park which was later followed by Chris Waddle. Melling's career became a series of quickfire moves. The longest spell he had with any of his six League clubs was at Mansfield, where he spent just over one season. In all, he accumulated 40 goals in 130 League appearances.

Two World Cups

Antonio Michael (TONY) **MEOLA** *(1990)*
b Belleville, New Jersey, USA 21/2/1969
FMC 1 (-)
University of Virginia, USA; Brighton & Hove Albion (non-contract 8/90); Watford (non-contract 9/90 until 12/90); Fort Lauderdale Strikers, USA (by 8/91); New York/New Jersey Metrostars, USA (4/96)
USA FULL
The son of a US immigrant who had been a professional in Italy during the 1960s, he came to England in search of a career, but got only one League game for Brighton, and a cup tie at Watford in which he conceded a soft goal in a 2-1 defeat. Nevertheless, at 25 he'd kept goal in two World Cups and was not far short of his 100th cap.

KEITH **MERCER** *(1973-1979)*
b Lewisham, London 14/10/1956
FL 109+25 (46), FAC 6 (4), FLC 10+4 (3)
St Albans Schools; Watford (sch 10/70, appr 7/73, pro 9/74); Southend Utd (£80,000 2/80); Blackpool (free 7/83 until 1/85)
Others have made their League débuts as apprentices, but this courageous bruiser of a striker actually did so *before* becoming one. He was still at school, and aged 16 years and 125 days, when he appeared as a substitute at Tranmere to become the club's youngest-ever senior player. A proneness to injury eventually caused his early retirement with ligament and cartilage problems.

Was still at school

Henry **(HARRY) MIDDLETON** *(1911-1912)*
b Newcastle-upon-Tyne, Northumberland
SL 23 (5), SCC 1 (-)
Scotswood; Newcastle Utd (am 7/06, pro 4/07); Brighton & Hove Albion (cs 1909); Watford (2/11); Darlington (6/12); Blyth Spartans (7/13 until 1/14)
A late-season signing who scored on his début, led the attack for a few games - impressively, some thought, although opinions were divided - and later played in other forward and half-back positions. He was retained for 1911/2 only after Newcastle United, who still held his Football League registration, had agreed to reduce the £250 fee on his head.

Opinions varied

William Percy **(DOSSIE) MILES** *(1929-1930)*
b Bournemouth, Hants 19/2/1898
d Weymouth, Dorset 1971
FL 14 (1), FAC 3 (-)
Bournemouth Trams (4 seasons); Bournemouth & Boscombe Athletic (5/24); Watford (free 7/29); Bournemouth Tramways (permit player 7/30)
During his amateur days he scored nearly two hundred goals in four years and represented Hampshire, but in his third season at Dean Court he was converted into a centre-half. It was in that position that this six-footer made his Watford appearances, at a time when the regular pivot, Neil McBain, was being used in the forward line.

Moved into defence

KEITH *Derek* **MILLEN** *(1994-1996)*
b Croydon, Surrey 26/9/1966
FL 73+1 (2), FAC 7 (-), FLC 4 (-)
Southampton (sch 12/80 until 3/82); Crystal Palace youth team; Brentford (youth team, pro 11/83); Watford (£65,000 plus B.J.Ashby, valued at £35,000, 3/94)
Almost ten years of professional service at Griffin Park encompassed an Associate Members Cup Final appearance at Wembley in 1985 and a Third Division championship medal in 1992. He and Colin Foster were signed simultaneously late in 1993/4 to form a tall central-defensive pairing at Vicarage Road, to help stave off relegation, which they did.

Wembley appearance

Amateur Cup and cap

Herbert Edwin James (TED) **MILLER** *(1922)*
b Watford, Herts 14/12/1897
d Watford, Herts 6/1/1985
FL 2 (-)
Watford Old Boys; Watford Corinthians; St Albans City; Watford (am by 10/19): Charlton Athletic (am 1/23); Millwall (am 8/24); Barnet (9/24); Clapton (9/24); St Albans City; Queens Park Rangers (am 9/25); Chesham Utd (2/26); Hampstead Town (by early 1928/9)
ENGLAND AMATEUR
One of three footballing sons of a Watford signwriter, he spent his entire career as an amateur, and his list of clubs has marked similarities to that of his brother Rev. He won his only Amateur cap whilst with St Albans City in March 1924, and the following year helped Clapton to win the Amateur Cup. His two League appearances were on the left wing.

First modern Cornishman

KEVIN **MILLER** *(1994-1996)*
b Falmouth, Cornwall 15/3/1969
FL 86 (-), FAC 6 (-), FLC 6 (-)
Newquay; Exeter City (3/89); Birmingham City (£250,000 5/93); Watford (£260,000 8/94)
The club's first Cornishman for 95 years, he was signed to restore a command of the penalty area to which Vicarage Road became accustomed from its goalkeepers in the days of Tony Coton and David James. His departure from Birmingham was part of the orgy of comings and goings at St Andrews which followed the appointment of Barry Fry as manager.

Three major cup wins

PAUL Richard **MILLER** *(1988-1989)*
b Stepney, London 11/10/1959
FL 22 (1), FAC 5 (-), FMC 3 (-)
Tottenham Hotspur (sch 1/75, appr 4/76, pro 5/77); Skeid, Norway (loan 1978); Charlton Athletic (£130,000 2/87); Watford (£85,000 10/88); AFC Bournemouth (£50,000 8/89); Brentford (loan 11/89); Swansea City (free 1/91); Wingate & Finchley youth-team coach (cs 1991)
At centre-half the club briefly had the benefit of his know-how borne of more than two hundred First Division appearances and three major cup triumphs as a Tottenham player. Under the captaincy of future Watford manager Steve Perryman he helped to win FA Cup twice, and the UEFA Cup in 1983/4, when he scored in the Final.

Good Merseyside spell

Peter Steedman **MILLER** *(1930-1931)*
b Bo'ness, West Lothian 15/4/1908
d Bo'ness, Lothian 19/5/1979
FL 14 (1), FAC 2 (1)
Bo'ness Utd; Grange Rovers (pro 5/27 until 6/29); Falkirk (8/29); Watford (free 7/30); New Brighton (free 8/31); Le Havre, France (6/35); Rotherham Utd (1/36); Port Vale (6/36 until cs 1937)
The highlight of his Vicarage Road season was a 3-1 FA

Cup away win against Second Division Oldham Athletic, in which he scored. An inside-forward, he'd had experience of top-flight football in Scotland, and on leaving Watford became a first-teamer for four years at New Brighton in the Third Division (North), before a brief flirtation with continental football.

*Redvers Buller (**REV**)* **MILLER** *(1922)*
b Watford, Herts 24/10/1899
FL 1 (-)
Watford Corinthians: St Albans City; Watford (am by 11/22); Charlton Athletic (am 1/23); Millwall (am 8/24); Barnet (9/24); St Albans City (10/24); Chesham Utd (2/26); Queens Park Rangers (pro 7/26 until cs 1927)
The circumstances of his one League appearance were unusual: he stood in at outside-left at Reading when his brother Ted withdrew. A regular Herts player for several years, he eventually turned professional, but was only a reserve player at QPR. A third brother, Harold, played for England in 1923 and turned out for Watford in the Second World War.

Unusual selection

*Henry Joseph (**HARRY**)* **MINGAY** *(1927)*
b Luton, Beds 19/10/1895
d Luton, Beds 1969
FL 2 (-), FAC 1 (-)
Blackpool (2/19); Clapton Orient (8/24); Luton Town (5/25 until cs 1927); Watford (11/27 until 12/27, and 3/28 until cs 1928); Bedford Town (9/28)
A goalkeeping problem (Joe Hewitt and Bill Yates were both injured) led to his initial one-month engagement, and similar difficulties brought him back later in the season, although all his first-team action was in the first spell. He had last been with his home-town club, but was discovered when serving with the RAMC at Blackpool in wartime.

Army discovery

***FRANK** Rollason* **MITCHELL** *(1952-1957)*
b Goulburn, Australia 3/6/1922
d Lapworth, West Midlands 2/4/1984
FL 193 (-), FAC 12 (-), SFC 3 (-)
Coventry City (am 8/38); Birmingham (pro 9/43); Chelsea (5-figure fee 1/49); Watford (£7,500 7/52 until cs 1957). Guested for Arsenal, Birmingham, Northampton Town and Portsmouth in WW2.
ENGLAND 'UNOFFICIAL'
A cool and commanding left-half and captain whose cultured passing adorned the Watford side for five years. He had settled in England after service with the Australian Navy, played v Scotland in the Bolton Disaster Fund international, and led Birmingham to the Second Division championship. He also played First Class cricket for Warwickshire.

Cool and cultured

Shipyard apprentice

T.W. (TOMMY) ***MITCHELL*** *(1912-1914)*
b Wallsend, Northumberland
SL 60 (9), FAC 3 (-), SCC 2 (-)
Hebburn Argyle; Watford (5/12 until cs 1914); Wallsend St Lukes (permit player 8/21)
Having just completed a shipyard apprenticeship whilst playing for Hebburn Argyle, he moved south to spend most of the next two seasons as Watford's outside-right. He was quick and, although inclined to centre erratically, was seen by some as the club's best in the position for some time. All his goals, including one on his début, came in 1912/3.

Four border crossings

Joseph (JOE) ***MOFFAT*** *(1908-1909)*
b Scotland
SL 18 (-)
Abercorn (7/96); Bo'ness (12/96); Wishaw Thistle (2/97 - reinstated as an amateur 8/97); Bo'ness (pro 11/97); Walsall (6/99); Tottenham Hotspur (5/00); Bo'ness (8/01); St Mirren (9/01); Manchester City (5/03); Kilmarnock (free 5/06); Nelson (7/07); Heart of Midlothian (cs 1908); Watford (8/08); Aberdeen (cs 1909 to cs 1910)
SCOTLAND JUNIOR
Far from averse to a change of club, he'd had plenty of experience on both sides of the border, and played at the top level with Manchester City, before spending a season at Cassio Road. He was at home in any of the three half-back positions, but played mainly in the centre for Watford, for whom his last three games were all victories.

Rare feat on loan

Thomas John (TOMMY) ***MOONEY*** *(1994-1996)*
b Middlesbrough, Yorks 11/8/1971
FL 77+4 (11 inc 2p), FAC 2+1 (1), FLC 7 (1)
Middlesbrough Schools; Billingham Synthonia; Aston Villa (tr 12/88, pro 11/89); Scarborough (free 7/90); Southend Utd (£100,000 7/93); Watford (loan 3/94, £95,000 7/94)
Released by Graham Taylor at Villa Park without a first-team game, he did well enough at Scarborough as a physically strong, battling forward to attract a six-figure fee. In the course of helping Watford to avoid relegation in 1984, he recorded the rare feat of scoring against his own club whilst on loan to another. He later had a run at left-back.

No win in 11 - then 8-1

John (JACK) ***MOORE*** *(1909-1910)*
b Wellington, Salop
SL 20 (2), FAC 3 (2)
Burton Utd (1904/5); Derby County (1/05); Oldham Athletic (9/07); Watford (7/09 until cs 1910)
Able to play on both wings, which he did for Watford, he had to wait eleven games for his first win in a first-team shirt - but it was by 8-1, in the FA Cup against Bromley, and Moore scored two. Then in his next match Wycombe Wanderers were beaten 4-0 in the same competition. First Division Woolwich Arsenal ended the run in the next round.

JAMIE David **MORALEE** *(1994-1996)*
b Wandsworth, London 2/12/1971
FL 40+9 (7), FAC 5 (-), FLC 6+1 (-)
Surrey Schools; Crystal Palace (tr 7/88, pro 7/90); Millwall (free 9/92); Watford (£425,000 7/94 until cs 1996)
A loose-limbed rag doll of a forward who was released by Crystal Palace to join Millwall when Chris Armstrong moved in the opposite direction for £1 million. After a good goalscoring start at The Den, his output fell dramatically, but despite scoring only five times in his last 43 Millwall games he was brought to Watford for the club's third-highest fee.

Diminishing returns

John (JACK) **MORAN** *(1932-1935)*
b Haydock, Lancs 9/2/1906
d Haydock, Lancs 12/10/1959
FL 100 (-), FAC 6 (-), 3SC 5 (-)
Earlestown; Wigan Borough (am 10/24, pro 4/25); Tottenham Hotspur (5/31); Watford (9/32); Mansfield Town (3/36 until cs 1937)
After a good career with Wigan Borough he left shortly before that club's demise, and played in a dozen Second Division games at White Hart Lane. Steady and consistent, rather than polished, he had three years as Watford's senior left-back - and the club's entertainer - before losing his place to Jim Lewis. He'd once been a miner.

Left ill-fated club

Emlyn (TOM) **MORGAN** *(1935-1938)*
b Troedrhiwfuwch, Glam 16/9/1914
d Rhymney, Mon 28/10/1983
FL 108 (6 inc 4p), FAC 5 (-), 3SC 12 (2 inc 1p)
New Tredegar; Watford (am 3/35, pro 5/35 until cs 1940)
One of ten Welshmen on the books at one time, he had a few reserve-team games as an amateur at the end of 1934/5, and the following season took the senior right-half spot as Bill Findlay's playing days drew to a close. He quickly established himself as a resourceful player, but serious cartilage trouble, and then the war, finished a promising career.

Career cut short

IAN Arthur **MORGAN** *(1973-1974)*
b City of London 14/11/1946
FL 15+1 (1), FAC 2 (-)
Queens Park Rangers (am 6/63, appr 11/63, pro 9/64); Watford (loan 10/73, £10,000 11/73 until 8/75); Barking (by 3/76); club manager in Norway
The Morgan twins on either wing were a familiar sight in QPR line-ups of the 1960s, and Roger went on to play for Tottenham Hotspur. Ian was brought to Watford by his former captain, Mike Keen, but soon sustained an injury which eventually brought about the cancellation of his contract and his retirement from full-time football.

Under Keen at QPR

Berkamstedian

John **SYDNEY / (TAFFY) MORGAN** *(1902-1904)*
b Barking, Essex 2/2/1876
d Hemel Hempstead, Herts 8/8/1951
SL 15 (9), FAC 1 (-), SEL 2 (1)
Sunnyside, Berkhamsted; Berkhamsted Town; Apsley; Casuals; Ilford (am 1/03); Watford (am); Old Berkhamstedians
WALES AMATEUR
He first played at Berkhamsted School, where he later taught classics and geography for 36 years and was the Old Boys association secretary for half a century. A centre-forward who played in spectacles, he once scored seven for Ilford. He became president of his adopted home town's senior football club, and (as late as 1928) captain of its cricket counterpart.

Ever-present at 35

LEWis **MORGAN** *(1946-1947)*
b Cowdenbeath, Fife 30/4/1911
d Portsmouth, Hants 22/9/1988
FL 50 (-), FAC 4 (-)
Crossgates Primrose (7/28); Lochgelly Celtic (cs 1929); Bowhill Rovers (6/30); Dundee (4/31); Portsmouth (8/35); Watford (7/46); Chelmsford City (free 5/48)
SCOTLAND SCHOOLS; SCOTTISH LEAGUE
An ever-present at right-back in 1946/7 at the age of 35, he played in every first-team game from his arrival until he was replaced by the newly-signed Jimmy Jones. His pre-war career had been a good one, bringing inter-league representative honours before he left Scotland, and an FA Cup-winner's medal with Portsmouth in 1939.

Season of penalties

William **(BILLY) MORGAN** *(1903-1904)*
SL 20 (9 inc 8p), FAC 2 (1p), SEL 13 (4 inc 3p)
Horwich; Newton Heath (1/97); Bolton Wanderers (3/03); Watford (7/03); Leicester Fosse (5/04); New Brompton (8/06); Newton Heath Athletic (3/10)
His one Watford season, in which he played in every first-team game and scored 12 penalties, brought the Southern League Second Division championship to Cassio Road. He was the right-half in a team which won all 19 competitive home matches (goals 92-12), and 11 of 16 away. His previous experience included 146 Football League appearances.

Snappy dresser

Harold **(HARRY) MORRIS** *(1925-1928)*
b Bolsover, Derbys 2/9/1902
d Bolsover, Derbys 1976
FL 50 (4)
Bolsover Town; Bolsover Colliery (cs 1924); Worksop (briefly 8/24); Bolsover Colliery; Watford (8/25); Mansfield Town (6/28); Barnsley (£350 6/29); Shirebrook (8/30)
A dapper, well-turned-out individual who spent three years on Watford's books as a hardworking forward or half-back. Immediately before and after his Vicarage Road service he scored heavily in non-League football, with 45 goals for his home-town club in 1924/5, and 46 when Mansfield won the Midland League championship four seasons later.

MARK John **MORRIS** *(1987-1989)*
b Morden, Surrey 26/9/1962
FL 41 (1), FAC 7 (-), FLC 5 (1)
Wimbledon (sch 10/78, appr 7/79, pro 10/81); Aldershot (loan 9/85); Watford (£40,000 7/87); Sheffield Utd (£175,000 7/89); AFC Bournemouth (£100,000 7/91)
After a difficult start he performed solidly and consistently at centre-half as Watford struggled unavailingly to retain their First Division status. His transfer to Bramall Lane brought in a useful profit, and it was the third time that he'd been signed by Dave Bassett. He was with Wimbledon throughout their climb through the divisions.

Bassett favourite

PATrick Joseph **MORRISSEY** *(1971-1974)*
b Enniscorthy, Co Wexford 23/2/1948
FL 101+6 (27 inc 2p), FAC 5 (1), FLC 5 (1)
Hackney Schools; Coventry Schools; Coventry City (appr 4/63, pro 7/65); Torquay Utd (7/68); Crewe Alexandra (7/69); Chester (£3,500 10/71); Watford (£8,000 12/71); Aldershot (valued at £10,000 in part-exchange for R.D.W.Joslyn 11/74); Swansea City (loan 10/77); Dartford (free 11/77); Hayes (by 11/79); Slough Town (by 10/80); Carshalton Athletic (cs 1981); Hendon (by 1982) Chesham Utd (1982, player-manager 11/82 until 3/85); Dunstable Town (4/85, later manager); Buckingham Town manager (cs 1988); Chesham Utd manager (10/88); Southall player-manager (cs 1989 until 2/90); Hemel Hempstead manager (by 10/93); also Colney Heath Veterans (player by 12/94); Colney Heath manager (by 12/95)
REPUBLIC OF IRELAND UNDER-23
Although Ireland-born, he lived in England from the age of five, and as a schoolboy played representative football in both London and the Midlands, where his professional career began. A forward, he scored on his Watford début, and then managed only one more goal in his next 24 games, but later hit a televised hat-trick in the snow at Oldham.

TV hat-trick

Stephen Joseph (STEVE) **MORROW** *(1991)*
b Carrickfergus, Co Antrim 2/7/1970
FL 7+1 (-), FMC 1 (-)
Arsenal (sch 12/84); Bangor, Northern Ireland; Arsenal (tr 7/87, pro 5/88); Reading (loan 1/91); Watford (loan 8/91); Reading (loan 10/91); Barnet (loan 3/92)
NORTHERN IRELAND SCHOOLS, YOUTH, UNDER-23 and FULL
He played in the Irish League at 15, began 1991/2 as Watford's left-back (on loan), and with Arsenal was a winner in the FA Youth Cup, European Cup Winners Cup and Football League Cup, which he won with his first goal in senior football and then broke an arm in the celebratory horseplay after the final whistle. One of the few professionals to wear contact lenses.

First goal won a trophy

All-round sportsman

GEOFFrey Dalgleish **MORTON** *(1948-1951)*
b Acton, Middx 22/7/1922
FL 107 (-), FAC 6 (-)
Harrow Schools; Chelmsford City; Watford (free 10/48); Southend Utd (about £1,000 2/52); Exeter City (9/54 until cs 1955). Guested for Chelsea in WW2.
No other Watford goalkeeper can match his eight successive clean sheets in the League. He was converted from an outfield player whilst representing Harrow Schools and, after retiring with a hand injury, spent 30 years as sports coach at Malvern College. He was a schoolboy boxing champion, and also played tennis and cricket for Middlesex.

Batted with W.G.

ALFred Samuel **MOULE** *(1928-1929)*
b Canning Town, Essex 31/7/1894
d Sompting, Sussex 5/2/1973
FL 11 (4)
West Ham Schools; West Ham Corinthians; Catford Southend; Leytonstone; Millwall (am 3/20, pro 5/20); Norwich City (5/27); Watford (free 7/28); Margate (free 8/29, player-manager 8/30)
In his prime he was Millwall's leading scorer three times, and at 34 began his Watford career at centre-forward with four goals in his first five matches, but later bowed out with three games at right-half. As a cricketer he played professionally for Essex, and for Devon until he was 43. As a youth he'd batted with W.G.Grace in a club match.

Field day against Newport

Albert Edward Pilkerton **(EDDIE) MUMMERY** *(1921-1925)*
(formerly Albert Edward **PILKERTON***)*
b Norwich, Norfolk 18/8/1897
d Great Yarmouth, Norfolk 31/1/1937
FL 119 (23), FAC 7 (-)
Lichfield, Yarmouth (1912/3); Coalville Swifts; Watford (5/20); Clapton Orient (free 8/26); Yarmouth (11/26, trainer 1928 until death)
Talented but wildly inconsistent, he was a versatile forward or half-back who is unique in having scored five times in a Football League match for Watford. He became a publican back in Norfolk, and was still involved in football when he expired prematurely, from an attack of influenza. When very young he'd enlisted for First World War service.

Billy Meredith colleague

Stewart **MUNN** *(1901-1904)*
b Greenock, Renfrewshire 22/12/1872
d Shotts, Lanarks 21/8/1959
SL 37 (-), FAC 2 (-), SEL 7 (-)
Maryhill; Third Lanark (1893/4); Burnley (cs 1894); Grimsby Town (7/95); Manchester City (11/97 until cs 1901); Watford (10/01 until cs 1905); Hitchin Town (1/06)
A First Division half-back briefly with Burnley, and later with Manchester City in Billy Meredith's heyday. His first-team status at Watford was mostly before the arrival as manager of John Goodall. For a time he was a member of the road staff of the Watford Urban District Council.

*James (JIMMY) **MURRAY** (1902-1903)*
b Dalmellington, Ayrshire 9/6/1880
d Glasgow 29/10/1933
SL 27 (6), FAC 2 (-), SEL 2 (2)
St Augustine's; Benwhat Heatherbell; Aston Villa (4/00); Small Heath (11/01); Watford (6/02); Kettering (5/03); Wellingborough (free 11/03)
SCOTLAND JUNIOR
Well-built and quick, with a long, raking stride, he was signed by Aston Villa after playing for the Scottish Junior FA at Small Heath's ground, and later spent one season as Watford's inside-left. The club has been playing in FA Cup ties since 1886, but Murray remains the only Watford player to have been sent off in the competition.

Unrepeated FA Cup fate

*John **EDWARD MYERS** (1897)*
b Kettering, Northants, July 1872
d Watford, Herts 21/4/1930
SL 3 (-)
Watford Swifts (by 1890); West Herts (1892); Bushey (by 12/92); Old Fullerians; Crouch End (10/96); West Herts (am 1897/8)
He played twice in friendly matches in 1892 (once in goal and once as a half-back) and reappeared in the first team as goalkeeper in 1897/8. He served as auditor to the club, the West Herts FA, the Herts FA, and the All-England Club at Wimbledon (the tennis journalist Wallis Myers was his brother), and as chairman of the Watford Divisional Liberal Party.

Accountancy services

***WARREN** Anthony **NEILL** (1996)*
b Acton, Middx 21/11/1962
FL 1 (-)
Queens Park Rangers (sch 9/77, appr 7/79, pro 9/80); Portsmouth (£110,000 7/88 until cs 1995); Queens Park Rangers Under-13 coach; Watford (1/96)
ENGLAND SCHOOLS
Having retired with sciatica, he helped Watford Reserves when raising a side was a problem. Then, as the injury crisis intensified, this experienced right-back found himself in the first team. In the 1982 FA Cup Final replay he stood in for his subsequent Watford manager, Glenn Roeder, who was suspended after the first game was drawn.

Replaced Roeder

*James Robert **NESS** (1911)*
b Scarborough, Yorks 1887
SL 4 (2), SCC 1 (-)
Everton (am 9/10, pro 10/10); Watford (8/11 until cs 1912)
This 13-stone centre-forward, son of a Scarborough policeman, scored in the 1911 preseason trial match and went straight into the first team, but soon vanished from the scene. His Southern League goals came in a 2-4 defeat at Brentford. His brother Harry played in FA Cup Finals for Barnsley and, as full-back partner of Charlie Gladwin, Sunderland.

Robert T. **NEWMAN** *(1922)*
FL 1 (-)
Watford (9/22 until cs 1923)
Invited down from the North-East for a trial, he impressed sufficiently to be given an engagement. His impact at first-team level was minimal, being limited to a single League appearance at inside-left, in a 5-1 defeat at Millwall. He nevertheless had the distinction of playing in the first game at Vicarage Road - the 1922 pre-season public trial match.

Début embarrassment

Thomas Bruce **(TOMMY) NIBLO** *(1906-1907)*
b Dunfermline, Fife 24/9/1878
d Tynemouth, Northumberland 1933
SL 30 (8), FAC 2 (-), SEL 1 (-), UL 9 (3)
Cadzow Oak; Hamilton Academical; Linthouse (8/96); Newcastle Utd (£90 4/98); Middlesbrough (4/00); Newcastle Utd (cs 1900); Aston Villa (1/02); Nottingham Forest (4/04); Watford (5/06); Newcastle Utd (7/07, coach 1/08); Hebburn Argyle player-manager (8/08); Aberdeen ("big fee" 12/08); Raith Rovers (8/09 until cs 1910); Cardiff City (by 12/10 - Cardiff were fined by the Southern League for irregularities in connection with the signing, and ordered to pay Watford £10); Blyth Spartans (4/11). Guested for Fulham and Crystal Palace in WW1.
SCOTLAND FULL
Despite an excellent pedigree in,the game (he had played against England at Celtic Park two years earlier), he was only 27 when he joined Watford. Entrusted with a penalty on his début, he failed to score. He played everywhere in the forward line whilst at Cassio Road, but mainly at inside-left, and hit a Southern League hat-trick against Leyton.

Played rugger as well

KEN*neth William* **NICHOLAS** *(1959-1964)*
b Northampton 3/2/1938
FL 198 (4), FAC 19 (2), FLC 2 (-)
Arsenal (am 5/55, pro 5/55); Watford (free 5/59); Guildford City (free 6/65); Hastings Utd (by 11/66 until at least 4/68); Tonbridge; Faro, Portugal
ENGLAND SCHOOLS and YOUTH
After failing to make the first team in four years as an Arsenal professional, he joined Watford with John Sanchez and virtually monopolised the No 3 shirt from the start. Neat and thoughtful, he was no goalscoring full-back, but once hit two in a League game at Colchester. In addition to his soccer honours, he played rugby for England Grammar Schools.

International captain

PETER NICHOLAS *(1991-1992)*
b Newport, Mon 10/11/1959
FL 40 (1), FAC 1 (-), FLC 4 (-), FMC 1 (-)
Crystal Palace (sch 9/74, appr 7/76, pro 12/76); Arsenal (£400,000 3/81); Crystal Palace (loan 10/83, £150,000 8/84); Luton Town (£150,000 1/85); Aberdeen (£350,000 8/87); Chelsea (£350,000 8/88); Watford (£175,000 3/91); Chelsea youth-team manager (7/92 until cs 1993); Brentford youth-team manager (10/93); Crystal Palace (youth-team manager cs 1994, assistant first-team coach 6/95)
WALES SCHOOLS, UNDER-21 and FULL

A busy and perceptive midfield organiser, he was a short-term signing who brought masses of top-level experience to help fight a successful battle against relegation. He captained Wales, and as a Watford player won his 73rd Full cap to set what was then a national record. With Crystal Palace he won FA Youth Cup-winner's medals in 1977 and 1978.

*George **FRED**erick* ***NIDD*** *(1900-1916)*
b Boston, Lincs 1869
d Watford, Herts 1956
SL 55 (-), FAC 5 (-), WW1 1 (-)
Everton (8/89); Southport Central; Everton (1/93); Preston North End (2/94, reinstated am 9/95); Southport Central (1895/6); Bury (pro 12/95); Stalybridge Rovers (1896); Halliwell Rovers (3/97); Lincoln City (9/97); Grimsby Town (9/98); Watford (free 8/00); Brentford (5/02); Fulham (6/03); Grays Utd (8/04); Clapton Orient (3/05); Watford (9/07). Guested for Watford in WW1.
Although really a full-back, he had brief experience as a goalkeeper with both Grimsby and Watford, and the age of 47 was persuaded to play in goal the day after Skilly Williams joined the colours; Watford lost 8-2 at home. He was a talented athlete and a tenor of repute, and settled in the town once his extensive football wanderings were over.

Brief comeback at 47

*William (**BILL**)* ***NOCK*** *(1898)*
b Newtown, Montgomeryshire 1876
d Rochdale, Lancs 10/11/1931
SL 3 (3)
Newtown (by 3/95); West Herts (2/98 until cs 1898); reinstated am (5/98); Vulcans (by 1/01); Newtown (1/02); Newtown North End (by 12/02); Newtown (until at least 11/07)
WALES FULL
Briefly a West Herts forward less than a year after winning his one international cap (against Ireland), he scored two goals in his third and final Southern League game shortly before applying successfully for reinstatement as an amateur. He later held a managerial position in a Rochdale shirt factory, and was a member of a very musical family.

LEE Martin ***NOGAN*** *(1991-1994)*
b Cardiff, Glam 21/5/1969
FL 97+8 (26), FAC 2 (1), FLC 5+2 (3), AIC 1+2 (-)
Cardiff Schools; Oxford Utd (tr 8/86, pro 3/87); Brentford (loan 3/87); Southend Utd (loan 9/87); Watford £300,000 12/91); Southend Utd (loan 3/94); Reading (£250,000 1/95)
WALES UNDER-21, 'B' and FULL
Steve Perryman knew him at The Manor Ground, took him on loan at Brentford, and signed him for Watford when Oxford were in desperate need of money immediately after Robert Maxwell's death. Nogan, a forward whose brother followed him into League football, won his first Full cap, as a substitute, soon after moving to Vicarage Road.

Sold after Maxwell death

Top golfing footballer

PHILip **NOLAN** *(1947-1954)*
b Edmonton, Middx 29/12/1923
FL 91 (8), FAC 4 (-),
Walthamstow Avenue; Hayes; Watford (am, pro 10/47); Bedford Town (7/55); De Havilland, Leavesden (11/57); Fishburn (by 10/60)
A latecomer to the professional ranks, he made his League début as an amateur and scored four goals in his first three games as an inside-forward, but was later to settle down as a loyal and enthusiastic centre-half. He was also an accomplished golfer, and in 1954 won the Professional Footballers Association championship, an annual event for two decades.

G.W. (GEORGE) **NORMAN** *(1912)*
SL 8 (4)
Clapton; Watford (am 10/11)
An amateur centre-forward who represented London v Southern Counties in a trial match a year before his brief Watford first-team career, which began with a 7-1 defeat at Brighton, and then a 4-2 win (Norman 2) against Stoke a week later. Any intention to make further use of his services the following season was thwarted by his emigration to New Zealand.

Decorated in Great War

Ernest Joseph (JOE) **NORTH** *(1926-1927)*
b Burton-on-Trent, Staffs 23/9/1895
d Havant, Hants 24/8/1955
FL 6 (-)
Atlas & Norfolk, Sheffield; Arsenal (am 11/19, pro 12/19); Reading (5/22); Gillingham (7/23); Norwich City (8/24); Watford (free 6/26); Northfleet coach (cs 1927)
That handful of League appearances encompassed all three inside-forward positions. Fred Pagnam, his Watford manager, had been the senior centre-forward at Highbury when North was trying to establish himself there, after war service which brought him the Military Medal. He played First Class cricket in the 1920s, and became a Minor Counties umpire.

A short but full life

Michael Terence (MICK) **O'BRIEN** *(1931-1933)*
b Kilcock, Co Dublin 10/8/1893
d Uxbridge, Middx 21/9/1940
FL 61 (5p), FAC 10 (1p)
Walker Celtic; Wallsend; Blyth Spartans; Newcastle East End; Alloa (3/19); Brentford (5/19); Norwich City (8/19); South Shields (12/19); Queens Park Rangers (5/20); Leicester City (3/22); Hull City (£750 6/24); Brooklyn Wanderers, USA (5/26); Derby County (12/26); Walsall (6/28); Norwich City (5/29); Watford (6/31); Queens Park Rangers manager (5/33 until 4/35); Brentford assistant-manager (11/35); Ipswich Town manager (5/36 until 8/37)
IRELAND & REPUBLIC OF IRELAND FULL
A centre-half who captained his country when on Watford's books, and a devout Catholic of strong opinions who left professional football after leading Ipswich Town to the Southern League championship. He served on *HMS Chester* at the Battle of Jutland and led an extraordinarily full life until his early death following a succession of personal setbacks.

<u>*Robert* ***VIC****tor* **O'BRIEN**</u> *(1934-1946)*
b Coventry, Warwicks 1/5/1909
FL 179 (9), FAC 23 (1), 3SC 19 (1), WW2 63 (4 inc 1p)
Morris Motors; Coventry City (am 11/30, pro 2/31), <u>Watford</u> (6/34); Bedworth Town (1946 until 1951). Guested for Birmingham, Coventry City and Morris Motors in WW2.
Versatile in the extreme, he occupied every playing position as a guest player during the war, appearing even in goal for Coventry. He once scored six goals as an inside-forward for the Reserves in his first season at Vicarage Road, but later settled down at right-back. He barely missed a game in the last four peacetime seasons, and became club captain.

Versatility the keynote

<u>*Roelof Johannes Gysbertus* ***(RALPH)*** **OELOFSE**</u> *(1953-1954)*
b Lichtenburg, South Africa 12/11/1926
FL 15 (-)
Berea Park, South Africa; Chelsea (10/51); <u>Watford</u> (nearly £2,000 7/53 until cs 1954)
SOUTH AFRICA 'UNOFFICIAL'
Expressing no personal preference for either position, he was a well-built full-back or centre-half who returned home in July 1954 after nearly three seasons in English football. Watford had retained his registration and placed him on the official open-to-transfer list at £1,500. He went on to represent South Africa against both Australia and England.

Played against England

<u>*Henry Spoors* ***(HARRY)*** **OLIVER**</u> *(1948-1952)*
b Sunderland, Co Durham 16/2/1921
d Sunderland, Tyne & Wear 11/1/1994
FL 122 (2p), FAC 6 (2p)
Houghton Colliery Welfare; Hartlepools Utd (am 10/37, pro 3/38); Brentford (£1,500 5/38); <u>Watford</u> (£2,000 5/48); Canterbury City (7/52 until 10/56). Guested for Leeds Utd and York City in WW2.
ENGLAND SCHOOLS
Soon after his 17th birthday he attracted a good fee from First Division Brentford, where he spent ten years but played in only 18 peacetime League games. A big man who moved from full-back to centre-half, he endeared himself to the Vicarage Road crowd with his forthright defending. His transfer fee was paid by the club's landlords and benefactors, Benskins.

Benskins paid the fee

<u>***KEN****neth* **OLIVER**</u> *(1963-1964)*
b Pelton, Co Durham 26/11/1938
FL 58 (26), FAC 4 (2), FLC 1 (-)
Chester-le-Street Schools; Lumley Juniors; Sunderland (5/58 until cs 1959); South Shields; Barnsley (2/60); <u>Watford</u> (£5,000 7/63); Workington (part-exchange for D.Carr) 2/65); Bournemouth & Boscombe Athletic (1/67 until 1/68); Bradford City coach (by 8/70 for 3 years); Newcastle Utd

Livesey's partner

reserve-team coach (3 years); Birmingham City (youth-team coach, first-team coach 1977/8); Walsall coach (by 1980); Tottenham Hotspur youth-team coach (1982 until 1984); coach in Qatar and Saudi Arabia (3 years); Carlisle Utd trainer-coach (by 10/86); Walsall physiotherapist (briefly 4/87)
A hard-working inside-forward who provided good goalscoring support for Charlie Livesey in the unsuccessful 1963/4 promotion chase. He was first a professional at Roker Park, but dropped to a lower status before getting his League career started at Oakwell. He was finished as a player when a kneecap was removed by surgery in the summer of 1967.

Effective stand-in

Joseph Henry **ORME** *(1911-1913)*
b Staveley, Derbys 8/11/1884
d Nottingham, June 1935
SL 13 (-), SCC 1 (-)
Clay Cross Zingari (5/04); New Tupton Ivanhoe (5/06); Clay Cross Zingari (5/07); North Wingfield Red Rose (5/08); Chesterfield Town (cs 1909); Pinxton Colliery; Watford (7/11); Millwall (£100 5/13); Nottingham Forest (9/18 until cs 1921); Heanor; Shirebrook (5/22); Butterley Co Works (permit player 12/27). Guested for Notts County in WW1.
He'd moved around as a professional within a tiny Derbyshire radius before becoming Joe Webster's goalkeeping understudy, and keeping clean sheets in his first three Southern League games, spread over 15 months. He spent the summer of 1912 as a professional with Rickmansworth Cricket Club, and in 1915 was sent off in an FA Cup tie at Millwall.

First Division defender

William **(BILLY) ORR** *(1906-1907)*
b Scotland
d Glossop, Derbys 21/12/1912 (aged 37)
SL 5 (-), UL 7 (-)
Ayr Parkhouse (by 1/97); Glossop North End (3/99); Manchester City (7/01); Fulham (cs 1903); Glossop (5/04); Watford (8/06); Glossop (9/07)
He was a regular First Division full-back or half-back with both his first two English clubs, and at one time was well-known in the game for wearing a cap whilst playing. Although in the first team just before being released, he had been only a minor figure in his one Cassio Road season, his best days being by that time behind him.

John Frederick **OSBORN** *(1897)*
SL 5 (-)
Watford Wanderers (by 3/95); West Herts (by 2/97 until 11/97); Small Heath (pro 6/99 until cs 1900)
After keeping goal for the Reserves in 1896/7, he was approached by Apsley, and before giving a decision he asked the West Herts committee if he could have trial in the first team. The request was granted, but he left the district soon afterwards, having played in the club's last all-amateur XI, and also the first to include professionals.

Part Two

E.J. **OSBORNE** *(1897)*
SL (2 (-)
Brentford (2 seasons); West Herts (cs 1897)
Like his near-namesake, he played - at left-half - in the two Southern League matches which marked the end of the purely amateur era at Cassio Road and the adoption of professionalism. Apart from a few friendlies, these were his only first-team appearances. He'd joined the club from Brentford after moving to Watford for business reasons.

John (JOHNNY) **OSBORNE** *(1948-1949)*
b Renfrew 14/10/1919
d Leicester 19/9/1981
FL 34 (13), FAC 1 (-)
Linwood Thistle; Leicester City (9/38); Watford (one of four players signed for £4,750 1/48); Rugby Town (cs 1949)
Although a Filbert Street professional for more than ten years, he didn't make his League début until Leicester shipped him out as part of the five-man package deal (including one on loan). He went into the Watford team at left-half, but was to spend most of his time in the inside-forward positions. His 13 goals all came in a sequence of 15 games.

Ten-year wait

David **OVENSTONE** *(1937)*
b St Monance, Fife 20/6/1913
d Cardiff, South Glamorgan, January 1983
FL 1 (-), 3SC 1 (-)
St Monance Swifts; Rosslyn Juniors; Raith Rovers (am 6/32, pro 9/32); Queens Park Rangers (6/35); Cardiff City (5/36); Watford (free 6/37); Southport (11/37); Barry Town (3/38); Broughty Ex-service (am 6/38); Forthill Athletic (am 9/38, pro 7/39 until 8/40)
Just five months after joining the club he was on the move again, having briefly featured as a first-team winger. One of his two competitive appearances was in the divisional cup final, which had been held over from the previous season. Watford and Millwall shared the cup after two drawn games. He began and ended his career in Scotland's lower leagues.

Drawn cup final

BRIAN Ernest **OWEN** *(1963-1970)*
b Harefield, Middx 2/11/1944
FL 148+5 (17), FAC 11 (3), FLC 4+2 (-)
Hayes Schools; Watford (am 8/61, appr 9/61, pro 6/62); Colchester Utd (free 5/70); Wolverhampton Wanderers (player/coaching staff free 1/72, trainer-coach 1976/7 until 1978/9); Peterborough Utd staff (1979); coach in USA (cs 1979); Ipswich Town (youth-team manager cs 1979, reserve-team coach 1982/3); England joint youth-team physiotherapist 9/79); England Under-21 trainer (by 11/84); Crystal Palace physiotherapist (cs 1988); Watford scout (by 2/89); Colchester Utd physiotherapist (cs 1989); Luton Town (reserve-team physiotherapist 1991/2, first-team physiotherapist 1992); Cambridge Utd assistant-manager (12/92); Colchester Utd physiotherapist (cs 1993)
Loyal and dedicated, he had a long career at Watford as a

Went out at the top

strong-running winger, in spite of many spells in the Reserves. He took part in the 1970 FA Cup semi-final, and scored a spectacular freak goal a year earlier, as the club homed in on the Third Division championship. His playing career ended with a handful of appearances in the First Division.

Sent off when he returned

Michael David (MIKE) ***PACKER*** *(1968-1973)*
b Willesden, Middx 20/4/1950
FL 57+11 (2 inc 1p), FAC 6+2 (-), FLC 1 (-)
Willesden Schools; Watford (appr 7/65, pro 4/68); Crewe Alexandra (loan 3/72); Colchester Utd (free 6/73 until cs 1983); Wivenhoe Town (by 3/84)
He was a Colchester defender for a decade (during which he was sent off in a League game at Vicarage Road), having already spent eight seasons with Watford. This included three years as an apprentice after he'd won local honours as a schoolboy in London. He played in the 1970 FA Cup semi-final, but was never able to establish a permanent first-team place.

Successful trial

FREDerick William ***PACKHAM*** *(1926-1927)*
b Birmingham, Warwicks 2/10/1901
d Hendon, London 1974
FL 5 (-)
Barnet; Fulham (pro cs 1924 until cs 1926); Watford (9/26 until cs 1927); Dartford; Hendon Garage LGOC (permit player 10/28); Cricklewood Garage LGOC (permit player 3/30)
A successful trial at the beginning of 1926/7 led to his engagement after he'd played five League games in two seasons on Fulham's right wing. He doubled this total at Vicarage Road (four defeats and a draw), but played no other League football. He had a trial with Brighton & Hove Albion in August 1927, but nothing came of it.

R. ***PADLEY*** *(1903)*
SEL 1 (-)
Bushey Heath; Watford (am 12/02)
His brief flirtation with first-team football brought two good home wins. After playing centre-forward against Brighton & Hove Albion, who were beaten 6-1 in the South-Eastern League, he was retained (at outside-right) for a Good Friday friendly six days later. Kensington Town were the visitors, and went down 5-1.

Had to wait

ROBERT John ***PAGE*** *(1993-1996)*
b Llwynypia, Mid-Glamorgan 3/9/1974
FL 24+4 (-), FAC 1+1 (-)
Watford (sch 12/88, tr 7/91, pro 4/93)
WALES SCHOOLS, YOUTH and UNDER-21
A youth-international captain who began his association with Watford by travelling from South Wales during the school holidays. Although never looking inexperienced or out of his depth when selected, he was made to wait a long time for a decent first-team run. Principally a central defender, he started his League career at right-back.

FRED PAGNAM (1921-1927) - SEE PART FIVE

Long League career

Charles Anthony (**CHARLIE**) **PALMER** *(1981-1984)*
b Aylesbury, Bucks 10/7/1963
FL 10 (1), FLC 2 (-), FLT 2 (-), UEFA 4 (-)
Watford (appr 10/79, pro 7/81); Derby County (free 7/84); Hull City (£30,000 2/87); Notts County (loan 2/89, £25,000 3/89); Walsall (free 8/94)
One of the young players pressed into UEFA Cup service for Watford, he forced the own-goal which closed a two-goal deficit against Kaiserslautern in the First Round. He was then a right-back, but later in his career played in the centre of defence, gathering extensive League experience over a long period after he'd left Vicarage Road.

Won trophies

F. (**FRED**) **PALMER** *(1907-1910)*
SL 16 (-), SEL 1 (1), SCC 2 (1)
Watford (am 1907); André & Sleigh (by 1910/1); St Albans City (by 1/12)
As an amateur wing-half he had a number of first-team games alongside another unpaid player, centre-half Fred Fayers. Palmer represented the county, captained the Bushey works team, André & Sleigh, when they won the Printers & Allied Trades Cup in 1910/1, and took part in St Albans City's Spartan League championship success a year later.

First for 74 years

Stephen Leonard (**STEVE**) **PALMER** *(1995-1996)*
b Brighton, Sussex 31/3/1968
FL 35 (1), FLC 2 (-)
Cambridge University; Ipswich Town (8/89); Watford (£135,000 9/95)
After 74 years, Watford were again represented in a League game by a university blue when he was signed to improve stability in midfield. He also proved reliable as a defender. Possessing height, strength and energy, he'd captained Cambridge in his second Varsity Match, in 1989, and subsequently played Premier League football for Ipswich Town.

Stepped up with Walsall

Thomas **PANGBORN** *(1901-1902)*
b Birmingham, Warwicks 1870
d Birmingham, Warwicks 1926
SL 24 (5), FAC 2 (-)
Walsall Town Swifts (by 1891); Worcester Rovers; West Bromwich Albion (6/95); Ashton North End (10/95); Bury (10/96); Grimsby Town (8/98); Ashton North End (11/98); New Brompton (6/99); Tottenham Hotspur (5/00); Reading (2/01); Watford (8/01 until cs 1902)
He'd moved around extensively as a professional player before spending a season as Watford's inside-left, during which he scored a Christmas Day hat-trick in a friendly match. He played in Walsall's first Football League match, having joined that club when it was in the Football Alliance, and he was a First Division player with Bury.

Big-time success

Harry **HAROLD PANTLING** *(1911-1915)*
b Leighton Buzzard, Beds 16/5/1891
d Sheffield, Yorks 21/12/1952
SL 35 (-), FAC 2 (-), SCC 2 (-), WW1 2 (1)
Callow Land Juniors; Watford (am 1908, pro 7/11); Sheffield Utd (£500 5/14); Rotherham Utd (£50 8/26 until cs 1927); Heanor Town (11/27). Guested for Watford in WW1.
ENGLAND FULL
After playing at full-back and wing-half he was sold with Ashbridge as a matter of economic necessity. In 1923 he played for England, and two years later won an FA Cup-winner's medal. He saved a penalty in the first-ever game at Maine Road, Manchester, after the Sheffield United 'keeper had been injured. A roughish character, both on and off the field.

Machine-gunner

John Martin **(JACK) PAPWORTH** *(1925)*
b Deptford, London 8/11/1894
d Deptford, London 13/11/1942
FL 27 (12)
St Nicholas, Deptford; Fulham (am 2/14, pro 5/19); Watford (£150 2/25); Dartford (12/26)
Goals were in short supply when Watford bought him late in 1924/5 to fill the centre-forward berth, but he didn't score until his sixth game, the first five having produced two goals and not a single point. He'd competed with George Edmonds for a first-team place at Fulham. During the Great War he became a sergeant-major in the Machine Gun Corps.

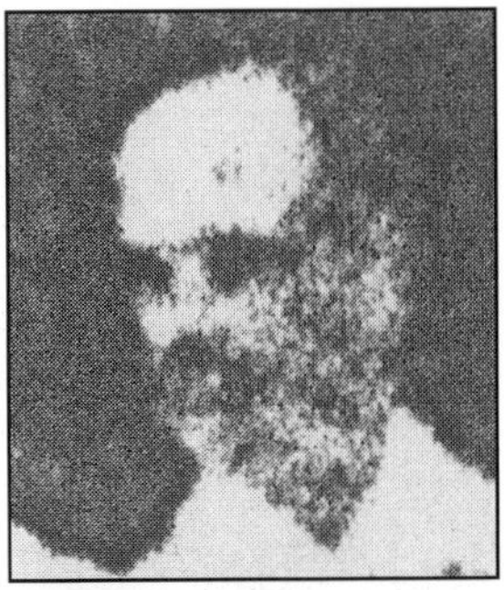
Church official

Henry James **PARIS** *(1896-1897)*
b Bromley, Kent 1876
d Watford, Herts 21/11/1947
SL 6 (-)
West Herts (by 1896)
Of his Southern League appearances. five were at full-back and the other at left-half. Four of the games were against military opposition, including two 3-0 defeats at the hands of the 1st Bn Scots Guards. He was a railway administrator with the LNWR, played cricket for the county, and was prominent in church affairs in the Watford district.

Lost record-breaking form

Richard **(DICK) PARKER** *(1927-1928)*
b Stockton-on-Tees, Co Durham 14/9/1894
d Stockton-on-Tees, Co Durham 1/1/1969
FL 13 (2), FAC 1 (1)
Norton Utd (1913/4); Thornaby Corinthians; Stockton; Sunderland (6/19); Coventry City (£1,500 1/20); South Shields (£1,000 10/20); Wallsend (1921); Queens Park Rangers (7/22); Millwall ("substantial fee" 7/24); Watford (£1,100 11/27 until cs 1928)
Spotted in army football in France, he began his League career as Sunderland's first post-war centre-forward, but was soon on his travels. Just before moving to Vicarage Road, he scored 37 League goals in a season - a Millwall record which still stands - but proved a waste of Watford's record fee, and retired whilst on the transfer list at £1,000.

*Robert (**BOB**)* **PARKINSON** *(1900-1901)*
b Preston, Lancs 27/4/1873
SL 15 (5)
Preston Ramblers; Preston Athletic; Fleetwood Rangers; Rotherham Town (12/94); Luton Town (5/95); Blackpool (5/96); Warmley (8/97); Nottingham Forest (10/98); Newton Heath (11/99); Watford (11/00); Swindon Town (cs 1901)
His brief reign as Watford's centre-forward ended when he was dropped in April 1901, the Committee announcing that they had no further need of his services. His Football League début was on Christmas Day 1894, he played in Blackpool's first League game, and he captained Warmley when they had a Southern League home goals tally of 72 for, and none against.

MARTIN **PATCHING** *(1979-1983)*
b Rotherham, Yorks 1/11/1958
FL 24+1 (3), FAC 3+1 (2), FLC 4 (1), FLT 2+1 (-)
Woverhampton Wanderers (sch 12/73, appr 7/75, pro 3/76); Watford (£100,000 12/79 until 11/83); Northampton Town (loan 1/83); Dunstable Town (2/85); Staines Town (by 10/87)
ENGLAND SCHOOLS and YOUTH
A goal at Preston in a 2-1 win was a good start to his Watford career, but injury was to curtail his midfield appearances. Returning after a long absence, he scored spectacularly against Liverpool in his last game at Vicarage Road, to help clinch second place the League, but was soon forced into retirement, although he did later play in non-League football.

Memorable home finale

*Alexander Montgomerie (**SANDY**)* **PATE** *(1965-1967)*
b Lennoxtown, Stirlingshire 15/8/1944
FL 14+1 (-)
Anniesland Waverley; Renfrew Juniors (am 12/61, pro 2/65); Watford (nearly £1,000 2/65); Mansfield Town (£2,500 10/67 until cs 1978)
He had success very early in his career, helping Anniesland Waverley to win the Scottish Juvenile Cup. Becoming a professional immediately before he moved south, he enabled Renfrew to collect a transfer fee. Having done little at Vicarage Road, he became a fixture at right-back for Mansfield, where he was ever-present in six consecutive seasons.

Rare feat at Mansfield

Robert Banting John **PATEN** *(1897)*
b St Albans, Herts 11/5/1875
d Estoril, Portugal 13/11/1948
SL 1 (1)
St Albans; West Herts (am)
Four years after making a single friendly appearance, he wrote in October 1896 to offer the club his services. The Committee picked him for a couple more friendlies, but decided not to take up the offer. Later, however, he played at outside-right in the season's final Southern League game, and only five other Watford players can match his goals-per-game ratio.

Clever Scot

Thomas (TOMMY) **PATERSON** (1952-1954)
b Lochore, Fife 3/4/1927
FL 45 (7), FAC 3 (-)
Raith Rovers (1/46); Lochgelly Albert (7/46); Leicester City (3/48); Newcastle Utd (£2,500 6/50); Watford (£750 7/52); Berwick Rangers ("small fee" 7/55 until cs 1957)
The archetypal Scottish ball-player and intelligent passer, he had a couple of First Division games for Newcastle in Milburn's heyday, before his three-season stint at Vicarage Road. Watford used him at wing-half briefly, when Frank Mitchell was injured, as well as in his more familiar inside-forward role. He made his home back on Tyneside.

John (JOHNNY) **PATON** (1952-1955) - SEE PART FIVE

Dundee survivor

James Arklay Jackson (JIM) **PATON** (1929-1930)
b Mains, Forfarshire 14/2/1903
d Dundee, Tayside 3/1/1994
FL 5 (-)
Kilmarnock (am 8/26); Dundee (am 3/28, pro 4/28); Watford (free 8/29 until cs 1930); Training Bn RE (permit player 2/31)
In a season when seven different full-back pairings were used, he played in the opening four League games at left-back before Joe Davison regained his place. His one other League appearance was in a 6-1 defeat at Fulham. Not long before his death he attended Dundee's centenary celebrations, and was believed to be that club's oldest surviving player.

Shot down over Germany

Thomas Gracie (TOMMY) **PATON** (1948-1952)
b Saltcoats, Ayrshire 22/12/1918
d Folkestone, Kent 14/12/1991
FL 141 (1), FAC 8 (-)
Ardeer Recreation (am 7/36); Wolverhampton Wanderers (pro 6/37); Swansea Town (10/38); Bournemouth & Boscombe Athletic (2/39); Watford (£1,000 1/48); Folkestone (8/52 until late 1950s); Sheffield Wednesday scout (by 9/59). Guested for Leeds Utd, Manchester City, Queens Park Rangers and Tottenham Hotspur in WW2.
Watford signed him as an inside-forward, but he settled down at wing-half and became club captain. He played his last 143 League and Cup games without scoring even once. As a wartime officer in Bomber Command he was taken prisoner after being shot down near Heidelberg. His brother captained Motherwell in the 1951 Scottish FA Cup Final.

Epitomised his era

John Richards **PAULL** (1892-1899)
b Truro, Cornwall 16/4/1869
d Truro, Cornwall 14/10/1953
SL 13 (-), FAC 6 (-), FAAC 5 (-), HSC 7 (-)
Pembroke College, Cambridge (1888); Cambridge University (until 1891); Corinthians; played in Dresden, Germany (1891/2); West Herts (1892 until 1899); also Truro in the 1890s
The epitome of the Victorian amateur, he was a highly accomplished and scrupulously fair full-back, and the club's first Southern League captain. Twice a Cambridge

blue, he returned to his *alma mater*, Aldenham, as a knuckle-rapping schoolmaster and the founder of Paull's House. He represented Herts - and Cornwall as footballer, county councillor and JP.

DEREK Richard **PAYNE** *(1994-1996)*
b Edgware, Middx 26/4/1967
FL 33+3 (1), FAC 2+1 (-), FLC 3 (-)
Middlesex Schools; Kingsbury Town; Burnham; Northwood; Hayes; Barnet (£12,000 12/88); Southend Utd (free 7/93); Watford (valued at £100,000 in exchange for K.B.L.Dublin 7/94 until cs 1996)
After making progress in the lower leagues, he was an industrious little midfield player with Barnet when they won promotion to the Football League. One of those who were given free transfers in 1993 as a result of the ludicrous financial situation at Underhill, he did the fashionable thing and rejoined manager Barry Fry at Southend.

Rose with Barnet

JOHN **PEARCE** *(1971)*
b Watford, Herts 12/12/1950
FL 0+1 (-)
Watford (am 10/67, pro 6/69 until 11/71); Wealdstone (until late 1973)
This was the briefest of all Watford careers in League football. He played in three first-team friendlies, but his only serious action was as a substitute, and it lasted eight minutes. A defender and a part-time professional, he left the club in mid-season with a cash settlement of his contract. Less than two years later his career was ended by a broken leg.

Shortest League career

GARY Kenneth **PENRICE** *(1989-1996)*
b Bristol, Glos 23/3/1964
FL 45+5 (18), FAC 4 (1), FMC 1 (1)
Bristol Rovers (sch 4/78 until 3/80); Bristol City (appr 6/80); Mangotsfield Utd; Bristol Rovers (11/84); Watford (£500,000 11/89); Aston Villa (£875,000, less 15% 'sell-on' profit to Bristol Rovers, 3/91); Queens Park Rangers (£625,000 10/91); Watford (£200,000 11/95)
Both the Bristol clubs rejected him before Rovers eventually gave him a contract. He broke new ground for a Watford player by scoring in each of his first six games, having attracted the club's second-highest outgoing transfer fee. A small, nimble and mobile forward, sharp in the penalty area, he returned to Vicarage Road after a career in the top flight.

Record start at Watford

F. **PHEBY** *(1906)*
UL 1 (-)
Chesham Generals; Wycombe Wanderers (until at least 12/09); Watford (am 10/05)
When the club competed in the South-Eastern and United Leagues, it was not unusual for a local amateur to be tested in one of these lesser competitions. Pheby's chance - and his only first-team appearance of any kind - came at outside-left in a 1-1 draw against Clapton Orient. He once scored seven goals for Wycombe Wanderers.

Transformed

KEVIN **PHILLIPS** *(1995-1996)*
b Hitchin, Herts 25/7/1973
FL 41+2 (20 inc 2p), FAC 2 (-), FLC 2 (1)
Southampton (sch 10/87, tr 7/89); Baldock Town (cs 1991); Watford (£10,000 12/94)
From the age of 12 until the end of his traineeship, he was associated with Southampton as a full-back, and it was at Baldock that he was successfully transformed into a sharp and skilful little striker. When given his first-team chance at Watford, he responded with no fewer than 21 goals in 12 months, before injury intervened.

Three Wembley finals

HAROLD James **PHIPPS** *(1952-1953)*
b Dartford, Kent 15/1/1916
FL 47 (-)
Middlesex Regiment; Charlton Athletic (am 9/42, pro 10/43); Watford (£300 5/52); Bexleyheath & Welling player-manager (free 7/54); Crystal Palace scout (1958/9). Guested for Bournemouth & Boscombe Athletic, Chelsea and Fulham in WW2.
He made his name in army football as a member of the Middlesex Regiment for 15 years from 1931, and played in Charlton's defence in three Wembley finals, one in wartime and two in the FA Cup, in which competition he got a winner's medal in 1947. He was 36 when he joined Watford, and all his appearances for the club were at centre-half.

Two in first away game

William Edward (BILL) **PICK** *(1930-1931)*
b Clay Cross, Derbys 5/6/1903
d Clay Cross, Derbys 27/8/1981
FL 26 (5), FAC 4 (-)
Danesmoor Rovers; Bury (am 12/24, pro 2/25); Lincoln City (4/26); Portsmouth (8/26); Newport County (7/27); Coventry City (for cash plus player-exchange 11/28); Watford (12/30); Barrow (for cash plus J.Wilson 7/32); Stockport County (9/33 until 10/33); Sutton Town; Danesmoor Miners' Welfare (permit player 9/35)
Signed in mid-season to strengthen the left-wing position, he soon displayed his pace and hard shooting, and scored twice at Walsall in his first away game, but was superseded the following September by another ex-Coventry man, Jack Barnes. Pick played all his League football in the two geographical sections of the Third Division.

Problem position

LESlie **PILKINGTON** *(1950-1951)*
b Darwen, Lancs 23/6/1925
FL 5 (-)
Darwen Corries; Arsenal (3/48); Watford (£350 3/50 until cs 1951)
On the field a clever and intelligent outside-right who was possibly deficient in the more physical aspects of the game, he was an amusing character off it, with a broad Lancashire accent. A product of Arsenal's scouting network, he was one of eight players tried in Watford's No 7 shirt in 1950/1, and left the club whilst transfer-listed at £500.

W. PILLON *(1907)*
SEL 1 (-)
Tufnell Park; Watford (am 12/07)
He played only once for Watford's first team - on the right wing in a 4-2 South-Eastern League defeat at Cassio Road against Clapton Orient in 1907/8. By that season the club almost invariably fielded a reserve eleven in the competition, but on this occasion seven of the team had played four days earlier in a Southern League fixture.

GEOFFrey PITCHER *(1995-1996)*
b Sutton, Surrey 15/8/1975
FL 4+9 (2), FAC 2 (-), FLC 1+1 (-)
Surrey Schools; Millwall (sch 9/90, tr 9/91, pro 3/93); Watford (£25,000 7/94 until cs 1996)
He joined Watford having spent four years at Millwall as a tenacious little midfield player, without making the first-team. After one away League appearance as a substitute for Watford, he faced his former club at Vicarage Road in a game televised live, and with a fine sense of occasion he scored the only goal of the match.

Sense of occasion

GARY Edward PLUMLEY *(1987)*
b Birmingham, Warwicks 24/3/1956
FAC 1 (-)
Leicester City (appr 8/72, pro 12/74 until 1/76); Newport County (6/76); Hong Kong football; Hereford Utd (non-contract 1982); Newport County (12/82); Happy Valley, Hong Kong; Cardiff City (8/83); Newport County (loan 8/84); Newport County (non-contract 8/85); Caerleon; Ebbw Vale; Newport County (non-contract 3/87); Watford (non-contract 4/87)
His record of having played in an FA Cup semi-final in his only Watford appearance at any level is probably unique in football history. A son of the club's chief executive, he was plucked from near-retirement and registered on non-contract forms in an injury crisis, but had an unhappy time in goal against Tottenham Hotspur, who won 4-1.

One for the pub quiz

BRIAN Edward POLLARD *(1977-1979)*
b York 22/5/1954
FL 68+3 (8), FAC 4+1 (-), FLC 8+1 (-)
York City (sch 12/69, am 9/70, pro 3/72); Watford (£30,000 11/77); Mansfield Town (£60,000 1/80); Blackpool (free 8/81); York City (free 9/81); Scarborough (free, cs 1984); Chesterfield (non-contract 9/84); Hartlepool Utd (until 2/85); North Ferriby (by 10/85); Harrogate Railway (by 9/87); Watford scout (by 2/89)
ENGLAND YOUTH
Immediately after dropping from the Second Division to the Fourth in consecutive seasons with York City, he moved in the opposite direction in successive promotions with Watford. His fast, direct wing-play, and a spectacular goal, had impressed when York won 3-1 at Vicarage Road, and he became the final piece in the Division 4 championship jigsaw.

Two down, then two up

League goal at 16

RICHARD John **POOLE** *(1976-1977)*
b Heston, Middx 3/7/1957
FL 3+4 (1), FLC 2 (-)
Brentford (appr 7/72, pro 7/75); Watford (7/76 until cs 1977)
His Watford engagement began with a trial period lasting three months, during which he made the first team. A tall, lean forward, he scored in a 4-1 win over Exeter City, to add to his only other League goal, two-and-a-half years earlier, when he was 16 years old and had over a year of his Brentford apprenticeship to run. He emigrated to France.

Eventually re-signed

William Arthur **POOLE** *(1923-1925)*
b Handsworth, Staffs 1900
FL 42 (8), FAC 1 (1)
Kidderminster Harriers; Merthyr Town (5/21); Stoke City (3/22); Watford (£250 7/23); Coventry City (9/25); Kidderminster Harriers (cs 1926); Merthyr Town (7/28); Walsall (2/32 until cs 1932)
Most of his Watford appearances were at centre-forward, but he'd been primarily a defender with his previous League clubs. He had two seasons at Vicarage Road, but was transfer-listed in March 1924, and at first declined to re-sign for 1924/5, eventually doing so in October, when he went straight back into the first team.

Hatfield's first pro

Andrew (ANDY) **PORTER** *(1960-1963)*
b Stewarton, Ayrshire 21/1/1937
FL 72 (4), FAC 5 (-), FLC 3 (-)
Darvel Juniors (am 7/55, pro 5/56); Watford (6/59); Guildford City (£1,000 5/63); Hatfield Town (cs 1966 until 1970); Sunday football
A lanky, stylish wing-half who was less than fairly treated by the Vicarage Road crowd. He was recruited from Scottish Junior football after completing his National Service, and when his Watford days were over became captain of Guildford City, and then Hatfield Town's first professional player. His career at that level was ended by a broken leg.

School-holiday trips

GARY Michael **PORTER** *(1983-1996)*
b Sunderland, Co Durham 6/3/1966
FL 358+38 (46 inc 13p), FAC 25+2 (3 inc 2p), FLC 28+2 (4), FMC 7+1 (2p), AIC 3 (-)
Watford (sch 4/80, appr 7/82, pro 3/84)
ENGLAND YOUTH and UNDER-21
Physically small, he forged an exceptionally long Watford career in midfield, and sometimes at left-back, on the strength of a football brain and the passing, shooting and dead-ball skills of a cultured left foot. He came south for school-holiday sessions from the age of 13, and at 17 was an England Youth captain with First Division experience.

MALCOLM ***POSKETT*** *(1980-1982)*
b Middlesbrough, Yorks 19/7/1953
FL 57+6 (17), FAC 5+1 (6), FLC 9 (6), FLT 2 (2)
South Bank; Middlesbrough (4/73); Hartlepool (7/74 until cs 1975); Whitby Town (1975/6); Hartlepool (£25 11/76); Brighton & Hove Albion (£60,000 plus half of 'sell-on' profit 2/78); Watford (£110,000 1/80); Carlisle Utd (£25,000 8/82); Darlington (7/85); Stockport County (1/86); Hartlepool Utd (loan 3/86); Carlisle Utd (loan 8/86, permanent transfer 9/86, player/acting-manager 11/87); Morecambe (cs 1988); Whitby Town (by 12/90); Workington (briefly, early 1991/2)
He spent most of his career with clubs at various levels in the far north of England, but it was from the south coast that this striker moved to Vicarage Road, where he was to specialise in cup-tie goals. His strike rate in League matches fell well short of that achieved in knockout competitions, and his first four goals for the club were all in the FA Cup.

Cup-tie specialist

CLIFFord George ***POWELL*** *(1988)*
b Harlesden, London 21/2/1968
FMC 0+1 (-)
Gadeside Rangers; Watford (sch 5/82, appr 7/84, pro 2/86); Hereford Utd (loan 12/87); Sheffield Utd (free 3/88 until 11/91); Doncaster Rovers (loan 3/89); Cardiff City (loan 11/89)
Before a knee injury finished his career, he played very briefly in League football as a big centre-half for each of four other clubs, but his only senior competitive action in a Watford shirt was in a cup game at Ipswich. The club treated it as a reserve-team fixture, and Powell was an extra-time substitute as a two-goal lead became a 5-2 defeat.

Extra-time sub

James (JIMMY) ***POXTON*** *(1934-1935)*
b Staveley, Derbys 2/2/1903
d Walsall, Staffs 14/12/1971
FL 23 (9 inc 2p), FAC 2 (-), 3SC 1 (1)
Eckington; West Bromwich Albion (6/24); Gillingham (part-exchange 3/28); Millwall (5/29); Watford (free 7/34); Walsall (free 5/35 until cs 1936); Shirley Town (by 3/37 until cs 1940)
An ex-miner and an experienced footballer by the time he came to Vicarage Road. He produced a useful goalscoring return for an outside-left, but lasted only half a season in the first team and was released in the summer. His earlier career included particularly good service at Millwall, where he spent most of his five years in the senior eleven.

Released despite goals

Hugh ***PRENTICE*** *(1910)*
b Scotland
SL 1 (-)
Bathgate (10/05); Broxburn Athletic (cs 1908); Dykehead (cs 1909); Armadale (cs 1910); Watford (briefly 11/10)
Already established in Scottish Junior circles, he was brought down for a trial at Cassio Road early in Harry Kent's managership, and played in a Southern League home game against Coventry City. Watford lost 0-2 and Prentice gave a very poor account of himself as leader of the attack. He was considered unworthy of further attention, and left the club.

Transfer coincidence

JOHN David **PRICE** *(1959)*
b St Pancras, London 31/12/1932
FL 22 (-), FAC 3 (-), SFC 1 (-)
Eastbourne Utd; Tottenham Hotspur (am 11/53, pro 9/54); Aldershot (1/57); Watford (exchange for W.K.Shipwright 6/59); Sittingbourne (free 7/60)
Big and strong, he played in 26 consecutive games at right-back after joining the club, but didn't appear again once Bobby Bell had regained the position. A coincidence surrounded the exchange deal with Aldershot which brought Price to Vicarage Road, he and Bill Shipwright having once been colleagues in youth football in North London.

Début goal chalked off

John Leonard (JACK) **PRICE** *(1900-1901)*
b Birmingham, Warwicks 1877
SL 26 (6), FAC 3 (3 inc 1p)
Shenstone Boys' Club; Small Heath (9/97); Watford (7/00); Doncaster Rovers (£15 to Small Heath 8/01); Stockport County (6/03 until at least cs 1905); Fulham reserve-team trainer (by 10/09)
At Small Heath he was a colleague of Tot Farnall, Micky Good and Charlie Hare, all of whom played with him at Cassio Road. He was a versatile member of the forward line throughout his one Watford season. Although he scored on his début, the game later became void when the opposition (Chatham) resigned from the Southern League in mid-season.

Brief career, big games

NEIL **PRICE** *(1982-1984)*
b Hemel Hempstead, Herts 15/2/1964
FL 7+1 (-), FAC 2 (-), FLT 0+1 (-), UEFA 2 (-)
Watford (sch 8/78, appr 7/80, pro 2/82); Plymouth Argyle (loan 2/84); Blackpool (loan 3/85 until cs 1985); Swansea City (free 7/85); Blackpool (non-contract 12/85); Wycombe Wanderers (2/86); Staines Town (by 10/88); Wealdstone (£5,000 12/89); Staines Town player-manager (6/91 until 1/92); Walton & Hersham manager (cs 1993 until 3/95); Hendon manager (11/95)
A left-back whose very brief career in senior football included a début in front of 60,000 Bulgarians, an FA Cup semi-final and Final, and a sending-off at Highbury. The Wembley game was his last for Watford as a first-team player. He had already won an FA Youth Cup winner's medal, a feat emulated by his brother Josh at Vicarage Road five years later.

Part Two

Scored only in the Cup

GEORGE **PRIOR** *(1924-1930)*
b Ashington Northumberland 2/3/1898
d Ashington, Northumberland 1977
FL 174 (-), FAC 15 (3)
Ashington; Sheffield Wednesday (2/21); Watford (part-exchange for G.Toone 8/24); Ashington (player-coach free 8/30, also groundsman from 6/31)
Playing almost entirely as a full-back, reliable and particularly sound in the tackle, he became very popular during his stay at Vicarage Road. His ability to score only in the FA Cup was due partly to a brief run at centre-forward, during which he scored in two ties. He had a brother and a son who both played in the First Division.

New Zealand success

KEITH Bernard **PRITCHETT** *(1976-1982)*
b Glasgow 8/11/1953
FL 133+7 (9 inc 6p), FAC 10 (-), FLC 18 (3 inc 1p), FLT 2+1 (-)
Wolverhampton Wanderers (4/72); Doncaster Rovers (free 7/73 until cs 1974); Queens Park Rangers (1/75); Brentford (free 7/76); Watford (£4,000 11/76); Blackpool (free 11/82 until 5/84); Mt Roskill, New Zealand (by 1986); Waitakere City, New Zealand, player-manager (by 10/89); New Zealand national coach (3/96)
Three times a free-transfer man, he then became a bargain buy for Watford, a Fourth Division club when he arrived and in the top flight when he left. A good striker of the ball, he lost and then regained the first-team left-back shirt several times. After emigrating to New Zealand he became a successful manager and a football journalist.

Top scorer for big clubs

JOHN **PROUDFOOT** *(1902)*
b Airdrie, Lanarks 27/10/1874
d Glasgow 22/4/1934
SL 12 (5), FAC 1 (-)
Partick Thistle (by cs 1893); Blackburn Rovers (2/97); Everton (5/98); Watford (5/02); Partick Thistle (9/03); Hamilton Academical (cs 1904 until cs 1905)
After representing Glasgow three times in inter-city games, he was Blackburn's and then Everton's top First Division scorer in his first two English seasons. His spell as Watford's centre-forward ended when he was suspended *sine die* for "insubordination" in December 1902. His brother David was also a pro who crossed the border.

15 games, 5 managers

CHRIStopher John **PULLAN** *(1987-1990)*
b Durham City 14/12/1967
FL 5+7 (-), FLC 1 (-), FMC 2 (-)
Beds, Bucks & Herts Schools; Watford (sch 2/86, pro 7/86 until 2/91)); Halifax Town (loan 2/89); Maidstone United (3/91 until cs 1991)
Discovered whilst playing in a schools inter-county match at Vicarage Road, he served under five managers as a stocky full-back or midfielder, but couldn't establish himself as a first-team player and was eventually released from his contract in mid-season.

Lively customer

TREVOR Anthony **PUTNEY** *(1991-1993)*
b Harold Hill, Essex 9/4/1960
FL 42+10 (2), FAC 2 (-), FLC 8 (-), FMC 1 (-), AIC 2 (-)
Havering Boys; Brentwood & Warley; Ipswich Town (6/80); Norwich City (player-exchange 6/86); Middlesbrough (£300,000 8/89); Watford (£100,000 8/91); Leyton Orient (£40,000 7/93); Colchester Utd (loan 8/94, loan 10/94, free 12/94 until cs 1995)
Under Bobby Robson he became a versatile member of the excellent Ipswich Town squad of the early 1980s. After a Middlesbrough career which was interrupted by a leg fracture, he spent two seasons at Vicarage Road as a quick-witted midfield player on the pitch, and an extremely chirpy personality off it. Another injury ended his career, at Colchester United.

Frederick Tom **PUTTERILL** *(1896-1897)*
b Brailes, Warwicks 1871
d Cheltenham, Glos 12/4/1953
SL 4 (-), FAAC 1 (1)
West Herts; Watford St Mary's (by 1/98)
One of the small band of players who turned out for the club in the FA Amateur Cup, he scored at Cheshunt in what was his first competitive game, but the home side won 5-2. His four Southern League appearances at inside-left quickly followed, and in one of them a Southall player was sent off for striking him, but they still won 4-1.

Only three younger

DAVID Allen **PYGALL** *(1956-1960)*
b Watford, Herts 23/1/1939
FL 20 (2), SFC 1 (-)
Herts Schools; Watford (groundstaff 8/54, pro 1/56); also Croxley Boys Club (10/54); Dover (8/61); Rugby Town (cs 1962); Highlands Park, South Africa (cs 1963); Bedford Town (1/67); Dunstable Town (by 4/68); Bletchley; Ringwood City, Australia (1969); retired in Australia 9/74
A delicately-skilled inside-forward, he was an England Schools trialist before joining the Vicarage Road groundstaff at 15. Less than two years later he was in the first team, and only three younger players have represented the club in a senior competitive game. He won a South African League championship medal in 1964.

Goal-merchant

Michael (MICK) **QUINN** *(1995)*
b Liverpool, Lancs 2/5/1962
FL 4+1 (-)
Derby County (appr 7/78), Wigan Athletic (9/79); Stockport County (free 7/82); Oldham Athletic (£52,000 1/84); Portsmouth (£150,000 3/86); Newcastle Utd (£680,000 8/89); Coventry City (£250,000 11/92); Watford (loan 3/95); Thessoloniki, Greece (free, cs 1995)
Heavy and unathletic even in his prime as a successful hitman with no fewer than 230 Football League goals to his credit, he was clearly a spent force when brought to Watford on loan, on Premier League wages. The lack of a competent senior striker had long been evident, and Quinn, like others before him, was unable to provide adequate temporary cover.

Andrew Thomson **RALSTON** *(1905)*
b Trodigal, Argyllshire 26/3/1880
d Ealing, Middx 31/1/1950
SL 2 (1)
London Caledonians (player for 25 years until early 1920s, hon secretary for 20 years); Watford (am, cs 1904); also Civil Service (by 9/04); Southend Utd (am 12/11). Guested for Tottenham Hotspur in WW1.
Born to a Kintyre farming family, he moved south and began a very long association with London Caledonians, also representing both Herts and London. For Watford he played right-back against Tottenham Hotspur, whom he represented in over a hundred wartime games, and at right-half against Brighton & Hove Albion, when he scored in a 5-1 win.

Spurs wartime stalwart

CRAIG Darren **RAMAGE** *(1994-1996)*
b Derby 30/3/1970
FL 89+4 (24 inc 3p), FAC 7 (-), FLC 7 (2)
Derby Schools; Chesopeke; Derby County (sch 11/84, tr 2/87, pro 7/88); Wigan Athletic (loan 2/89); Watford (£90,000 2/94)
ENGLAND UNDER-21
A creative attacking player and, although frustratingly capricious, the club's purest natural talent of the 1990s. He was held back by knee-ligament operations at the Baseball Ground - so much so that, on joining Watford when nearly 24, he had made barely 50 Football League appearances. He had nevertheless been capped three times at Under-21 level.

Natural talent

John Edward **RAND** *(1926-1927)*
b Cockfield, Co Durham 19/6/1902
d New Ollerton, Notts 3/6/1970
FL 6 (-)
Cockfield Albion; Everton (am 4/25, pro 5/25); Watford (free 8/26 until cs 1927); Flint (10/27); Connah's Quay (8/28); Darlington (6/29); Scarborough (7/30); West Stanley (8/32)
He came to Vicarage Road on trial after being released by Everton, and was signed on between the two pre-season public trial games. Picked for only a handful of first-team games at inside-right, he was well among the goals soon afterwards at Flint, for whom he scored 38 times in a season. He also played club cricket to a good standard.

Andrew George (ANDY) **RANKIN** *(1971-1979)*
b Bootle, Lancs 11/5/1944
FL 299 (-), FAC 13 (-), FLC 17 (-)
Everton (am 5/61, pro 10/61); Watford (£12,500 11/71); Huddersfield Town (loan 12/79, free 1/80 until cs 1982)
ENGLAND UNDER-23
Only Skilly Williams kept goal more often for Watford and, like Williams, he won the full-hearted approval of the home spectators. His peak moment was an astounding save which secured a League Cup victory at Old Trafford. Before moving to Vicarage Road he'd made 85 First Division appearances and won an Under-23 cap against Wales.

Second only to Skilly

Watford v Portsmouth, 1907.
The period charm of Cassio Road and its Victorian pavilion contrasts sharply with the multi-million-pound developments at Vicarage Road (below). The move took place in 1922, and a privileged band of 20 players represented the club on both grounds in senior competitive matches:
G.H. Barnes, H. Bellamy, W. Carter, W.J. Coutanche, G.H. Cutts, G.W.N. Edmonds, F.J. Gregory, F. Horsman, J. Johnson, W. Marshall, A.E.P. Mummery, F. Pagnam, R. Slade, F.W. Smith, J. Strain, G. Toone, E.E. Wallington, C.W. White, J.T. Wilkinson and R.G. Williams.

International caps awarded to Watford players were once few and far between, but this group all got the call in 1982/3. BACK - **Graham Taylor** *(England Youth manager); MIDDLE ROW -* **Kenny Jackett** *(Wales),* **Derick Williams** *(England Youth),* **Gerry Armstrong** *(Northern Ireland); FRONT ROW -* **Nigel Callaghan** *(England Under-21),* **Luther Blissett** *(England),* **John Barnes** *(England),* **Gary Porter** *(England Youth).*

Six years after they'd shared 4th Division status with Halifax Town, Newport County and Southport, Watford took on more exotic opponents in the UEFA Cup. In action here during the 3rd Round home leg against Sparta Prague, **Steve Sims** *(right) prepares to flick on a left-wing corner, while* **John Barnes** *loiters behind him, with intent.*

*Watford-born **Kenny Jackett**'s long unbroken association with the club was rewarded by his appointment as team manager in May 1996. None of his predecessors had been born in the town - or, indeed, anywhere in the whole of Hertfordshire. The only five previous managers of anything like 'local' origin were John Goodall (born Westminster), Len Goulden (Homerton), Mike Keen (High Wycombe), Dave Bassett (Wembley), Steve Perryman (Ealing) and Glenn Roeder (Woodford).*

***Maurice Johnston** was seldom out of the news for long, for a variety of reasons which were by no means all connected with football. Neverthe-less, his goalscoring panache brought him the only Full caps ever awarded by the Scottish FA to a player on Watford's books. Other Full international honours have been bestowed on the club by Wales (to 8 different players), Northern Ireland (4), England and the Republic of Ireland (2 each), and Canada and the USA (1 each) -* *SEE PART SIX.*

Watford's progress to the 1984 FA Cup Final focused attention on the goalscoring partnership of ***Maurice Johnston*** *and* ***George Reilly****, who headed the semi-final winner. Here he takes a tumble at Wembley. The other Watford players are 18-year-old* ***Lee Sinnott*** *(left) and Johnston.*

More Cup Final action, with ***Nigel Callaghan*** *(yellow shirt) disputing possession with John Bailey. The other Everton player is* ***Kevin Richardson****, later transferred to Vicarage Road. The familiar protective headband of* ***Steve Terry*** *can be seen in the background.*

David James *looked set to start the 1990/1 season as Watford's No 2 goalkeeper, with no League experience, but was unexpectedly promoted to the first team. He missed only three games in two seasons, and was then the subject of a major transfer to Liverpool. He is one of six goalies who have won international caps at various levels whilst on Watford's books, the others being Pat Jennings, Tony Meola, Simon Sheppard, Mike Walker and Derick Williams.*

Well-versed in the requirements of top-class football at both club and international level, the cool and experienced **John McClelland** *was an immediate and outstanding success when signed to bring order to a struggling First Division defence in 1984. As a Watford player he won 20 Full caps for Northern Ireland, a total exceeded by only Kenny Jackett (31 for Wales), John Barnes (31 for England) and Gerry Armstrong (21 for Northern Ireland).*

Cold statistics can be used in two ways to illustrate the athletic ***Paul Furlong****'s value to Watford. His 41 goals made him comfortably the top scorer in his two Vicarage Road seasons, and the transfer to Chelsea brought the club a profit of more than £2 million. Before becoming a full-time footballer, he had won England Semi-Professional honours, a distinction he shares with Tony Agana, Steve Butler, Andy Hessenthaler and Roger Willis.*

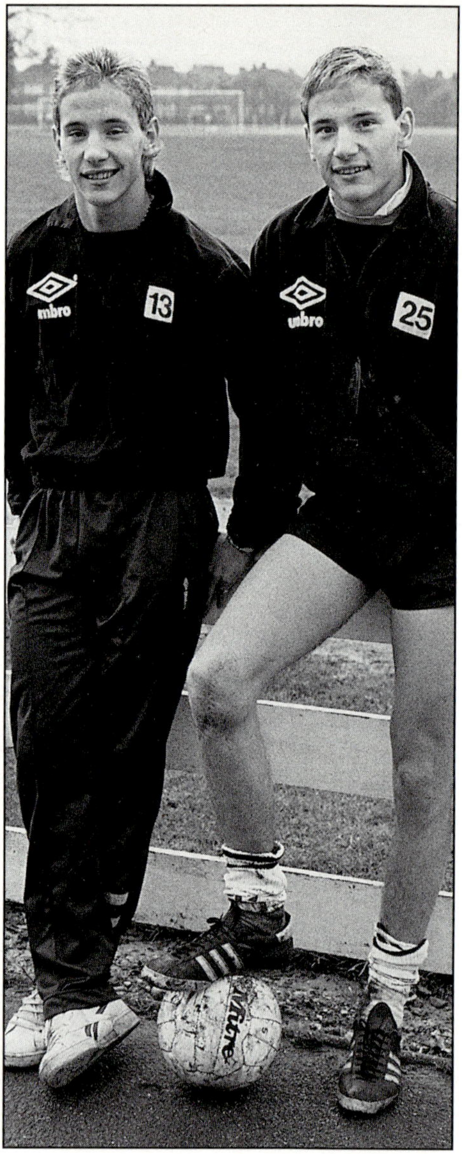

In January 1996 the ***Holdsworth twins*** *made FA Cup history when they were in direct opposition in a 3rd Round tie -* ***David*** *at centre-half for Watford and* ***Dean*** *as Wimbledon's centre-forward. Eleven years earlier they had both been members of the Watford team which reached the FA Youth Cup Final. Here they're seen relaxing during the 1986/7 season, when they became full professionals at Vicarage Road. David, the elder by 40 minutes, is on the left.*

No one has ever played in Watford's first team in more consecutive peacetime seasons than **Gary Porter**, *a survivor of seven changes of manager. Only seven other players have made over four hundred senior competitive appearances for the club - Luther Blissett, Duncan Welbourne, Tommy Barnett, Arthur Woodward, Kenny Jackett, Johnny Williams and Wilf Rostron. (This milestone was also passed by both Charlie White and Taffy Davies, if their wartime appearances are included.)*

Nigel Gibbs*'s Vicarage Road career petered out horribly following a serious injury sustained in 1992, soon after he became club captain, having made the No 2 shirt his own. He had been been associated with the club continuously since training sessions which began when he was 12 years old. He's one of 24 players who have become youth internationals whilst on Watford's books, and one of 15 to do so at Under-21 level -* *SEE PART SIX.*

Andy Hessenthaler *played at international level as a semi-professional, and didn't become a full-time footballer until he was 26. His battling, muck-and-nettles approach in midfield, and a rare ability to sustain the effort for 90 minutes, brought him the Watford captaincy.*

After being rejected by Southampton at 17, **Kevin Phillips** *was converted by Baldock Town from full-back to striker. At Watford he responded to a second chance of a full-time career with 21 first-team goals within a year of his début. The club had paid only £10,000 for his signature.*

Cost money at 39

Beaumont (BILL) **RATCLIFFE** *(1945-1949)*
b Barnburgh, Yorks 24/4/1909
FL 24 (-), FAC 1 (-), WW2 1 (-)
Bolton Albion; Bradford Park Avenue (am 12/30); New Brighton (10/31); Oldham Athletic (6/35); Reading (5/46); Watford (£750 5/48); Runcorn player-manager (6/49). Guested for Arsenal, Chester, New Brighton, Reading, Southport, Tranmere Rovers and Watford in WW2.
Having first played League football for New Brighton 17 seasons earlier, he cost what was, in the 1940s, a tidy sum for a 39-year-old, and gave the club barely half a season as the first-team pivot. Eddie Hapgood, the Watford manager who signed him, had met him in the RAF during the war, before Ratcliffe was wounded and captured in Italy.

Hit by injury

Charles Robert (CHARLIE) **RATTRAY** *(1934-1935)*
b Fleetwood, Lancs 11/5/1911
d Fleetwood, Lancs 1/10/1995
FL 19 (-), FAC 3 (1), 3SC 4 (-)
Fleetwood Windsor Villa; Blackpool (11/29); Watford (undisclosed fee 6/34); Mansfield Town (6/36); Port Vale (5/37); Accrington Stanley (6/38 until cs 1939); Fleetwood (by 1/40)
After beginning his League career in the First Division, he became Watford's senior right-winger as soon as he joined the club, but injury cost him his place, and he regained it only very briefly before spending his second season in obscurity. He'd been employed in the Fleetwood fishing industry prior to taking up football professionally.

William **RAY** *(1897-1898)*
SL 20 (10)
Macclesfield; Burslem Port Vale (1/94 until cs 1895); West Herts (10/97 until cs 1898)
One of the club's earliest professionals, he helped to achieve third place in the Southern League Second Division as the regular inside-right. His useful goals return owed much to a burst of five in the last three games, including an away hat-trick in a 6-1 win against Old St Stephens, and he claimed a further 15 in no fewer than 21 first-team friendlies.

Ernest (ERNIE) **READING** *(1904-1905)*
SL 6 (-), SEL 4 (1)
Chesham Generals (by 11/99); Chesham Town (cs 1899); Watford (2/04 to cs 1905)
The club lost all his Southern League games, but he had a better time in the South-Eastern League against Eastbourne Old Town, who were beaten 10-0. Having been fined 10/- for failing to turn up for a reserve-team match in November 1904, he repeated the offence on Boxing Day. The Committee demanded a doctor's certificate, which he subsequently produced. He played at both centre-forward and outside-right.

Dramatic scoring feat

NEIL David **REDFEARN** *(1988-1989)*
b Dewsbury, Yorks 20/6/1965
FL 24+2 (4), FAC 6 (3 inc 1p), FLC 1 (-), FMC 3 (-)
Yorkshire Schools; Nottingham Forest (appr 7/81 until 2/82); Bolton Wanderers (6/82); Lincoln City (loan 3/84, £8,250 8/84); Doncaster Rovers (£20,000 8/86); Crystal Palace (£85,000 7/87); Watford (£150,000 11/88); Oldham Athletic (£100,000 1/90); Barnsley (loan 9/91, £180,000 10/91)
A strong, tenacious midfield player with a good shot and a good scoring record. He's very probably the only player in

FA Cup history to have scored with his team's first kick of the match, which he did direct from a free-kick for Watford in a tie against Newcastle United. His father had a useful career as a lower-divisions player with northern clubs.

Became a golf pro

ALFred George **REED** *(1935-1939)*
b Exeter, Devon 21/3/1910
d Exeter, Devon 1/11/1961
FL 126 (5), FAC 7 (-), 3SC 12 (-), WW2 2 (-)
Friernhay; Llanelly; Lovells Athletic; Charlton Athletic (6/33); Watford (6/34 until 5/46). Guested for Torquay Utd in WW2
He enjoyed the best period in the club's pre-war history, fourth place in the Third Division (South) being achieved in each of his three seasons as a first-team wing-half. He was over six feet tall and had a powerful long-range shot. A keen golfer, he became a professional, but later had a leg amputated as a result of a war wound.

Foiled by David James

MELvyn John **REES** *(1987-1988)*
b Cardiff, Glam 25/1/1967
d Derby 30/5/1993
FL 3 (-), FAC 1 (-), FMC 1 (-)
Cardiff City (sch 3/81 until 6/82); Plymouth Argyle (sch 12/82); Cardiff City (non-contract 8/83, pro 9/84); Watford (£63,000 7/87); Crewe Alexandra (loan 8/89); Southampton (loan 11/89); Leyton Orient (loan 1/90); West Bromwich Albion (£45,000 9/90); Norwich City (loan 1/92); Sheffield Utd (£25,000 3/92 until death); Chesterfield (loan 1/93)
WALES YOUTH
After three years understudying Tony Coton he seemed set for a first-team run in goal when Coton was transferred, but was suddenly superseded by the young David James, and soon left the club. Before he was 21 he'd played in all four divisions of the League. Having fought off one attack of cancer, he succumbed to a recurrence at the age of 26.

Six in a row

James (JIMMY) **REID** *(1905-1906)*
b Bellshill, Lanarks, circa 1880
SL 19 (7), FAC 3 (2), SEL 4 (1), UL 9 (6)
Hibernian (8/98); Burslem Port Vale (7/99); West Ham Utd (6/00); Gainsborough Trinity (6/01); Worksop (7/02); Notts County (5/03); Watford (5/05); Tottenham Hotspur (5/06); Reading (during 1907/8); New Brompton (8/08); Worksop Town (cs 1910)
Early in his one Watford season he scored in each of six successive competitive appearances, and eventually signed off with two against Millwall. He'd played in the First Division in both Scotland and England, and became Tottenham's leading Southern League scorer in 1906/7.

JOHN **REID** *(1956)*
b Edinburgh 23/7/1935
FL 1 (1)
Tranent Juniors (2/52); Airdrieonians (8/54); Watford (loan 12/56 until 4/57); Norwich City (6/58); Barrow (7/59 until 1960)

A happy Christmas

Signed on loan after being recommended by National Service colleague Jimmy Strain (they were stationed at RAF Uxbridge), he played outside-right and scored on Christmas Day, but chose not to play in the return game at Ipswich on Boxing Day, preferring to be at home with his young bride, and didn't play in the first team again. He later served in the Scottish Police for 30 years.

Played for Lge champions

Michael James (MICKY) ***REID*** *(1952-1953)*
b Wolverhampton, Staffs 7/8/1927
d Portsmouth, Hants 10/4/1975
FL 19 (8)
Wolverhampton Wanderers (am 11/47, pro 2/48); Bournemouth & Boscombe Athletic (2/49); Portsmouth (7/50); Watford (£1,000 12/52); Yeovil Town (7/53); Bedford Town (by 3/57); Poole Town (1957/8)
A centre-forward signed in mid-season, he displaced Cyril Thompson and got off to a bad start with a 5-1 defeat away to Bristol City, but then scored in each of his first three home games. For a man who in 1950/1 played in the First Division for the reigning champions, his career total of only 29 Football League appearances is surprising.

Header ensured big day

GEORGE Gerard ***REILLY*** *(1983-1985)*
b Bellshill, Lanarks 14/9/1957
FL 46+2 (14), FAC 8 (4), FLC 5 (1)
Corby Town; Northampton Town (6/76); Cambridge Utd (£140,000 10/79); Watford (£90,000 8/83); Newcastle Utd (£200,000 2/85); West Bromwich Albion (£150,000 12/85); Cambridge Utd (free 7/88); Barnet (3/89 until 2/90); Alvechurch (12/90); Cambridge City (by 3/92)
Having left Scotland in infancy, he developed as a player in Northamptonshire before embarking on a League career as a beanpole centre-forward. The transfer fee received by Northampton was then a Fourth Division record, and it was not broken until Richard Hill joined Watford from the same club. He scored the goal which took Watford to Wembley.

Ajax coach for decades

John (JACK) ***REYNOLDS*** *(1907-1908)*
b Manchester, Lancs 23/9/1881
d Amsterdam, Netherlands 8/11/1962
SL 27 (4), FAC 1 (-), SEL 1 (-)
Manchester City (5/02); Burton Utd (5/03); Grimsby Town (4/04); Sheffield Wednesday (£275 6/05); Watford (5/07); New Brompton (5/08); Rochdale (cs 1911); coach in Switzerland (1912); Ajax, Netherlands, coach (1918 until 1948)
He was Watford's principal right-winger in 1907/8. His 30 years as Ajax coach - they were champions five times in the Thirties - were interrupted when he was interned in a camp in Germany for four-and-a- half years, during which he was erroneously reported to have died. A brother played for Manchester City, Burton United and Grimsby Town, as did Jack.

*Joseph William (**JOE**)* ***REYNOLDS*** *(1930)*
b Leicester 25/12/1906
d Leicester, January 1993
FL 6 (-)
Luton Town (11/27); Watford (free 8/29 until cs 1931); Market Harborough (10/31)
Almost entirely a reserve-team player at Kenilworth Road, he had just a couple of League games in almost two seasons there. His first two months with Watford were a trial period, and it was in his second season that he made his half-dozen Third Division (South) appearances, all at right-half. His début saw his former employers beaten 1-0.

Pleasing début result

PATrick James ***RICE*** *(1980-1984)*
b Belfast 17/3/1949
FL 112 (1), FAC 10 (-), FLC 9 (-), FLT 5 (-), UEFA 0+1 (-)
Arsenal (am 7/64, appr 12/64, pro 3/66); Watford (£20,000 11/80); Arsenal (youth-team coach 7/84, joint-first-team coach 4/96)
NORTHERN IRELAND YOUTH, UNDER-23 & FULL
His influential captaincy from right-back, based on vast experience with Arsenal and in 49 Full international appearances, contributed greatly to Watford's advance to, and immediate success in, the First Division. His Highbury career encompassed an FA Youth Cup win, the Football League and FA Cup double, and (as captain) a second FA Cup win.

Had done it all

*David (**DAVE**)* ***RICHARDS*** *(1931-1933)*
b Wolverhampton, Staffs 1/10/1896
d Hammersmith, London 25/6/1971
FL 35 (-), FAC 8 (-)
Larkhall Thistle; Port Vale (8/22); Dundee Utd (7/23); Luton Town (5/25); Watford (free 5/31); Queens Park Rangers trainer (6/33); Chelmsford City trainer (8/39); Brentford trainer (8/50)
Heftily-built full-backs were once the norm, and Richards was exactly that. English-born but raised in Lanarkshire, he joined Dundee United when they entered the Scottish League, and led them to the Second Division title. He also captained Luton for six years. He was a qualified masseur, and a trained singer who ran concert parties.

Led Luton for six years

IAN Paul ***RICHARDSON*** *(1983-1985)*
b Ely, Cambs 9/5/1964
FL 5+3 (2), FLC 1+1 (-), UEFA 5 (3)
Watford (sch 6/79, appr 7/80, pro 5/82); Blackpool (loan 12/82); Rotherham Utd (loan 2/85); Chester City (£15,000 11/85); Scunthorpe Utd (£15,000 10/86); Staines Town (free, cs 1989); Stevenage Borough (loan by 10/89); St Albans City (10/90)
A lightweight, pacy forward, he achieved instant but fleeting fame through television coverage of his senior début, in which he scored twice to help overturn a two-goal UEFA Cup deficit against Kaiserslautern. He'd been runner-up in the 100 metres in the national schools championships at the age of 15, and helped Watford to win the FA Youth Cup.

Dream start

Patience rewarded

J.W. (JACK) **RICHARDSON** *(1897-1909)*

SL 166 (2), FAC 16 (3), BCCL 2 (1), SEL 11 (-), UL 22 (2)

West Herts (am 1895, pro 10/99); Canadian football

He became a popular warhorse of a player who, after nine years with scarcely a look-in (originally as an amateur), amassed more Southern League appearances for the club than anyone except Charlie White and Billy Biggar, featuring mainly at left-half. He later represented Toronto, where he was a business associate of Harold Pantling's brother.

String of honours

KEVIN **RICHARDSON** *(1986-1987)*

b Newcastle-upon-Tyne, Northumberland 4/12/1962

FL 39 (2), FAC 7 (-), FLC 3 (-), FMC 1 (-)

Everton (sch 7/78, appr 5/79, pro 12/80); Watford (£225,000 9/86); Arsenal (£250,000 8/87); Real Sociedad, Spain (£750,000 6/90); Aston Villa (£450,000 7/91); Coventry City (£300,000 2/95)

ENGLAND FULL

His eleven months at Vicarage Road were a relatively low-key interlude in a career which brought a string of honours in the three major domestic competitions and the European Cup Winners Cup - and an England cap at the age of 31. An unspectacular but astute support player in midfield, he was in the Everton team which beat Watford at Wembley.

Scottish Cup Final goal

LEE *James* **RICHARDSON** *(1989-1990)*

b Halifax, Yorks 12/3/1969

FL 40+1 (1), FAC 1 (-), FLC 1+1 (-)

Halifax Town (sch 4/85, tr 8/86, pro 7/87); Watford (£175,000 2/89); Blackburn Rovers (£250,000 including A.J.Kennedy in part-exchange 7/90); Aberdeen (£150,000 9/92); Oldham Athletic (£325,000 8/94)

After beating his older brother into League football at Halifax, he was announced by Steve Harrison as an investment for the future when he came to Vicarage Road. Nevertheless he spent most of his time with the club in the first team. A midfield player, he scored Aberdeen's only goal in the 1993 Scottish FA Cup Final, which Rangers won 2-1.

Finished at 22

FRED*erick William* **RIDDELL** *(1908-1909)*

b Newhall, Derbys 1887

d Nottingham 16/10/1959

SL 6 (-)

Newhall Swifts; Derby County (5/07); Watford (8/08); Norwich City (5/09 until cs 1910); scout for a succession of clubs under Major Frank Buckley

During his Baseball Ground days he collected a winner's medal in the Derbyshire Senior Cup (South Division) and made three Football League appearances. He was reported to have refused Derby's offer of renewed terms before joining Watford as a versatile attacking player. His career ended when he sustained a broken leg whilst with Norwich City.

Thomas (TOMMY) **RIGG** *(1946-1948)*
b Bedlington, Northumberland 20/2/1920
FL 80 (-), FAC 5 (-)
Middlesbrough (2/39); Watford (6/46); Consett (free, cs 1949); Gillingham (8/51); Gateshead trainer (cs 1956); Ashington physiotherapist (by 1982 until at least 1984). Guested for Arsenal, Bournemouth & Boscombe Athletic and Southampton in WW2.
Watford's first post-war Football League goalkeeper and a relative of Jimmy Kelly, he stayed until 1949 and then declined to sign for a fourth winter, whereupon he was released and returned to the North-East. Two seasons in non-League football were followed by five years with Gillingham, for whom he played nearly two hundred times in the Third Division (South).

Career revived by Gills

STUART *Alan* **RIMMER** *(1988)*
b Southport, Lancs 12/10/1964
FL 10 (1), FLC 0+1 (1)
Everton (sch 2/79, appr 5/81, pro 10/82); Hamilton, New Zealand (loan); Chester City (loan 1/85, £10,000 plus half of 'sell-on' profit 3/85); Watford (£205,000 3/88); Notts County (£200,000 11/88); Walsall (£150,000 1/89); Barnsley (£150,000 3/91); Chester City (£150,000 8/91); Rochdale (loan 9/94); Preston North End (loan 12/94)
ENGLAND YOUTH
A nippy striker who had few chances at Watford. He's the only player to have hit a hundred League goals for Chester, for whom he scored four away from home on his 21st birthday. In his first two games for Walsall he missed a penalty at home (they lost 7-0 to Chelsea) and then scored a hat-trick at Sunderland to end Walsall's run of 15 League defeats.

Crazy start at Walsall

ALEXander Watson **RITCHIE** *(1933-1934)*
b Airdrie, Lanarks 2/4/1904
d Mossend, Lanarks 13/7/1954
FL 17 (3)
Fauldhouse Utd; Airdrieonians (9/22); Armadale (4/23); St Bernards (5/23); Raith Rovers (5/23); Peebles Rovers (8/23); Raith Rovers (12/23); Dunfermline Athletic (3/26); Raith Rovers (5/26); Blackpool (7/28); Reading (3/31); Watford (6/33); Bournemouth & Boscombe Athletic (8/34); Third Lanark (6/35); Hibernian (free 8/36 until cs 1937); Albion Rovers (9/37 until 10/37); Reading scout in Scotland (1938)
In his two full Reading seasons he comfortably outscored Frank McPherson, who'd hit 55 goals in 61 League games in his first spell as a Watford player. The pair then moved to Vicarage Road together, and Ritchie began and ended the season as the first-team right-winger. He'd been a forward with Blackpool when they first got into the First Division.

Outscored McPherson

Golf-club captain

Robert (BOB) **RITCHIE** (1949)
b Glasgow 1/2/1920
FL 1 (-)
Rickmansworth Town; Watford (2/48); Margate (free 8/50); Leavesden Hospital (permit player 9/52)
His only first-team game of any kind was at inside-left when Watford suffered a 3-1 defeat away to Port Vale in January 1949. He'd made his name locally before becoming a part-time professional, and had played army football in the western desert and in Germany. He was elected captain of Rickmansworth Golf Club in 1956.

Just two substitutions

ALAN Desmond **RIVERS** (1967)
b Portsmouth, Hants 27/1/1946
FL 0+2 (-)
Luton Town (am 10/61, appr 11/62, pro 1/64); Watford (7/67 until cs 1968); Crewe Alexandra (12/71 until 1/72); Rangers, South Africa (3 years)
On completion of his Kenilworth Road apprenticeship he spent two-and-a-half seasons as a full professional, and played in Luton's defence on 30 occasions in the Football League. His only senior experience for Watford in competitive football was in the No 12 shirt - in a 2-1 win at Tranmere Rovers and a 1-0 defeat at Brighton & Hove Albion.

Headlines at 18

IWAN Wyn **ROBERTS** (1986-1990)
b Bangor, Caernarvonshire 26/6/1968
FL 42+23 (9), FAC 1+6 (-), FLC 6+2 (3), FMC 3 (-)
Watford (tr 5/85, pro 7/86); Huddersfield Town (£240,000 8/90); Leicester City (£300,000 11/93)
WALES YOUTH, 'B' and FULL
At the age of 18 he hit the headlines with a winner against Manchester United. A striker with a good balance of skill, strength and mobility, he scored freely for Huddersfield to earn a second chance in the higher divisions. In 1988 he scored twice for Watford Reserves at Ipswich, and did the same for the first team at the same ground four days later.

Ten years on the move

Joseph (JOE) **ROBERTS** (1926-1927)
b Tranmere, Cheshire 2/9/1900
d Watford, Herts 9/3/1984
FL 20 (5)
Oswestry Town; Watford (8/26); Queens Park Rangers (free 5/27); York City (8/28); Halifax Town (6/29); Southport (3/30); Clapton Orient (5/31); Luton Town (8/32); Millwall (12/32); Barrow (7/33); Luton Town (cs 1934); Cardiff City (8/35); Worcester City (8/36)
Nearly 26 when he entered League football, he then roamed extensively in the next ten years and acquired a remarkable sequence of employers, mostly at Third Division level. His five League goals as Watford's outside-left included three in two games against Swindon Town. He later had a newsagents business in Vicarage Road.

Thomas (TOMMY) ***ROBERTS*** *(1954)*
b Liverpool, Lancs 28/7/1927
FL 1 (-)
Skelmersdale Utd; Blackburn Rovers (12/51); Watford (12/54); Chester (2/56 until 6/56)
A left-back who proved a great disappointment after going straight into the first team on signing for Watford, having impressed as a guest player in a friendly game against Liverpool. He was dropped immediately and didn't get another chance. In three years at Blackburn he'd had a few Second Division games as understudy to England's Bill Eckersley.

Quickly out of favour

Leonard Verdun (LEN) ***ROBERTSON*** *(1946)*
b Middlesbrough, Yorks 1/3/1916
d Cleveland 1979
FL 6 (2), WW2 3 (-)
Hartlepools Utd (am 5/44, pro 8/45); Watford (6/46); Bradford City (free 3/47); Hull City (free 4/47); Accrington Stanley (7/48 until 7/49). Guested for Grimsby Town, Southport and Watford in WW2.
Signed after playing as a guest late in 1945/6, he was an inside-forward in Watford's first post-war Football League games. He scored the club's first peacetime League goal for more than seven years, but it wasn't enough to stop Queens Park Rangers taking both points. He was soon in the Reserves, and returned north before the end of the season.

FREDerick Charles ***ROBINS*** *(1894-1899)*
b Gravesend, Kent 15/6/1872
d Hythe, Kent 5/2/1927
SL 46 (2), FAC 8 (1), FAAC 5 (-), HSC 4 (-), BCCL 6 (1p)
Faversham; Sittingbourne (1891 until 1893); West Herts (1/94 until 10/99, joint hon secretary 4/01, hon secretary); also Luton Town (am 3/94); also Crouch End (1894 until 1896); also Northfleet (1895/6); also London Caledonians (1896/7 and 1897/8); also Gravesend; Southern League management committee (5/09 until WW1)
It was a teaching appointment at the London Orphan (later Reed's) School that brought him to Watford. He retired with a knee injury early in his third season as the club's centre-half and captain. After war service in France as an officer in the RASC he returned to Kent. He married Charlotte Grover, sister of the club's founder.

Player and administrator

E. ***ROBINSON*** *(1913)*
b circa 1891
SL 1 (-)
Hebburn Argyle; Watford (5/12 until cs 1913)
Sturdily built, he had just completed a shipyard appenticeship and was said to be coveted by other clubs when Harry Kent signed him as a promising centre-half after a season of North-Eastern League football in which he'd played especially well against Newcastle United Reserves. In the first team at Cassio Road he played just once, in mid-season.

Picked only once

Strong-man in reserve

REGinald **ROBINSON** *(1937-1938)*
b Sheffield, Yorks 11/2/1910
d Scunthorpe, Lincs 17/3/1993
FL 2 (-), 3SC 5 (-)
Scunthorpe & Lindsey Utd; Huddersfield Town (am 6/33, pro 9/33); Exeter City (6/35); Watford (exchange for W.Brown 6/36 until cs 1939)
All his first-team action as a Watford player was during the second of his three seasons with the club, when he played in all three half-back positions. The possessor of a good physique, he'd been Exeter's regular centre-half, but Jimmy Armstrong's form kept him in the Reserves at Vicarage Road. He was an uncle of the well-known referee, Maurice Fussey.

Mysterious loan spell

MARK Andrew **ROBSON** *(1989)*
b Newham, London 22/5/1969
FL 1 (-)
Exeter City (appr 8/85, pro 12/86); Tottenham Hotspur (£50,000 7/87); Reading (loan 3/88); Watford (loan 10/89); Plymouth Argyle (loan 12/89); a Scandinavian club (loan); Exeter City (loan 1/92); West Ham Utd (free 8/92); Charlton Athletic (£125,000 11/93)
A frail-looking winger, but sparky and skilful. He had little opportunity to show these attributes when he became Watford's first loan player for 12 years, being mysteriously pulled off at half-time in his first game and never picked again. A career littered with temporary transfers and injury problems eventually blossomed at West Ham.

GLENN Victor **ROEDER** *(1989-1991)* - *SEE PART FIVE*

The first League goal

PETER Mann **RONALD** *(1914-1921)*
b Walker, Northumberland 5/11/1889
d Watford, Herts 21/4/1953
SL 70 (19), FL 29 (10), FAC 3 (-), SCC 1 (-)
Hebburn Argyle; Watford (unspecified fee 6/14); Nottingham Forest (£500 6/21); West Stanley (cs 1923); Watford (Reserves 1924/5, assistant-trainer 8/25 until 6/46)
A Southern League championship medal came his way within a year of his arrival as a clever inside-right, and he eventually attracted a useful fee from Nottingham Forest, in whose first team he played only occasionally. He scored Watford's first Football League goal, and on leaving the club in 1946 was awarded £50 in recognition of his long service.

Captain in 1946/7

Robert (BOBBY) **ROSS** *(1943-1947)*
b Glasgow 2/2/1917
FL 33 (6 inc 5p), FAC 2 (-), WW2 25 (1)
Blenburb (6/35); Rangers (11/36); Ayr Utd (9/38); Rangers (4/39); Dundee Utd (4/40); Rangers (4/40); Dumbarton (3/46); Watford (7/46); Dumbarton (£250 7/47 until cs 1948). Guested for Reading and Watford in WW2.
After making himself known at Vicarage Road during a lengthy guest spell in 1943/4, he came back as a *bona fide* Watford player for the first normal post-war season, which he spent as the first-team right-half and captain. The club at

first included him in its retained list for another year, but he returned to native parts in the summer.

John WILFred **ROSTRON** *(1979-1989)*
b Sunderland, Co Durham 29/9/1956
FL 306+11 (22), FAC 43+1 (2), FLC 30+1 (3), FLT 4+1 (-), UEFA 6 (3), FMC 1 (-)
Arsenal (sch 9/72, appr 7/73, then pro 10/73); Sunderland (£40,000 7/77); Watford (£150,000 10/79); Sheffield Wednesday (free 1/89); Sheffield Utd (loan 9/89, permanent transfer 11/89); Brentford player/assistant-manager (free 1/91 until 6/93); Gateshead (assistant-manager 10/93, caretaker-manager 11/93); Sunderland Ryhope Colliery Welfare manager (12/93 until cs 1994)
ENGLAND SCHOOLS
Converted into a plucky and resourceful left-back after being signed as a winger, he was high on the crowd's list of favourite players during Watford's golden era. In a sequence of 40 consecutive FA Cup ties, the only one he missed (through suspension) was the 1984 Final, for which he would have led the team out at Wembley.

Missed one tie in 40

BRIAN **ROWAN** *(1971-1972)*
b Glasgow 28/6/1948
FL 8+4 (-), FAC 1 (-)
Baillieston Juniors (am 6/67); Aston Villa (4/69); Toronto Metros, Canada (free 4/71 until 8/71); Watford (free 10/71 until 3/72); Toronto Metros, Canada (5/72); New York Cosmos, USA (7/75 until 8/76)
SCOTLAND JUNIOR
In terms of results, this was the worst of all Watford careers, his appearances as a first-team defender in the dreadful 1971/2 season having produced 12 defeats and draw. He'd previously played in Canada, and when his Watford contract was cancelled by mutual consent he went straight back across the Atlantic - and who would blame him?

Won 0, Drew 1, Lost 12

PAUL **RUMBLE** *(1988)*
b Hemel Hempstead, Herts 14/3/1969
FMC 1 (-)
Herts, Beds & Bucks Schools; Watford (sch 5/83, tr 5/85, pro 3/87); Scunthorpe Utd (loan 8/88); Maidstone Utd (free 7/89 until 10/91); Hemel Hempstead Town (by 2/92); Staines Town (9/92)
Like Cliff Powell, he owes his status as a 'first-team' player to the decision to field an entire reserve team in a cup tie at Ipswich - a selection not universally popular among spectators who travelled to Suffolk on that January night. Left-back Rumble had won county honours as a schoolboy, and later played over 50 League games for Maidstone.

Reserve eleven fielded

David Page **(DAVE) RUSSELL** *(1926)*
b Crossgates, Fife 13/11/1895
d Kirkcaldy, Fife 15/8/1972
FL 7 (-)

Followed a legend

Hearts of Beath; Kilsyth Rangers; Doncaster Rovers (8/23); Leeds United (1/25); Watford (free 6/26); Lincoln City (free 7/27 until cs 1928)
SCOTLAND JUNIOR
Signed as the goalkeeping replacement for Skilly Williams, who surprisingly had not been retained, he played in the first seven League games of 1926/7, but then took a permanent back seat after a four-goal drubbing at Plymouth. He'd been capped at Junior level before leaving Scotland, and briefly played First Division football for Leeds.

Spotted in the Reserves

GEORGE Henry ***RUSSELL*** *(1926-1927)*
b Atherstone, Warwicks 1902
FL 12 (1p)
Atherstone Town; Portsmouth (5/25); Watford (free 6/26); Northampton Town (free 5/27); Bristol Rovers (£110 1/31); Atherstone Town (8/32); Cardiff City (12/32); Newport County (free 8/34); Stafford Rangers (1935); Bangor City player-manager (1936); Cradley Heath (2/37); Stafford Rangers (8/38)
Two good performances against Watford Reserves in 1925/6 were a prelude to his move from Fratton Park. In his League appearances he played twice at centre-forward, but otherwise as a physically strong full-back. His goal, from the penalty spot, was one of four in a comprehensive defeat of Northampton Town, whom he joined at the end of the season.

Record crowd for début

John (JACK) ***RUTHERFORD*** *(1931-1933)*
b Nenthead, Cumberland 6/11/1908
FL 31 (-), FAC 1 (-)
Crawcrook Celtic; Gillingham (6/28); Watford (8/31); West Ham Utd (free 6/33); Swindon Town (6/35); Dartford (6/36); Hartlepools Utd (10/37); Barrow (9/38 until WW2)
Tom Holland having been injured against Norwich City on Christmas Day, Rutherford made his Watford début in goal in the return game a day later, when the gates were closed on a record crowd of 17,000 at The Nest. Norwich won 4-1. The League awarded him a free transfer after he'd been listed at £150, and he became a Second Division regular in 1933/4.

Accrington to Tottenham

JOHN Johnston ***RYDEN*** *(1961-1962)*
b Alexandria, Dunbartonshire 18/2/1931
FL 24 (1), FLC 2 (-)
Duntocher Hibs (12/49); Alloa (7/50); Accrington Stanley (2/54); Tottenham Hotspur (£10,000 11/55); Watford (£4,000 6/61); Romford (free 10/62); Hastings Utd; Tunbridge Wells Rangers; Bexley Utd player-manager (cs 1966 until 1968)
A tough half-back who'd captained Tottenham Hotspur. At Watford he rejoined former team-mates Tommy Harmer and Alf Stokes, who themselves had been playing colleagues of manager Ron Burgess. Ryden led the club briefly after Holton's departure, and his only Watford goal sparked a late rally which saw Queens Park Rangers beaten after they'd led 2-0.

<u>*JOHN* ***SANCHEZ***</u> *(1960-1961)*
b Paddington, London 21/10/1940
FL 19 (-)
Arsenal (am 5/57, pro 10/57); <u>Watford</u> (free 5/59); King's Lynn (free 6/61); Gravesend & Northfleet (by 1/63); football in Australia (2/63); George Cross, Australia, coach (9/74)
ENGLAND SCHOOLS and YOUTH
He and Ken Nicholas, both of whom had been capped as youth players but failed to make Arsenal's first team, joined Watford together. A left-half who was very tough in the tackle, Sanchez later helped Gravesend & Northfleet to hold Sunderland in the 4th Round of the FA Cup, but he emigrated to Australia before the replay.

Emigrated in mid-tie

<u>*ARTHUR Ernest* ***SANS***</u> *(1906)*
b Edmonton, Middx 1886
d Edmonton, Middx 1954
SEL 1 (-)
Wood Green; <u>Watford</u> (am by 1/06); Crystal Palace (pro 9/06); Tottenham Hotspur (9/07); Maidstone Utd (10/07)
Picked for just one first-team game, he took the outside-left position which in Southern League games at that time was briefly occupied by the celebrated Fred Spiksley. Sans made a couple of Southern League appearances after turning pro with Crystal Palace. In 1909 he applied unsuccessfully to the FA for reinstatement as an amateur.

<u>*Kenneth Graham (KENNY)* ***SANSOM***</u> *(1994)*
b Camberwell, London 26/9/1958
FL 1 (-)
Crystal Palace (sch 3/75, appr 4/75, pro 12/75); Arsenal (valued at £1 million in player-exchange 8/80); Newcastle Utd (£300,000 12/88); Queens Park Rangers (£300,000 6/89); Coventry City (£100,000 3/91); Everton (free 2/93); Brentford (free 3/93); Petersfield Town (8/93); Wycombe Wanderers (9/93); Luton Town Reserves (10/93); Bromley (11/93); Chertsey Town (12/93 until 7/94); <u>Watford</u> player-coach (8/94 until 2/96); also Sydenham Sports (10/95); Slough Town (3/96)
ENGLAND SCHOOLS, YOUTH, UNDER-21, 'B' and FULL; FOOTBALL LEAGUE
When he played at Barnsley, he became Watford's oldest League débutant since 1952, and their most experienced player ever, with 86 Full internationals at left-back and getting on for 800 club games behind him. He played League football at 16, and was a winner in the FA Youth Cup with Crystal Palace and the Football League Cup with Arsenal.

The most experienced

<u>*REGinald Francis Edward* ***SAPHIN***</u> *(1951-1954)*
b Cricklewood, Middx 8/8/1916
FL 57 (-), FAC 2 (-)
Hayes; Walthamstow Avenue; Queens Park Rangers (5/46); <u>Watford</u> (7/51 until cs 1954, assistant trainer by 3/57, youth-team manager 1960 until 1/63). Guested for Brentford and Ipswich Town in WW2.

Turned pro at 29

Nearly 30 when he turned professional, he'd already guested regularly for Ipswich in 1945/6. He eventually retired after three seasons as one of Watford's goalkeepers, and was the first choice until superseded by Dave Underwood after conceding five at Norwich. He played only once more in the League, 18 months later, and kept a clean sheet.

Artilleryman

Herbert John **SAUNDERS** *(1909)*
b Crewe, Cheshire, 1884
SL 2 (-)
Leith Athletic (am 11/06 until cs 1907); Sheerness Garrison; Watford (am 1/08); Oxhey; New Bushey; Watford (pro 5/08 until cs 1909)
A brawny soldier, he'd been in the Royal Garrison Artillery when he joined Watford. Due to the long and almost uninterrupted incumbency of Billy Biggar, he played only twice in the first-team goal - in a 4-1 win against Northampton and a 5-1 defeat at New Brompton a week later. For a while he ran a confectionary shop in The Parade.

£50 goalkeeper

James E. **SAUNDERS** *(1910)*
b Birmingham, Warwicks
SL 4 (-), SCC 1 (-)
Glossop (3/00); Middlesbrough (2/01); Newton Heath (8/01); Nelson (1905/6); Lincoln City (10/06); Chelsea (5/09); Watford (£50 5/10 until cs 1911); Lincoln Liberal Club
He began the 1910/1 season in the first-team goal, but was soon replaced by Joe Webster, who settled into a long occupancy and left Saunders with no further opportunities. At Lincoln his manager was David Calderhead, who later signed him for Chelsea, for whom his only two Football League games were on Christmas Day and Boxing Day 1909.

Easily the top manager

RONald **SAUNDERS** *(1964-1965)*
b Birkenhead, Cheshire 6/11/1932
FL 39 (18), FLC 2 (-)
Birkenhead & Liverpool Schools; Everton (am 10/49, pro 2/51); Tonbridge (7/56); Gillingham (£800 5/57); Portsmouth (£8,000 9/58); Watford (£15,000 9/64); Charlton Athletic (£10,000 8/65 until 4/67); Yeovil Town manager (5/67 until 1968); Oxford Utd manager (3/69 until 6/69); Norwich City manager (7/69); Manchester City manager (11/73 until 4/74); Aston Villa manager (6/74); Birmingham City manager (2/82 until 1/86); West Bromwich Albion manager (2/86 until 9/87)
ENGLAND YOUTH
As a player he was a gritty centre-forward whose best years were at Portsmouth (140 goals in 234 League games). As a manager, dour and single-minded, he was easily the most successful of all ex-Watford players. In the League Cup he led three clubs to the Final in successive years, and won it twice, as well as the League itself, with Villa.

William (BUMPER) **SAUNDERS** (1896-1900)
SL 33 (19 inc 1p), FAC 2 (1), FAAC 2 (-), HSC 2 (2 inc 1p), BCCL 5 (5)
West Herts (am 1895, pro 10/97)
Ever-present at inside-right, and leading scorer, in Watford's first Southern League season, he also hit the club's first goal in the competition. In the space of six days in 1898 he thrice scored four times in a game - twice for the Reserves and once for the first team. And a year later he kept goal for the Reserves in an 11-0 win, sporting an over-coat and pipe.

Overcoat and pipe

Harry **SAVAGE** (1921-1922)
b Frodsham, Cheshire 1897
d Runcorn, Cheshire 1968
FL 7 (1)
Crewe Alexandra (1919); Sheffield Utd (£750 5/20); Watford (£250 6/21 until cs 1922)
A winger on whom Watford wasted what was then their record fee, although it was only half the original asking price. He'd played amateur football before the Great War, and for army sides during it, and on joining Sheffield United went straight into their First Division line-up. Watford listed him at £200 after his modest season.

Record fee wasted

Henry (HARRY) **SCOTT** (1933)
b Newburn, Northumberland, circa 1897
FL 1 (-)
Newburn Grange; Sunderland (1/22); Wolverhampton Wanderers (6/25); Hull City (11/26); Bradford Park Avenue (part-exchange 6/28); Swansea Town (7/32); Watford (free 7/33); Nuneaton Town (free 7/34); Vauxhall Motors (permit player 9/35)
A tall inside-forward, and a veteran when he came to Vicarage Road, he was dropped after playing in the opening League game of the season, and didn't get back in. He'd had 39 games in Swansea's Second Division team the previous season, but that was easily the nearest he came to a full winter of Football League action with his various clubs.

Opening game his last

STEWART McNab Adam **SCULLION** (1966-1976)
b Bo'ness, West Lothian 18/4/1946
FL 304+8 (49 inc 7p), FAC 22 (3), FLC 14 (3)
Chesham Utd; Charlton Athletic (am 12/64, pro 3/65); Watford (makeweight in C.C.Holton transfer 2/66); Sheffield Utd (£25,000 5/71); Watford (£15,000 12/73); Tampa Bay Rowdies, USA (loan 5/75 until 8/75, £8,000 2/76); Wimbledon (9/76); Portland Timbers, USA (4/77 until 8/77); Hayes (by 11/77); Portland Timbers, USA (3/78 until 8/79)
A total outlay of only £15,000 brought the club two good spells from this crowd-pleasing individualist. His sometimes dazzling wing skills embroidered the otherwise workmanlike team (albeit a highly successful one for a time) built by Ken Furphy. When in the USA Scullion played in a representative match against England for 'Team America'.

Embroiderer

Experiment let him in

FRANK Burnett **SEARLE** *(1933)*
b Hednesford, Staffs 30/1/1906
d Waltham Forest, London 16/6/1977
FL 4 (-), FAC 1 (-)
Willenhall (1926); Bristol City (12/26); Charlton Athletic (5/28); Chester (2/33); Watford (free 7/33 until cs 1934); Clapton Orient (9/34 until cs 1938)
During his one Vicarage Road season he had just a single first-team run - at left-half, when Arthur Woodward, who otherwise monopolised the position, was pushed forward to ginger up the attack. The ploy worked at first (three good wins and a draw in the League), but was then abandoned after a three-goal home defeat by Reading in the FA Cup.

Legendary deeds

TREVOR John **SENIOR** *(1987-1988)*
b Dorchester, Dorset 28/11/1961
FL 22+2 (1), FAC 3+1 (2), FLC 3+1 (1), FMC 1 (1)
Dorchester Town; Portsmouth (£20,000 12/81, plus £15,000 of 'sell-on' fee); Aldershot (loan 3/83); Reading (£35,000 8/83); Watford (£325,000 7/87); Middlesbrough (£200,000 3/88); Reading (£150,000 10/88); Woking (free 7/92); Weymouth (free 8/93); Basingstoke Town; Dorchester Town (11/93); Farnborough Town (12/93); Weymouth (5/94, joint-acting-player/manager 9/94, player-manager 12/94; Farnborough Town (6/95 until cs 1996); Newport, Isle of Wight (loan 1/96); Dorchester Town football-in-the-community officer (2/96)
He found goalscoring difficult in the top flight, but as a tall, marauding centre-forward performed legendary deeds for Reading. A hat-trick in under five minutes on his Elm Park début prefaced a club career of 291 League games, in which he amassed 153 goals. He was at Watford during the grim months immediately following Graham Taylor's departure.

Sent off twice

Albert (ALBIE) **SHARP** *(1898-1901)*
b St Albans, Herts 1878
d London
SL 58 (1), FAC 11 (2), BCCL 13 (-)
St Albans Abbey; Stanville (1895/6); St Albans Town (pro 8/97); Watford (5/98); Luton Town (5/01 until cs 1903)
He had a run at wing-half towards the end of his Watford career, but was essentially a full-back who, after representing the county, had turned professional with the short-lived St Albans club. His two-year stint at Luton was ended by injury. Remarkably for an era in which the punishment was rare, he was sent off twice as a Watford player.

Gold-medallist

IVAN Gordon **SHARPE** *(1908)*
b St Albans, Herts 15/6/1889
d Southport, Lancs 9/2/1968
SL 7 (1)
St Albans; Watford (am 10/07); Glossop (am 8/08 until 9/11); Derby County (am 10/11); Leeds City (am 6/13 until 11/19); Leeds Utd (am 1920)
ENGLAND and GREAT BRITAIN AMATEUR

A leading sports journalist for many years, he played his football as an amateur left-winger. He didn't impress the Cassio Road crowd, but went on to success elsewhere - notably in 1912, when in addition to being married he helped Derby County to the Second Division championship and won an Olympic gold medal with Great Britain.

ARTHUR **SHAW** *(1955)*
b Limehouse, London 9/4/1924
FL 3 (-)
East London Schools; Whitton Rovers; Hounslow Town (1941); Queens Park Rangers (am 1941/2); Southall (1945); Hayes (1945/6); Brentford (5/46); Arsenal (4/48); Watford ("moderate fee" 6/55); Gravesend & Northfleet (8/56). Guested for Hounslow Town in WW2.
After representing East London Schools he played his club football on the other side of town before moving to Highbury, where he won a League championship medal in 1952/3, as did Cliff Holton and Lionel Smith. A versatile player, and physically big, he wore the No 4 shirt in his League games for Watford. He was also a professional gambler.

League championship win

JOHN **SHAW** *(1942-1946)*
b Oldham, Lancs 2/10/1916
d Shaw, Lancs 22/10/1973
FAC 9 (-), WW2 98 (1)
South Shore Wesleyans; Lytham (12/33); Oldham Athletic (3/34); Mossley (7/36); Grimsby Town (5/37); Birmingham (3/39); Watford (£800 10/45 until 7/46). Guested for Crewe Alexandra, Luton Town, Reading and Watford in WW2.
He'd played in all five outfield defensive positions as a guest player for three seasons, but whilst on the club's books in 1945/6 he was the regular centre-half. His pre-war career had included service with three Football League clubs, but first-team appearances were rare. He did, however, play a handful of First Division games for Grimsby.

Long-term guest

Edward **SHAWCROFT** *(1921)*
b Barlow, Derbys 1893
d Chesterfield, Derbys 1968
FL 1 (-)
Barlow; Chesterfield Town (cs 1913); Clay Cross; Welbeck Colliery; Watford (6/21 until cs 1922); Dinnington Main (permit player 10/22); Newbold Rovers (permit player 5/24); Barlow Rangers (permit player 9/28); Barlow Welfare (permit player 2/33)
Among the less successful of Harry Kent's many recruits from minor football in the East Midlands, he made his one League appearance in mid-season - at centre-forward in a 1-1 draw at Queens Park Rangers. This was immediately prior to the signing of Fred Pagnam, who thereupon took up a long occupancy of the position.

Made way for Pagnam

SIMON **SHEPPARD** *(1993-1994)*
b Clevedon, Somerset 7/8/1973
FL 23 (-), FAC 1 (-), FLC 4 (-), AIC 2 (-)

Third England 'keeper

Westown Harriers; Watford (sch 10/87); FA School of Excellence; Watford (tr 7/89, pro 4/91); Scarborough (loan 3/94); Reading (free 9/94, but Watford to receive 40% of any 'sell-on' fee)
ENGLAND SCHOOLS and YOUTH
Three Watford youth-team goalkeepers of the 1980s won England caps at one level or another, and Sheppard was the third of them, following Derick Williams and David James. As a schoolboy he played for Bristol City's nursery club, Westown Harriers, but it was with Watford that he became officially linked at the age of 14.

Walsall scorer v Arsenal

William (BILL) SHEPPARD (1927-1929)
b Ferryhill, Co Durham 1906
d Hemel Hempstead, Herts 27/12/1950
FL 89 (37 inc 3p), FAC 6 (2)
A County Durham club; Liverpool (am 12/25, pro 12/25); Watford (7/27); Queens Park Rangers (free 6/30); Coventry City (5/31); Walsall (1/33); Chester (free, cs 1934); Walsall (10/34 until cs 1935); Odhams (by 9/37)
Two goals on his début paved the way for a total of 25 in his first season as the club's inside-left. It was a striking rate which he was unable to maintain, but he was to become one of Walsall's scorers in their historic FA Cup win over Arsenal. Seventeen years later he died on a Christmas visit to the *King Henry the Eighth* pub, Hemel Hempstead.

Spanned Taylor's decade

Stephen (STEVE) SHERWOOD (1977-1987)
b Selby, Yorks 10/12/1953
FL 211 (1), FAC 23 (-), FLC 23 (-), FLT 6 (-), UEFA 6 (-)
West Riding Schools; Chelsea (appr 9/70, pro 7/71); Brighton & Hove Albion (loan 10/73); Millwall (loan 10/73); Brentford (loan 1/74 until cs 1975); Hartford Bicentennials, USA (loan 4/76 until 8/76); Watford (£3,000 11/76); Grimsby Town (free 7/87); Northampton Town (free 7/93); Grimsby Town (non-contract 8/94); Immingham Town (10/94); Lincoln City (non-contract 3/95); Stalybridge Celtic (8/95); Gateshead (10/95)
The only player on Watford's books throughout Graham Taylor's first Watford spell. A gentle giant of a goalkeeper, he scored in the First Division with a wind-assisted drop-kick, and won successive promotions with both Watford and Grimsby. His father played League football before the war, and his brother John won Olympic bronze as a hurdler.

Led the Blackburn triumph

TIMothy Alan SHERWOOD (1987-1989)
b St Albans, Herts 6/2/1969
FL 23+9 (2), FAC 9 (-), FLC 4+1 (-), FMC 4+1 (-)
Herts Schools; Forest Utd; Watford (tr 5/85, pro 2/87); Norwich City (£175,000 7/89); Blackburn Rovers (loan 2/92, £500,000 2/92)
ENGLAND UNDER-21 and 'B'
Although he developed into a First Division player at Watford, it was after leaving Vicarage Road that his career took him to international honours. As a forceful and energetic midfield player he became captain of the multi-

million-pound Blackburn Rovers team which won the FA Premier League.

*James HerBERT **SHINNER** (1909-1910)*
b Dudley, Worcs 1877
SL 18 (-), SCC 4 (-)
Dudley; Middlesbrough (10/02); Aberdeen (8/03); Bradford City (cs 1904); Doncaster Rovers (10/04); Brentford (1/05 until cs 1905); Barrow (5/06); Bristol City (5/07); Southend Utd (9/08); Watford (9/09); Bristol City (£15 7/10)
He learnt his football in the Royal Navy, and was also a talented performer on the athletic track, winning many professional handicaps. His career in the game took him to various points in the far north, south, east and west of Britain, and in his season with Watford he shared the full-back duties with the established pair of Betts and Lockett.

Began as a sailor

*NEIL Jason **SHIPPERLEY** (1994-1995)*
b Chatham, Kent 30/10/1974
FL 5+1 (1)
Chelsea (sch 2/91, tr 7/91, pro 9/92); Watford (loan 12/94); Southampton (£1.2 million 1/95)
ENGLAND UNDER-21
He had more than half a season of Premier League football at Stamford Bridge, but then dropped behind more experienced strikers in the queue for first-team shirts, and was sold to Southampton just after his Watford spell. His father played over three hundred League games, almost entirely for Charlton Athletic and Gillingham, as a mountainous centre-half.

Sold after Watford loan

*William Kenneth (BILL) **SHIPWRIGHT** (1954-1959)*
b Somers Town, London 22/12/1932
FL 146 (-), FAC 7 (-), SFC 6 (-)
Medburn Old Boys; Watford groundstaff (3/50 until 4/51); St Helen's, Watford; Chesham Utd; Watford (pro 4/53); Aldershot (exchange for J.D.Price 6/59); Yiewsley (7/63 for two seasons); Wokingham manager (one season); Hillingdon Borough manager (2/73 until cs 1974)
Just before doing his National Service he played for both Chesham United and, as a member of the groundstaff, for Watford's Midweek League side. After being demobbed he had six years with the club as a sturdy centre-half and right-back. He captained RAF Egypt, and later also Aldershot, whom he joined in exchange for a former youth-football colleague.

RAF captain in Egypt

*James **SHORT** (1920-1921)*
b Hucknall, Notts
FL 21 (7 inc 2p)
Arnold St Mary's; Notts County (12/17); Birmingham (5/19); Watford (5/20); Ilkeston Utd (free 8/22); Norwich City (5/23 until cs 1924); Newark Town (9/24 until 1927); Grantham Town; Lewison, Nottingham (permit player 9/27)
Having scored two wartime hat-tricks for Notts County, he hit eight goals for Birmingham in his first seven peacetime

Post-war goal rush

League games. He nevertheless moved to Watford at the end of the season as a forthright centre-forward or inside-forward, and then had a winter in non-League football before joining Norwich. He'd been wounded in the Great War.

Home defeat

GEORGE Frederick **SIMONS** *(1905)*
b Watford, Herts 21/1/1882
d Abbots Langley, Herts 27/10/1953
SL 1 (-)
Apsley; Park Royal; St Albans; Watford (am 1904/5); Leavesden Asylum (by 11/08)
He served in the Boer War as a youth, was a prominent cyclist, and played amateur football locally. His Southern League appearance was at right-back in a 3-0 home defeat by West Ham United. He became proprietor of the butcher's business which had been in the family since the 18th century, and his son kept wicket for Hertfordshire for many years.

Anglo-Scot

COLIN Robertson **SIMPSON** *(1996)*
b Oxford 30/4/1976
FL 0+1 (-)
Chinnor Boys; Watford (sch 10/90, tr 7/92, pro 7/94)
Born in England to Scottish parents, he began his association with Watford long before being eligible to sign schoolboy forms at the age of 14. Essentially a winger, he developed into a versatile forward who made his League début as a substitute, with the club seven games from a return to the lower divisions after a absence of 17 seasons.

Third Division record

STEVEn Frank **SIMS** *(1978-1987)*
b Lincoln 2/7/1957
FL 169+2 (5 inc 1p), FAC 21 (-), FLC 14 (3), FLT 8 (-), UEFA 4+1 (-)
Lincoln Utd; Leicester City (appr 8/73, pro 7/74); Watford (£175,000 12/78); Notts County (£50,000 9/84); Watford (£50,000 10/86); Aston Villa (£40,000 6/87 until cs 1990); Burton Albion (9/90); Lincoln City (non-contract 10/90); AFC Bournemouth (non-contract 2/91); Boston assistant-manager (cs 1991); coach at Port Vale School of Excellence (by 12/91); Stafford Rangers (non-contract 12/91); Shepshed Albion (1/92); Aston Villa part-time youth coach (by 11/92); Coventry City youth-development officer (7/94)
ENGLAND UNDER-21 and 'B'
Watford paid what was then a record fee for a Third Division club for this strapping centre-half and long-throw specialist, who went on to help the club establish itself in the top flight. Graham Taylor was later to sign him a second time - and then yet again for Aston Villa. Sims's father, another centre-half, made three League appearances for Lincoln City.

ROY **SINCLAIR** *(1969-1972)*
b Liverpool, Lancs 10/10/1944
FL 32+11 (3), FAC 1 (-), FLC 2 (-)
Liverpool Schools; Liverpool (am 5/61); Tranmere Rovers (10/63); Watford (£11,000 3/69); Chester (loan 12/71); Tranmere Rovers (free 7/72 until 2/74); Seattle Sounders, USA (5/74); Denver Dynamos, USA (5/75 until 8/75); Detroit Express, USA (4/78 until 7/78)
Although no great scorer (he was essentially a midfield worker) he drove home the winner against Plymouth Argyle which propelled Watford into the Second Division for the first time. This was one of only 22 League goals of his career, three of which came on his 21st birthday. He later became an insurance manager and a football referee in Seattle.

Promotion goal

LEE **SINNOTT** *(1983-1987)*
b Pelsall, Staffs 12/7/1965
FL 71+7 (2), FAC 11 (-), FLC 6 (-)
Rushall Olympic (1981/2); Walsall (appr 9/81, pro 11/82); Watford (£95,000 9/83); Bradford City (£100,000 7/87); Crystal Palace (£350,000 8/91); Bradford City (loan 12/93, permanent 1/94); Huddersfield Town (£105,000 12/94)
ENGLAND YOUTH and UNDER-21
A tall, physically strong defender with a long-range throw-in, he played in the League at 16 and then captained the national youth team (his colleagues included David Bardsley and Perry Suckling) under Graham Taylor, who soon afterwards brought him to Vicarage Road. Within eight months he became one of the 20 youngest FA Cup finalists of all time.

Cup finalist at 18

Arthur Harold **SKILTON** *(1908-1910)*
b Harrow, Middx 1888
d Southend, Essex 8/5/1953
SL 15 (5), SCC 2 (-)
Watford (am 1908 until 1910)
An amateur forward who made sporadic appearances in the first team in the 1908/9 and 1909/10 seasons, and didn't experience defeat until the tenth of them. His brother Percy also played as an amateur in professional company, and was present more often than not in the Queens Park Rangers side which won the Southern League in 1907/8.

Ralph (**REG**) **SLADE** *(1921-1929)*
b Amersham, Bucks 25/3/1896
d Bushey, Herts, June 1983
FL 119 (-), FAC 5 (-)
Amersham; Watford (am 8/20, pro 1/21 until 4/30)
He served as a part-time professional for nearly a decade, including two successive seasons as a first-team regular. A strong, hard-working full-back, he retired after suffering a broken leg and head injuries when his motorcycle collided with a lorry in Radlett Road. At one time his Vicarage Road appearances involved bookmaking activities on dog nights.

Vicarage Road bookie

European Cup semi-final

RoBERT **SLATER** *(1965-1969)*
b Musselburgh, Midlothian 5/5/1936
FL 134 (-), FAC 9 (-), FLC 9 (-)
Tranent Juniors (1/53); Falkirk (8/53); Liverpool (5/59); Dundee (7/62); Watford (free 5/65, trainer 1971 until cs 1973); Evergreen chairman (7/74); Dundee chief scout (by 8/88)
SCOTLAND UNDER-23
Either side of his Liverpool spell, during which he won a Second Division championship medal under Bill Shankly, he helped Falkirk to win the Scottish FA Cup and reached the European Cup semi-finals with Dundee. He was Watford's senior goalkeeper for three years until Mike Walker was signed early in the Third Division championship-winning season.

Off injured twice running

Thomas **ARTHUR SLATER** *(1933)*
b Chester-le-Street, Co Durham 25/2/1908
d Luton, Beds 1976
FL 29 (-), FAC 1 (-)
Murton Colliery Welfare; Clapton Orient (8/26); Port Vale (6/30); Watford (free 8/32); Vauxhall Motors (permit player 8/34)
His first-team appearances in Watford's goal came in a single sequence which spanned the 1933 close season. In both his last two games he was taken off injured, whereupon the club bought Jim McLaren. Late in the following season he suffered another bad knock whilst playing for Vauxhall Motors. He'd been a car mechanic before becoming a full-time pro.

Muddle over pro status

Robert **(BOBBIE) SLAUGHTER** *(1894-1900)*
b Bushey, Herts 1874
SL 33 (18), FAC 8 (7), HSC 2 (-) BCCL 13 (9)
Melrose (by 2/93); West Herts (am 1/94); Watford Church Institute; Watford St Mary's; West Herts (pro 10/97); Watford St Mary's (11/97); Watford (4/98); Fulham (11/01); Watford (2/02); Chesham Town (11/02 briefly)
His turning professional at Cassio Road caused St Mary's, the club he'd just left in order to do so, to adopt professionalism themselves, fearing that they would lose other good players. Slaughter was peeved by this, and was allowed to return to St Mary's, where he remained until their demise. A goalscoring inside-forward, he'd played for the county.

Small name and size

DAVID SMALL *(1951-1952)*
b Dundee, Angus 17/7/1930
FL 5 (-)
Monifieth Tayside (am 7/48); Dundee North End (am 3/50); Watford (pro 6/50); Dunfermline Athletic (free 7/52); Montrose (7/53); Carnoustie Panmure (8/54); Dundee St Josephs (9/58 until cs 1959); Broughty Athletic (11/59 until cs 1960)
A ball-playing right-winger whose physical stature reflected his surname, he spent two seasons with Watford at a time when the club's fortunes were at a low ebb, the final Third Division (South) positions being 21st and 23rd, respectively, out of 24. He spent the rest of his career with clubs in and around familiar territory in the east of Scotland.

Wembley scorer

NEIL SMILLIE *(1985-1986)*
b Barnsley, Yorks 19/7/1958
FL 10+6 (3), FAC 2 (1), FLC 1 (-)
Essex Schools; Crystal Palace (sch 1/74. appr 7/74, pro 10/75); Brentford (loan 1/77); Memphis Rogues, USA (loan 4/78 until 8/78, and 5/79 until 8/79); Brighton & Hove Albion (player-exchange 8/82); Watford (£100,000 6/85); Reading (loan 12/86, free 3/87); Brentford (8/88); Gillingham (player/assistant-manager free 7/93, player/caretaker-manager 2/95 until 6/95); Wycombe Wanderers youth-team coach (7/95)
An old-fashioned winger with speedy and direct methods, he scored as a substitute on his Watford début, and all his four goals for the club contributed to excellent victories. He also scored for Reading when they won the Full Members Cup at Wembley, and extended his League career into his late thirties. His father played for Barnsley and Lincoln City.

Albert SMITH *(1929)*
b West Melton, Yorks
FL 5 (-)
Wombwell; Leicester City (4/28); Watford (a month's trial 8/29); Denaby Utd (10/29)
Unable to get a First Division place at Filbert Street, where Jim McLaren was ahead of him as the first-team goalie and Bill Findlay was also in the side, he was released. During a trial period at Watford he kept goal in five League games, four of which were lost, and at the end of the month was offered the choice of staying with the club or leaving. He left.

Upton Park reserve

Anthony (TONY) SMITH *(1966-1967)*
b Sunderland, Co Durham 31/12/1943
FL 3 (-)
Consett; West Ham Utd (11/63); Watford (5/66 until cs 1967); Hartlepools Utd (10/67 until cs 1968)
Brought down from the North-East by West Ham United at the age of 19, he spent nearly three seasons at Upton Park without making the first team. His three League matches in Watford's forward line, all away from home, produced one goal and one point. For Hartlepools he scored once in two Fourth Division games, in a season when they won promotion.

Dodgy FA Cup record

CHRIStopher SMITH *(1910-1912)*
SL 32 (-), FAC 1 (-), SCC 2 (-)
Hartlepools Utd (1908); Watford (7/10 until cs 1912)
Signed at the start of Harry Kent's long occupation of the manager's seat, he was a burly, bustling defender who, in his only FA Cup appearance for Watford, was a member of the eleven which suffered the club's record defeat in the competition. In a Molineux replay, Wolverhampton Wanderers won 10-0 after scoring eight times in the first half.

Travelled the world

*Ernest Edwin (***BERT***)* **SMITH** *(1925-1927)*
b Donegal 4/1/1890
FL 50 (1), FAC 5 (-)
Cardiff City (7/19); Middlesbrough (1/24); Emsworth (loan 1925); Watford (£250 8/25); Emsworth (free 4/27)
IRELAND FULL
Resident in South Africa when the Great War broke out, he served with the South African Artillery in France and Salonika. As a footballer he played for the British Army and in the Calcutta League before winning four caps as an outstanding Cardiff City centre-half who helped them into the First Divison. In his last League game Watford lost 6-0.

Made it with third club

*Edmund William Alfred (***EDDIE***)* **SMITH** *(1953-1955)*
b Marylebone, London 23/3/1929
d Westminster, London, April 1993
FL 38 (12), FAC 4 (1)
Chelsea (am 8/46); Wealdstone; Chelsea (pro 5/50); Bournemouth & Boscombe Athletic (8/52); Watford ("small fee" 7/53); Northampton Town (4-figure fee 1/55); Colchester Utd (6/56); Queens Park Rangers (7/57 until cs 1958)
Whilst a Chelsea junior he played amateur football for Wealdstone, and only with his third professional club, Watford, did he first appear in the Football League. An aggressive inside-forward, he made his first-team début in a friendly against Pegasus at the start of Vicarage Road's floodlight era, with over 11,000 present, and scored both Watford goals.

£125 well spent

FRANK *William* **SMITH** *(1921-1931)*
b Kettering, Northants 13/10/1897
d St Albans, Herts, July 1988
FL 319 (30), FAC 22 (1)
Kettering; Watford (£125 3/21 until cs 1932) London General Country Services, Watford (permit player 9/32)
Conscientious, consistent, and popular with both colleagues and spectators, he joined the club as an inside-forward and later settled at right-half. In 1925 he played in a representative match at Highbury in which experiments were made regarding the offside law, soon to be changed with dramatic effect. On retiring in 1932 he became a bus conductor.

67% pay rise

G. **SMITH** *(1902-1904)*
SL 3 (-), SEL 2 (-)
Melrose; Watford (am, cs 1902, pro 1/03 until cs 1906)
His Southern League appearances at right-half were consecutive, during the 1902/3 Christmas and New Year period, with the club *en route* to relegation. Conversely, the two South-Eastern League games were separated by more than two years. His weekly wage rose from 6/- to 10/- for 1904/5, and he re-signed in September 1905 at 10/- per match.

George **SMITH** *(1931)*
b Sunderland, Co Durham
FL 1 (-)
Easington Colliery; Watford (11/30); Clapton Orient (free 8/32); Darlington (7/33); Yeovil & Petters Utd (free 6/34)
In nearly two seasons as a Vicarage Road player he was picked only once for the first team, lining up at centre-half in a 1-0 win at Norwich on the final day of the 1930/1 League season. Three of the four Smiths in the match were Watford men, of whom he and Joe were both making the only Football League appearance of their careers.

Good win in only game

HARRY **SMITH** *(1908-1919)*
b Watford, Herts 1882
d Watford, Herts 1968
SL 35 (15), SCC 1 (1), WW1 43 (27)
Watford (am 1908 until cs 1922); also Watford Orient (late 1912/3)
A go-ahead centre-forward, he began his long amateur career with the club on leaving the 3rd Dragoon Guards, with whom served in the Boer War. When he suffered a broken leg at Southampton in November 1908, the opposition collected £14 for him and the Herts FA sanctioned a weekly allowance until he was fit to resume his employment.

Dragoon guardsman

John (JACK) **SMITH** *(1960-1961)*
b West Hartlepool, Co Durham 24/4/1936
FL 20 (8), FAC 3 (-)
Hartlepools Utd (youth team, pro 5/53); Watford (£3,000 7/60); Swindon Town (6/61); Brighton & Hove Albion (1/64); Notts County (9/66 until 12/68); Margate; Ramsgate Athletic player-manager (1971 until at least 1973); Bath City manager
A career total of 139 League goals included only eight during his Vicarage Road stint, although he began well enough with two against Notts County. He soon drifted out of favour, failing to score in his last nine competitive games, but moved on to good spells with both Swindon and Brighton, having originally done well with his local club.

Did better elsewhere

Joseph Kirby (JOE) **SMITH** *(1931)*
b Whitburn, Co Durham 11/6/1908
d Leicester, September 1993
FL 1 (-)
Whitburn; Leicester City (10/27); Watford (free 7/30 until 3/32); Market Harborough Town (8/32); Bentley Engineering (permit player 8/35 for many years)
Like his namesake George, he made his only appearance (at left-back) in the final game of 1930/1. He later had a long association with Bentley Engineering, whom he captained at both football and cricket. Of his four footballing brothers, two were England caps and three played in the same FA Cup semi-final in 1934.

Two brothers won caps

Best years were pre-war

John **TREVOR SMITH** *(1947)*
b West Stanley, Co Durham 8/9/1910
FL 10 (-), FAC 2 (-)
South Moors; Annfield Plain (1929/30); Charlton Athletic (5/33); Fulham (£1,000 3/35); Crystal Palace (£2,500 2/38); Yeovil Town (1946/7); Watford (6/47 until cs 1948); Bedford Town (by 4/49); Wingate manager (6/49). Guested for Fulham, Nottingham Forest, Notts County, Tottenham Hotspur and West Ham Utd in WW2.
A veteran inside-forward who had come south in 1933, and stayed. His experience with London clubs before the war included an FA Cup semi-final appearance with Fulham. He joined Watford as a part-time professional at the age of 36, and his brief first-team run ended with two FA Cup games against Torquay United, who won the replay 3-0.

Used to the big-time

LIONEL SMITH *(1954-1955)*
b Mexborough, Yorks 23/8/1920
d Stoke Newington, London 8/11/1980
FL 7 (-)
Mexborough Albion; Yorkshire Tar Distillers; Denaby Utd; Arsenal (am 5/39, pro 8/39); Watford (6/54); Gravesend & Northfleet player-manager (free 5/55 until 4/60). Guested for Notts County in WW2.
ENGLAND FULL; FOOTBALL LEAGUE
This six-footer from Yorkshire won six England caps at left-back, but he was more or less finished by the time he joined Watford. His Arsenal career had brought him a League Championship and an FA Cup runners-up medal in company with Cliff Holton. On resigning the manager's job at Gravesend he took over a pub in Stoke Newington.

Awful results

RON*ald* **SMITH** *(1955)*
b Aberystwyth, Cardiganshire 9/4/1934
FL 2 (-), SFC 1 (-)
Maidenhead Utd; Arsenal (7/54); Watford ("small fee" 6/55); Bedford Town (free 7/57)
His three senior matches at right-back were consecutive. They all ended in defeat, and 12 goals were conceded, ten of them in two home games. He was one of a succession of 1950s men who made the short trip from Highbury, where he was released after one season without making the first team. He became a part-timer in his second Watford season.

Axed and released

William Arthur **(BILL) SMITH** *(1959)*
b Lambeth, London 2/11/1938
FL 10 (-)
Crystal Palace (am 5/55, pro 12/56); Watford (8/57 until cs 1959); Headington Utd (a month's trial 11/59)
Following a substitute appearance in the 1957 pre-season public trial, he was taken on as the club's third goalkeeper. Although soon called up for National Service he played in Midweek League games, but had to wait more than a season and a half for his first-team chance, which ended when he was replaced by amateur Peter Storer.

Thomas **ALBERT SOAR** *(1906-1908)*
b Heanor, Derbys 20/5/1881
SL 33 (3), FAC 2 (1), SEL 1 (-), UL 9 (-)
Heanor St Mary's; Nottingham Forest (3/00); Alfreton Town (6/00); Newark (12/01); Derby County (£150 1/03); Fulham (5/03); Watford (5/06 until 3/08); reinstated am (5/09)
Highly rated at Fulham, he succeeded George Badenoch at Watford and became one of the best of their early outside-rights, his speed and trickery compensating for a lack of physical power. Having returned after missing most of 1907/8 through injury, he was soon forced into retirement at the age of 26. He was later reinstated as an amateur.

Highly-rated until hurt

JASON *Rafael* **SOLOMAN** *(1989-1994)*
b Welwyn Garden City, Herts 6/10/1970
FL 79+21 (5), FAC 1 (-), FLC 9 (1), FMC 1+1 (-), AIC 4 (-)
Panshanger Yellows; Watford (sch 11/84); FA School of Excellence; Watford (tr 7/87, pro 12/88); Peterborough Utd (loan 1/95); Wycombe Wanderers (£10,000 3/95 until cs 1996)
ENGLAND YOUTH
Determined and versatile, he was Barry Ashby's central-defensive partner when Watford won the FA Youth Cup in 1989. In League football he had experience at full-back, but went on to play mostly in midfield, covering large areas in both halves of the pitch. His formidable shooting power brought a spectacular goal at West Bromwich Albion.

Outstanding youth player

RON*ald Edward* **SPELMAN** *(1963-1965)*
b Blofield, Norfolk 22/5/1938
FL 40 (3), FAC 3 (-), FLC 1 (-)
City of Norwich School Old Boys Union; Norwich City (8/56); Northampton Town (11/60); Bournemouth & Boscombe Athletic (3/62); Watford (£2,000 9/63); Oxford Utd (free 5/65); Wisbech Town (8/66 until 1967); Gothic (11/68)
In his opening Watford appearance he gave an outstanding performance, and scored. This was not the first spectacular right-wing display he'd given at Vicarage Road, as four seasons earlier he'd inspired Norwich to victory in a top-of-the-table reserve game. Later in life he developed arthritis of the neck, diagnosed as a football-related condition.

Sparkling début

FRED*erick* **SPIKSLEY** *(1906)*
b Gainsborough, Lincs 25/1/1870
d Goodwood, Sussex 28/7/1948
SL 11 (5), UL 1 (-)
Gainsborough Trinity (1887); Sheffield Wednesday (1/91); Glossop (6/04); Leeds City (free 2/05); Southern Utd (5/05); Watford (2/06 until cs 1906); coach in Denmark (by 5/11); coach in Nuremberg, Germany (until 8/14); Reformers Club, Mexico, coach (by 10/24); Fulham coach; coach in Nuremberg, Germany (1926)
ENGLAND FULL; FOOTBALL LEAGUE
The finest left-winger of his day, he had a brilliant career with Sheffield Wednesday which brought him winners'

Best of his era

medals in the top two divisions and in the FA Cup, as well as seven England caps. In 1914 he was briefly interned by the Germans, then arrested by the British for deliberately injuring himself, to avoid active service. He died at the races.

FA Cup trio v Brentford

*ARTHUR **SQUIRES** (1909-1916)*
b Redbourn, Herts 1886
d West Clandon, Surrey 27/5/1953
SL 106 (20 inc 3p), FAC 10 (5 inc 1p), SCC 5 (-), WW1 11 (-)
Redbourn (by 1905); Watford (am 2/09, pro 5/09); Bristol Rovers (£200+ 5/13). Guested for Watford in WW1.
Watford were more than satisfied with his service on their left wing, which brought him selection for the Southern League representative team. An amateur inside-left when he made his first-team début, he was to return as a guest player whilst in the Army Veterinary Corps. His best scoring feat was an FA Cup hat-trick against Brentford.

Knew only victory

*Thomas (TOM) **STEEL** (1898-1899)*
d Watford, Herts 9/1/1942 (aged 67)
SL 1 (-), FAC 1 (-), BCCL 1 (-)
Melrose; Watford St Mary's (1892/3); Watford (pro 8/98 until cs 1899)
He threw in his lot as a professional at Cassio Road when St Mary's called it a day. His six first-team games at right-back, including friendlies, were all at home, and they produced six wins and a goal aggregate of 22-4. Several years later the committee paid 14/6d in settlement of a summons which had been issued against him.

Sherwood came back

*ERIC Graham **STEELE** (1979-1984)*
b Newcastle-upon-Tyne, Northumberland 14/5/1954
FL 51 (-), FAC 4 (-), FLC 8 (-), FLT 2 (-)
Newcastle Utd (am 2/71, pro 7/72); Peterborough Utd (12/73); Brighton & Hove Albion (£19,000 2/77); Watford (£100,000 10/79); Cardiff City (loan 3/83); Derby County (free 7/84); Southend Utd (free 8/87); Mansfield Town (loan 3/88); Notts County (non-contract 10/88); Wolverhampton Wanderers (non-contract 3/89); Derby County goalkeeping coach (by 3/96)
ENGLAND SCHOOLS UNDER-18
From the time of his arrival he had a good run in the first-team goal, but was rarely in action during his last three-and-a-half seasons with the club, Steve Sherwood being back in favour. Having moved to the Baseball Ground, Steele settled in the Midlands, and after a career of 348 League appearances became a restaurateur in Derbyshire.

Nightmare start

*GEOFFrey Gordon **STEINER** (1952)*
b Hackney, London 8/6/1928
FL 3 (-)
Barnet (circa 1947); Tottenham Hotspur (am); Watford (am 10/50, pro 11/50); Cheltenham Town (free cs 1953)
He had nearly three seasons as a full-back on the Vicarage Road staff, but his first-team action was limited to three

games at the end of the 1951/2 season. Having waited 18 months for his chance, he headed an own-goal after six minutes of his début, and finished with a Football League career of three defeats - 0-3, 0-2 and 0-1.

James (JIMMY) STEPHENSON (1922-1927)
b New Delavel, Northumberland
d Newcastle-upon-Tyne, Northumberland, February 1958 (aged 63)

FL 195 (18), FAC 14 (2 inc 1p)
New Delavel Villa; Aston Villa (5/13); Sunderland (£2,000 5/21); Watford (£500 9/22); Queens Park Rangers (free 7/27); Boston (free 8/28); New Delavel Villa; Ashington (1/31)
A class act on the right wing, he was one of a famous footballing brotherhood which included the great Clem, and was also an uncle of the cricketer/footballer, Bob Stephenson. Jimmy had top-flight experience with Aston Villa and Sunderland, and was virtually an automatic choice throughout his five full seasons at Vicarage Road.

Class act, class family

WORRELL Ricardo STERLING (1983-1988)
b Bethnal Green, London 8/6/1965
FL 82+12 (14), FAC 18 (2), FLC 7+2 (1), UEFA 0+1 (-)
Watford (sch 12/79, appr 7/81, pro 5/83); Peterborough Utd (£70,000 3/89); Bristol Rovers (£140,000 7/93)
It was a typically bold Graham Taylor move to throw this shy individual in at the deep end. His League début at Old Trafford as a 17-year-old began a first-team career of fits and starts over six seasons as a hard-working right-winger, but he was to become a fixture in the senior sides at Peterborough and Bristol Rovers, for whom he was signed by John Ward.

Old Trafford at 17

ALEXander STEWART (1910-1916)
b Dumfries
SL 149 (3p), FAC 11 (1p), SCC 6 (1p), WW1 9 (-)
Strathclyde (am); Ilkeston Utd (circa 12/09); Watford (7/10); Cardiff City (free cs 1919)
An accomplished and popular left-back, he relinquished the captaincy when he enlisted in The Footballers' Battalion in January 1915, but continued as a regular member of the Southern League championship-winning side. After sustaining severe shrapnel wounds in France, he unexpectedly resumed his career with Cardiff City after the war.

Badly hurt in France

JOHN STIRK (1978-1979)
b Consett, Co Durham 5/9/1955
FL 46 (-), FAC 3 (-), FLC 11 (-)
Consett; Ipswich Town (sch 10/71, appr 7/72, pro 6/73); Watford (£30,000 5/78); Chesterfield (£40,000 3/80 until cs 1983); North Shields (by 12/84)
ENGLAND YOUTH
After helping Watford into the Second Division as its ever-present right-back, he was discarded without playing for the club again in League football. All his 60 first-team appearances were consecutive. Having completed his

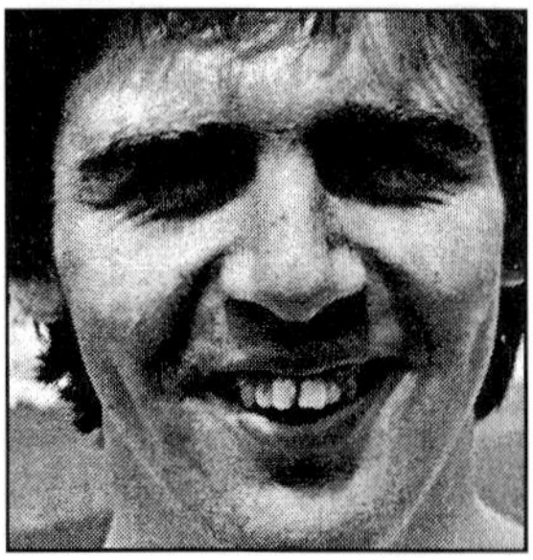
Discarded after long run

apprenticeship at Portman Road, he'd won two youth international caps and had a short run as a stand-in in the First Division.

Two great games

KENneth Sidney STOCKLEY *(1949-1950)*
b Watford, Herts 24/11/1926
FL 1 (-), FAC 1 (-)
Watford Schools; Luton Town (am 1943, pro 2/44); Watford (free 7/48 until cs 1952)
After captaining Watford Schools he was in Luton Town's first team at 16 during the war. His two senior matches in Watford's No 6 shirt were a 6-0 win against Ipswich Town, followed immediately by a drawn FA Cup tie against Preston North End in front of 25,000 at Vicarage Road. Leg injuries severely hampered his career, and ended it in 1952.

Unexpected second term

AlFRED STOKES *(1931-1933)*
b West Bromwich, Staffs 1904
FL 38 (-), FAC 4 (-)
Allan & Everitt's, Birmingham; Notts County (11/26); Coventry City (5/29); Watford (free 5/31 until cs 1933)
Originally discovered in works football, he came to Watford as a vigorous tackler and spent most of the 1931/2 season at right-half in the first team. Although given a free transfer, he was in fact subsequently re-engaged, but the signing of Bill Findlay pushed him into the background, and he played only four times in his second season.

Meteoric career

ALFred Frederick STOKES *(1961)*
b Hackney, London 13/10/1932
FL 14 (2), FLC 2 (1)
Clapton; Tottenham Hotspur (am 6/51, pro 2/53); Fulham (£10,000 7/59); Cambridge City (10/60); Watford (free 4/61); Nuneaton Borough (12/61); Ramsgate Athletic (£850); Hastings Utd; Guildford City
ENGLAND UNDER-23 and 'B'; FOOTBALL LEAGUE
Recruited to the professional ranks at the age of 20, he played only 80 League games for his First Division clubs, but collected 46 goals and several representative honours. He occupied all three inside-forward positions during his brief, undistinguished Watford career, and ended a flurry of non-League moves by emigrating to Australia in 1962.

First-team amateur

PETER Russell STORER *(1959)*
b Shoreditch, London 14/2/1935
FL 9 (-)
Sun Sports; Berkhamsted Town (by 1957); Watford (am 3/59); Hitchin Town; Hemel Hempstead Town (cs 1961)
He became well-known in local amateur football as a well-built goalkeeper, and had more experience for Watford's first team as an unpaid player than anyone since Ernie Grimsdell many years earlier. His appearances were in the last nine games of 1958/9, in addition to the notorious game which was abandoned when the Vicarage Road lights failed.

Joseph (**JOCK**) **STRAIN** *(1921-1927)*
b Scotland
FL 178 (6), FAC 15 (-)
Baillieston Juniors; Shettleston; Bo'ness (trialist); Watford ("small fee" 11/21); Hamilton Academical (free 8/27 until cs 1928); Baillieston Juniors (12/29 until cs 1930)
A hard-drinking Scot who gave equal dedication to his football as a never-say-die half-back. Spotted by Harry Kent as a Bo'ness trialist in a Scottish Second Division game, he was signed to stiffen the defence, which he undoubtedly did, at centre-half and later left-half. Although saddled with 'Jock' at Vicarage Road, he was known as 'Joe' back home.

Drank hard, played hard

James Henry (**JIMMY**) **STRAIN** *(1957)*
b Chesham, Bucks 28/11/1937
FL 3 (-)
Herts Schools; Berkhamsted Town; Chesham Utd; Watford (am 9/55, pro 11/55 until cs 1958); Millwall (9/58 until cs 1959); Gravesend & Northfleet; Amersham Town; coach in Denmark
With Bryan Atkinson and Ernie Bateman he was one of three locally-recruited centre-halves who stood in briefly for Roy Brown during the 1956/7 season. He first came to notice as a Berkhamsted schoolboy, and it was as a National Serviceman that he made his three League appearances. He made another five during his season at Millwall.

Three local centre-halves

PERRY John **SUCKLING** *(1992-1993)*
b Leyton, London 12/10/1965
FL 39 (-), FAC 1 (-), FLC 4 (-), AIC 2 (-)
Coventry City (sch 10/81, appr 4/82, pro 10/83); Manchester City (player-exchange 6/86); Chelsea (loan 12/67); Crystal Palace (£100,000 1/88); West Ham Utd (loan 12/89); Brentford (loan 10/91); Ernest Borel, Hong Kong (loan 1/92); Watford (free 7/92); Doncaster Rovers (free 7/94); Wits University, South Africa (free 3/96)
ENGLAND YOUTH and UNDER-21
A First Division goalkeeper at 16, and Coventry's youngest-ever senior player, he went on to win caps at two levels, and was eventually brought to Watford immediately after the halcyon era of Tony Coton and David James. He's one of the few modern 'keepers to have been beaten nine times in a League game. It happened in a Palace fixture at Liverpool.

Division 1 'keeper at 16

Hubert (**HUGH**) **SURTEES** *(1946-1949)*
b Durham City, 16/7/1921
FL 14 (1), FAC 2 (-), WW2 1 (-)
Bushey; Watford (am 4/46, pro 7/46); Crystal Palace (free 8/49); Snowdown Colliery (8/52); Biggleswade Town
As a misfortune to start a professional career, it's hard to imagine anything more cruel than the broken leg which he sustained in the 1946 pre-season trial match. He made his League début just over a year later in the outside-left spot, but soon lost his place, and appeared only twice more - on the opposite flank - in his last season and a half at Vicarage Road.

Cruel start to career

Disastrous loan

Robert Louis (BOBBY) **SVARC** *(1977)*
b Leicester 8/2/1946
FL 1 (-)
Leicester City (appr 10/61, pro 3/63); Lincoln City (12/68); Barrow (loan 9/70); Boston Utd (10/71); Colchester Utd (12/72); Blackburn Rovers (£20,000 10/75); Watford (loan 9/77)
At Lincoln he was a playing colleague of Graham Taylor, in whose ten-year Watford régime he was the only man to be engaged on loan. The move backfired after 17 minutes of action, when he sustained an injury which ended his career as a foraging striker. His best spell had been at Colchester, for whom he scored 59 times in 116 League appearances.

Lived to 97

John (JACK) **SWAN** *(1925-1927)*
(formerly John ***SWANN****)*
b Seaham Harbour, Co Durham 19/7/1892
d Hendon, London, January 1990
FL 54 (27 inc 1p), FAC 5 (4)
Seaham Colliery; Huddersfield Town (5/19); Leeds Utd (11/21); Watford (£750 or £1,000+ 9/25); Queens Park Rangers (£250 or £300 2/27); Thames (free 7/28); Lovell's Athletic (10/29)
A *sine die* suspension (Jimmy Broad was dismissed at the same time) ended his Watford career as an experienced, hard-shooting goalscorer. He'd earlier been suspended by Leeds United for going AWOL, but was that club's top scorer when it took the Second Division title the following season. He played for Huddersfield in the 1920 FA Cup Final.

Unique distinctions

BRIAN Ernest **TALBOT** *(1985-1986)*
b Ipswich, Suffolk 21/7/1953
FL 46+2 (8), FAC 8 (-), FLC 3 (-)
Ipswich Town (sch 3/67, appr 7/68); Toronto Metros, Canada (loan 5/71 until 6/71 and 5/72 until 7/72); Ipswich Town (pro 8/72); Arsenal (£450,000 1/79); Watford (£150,000 6/85); Stoke City (£25,000 10/86); West Bromwich Albion (£25,000 1/88, player-manager 10/88 until 1/91); Fulham (non-contract 3/91); Aldershot (non-contract 3/91, player-manager 4/91, player-manager/managing director 8/91 until 11/91); Sudbury Town (1/92); Kettering Town chief executive and chairman (3/92 until 5/92); Hibernians, Malta, manager (1993)
ENGLAND UNDER-21, 'B' and FULL
He joined Watford as PFA Chairman, an England 'B' captain, holder of six Full caps, and the only man ever to have helped different clubs to FA Cup Final wins in successive years. An energetic midfielder of nearly six hundred League appearances, mostly for Ipswich and Arsenal, he created League history at Aldershot by being simultaneously a player and a director.

Walter Scott (WALLY) **TATTERSALL** *(1910-1912)*
b Warsop, Notts 4/9/1888
d Warsop, Notts 30/12/1968
SL 64 (11), FAC 8 (-), SCC 3 (-)

Chesterfield Town (am 1/08, pro 5/08); Mansfield Mechanics; Watford (7/10); Tottenham Hotspur (£500 for Tattersall and A.Grimsdell 4/12 until cs 1915); Shirebrook; Welbeck Colliery (5/21)

After missing very few first-team games in two seasons on Watford's right wing, he was sold with Arthur Grimsdell to raise cash for summer wages, without which none of the players could have been retained. The son of a Nottinghamshire pork butcher, he had eight different inside partners in his Southern League appearances for the club.

Sold with Grimsdell

LESlie **TAYLOR** *(1980-1985)*
b North Shields, Northumberland 4/12/1956
FL 167+5 (13), FAC 21 (3), FLC 14 (4), FLT 3 (-), UEFA 1 (-)
Wallsend Boys' Club; Oxford Utd (appr 12/72, pro 12/74); Watford (£100,000 plus K.B.Cassells, valued at £50,000, 11/80); Reading (loan 10/86, £20,000 12/86); Colchester Utd (£20,000 1/89 until cs 1990; Oxford Utd Under-16s part-time coach (1992/3)

As a result of other players' injuries and suspension he led Watford at Wembley as the club's fifth captain of 1983/4. An exceptionally busy, unspectacular but important midfield performer during the club's peak years, he had already played over two hundred League games for Oxford, and went on to help Reading to win the Full Members Cup at Wembley.

Fifth choice at Wembley

James (JIMMY) **TENNANT** *(1902-1905)*
b Scotland
SL 83 (15), FAC 9 (6), SEL 26 (12)
Parkhead; St Bernards (11/97); Woolwich Arsenal (5/99); Middlesbrough (Tennant and P.Turner for £180 5/01); Watford (6/02); Royal Albert (6/05); Stenhousemuir (cs 1906); St Bernards (cs 1907 until cs 1909)
SCOTLAND JUNIOR

Watford was the fourth professional club for which he and Peter Turner had formed a left-wing pair. Before the other half of the double-act caught up with him at Cassio Road, Tennant was ever-present at outside-left when the club dominated the Southern League Second Division, and indeed missed only two Southern League games in three years.

Wandering double-act

STEVE Graham **TERRY** *(1980-1988)*
b Clapton, London 14/6/1962
FL 160 (14), FAC 20+1 (1), FLC 20 (4), FLT 2 (1), UEFA 2+1 (-), FMC 2 (-)
Watford (sch 5/78, appr 7/78, pro 1/80); Hull City (£100,000 6/88); Northampton Town (£75,000 3/90); Aylesbury Utd (free cs 1994); Walton & Hersham (9/94); Enfield (free 3/95)

A craggy, muscular centre-half, commanding in the air, he suffered five-goal defeats in both his first two away League games, but went on to enjoy much of the club's success in the early 1980s, and played in the FA Cup Final. Elsewhere he took his career total of League appearances past four hundred. His father was an England Amateur international.

Son of Amateur cap

William **TERVIT** *(1900)*
SL 1 (-)
Muirhouse Rovers; Watford (briefly on trial 2/00); Raith Rovers (11/00)
The first player Watford ever brought down from Scotland, he came from Edinburgh as a trialist. Having scored in a practice game, he earned himself a Southern League appearance at inside-right three days later, but nothing further came of the trial. His début for Raith Rovers was as a member of an unfamiliar line-up during a players' dispute.

Wealdstone forward

F. **THEOBALD** *(1910-1911)*
SL 3 (-)
Wealdstone (until at least 1922); Watford (am 1910)
Good enough to represent Middlesex, he was an amateur inside-forward whose regular club was Wealdstone. His Southern League appearances for Watford were all in the 1910/1 season - home matches against Brentford (0-2) and Northampton Town (2-2), and a five-goal defeat - the biggest of the season - at Brighton & Hove Albion.

Fraternal coincidence

David Watkin John **(DAVE) THOMAS** *(1948-1950)*
b Mile End, London 6/7/1917
d Dovercourt, Essex 30/3/1991
FL 105 (39), FAC 6 (4)
Romford; Plymouth Argyle (6/38); Watford (£3,500 1/48); Gillingham ("substantial fee" 10/50 until cs 1952); Sittingbourne (1953); Chatham Town; Gravesend & Northfleet trainer (by 1957/8). Guested for Brentford, Clapton Orient, Fulham, Gillingham, Grimsby Town and West Ham Utd in WW2.
A centre-forward built like a brick outhouse. He joined Watford for a club-record fee for one player, and made his début in mid-season with six other newcomers. In 1946/7 he scored 18 League goals in 41 games for Plymouth - exactly as did his brother. Later in life he suffered from heart trouble caused by the accumulative effects of football knocks.

Schoolboy prodigy

RODERICK *Clive* **THOMAS** *(1988-1992)*
b Park Royal, London 10/10/1970
FL 65+21 (9), FAC 0+1 (-), FLC 3+2 (-), FMC 1+1 (-), AIC 1 (-)
Parkfield; Watford (sch 2/85); FA School of Excellence; Watford (tr 7/87, pro 5/88); Gillingham (loan 3/92); Carlisle Utd (free 7/93)
ENGLAND SCHOOLS, YOUTH and UNDER-21
Once a schoolboy prodigy, he scored the winner in the 1989 FA Youth Cup Final, more than a year after making his League début at Highbury as a trainee. A darting, dribbling winger, short in stature and with an extremely low centre of balance, he failed to fulfil his early promise but was a member of Carlisle's outstanding Third Division side in 1994/5.

<u>CYRIL Alfred</u> **THOMPSON** *(1951-1953)*
b Southend, Essex 18/12/1918
d Folkestone, Kent 5/4/1972
FL 78 (36), FAC 5 (5)
Southend Utd (7/45); Derby County (7/48); Brighton & Hove Albion (3/50); Watford (exchange for R.H.Garbutt 3/51); Folkestone Town (7/53, trainer by 9/62)
His tally of 25 League and Cup goals in 1951/2 was Watford's peacetime best for 17 years. A powerfully-built centre-forward - and an excellent club cricketer - he scored 88 League goals in 202 appearances before going to Folkestone, where he settled. He was a prisoner of war for five years before starting his Football League career at nearly 28 years of age.

Five years a POW

<u>GARRY Linsey</u> **THOMPSON** *(1988-1990)*
b Birmingham, Warwicks 7/10/1959
FL 24+10 (8), FAC 7+1 (-), FLC 0+1 (-)
Coventry City (sch 2/75, appr 7/76, pro 6/77); West Bromwich Albion (£250,000 2/83); Sheffield Wednesday (£450,000 8/85); Aston Villa (£450,000 6/86); Watford (£325,000 12/88); Crystal Palace (£150,000 3/90); Queens Park Rangers (£100,000 8/91); Cardiff City (free 8/93); Northampton Town (free 2/95)
ENGLAND UNDER-21
After emerging from Coventry City's apprentice ranks, which also produced his younger brother Keith (a youth international), he won six Under-21 caps and became the subject of a succession of lucrative transfers. An aggressive striker, extremely strong in the air, he had a disappointing scoring record at Watford, and was soon in the Reserves.

Six 6-figure moves

<u>William (BILL)</u> **THOMPSON** *(1946-1947)*
b Berwick-on-Tweed, Northumberland 31/8/1916
d Sunderland, Tyne & Wear, February 1989
FL 9 (-), FAC 2 (-)
Ashington; Leeds Utd (8/35 until 4/38); Watford (7/46 until cs 1947)
His brief experience in the first-team goal incorporated several good home wins, but he had a fairly torrid time on the road, conceding 21 goals in his six away games, including 17 in the last four. He'd been on Leeds United's books before the war, but it was with Watford, at the age of 30, that he played all his League football.

Busy in away games

<u>ARTHUR</u> **THURLEY** *(1932)*
b Bishops Stortford, Herts 17/5/1908
d Harefield, Middx 14/6/1972
FL 4 (-)
Bishops Stortford; Watford (am 1/26, pro 11/27 until cs 1933); Racing Club de Calais, France; Red Star Olympique, France; Lyon Olympique, France; Villourbanne, France; Watford Labour Club (permit player 1/38)
Big, energetic and versatile - he even had spells in goal for the Reserves - he had just one first-team run of four games at centre-half in his long spell with the club. The last of the

Gave the continent a go

four was a five-goal defeat at Fulham. After returning from France in the 1930s he worked at Shrodells Hospital until his death. He also captained Watford Town Cricket Club.

Bricklayer

Thomas (**TOMMY**) **TIERNEY** *(1904)*
SEL 2 (-)
Witton Albion; Northwich Victoria (8/93); Chorley (1894/5); Blackburn Rovers (6/95); New Brighton Tower (8/97); Blackburn Rovers (4/98); New Brighton Tower (4/98); Chorley (11/98); New Brighton Tower (5/99); Luton Town (7/00); Gainsborough Trinity (8/02); Barrow in Furness (2/03); Glentoran (8/03); Watford (8/04 until cs 1905); Chorley (9/05)
He'd included a trip across the Irish Sea among his many moves before arriving at Cassio Road for a trial which resulted in his engagement for the 1904/5 season. He was also employed in the town as a bricklayer. He'd once been a First Division forward with Blackburn, but at Watford was picked only for a couple of South-Eastern League fixtures, at inside-right.

Useful with a cue

Her**BERT** Frank **TINKLIN** *(1936)*
b Selston, Notts 16/6/1910
d Worcester 15/7/1980
FL 8 (-), 3SC 2 (-)
Alfreton Town (1924/5); Grantham (pro 1928 until cs 1929); Loughborough Corinthians (one season); Nuneaton Town; Folkestone; Aldershot (4/35); Watford (free 5/36 until cs 1937)
When he eventually got into League football in 1935/6, he held a regular place in the Aldershot side and made 35 appearances. He followed this with ten games on Watford's left wing the following season, at the end which he was released. Before joining the club he claimed a bar billiards "world record" with a break of 18,000.

A.E. **TOOLEY** *(1904-1906)*
SL 1 (-), SEL 2 (-), UL 2 (-)
Leighton Cee Springs (by 9/02); Watford (am 1903 until 1/07)
As an amateur full-back he did make that handful of senior appearances, but his main contribution at Cassio Road was as captain of the Reserves for both 1905/6 and 1906/7. In January 1907 he stood down, and ended his association with the club, due to pressure of business. In his one Southern League game, Brighton & Hove Albion were beaten 5-1.

Son of England goalie

GEORGE TOONE *(1919-1924)*
b Nottingham 6/9/1893
d Nottingham 21/7/1950
SL 13 (-), FL 165 (-), FAC 12 (-)
Mansfield Mechanics; Notts County (8/13 until cs 1916, but registration held until 7/19); Watford ("small fee" 7/19); Sheffield Wednesday (exchange for £240 plus G.Prior 8/24 until cs 1928); Scarborough Penguins (10/28)
A prodigious worker and quick to spot danger, he was a half-back whose strengths were defensive ones, as borne out by his goals tally. His consistency was such that he played in every one of Watford's first 159 Football League games. He was at Hillsborough with Billy Chapman and Jimmy Trotter, and his father kept goal for England.

Charles **TRACEY** *(1930-1931)*
b Glasgow 17/8/1909
FL 3 (1)
Douglas Water Thistle (6/29); Kirkmuirhill Juniors (2/30); Watford (free 5/30 until cs 1931); Morton Reserves (11/31); Kings Park (1/32 until cs 1932); Morecambe (4/33); Newry Town; Bacup Borough (8/36); Morton (by 8/39); Luton Town (8/45). Guested for Hartlepools Utd and Wrexham in WW2.
Maximum points were obtained from his three League games. Thames were beaten 1-0 at home, Bristol Rovers 5-1 away, and Bournemouth & Boscombe Athletic, against whom he scored, 2-0 at home. A small and clever winger, he went home to Scotland after his Watford season, but later crossed the border again twice more.

Maximum points

RAYmond **TRAIN** *(1978-1982)*
b Nuneaton, Warwicks 10/2/1951
FL 91+1 (3), FAC 9 (-), FLC 8+1 (1), FLT 1+1 (-)
Bedworth Utd; Walsall (appr 9/67, pro 11/68); Carlisle Utd (£15,000 12/71); Sunderland (£80,000 3/76); Bolton Wanderers (£30,000 3/77); Watford (£50,000 11/78); Oxford Utd (£10,000 3/82); AFC Bournemouth (loan 11/83); Northampton Town (free 7/84); Tranmere Rovers (free 8/85); Walsall (free 8/86, reserve and youth-team coach by 10/88, caretaker-manager 12/88 until 1/89); Port Vale community officer (2/90); Middlesbrough reserve-team coach (by cs 1991)
He joined Walsall twice, separated by nearly two decades, during which he turned out for eight other League clubs, four of which (lastly Watford) he helped to promotion in the space of six seasons. As a tidy little midfield player he appeared in well over five hundred League games, in which he scored a mere 24 goals, including one on his Watford début.

Promotion specialist

Patrick **TRAINER** *(1904)*
b Scotland
SEL 1 (2)
Douglas Wanderers; Watford (trial 4/04)
Inexplicably, the club brought him down from Castle Douglas for one game, in which he scored twice - and this after travelling on the overnight train and reaching Watford at 9am - but decided to show no further interest. He played inside-right, with former Douglas Wanderers colleague George Badenoch (who also scored in the 4-1 win) on the wing.

James (JIMMY) **TROTTER** *(1931-1932)*
b Newcastle-upon-Tyne, Northumberland 3/1/1899
d Teynham, Kent 11/2/1985
FL 4 (1)
Parsons Turbine Works; Bury (11/19); Sheffield Wednesday (2/22); Torquay Utd (6/30); Watford (£375 12/31 until cs 1933); Charlton Athletic (trainer 1935, manager 9/56 until 10/61); also England trainer
A début goal and an injury which ended his career were all Watford got for their money, but at Hillsborough he'd led the Second and First Division scorers in successive years, and twice scored five. He was England's sponge-man many times, and after his long Charlton stint under former playing colleague Jimmy Seed he succeeded him as manager.

Division 1's top scorer

Alfred **_DOCWRA TURNER_** _(1899)_
b Islington, Middx 25/6/1879
d Probus, Cornwall 2/10/1926
SL 4 (1), BCCL 1 (-)
Old Rossalians; West Herts (4/96); Crouch End Vampires; Watford (am 2/99); Upton Park; Nottingham Forest (pro 12/02); Bristol City (1/05 until cs 1905)
As a 16-year-old he played for the club in three friendly matches. His competitive games on the right wing three seasons later were just before he left for South Africa with the Herts Co of the Imperial Yeomanry. He played representative football for London, Middlesex and Essex, and in the Football League for Forest and Bristol City.

Wolves career shattered

John Allan **TURNER** _(1929-1930)_
FL 13 (-), FAC 3 (-)
Silverwood Colliery; Dalton Brook; Stockport County (12/26); Wolverhampton Wanderers (6/28); Watford (free 9/29); Rotherham United (free 4/30 until cs 1930); Southampton Borough (permit player 11/30); Winchester City (permit player 9/33)
A product of minor football in the Rotherham area, he entered League football with Stockport and became the first-team goalie on moving to Wolves. A broken leg only seven games into the season, however, led to a year in the wilderness before his short first-team spell at Watford. After a very brief return to Yorkshire he turned up on the south coast.

Tennant's sidekick

PETER TURNER _(1904-1907)_
b Glasgow 18/12/1876
d East Kilbride, Lanarks 8/2/1970
SL 99 (20 inc 1p), FAC 9 (2), SEL 17 (8), UL 26 (8)
Parkhead; St Bernards (6/98); Woolwich Arsenal (5/00); Middlesbrough (£180 for Turner and J.Tennant 5/01); Luton Town (cs 1903); Watford (5/04); Clyde (5/07); Leyton (5/07 until cs 1908); Doncaster Rovers (1/09 until 2/09)
SCOTLAND JUNIOR
Jimmy Tennant's seemingly universal sidekick was an elegant and skilful inside-forward. Although perceived to lack shooting power, he topped Watford's list of scorers in 1905/6, in addition to his creative duties, with a total of 17 goals in all competitions. He missed very few games in his three years at Cassio Road, and none at all in his first season.

Soon dispensed with

Robert **_(BOB) TURNER_** _(1902)_
b Manchester, Lancs
SL 2 (-)
Gravesend Utd (5/97); Newton Heath (5/98); Brighton Utd (5/99); Thames Ironworks (12/99); Fulham (12/00); Glentoran (cs 1901); Watford (8/02 until 9/02); Rossendale Utd (10/02)
His experience before he reached Cassio Road included winning two cups with Gravesend United, three Football League games for Newton Heath, and a spell in Ireland. He started the 1902/3 season as Watford's centre-half, but in next to no time was suspended by the club, and a permanent parting of the ways quickly followed.

Edmund David (**DAVE**) **UNDERWOOD** *(1952-1963)*
b St Pancras, London 15/3/1928
d Durban, South Africa 25/1/1989
FL 176 (-), FAC 12 (-), SFC 2 (-), FLC 4 (-)
Kingsbury Town; Edgware Town; Queens Park Rangers (am 9/49, pro 12/49); Watford (2/52); Liverpool (£5,000 12/53); Watford (4-figure fee 7/56); Dartford (8/57); Watford (4/60); Fulham (free 7/63); Dunstable Town (7/65); Hastings Utd player-manager (cs 1966); Barnet (permit player 11/67); Wealdstone manager (by 11/68); Barnet chairman (by 8/77)
A genial, ebullient figure who had three spells as a goalkeeper at Vicarage Road, the first of which ended with the club's first £5,000 sale. He became the proprietor of a haulage business, and as Barnet's chairman he earned the gratitude of Jimmy Greaves for his help in the latter's fight to overcome much-publicised personal difficulties.

Joined three times

Edward **DENNIS** *Herbert* **UPHILL** *(1959-1960)*
b Bath, Somerset 11/8/1931
FL 51 (30 inc 3p), FAC 7 (6), SFC 1 (-)
Peasedown Colliery; Odd Down; Tottenham Hotspur (am 3/48); Finchley; Tottenham Hotspur (pro 9/49); Reading (part-exchange 2/53); Coventry City (10/55); Mansfield Town (3/57); Watford (4-figure fee 6/59); Crystal Palace (4-figure fee 10/60); Rugby Town (4/63); Romford; Dartford (2/64); Croxley Casuals (permit player (10/67)
Battling unselfishly and very productively at centre-forward, he shared 84 League and cup goals with Cliff Holton in the 1959/60 season. On leaving League football, in which he scored 147 times, he recorded a hat-trick on his début for Rugby Town. He later became a bookmaker in Watford, and stood for the Conservative Party in local elections.

Prolific and unselfish

John Allison Gray (**JOHNNY**) **USHER** *(1946-1948)*
b Hexham, Northumberland 6/9/1918
d Fulham, London 5/1/1989
FL 23 (3), FAC 3 (1)
Watford (am 3/46, pro 5/46); Folkestone (8/48)
Recommended to the club by Bobby Ross, with whom he served in Cairo, he was an enthusiastic utility player who spent two seasons on the Vicarage Road staff. He wore five different first-team shirts, and his goals included one in his first League game - a 4-3 away win against Bristol Rovers.

Vicarage Road via Cairo

Henry John (**HARRY**) **VANNER** *(1928)*
b Shoreditch, London 27/12/1898
d Bethnal Green, London 18/1/1975
FL 2 (-)
RN Depot, Chatham; Charlton Athletic (am 3/24); Watford (am 4/28); Erith & Belvedere
His football experience included appearances for Kent and for Royal Navy and Royal Marines representative teams. Watford gave him two Third Division (South) games on the right wing, and on the first occasion did so without League permission, after registering him later than the March 16th deadline. For this they were fined two guineas.

Unauthorised appearance

Mostly an amateur

*Edmund Algernon (**ALGY**)* ***VARLEY*** *(1898-1901)*
b Watford, Herts 10/4/1879
d Wembley, Middx 13/7/1945
SL 42 (9), FAC 6 (1), BCCL 12 (3)
Ealing; Watford Church Institute; West Herts (am 3/98); Watford St Mary's (am 4/98); Watford (pro 10/00); West Ham Utd (1/02); Shepherds Bush (2/03); Watford Amateurs (by 10/05); Shepherds Bush (am by 2/06)
The son of a dentist who practised near Marble Arch and in Watford, he followed his father into the profession, but did not qualify until 1921. As a winger he made most of his first-team appearances for the club before turning professional, and subsequently only Harry Smith has come anywhere near his total of games as an unpaid player.

Registration retained

*Thomas Heppell (**TOMMY**)* ***VARTY*** *(1950-1951)*
b Newcastle-upon-Tyne, Northumberland 2/12/1921
FL 34 (5), FAC 1 (-)
Newcastle Utd (am 5/39 until cs 1942); Darlington (am 4/44, pro 8/45); Watford (9/50 until cs 1951)
After scoring 31 times in 162 League games for Darlington, he began his Watford career with a 5-0 win over Gillingham. A versatile forward or wing-half, he played mainly at inside-left before going into business with his wife back in Darlington in August 1951. Watford nonetheless retained his registration, and listed him at £2,000 as late as 1953.

John ***WAKEFIELD*** *(1897)*
SL 1 (-)
Hucknall Portland; Notts County Reserves (1896/7); Northfleet (pro 5/97); West Herts (trial 10/97); Stapleford Town (7/98); Arnold (8/99)
Engaged on trial as soon as professionalism was adopted, he was picked for the club's first Southern League eleven to include paid men. The change of status was not an immediate success - eight goals were conceded for only the second time in the club's 16-year history - and inside-right Wakefield was deemed unworthy of further attention.

Administrative blunder

*Andrew (**ANDY**)* ***WALKER*** *(1930)*
b Paisley, Renfrewshire 27/9/1900
d Paisley, Renfrewshire 17/9/1963
FL 2 (-)
Renfrew; Bo'ness (6/26); St Mirren (4/28); Bo'ness (4/28); Reading (6/28); Bo'ness (loan 8/29); Watford (free 6/30); Dunfermline Athletic (6/31 until 7/32)
SCOTLAND JUNIOR
His curiously coincidental first-team career at Watford consisted of two games at centre-half, on Christmas Day and Boxing Day 1930. Both were 2-2 draws with Walsall with about 6,000 present. Reading had wanted a fee for him, but due to administrative negligence at Elm Park he became a free agent shortly before joining Watford.

Michael Stewart Gordon (**MICKY**) **WALKER** *(1968-1973)*
b Colwyn Bay, Denbighs 28/11/1945
FL 137 (-), FAC 14 (-), FLC 8 (-)
Berks & Bucks Schools; Oxfordshire Schools; Reading (am 4/61, pro 1/63); Shrewsbury Town (free 6/64); York City (6/66); Watford (£5,000 9/68); Charlton Athletic (loan 2/73); Colchester Utd (£4,000 6/73, reserve-team player-coach by 4/84, manager 5/86); Norwich City (reserve-team manager 11/87, manager 6/92); Everton manager (1/94 until 11/94)
WALES UNDER-23
He was the only Watford goalkeeper to become a League manager, and the first to represent the club in the Second Division. After some success as Norwich's manager he left in acrimonious circumstances to join Everton, where he struggled and was soon dismissed. He made 451 League appearances for Colchester, and his son Ian became an England goalkeeper.

Father of England cap

PAUL Graham **WALKER** *(1972)*
b Bradford, Yorks 3/4/1949
FL 2+1 (-), FAC 1 (-)
Bradford Park Avenue (youth team); Wolverhampton Wanderers (pro 10/66); Watford (loan 12/71); Swindon Town (loan 3/73); Peterborough Utd (free 7/73); Barnsley (free 7/75); Huddersfield Town (11/76 until 4/77)
Drafted into midfield on loan during a club-record run of ten successive defeats, he was unable to stem the tide, and indeed in the three games which he started, 12 goals were conceded. These included four in a home FA Cup tie against Third Division Notts County. Seventy-five games for Peterborough United represented the bulk of his League experience.

PETER Martin **WALKER** *(1954-1962)*
b Watford, Herts 31/3/1933
FL 172 (37), FAC 7 (2), SFC 7 (2), FLC 4 (3)
Whippendell Road Guild; Watford (am 7/49); Bushey Utd; Watford (pro 7/54); Kettering Town (free 7/62); Wisbech Town; Stevenage Town (by 1966/7); Dunstable Town (1/68)
Associated with his local League club from the age of 16, he played in both Egypt and Malta with Bill Shipwright whilst in the RAF on National Service, following which he signed professional forms. A versatile forward capable of moments of great skill, he became a prolific non-League scorer and went into business as a garage proprietor.

Played in Egypt & Malta

RONald William **WALKER** *(1955)*
b Westminster, London 10/4/1930
d Devizes, Wilts, June 1988
FL 3 (-)
Leytonstone; Watford (am 7/50); Walthamstow Avenue; Watford (pro 4/54 until cs 1955)
Signed by Watford on amateur forms long before he turned professional, he spent a season on the staff before being transfer-listed with a fee of £1,000 on his head. The League, however, awarded him a free transfer. An inside- or outside-left, he played in two of the popular floodlit friendlies of the time, and scored against Third Lanark.

Eventually turned pro

Half a season

Thomas **WALKER** *(1908)*
b Seaton Delavel, Northumberland
SL 15 (5)
Thornley; Sunderland (cs 1903); West Stanley (9/06); Fulham (5/07); Watford (1/08); Blackpool (7/08)
He spent a season-and-a-half as a reservc player at Craven Cottage before moving to Cassio Road in mid-season. Going straight into the first team, he was ever-present during his short time at the club, before moving on during the summer. He began in the centre-forward position, but for the last few weeks was used at inside-right.

George **WALLER** *(1901)*
SL 7 (-), FAC 2 (-)
Belper Town; Wolverton LNWR (7/97 to cs 1900); Bedford Queen's Engineering Works (11/00); Watford (9/01 until 12/01); Bedford Queen's Engineering Works (9/02)
A goalkeeper signed in mid-season when Hammett was released to take a job outside the game, he began his Watford career with a penalty save on his début. Ignominy quickly followed, however, for he was soon dismissed, after what was described as a series of poor displays, for "habits which render training ineffective".

Brilliant youth coach

John Thomas ***(TOM)*** **WALLEY** *(1967-1977)*
b Caernarvon 27/2/1945
FL 214+3 (17), FAC 16 (-), FLC 15 (1)
Caernarvon Town (am); Wrexham (am 11/63); Caernarvon Town (pro); Arsenal (£1,000 12/64); Watford (£9,000 3/67); Orient (£22,500 12/71); Watford (£3,000 5/76, youth-team coach 8/77, first-team coach 1/88 until 3/90); Millwall youth-team coach (8/90 until 3/96): also Wales Under-21 manager (2/96); Arsenal youth-team coach (4/96)
WALES UNDER-23 and FULL
A strong and determined wing-half who, before his career was ended by injury, played with the dedication which was to characterise his work as an outstanding youth coach who took Watford and Millwall to two FA Youth Cup Finals each. During his spell as first-team coach under Steve Harrison, his brother Ernie was in charge of the Reserves.

Consistency elusive

Edward Ernest ***(ERNIE / DICK)*** **WALLINGTON** *(1921-1922)*
b Rickmansworth, Herts 8/7/1895
d Croydon, Surrey 15/2/1959
FL 51 (5), FAC 2 (-)
Rickmansworth Town; Watford (Reserves 1/13, pro 2/20 until cs 1923); Arsenal (9/23); Watford Old Boys (reinstated amateur by 1926/7)
After turning out for the Reserves from the age of 17 he remained a Rickmansworth Town player until he eventually became a professional. An occasionally brilliant but wildly erratic right-winger, he had a good first-team run which ended - permanently - when Jimmy Stephenson was signed. Wallington's brother George also played for the Reserves.

*- **WALMESLEY** (1903)*
SL 1 (-)
Watford (trial 1/03)
He came down on trial, apparently recommended by the famous Preston North End goalkeepers, Trainer and McBride, and was put in goal for a home game against Millwall, without anyone at the club having seen him play. The folly of this was soon apparent, for he was spectacularly inept and conceded seven goals. He returned north within a day or two.

*James Thomas (**JIMMY**) **WALSH** (1974-1977)*
b Paddington, London 20/11/1954
FL 60+5 (-), FAC 1 (-), FLC 4 (-)
Watford (am 6/70, appr 11/70, pro 11/72); York City (free 6/78 until 4/81); Frickley Athletic; Slough Town (1981/2); Windsor & Eton (by 12/84)
He followed his apprenticeship with six seasons as a Vicarage Road professional, and had a good run at left-back before being superseded by the newly-signed Keith Pritchett. When released at the end of 1977/8, he had made just a couple of substitute appearances in the League during that Fourth Division championship-winning season.

Made way for Pritchett

*John (**JOHNNY**) **WALTER** (1905-1916)*
SL 1 (-), SEL 2 (-), UL 5 (1), WW1 3 (-)
Callow Land Old Boys; Watford (am); Clapton (1913/4)
A local amateur, he turned out for Watford Reserves, and for the the county, for a long period of time, and was notably versatile. All his peacetime experience as a first-time player was in 1905 and 1906, but he was to reappear much later, during the Great War, by which time he had also represented the prominent amateur club, Clapton.

Versatile county player

*Thomas Charles (**TOM**) **WALTERS** (1935-1942)*
b Tre-Alaw, Glam 15/6/1909
d Torquay, Devon 27/1/1968
FL 57 (24), FAC 2 (1), 3SC 7 (6), WW2 34 (16)
Merthyr Town; Bolton Wanderers (5/30); Crystal Palace (5/32); Exeter City (free, cs 1933); Torquay Utd (11/33); Watford (5/35); Clapton Orient (free 6/38); Dartford (free cs 8/39); Watford (4/40 until cs 1942)
A coalminer in the Valleys before embarking on his career as a centre-forward, he scored in each of his first three League games for Watford, and in the same season hit two hat-tricks in the space of five games. After the war he ran pubs in Watford, Abbots Langley and Croxley Green, and then died a few weeks after retiring to Devon at the age of 58.

Miner/footballer/publican

*David (**DAI**) **WARD** (1962-1963)*
b Barry, Glam 16/7/1934
d South Wales 12/1/1996
FL 59 (31), FAC 5 (1), FLC 2 (-)
Barry Town (8/50 until 11/54); also Cardiff City (am 1952); Bristol Rovers (11/54); Cardiff City (2/61); Watford (£7,000 5/62); Brentford (£8,000+ 10/63); Worcester City (8/65); Bath City (7/66); Cambridge Utd player/youth-team manager; Kettering Town coach; Cambridge City player-coach (by 1972 until 4/74)

Never stopped scoring

WALES FULL
Despite a dramatic decline in the club's performances in the second half of 1962/3, he continued to score consistently and his total of 29 League goals was the Third Division's best. A busy, energetic inside-forward, he'd won a cap whilst with each of his two previous League clubs, and on moving to Brentford he scored twice on his début, in a 9-0 victory.

Came through ordeal

DARREN Philip **WARD** *(1996)*
b Harrow, London 13/9/1978
FL 1 (-)
Watford (sch 10/93, appr 7/95)
As a 17-year-old trainee he was propelled into first-team action by injuries and suspension affecting all the senior centre-backs. With only a few reserve-team appearances behing him, he came through a tight relegation scrap at Luton with composure and a clean sheet. His goalkeeping brother, Lee, had been a Watford trainee before him.

Valued by Taylor

JOHN Peter **WARD** *(1979-1981)*
b Lincoln 7/4/1951
FL 22+5 (6), FAC 1+1 (-), FLC 1 (-)
Adelaide Park, Lincoln; Lincoln City (am 7/69, pro 3/71), Workington (loan 9/72); Watford (£15,000 7/79); Grimsby Town (free 6/81); Lincoln City (free 3/82); Watford (trainer-coach 5/82, assistant-manager 7/85 until 5/87); Southend Utd coach (9/87 for two weeks); Aston Villa assistant-manager (1/88 until 1/91); York City manager (11/91); also an England 'B' and Under-21 coach, and Under-21 manager; Bristol Rovers manager (3/93 until cs 1996)
He was used by Graham Taylor in a variety of roles, from his days as top scorer when Lincoln City won the Fourth Division championship to his coaching of international teams. His career as a striker at Watford was a modest one, but he returned to become a respected coach and assistant-manager, until being discarded when Dave Bassett arrived.

Played up front, too

KEITH Donald **WARN** *(1960)*
b Croxley Green, Herts 20/3/1941
FL 3 (-)
London Schools; Croxley Boys Club; Fulham youth team; Watford (am 8/57, pro 3/59); Dover (free 7/61); Kettering Town; Stevenage Town (by 2/64); Elizabeth City, Australia (by 2/67); Modbury, Australia, manager; Sun Sports (by 1972/3); Dickinsons (Croxley) manager (6/73); Bedmond Social manager (until 1977)
After his success as a goalkeeper at Durrants School, he went on to play for the county youth team. His three League games were in a Watford team on the verge of winning promotion from the Fourth Division, and he began with two clean sheets. He also played occasionally in the forward line, for both the youth team and the Reserves.

John (JACK) **WARNER** *(1926-1930)*
b Woolwich, London 1898
d Greenwich, London 23/8/1950
FL 110 (22), FAC 5 (3)
Custom House; Burnley (briefly 2/21); Manchester City (4/21); Watford (5/26); Thames (free 6/30 until cs 1932)
The big Manchester clubs provided Watford with a succession of players in the late 1920s, and Warner came from Maine Road with Arthur Daniels. A clever ball-player with a fair number of First Division games at inside-right, he moved to wing-half after two years at Vicarage Road, and then served Thames during their two seasons of League membership.

Londoner from Manchester

Thomas (TOMMY) **WATERALL** *(1914-1921)*
b Radford, Notts 24/10/1884
d Nottingham 8/11/1951
SL 72 (15), FL 36 (4), FAC 4 (1), SCC 1 (-)
Radford Institute (1904); Eleanor Utd (1905); Notts County (am 3/06, pro 4/06); Bradford Park Avenue (6/08); Mansfield Mechanics (cs 1909); Leicester Fosse (£10 7/13); Watford (7/14); Gillingham (free 7/21); Sheppey Utd (cs 1922); Sittingbourne (by 3/26). Guested for Stockport County in WW1.
A former miner, and one of three brothers who played League football, he scored all the goals in his first away game for Watford (a 3-0 win at Millwall) in the season in which they won the Southern League championship. He spent three winters as the club's senior outside-left, usually with Charlie White as his partner, and missed only a handful of games.

Soon showed his worth

MARK Stewart **WATSON** *(1993-1995)*
b Vancouver, Canada 8/9/1970
FL 18 (-), FAC 1+2 (-)
Vancouver 89s, Canada; Ipswich Town Reserves (9/93); Watford (11/93); Vancouver 86ers, Canada (free 8/95)
CANADA UNDER-21 and FULL
When already an established international he sought a career in English football, and after five weeks with Ipswich he impressed sufficiently as a cool, cultured central defender in Watford's reserve team to be taken on as a registered player. He had a first-team run in a struggling side, but then the signing Colin Foster and Keith Millen restricted his chances.

Edged out by new man

JOHN Gibson **WATT** *(1972)*
b Airdrie, Lanarks 23/11/1954
FL 0+1 (-)
Chesham Utd (1971); Watford (am 10/71, appr 10/71, pro 3/73); Hillingdon Borough (loan 11/73 until 3/74); Hayes (free, cs 1974); Chesham Utd; St Albans City player-coach (by 12/84 until cs 1987); Chesham Utd (by 2/88); Maidenhead manager (10/92)
His League career lasted 17 minutes, and was completed during his apprenticeship as a defender. Norwich City came to Vicarage Road on the last day of 1971/2, seeking to clinch

22,000 saw his one game

the Second Division championship, which they did in front of over 22,000. Watt was Watford's substitute, and he's the club's third-youngest post-war League débutant.

Got his first touch at 2-0

KEITH **WAUGH** *(1992-1993)*
b Sunderland, Co Durham 27/10/1956
FL 7 (-)
Sunderland (sch 10/71, appr 6/73, pro 7/74); Peterborough Utd (free 7/76); Sheffield Utd (£90,000 8/81); Cambridge Utd (loan 11/84); Bristol City (loan 12/84, free 7/85); Coventry City (£40,000 8/89); Watford (loan 12/90, free 2/91, youth-team manager 8/93 until 5/94)
He'd been David James's goalkeeping understudy for 14 months when he eventually made his first-team début - and Watford took a two-goal lead against Newcastle United before he'd touched the ball. The match finished 2-2. He was then 35 years old and a veteran of more than 450 League appearances - all of them after being released by his home-town club.

'Twixt Biggar & Williams

Joseph (JOE) **WEBSTER** *(1910-1914)*
b Nottingham 1883
d Northampton 15/10/1927
SL 131 (-), FAC 13 (-), SCC 4 (-)
Ilkeston Utd (6/07); Watford (7/10); West Ham Utd (£300 4/14); Watford trainer (7/20 until 5/24); Watford Old Boys trainer; Northampton Town trainer (7/26)
The second of three outstanding goalkeepers who successively served the club for more than two decades, he was good enough to play for the Southern League twice, and for The South v England in an international trial match. This was soon after he'd been falsely diagnosed as having tuberculosis. His untimely death followed an appendix operation.

Known in local circles

J. (JIMMY) **WEEDON** *(1897)*
SL 12 (-), HSC 2 (-)
The Grove; Kings Langley (by 1890); West Herts (1896)
Early in his career he represented The Grove, a club which disbanded soon after losing some of its best men, recruited as reserve-team players when West Herts Club & Ground was founded. Weedon himself was by then playing for Kings Langley. He made all his Southern League appearances as a wing-half in the latter half of the 1896/7 season.

2-1 away win not enough

George B. **WEEKS** *(1932)*
b London
FL 1 (-)
Millwall Utd (1925); Southall (3/28); Brentford (pro 5/29); Watford (free 7/32 until cs 1933); Ford Sports, Dagenham (permit player 10/34)
In three seasons at Griffin Park he made only two League appearances, but went straight into Watford's first team at left-back for the opening game of the 1932/3 season. Despite a 2-1 win at Norwich, he wasn't picked again. As a Southall player he'd been selected to represent the Athenian League against the Isthmian League.

Alexander (**ALEX / JOCK**) **WEIR** *(1943-1946)*
b Bathgate, West Lothian
FL 1 (-), FAC 4 (-), WW2 22 (5)
Stoneyburn Juniors (7/35); Preston North End (2/36 to cs 1936); Waterford (10/36 until 11/36); Shelbourne (8/38); Glenavon (8/39); Ballymena Utd (12/39); Glentoran (1940/1 until 1943/4); Watford (12/45); Northampton Town (free 9/47); Margate player-manager (7/48); Wembley Town coach; Berne, Switzerland, coach (6/50 until 1953); also Switzerland coach for 3 years; Hayes coach (1957); Hendon coach (1958/9); coach in Iceland, Burma and France; St Albans City manager (cs 1961 until cs 1963). Guested for Hartlepools Utd, Middlesbrough, Millwall, Tranmere Rovers and Watford in WW2.
LEAGUE OF IRELAND
He made his only peacetime League appearance on the right wing (in a five-goal Boxing Day defeat at Southend), but was primarily an inside-forward. He represented the League of Ireland v the Irish League, and remarkably played in national cup-winning teams on either side of the Irish border in successive seasons - for Shelbourne and Ballymena.

A great time in Ireland

DUNCAN WELBOURNE *(1963-1974)*
b Scunthorpe, Lincs 28/7/1940
FL 404+7 (22), FAC 28 (2), FLC 17+1 (1)
Scunthorpe & Lindsey Utd (am 2/56); Grimsby Town (pro 8/57); Watford (£1,300 11/63); Southport (free 6/74, player-coach by 9/75, acting-manager 9/75 until 1/76, commercial manager by 4/77 until early 1977/8)
An unbroken sequence of 280 League games bears testimony to his consistency as a tough-tackling wing-half or full-back who broke Tommy Barnett's 35-year-old appearances record for Watford. He was ever-present when the club won the Third Division title, and in the FA Cup semi-final run the following season. His brother played for Scunthorpe United.

Barnett caught at last

C.F. **WELCH** *(1902)*
SL 1 (1)
Richmond Association; Watford (am 1902/3); Ilford (10/04); also Cheshunt (12/04)
His only first-team game was on the right wing in a home Southern League defeat (1-4) against Portsmouth. It was the club's fifth successive loss, but Welch at least had the consolation of scoring. He was prominent in amateur circles, and went on to represent both Herts and London. He also played cricket for Pinner, Harrow Weald and Stanmore.

COLIN WEST *(1985-1986)*
b Wallsend, Northumberland 13/11/1962
FL 45 (20), FAC 8 (3), FLC 2+1 (-)
Sunderland (sch 1/79, appr 7/79, pro 7/80); Watford (£115,000 3/85); Rangers (£200,000 5/86); Sheffield Wednesday (£150,000 9/87); West Bromwich Albion (valued at £300,000 in part-exchange 2/89); Port Vale (loan 11/91); Swansea City (free 7/92); Leyton Orient (free 7/93)
In his relatively brief Vicarage Road career as a beefy centre-forward, he improved considerably on a hitherto modest scoring record in senior football. He then

Scoring rate boosted

became the first Souness signing at Ibrox, and later scored against Watford on his Sheffield Wednesday début. It was a former Watford colleague, Brian Talbot, who took him to The Hawthorns.

William **(BILLY) WHEELER** *(1909-1911)*
SL 24 (-), FAC 1 (-), SCC 1 (1)
Chesham Town; Watford (am, pro 5/10); Derby County (£25 4/11); Watford (12/11 until cs 1912); Peterborough (by 1/13)
Before turning professional he represented Herts and had a dozen Southern League games on Watford's left wing. On moving to Derby he played in the final game of 1910/1, but was not picked again. As a cricketer he represented Buckinghamshire once, in 1906, and was a Chesham CC stalwart who was still performing as a very portly figure in the mid-1930s.

Only the good die young

Charles William **(CHARLIE) WHITE** *(1909-1925)*
b Chesham, Bucks 13/1/1889
d Watford, Herts 23/7/1925
SL 211 (57), FL 134 (24), FAC 27 (5), SCC 8 (2), WW1 44 (10 inc 1p)
Chesham Generals; Chesham Town (1907); Watford (8/09 until death). Guested for Swindon Town in WW1.
An unassuming, unselfish and stylish inside-forward who was much revered, and in 1925 much mourned. He'd represented Berks & Bucks in 1908/9, later played for the Southern League, and was a younger brother of Tommy and a co-founder of Watford Harriers. An appendix operation kept him out of the run-in to the Southern League championship win.

Penrice follower

DEVON *Winston* **WHITE** *(1996)*
b Nottingham 2/3/1964
FL 9+7 (4)
Arnold Kingswell; Lincoln City (free 12/84); Boston Utd (free 10/86); Bristol Rovers (free 8/87); Cambridge Utd (player-exchange plus £100,000 3/92); Queens Park Rangers (£100,000 1/93); Notts County (£110,000 12/94); Watford (£100,000 2/96)
A very tall striker who was twice brought out of non-League football before settling to a career which incorporated top-flight experience with Queens Park Rangers. When Notts County won the 1995 Anglo-Italian Cup at Wembley, he and Tony Agana scored the goals, and Steve Cherry was in goal. He followed Gary Penrice to three different clubs.

Herbert Walter **(BERTIE) WHITE** *(1900)*
b Camberwell, London 24/4/1877
d Lambeth, London 1926
SL 10 (6), FAC 2 (1)
Surrey Wanderers; Watford (am 1900); Alleyn
A cousin of goalkeeper Guthrie Baker, he learned the game at Alleyn's School, for whose old boys' team he subsequently played. He earned selection for Surrey, London and Herts, his speed being a particular asset. In Watford's forward line he scored four times in his first three Southern League games, having already hit seven in a reserve-team match.

Robert Nelson (**BOB**) **WHITE** *(1930-1932)*
b Walbottle, Northumberland 5/12/1901
d Newburn, Tyne & Wear 10/7/1977
FL 20 (16), FAC 4 (4)
Prudhoe Castle; Huddersfield Town (9/23); Stoke City (5/24); Tranmere Rovers (5/25); Yeovil & Petters Utd (9/28); Wolverhampton Wanderers (5/29); Watford (free 5/30); Carlisle Utd (free 6/32); North Shields (7/34)
Despite that admirable goals ratio, he was never more than George James's centre-forward understudy. Even after scoring a hat-trick in his first League game for the club, he was dropped immediately to make way for the returning James. For Wolves he made three Second Division appearances, and scored twice in a 7-3 local-derby defeat at West Bromwich.

What more could he do?

Thomas Henry (**TOMMY**) **WHITE** *(1909)*
b Tring, Herts 12/11/1881
SL 3 (-), FAC 1 (1)
Chesham Generals (by 9/01); Grays Utd; Brighton & Hove Albion (3/04); Stockport County (5/06); Exeter City (7/08); Watford (8/09 until cs 1910)
In marked contrast to brother Charlie, he spent only one season at Cassio Road. They joined the club together, but Tommy was already a professional, and he left Exeter City to focus on his business activities in Chesham. The Whites are the only brothers since 1895 to have appeared together in a first-team forward line, which they did in an FA Cup tie.

Unlike Charlie, a rover

Vincent Harold **WHITE** *(1923-1924)*
b Walsall, Staffs 22/10/1897
d Southampton, Hants 27/8/1972
FL 7 (1)
Erdington; Wednesbury Old Athletic; Birmingham (am 5/20, pro 11/20); Redditch Town (loan 1922); Watford (free 6/23 until cs 1925)
It was in the first of his two seasons that he made his seven League appearances for Watford, and only the last was won. Although normally a wing-half, he scored his goal when playing inside-left. He'd earlier represented the Birmingham FA against Scotland in one of the contests styled 'Junior internationals' and then played twice in the First Division.

Picked to face Scotland

RON*ald George* **WIGG** *(1970-1973)*
b Dunmow, Essex 18/5/1949
FL 91+6 (20), FAC 4+2 (4), FLC 6+1 (3)
Leyton Orient (appr 3/65); Ipswich Town (4/67); Watford (£18,000 6/70); Rotherham Utd (£12,000 3/73); Grimsby Town (£20,000 1/75); Barnsley (£5,000 3/77); Scunthorpe Utd (£5,000 10/77); Columbus Magic, USA (free 3/79); Cleveland Force, USA (indoor league); Ohio South director of coaching, USA; also National Staff Coaching Board, USA (by 4/96)
He had an unenviable task as the principal striker - indeed, very often the only one - for three dismal seasons during which the club averaged well under a goal a game. The

Ploughed a lone furrow

amount Watford had paid was a club record, and subsequently Grimsby Town were also to lay out for his signature what was at the time their highest transfer fee.

- ***WIGZELL*** *(1904)*
SEL 1 (-)
Watford (trial 9/04)
Occupying a fleeting moment in the club's history, he came from the Sunderland area and "made his entrance and his exit on the same day", as was noted at the time. For a home South-Eastern League game versus Brighton & Hove Albion, which Watford lost 3-1, he took the inside-right position which normally belonged to player-manager Goodall.

Rare team-change

Henry (HARRY) ***WILBOURN*** *(1928)*
b Eckington, Derbys 10/2/1905
d Poole, Dorset, January 1991
FL 2 (-)
Anston Athletic; Sheffield Utd 10/24; Watford (free 6/27); Halifax Town (free 7/28 until cs 1929)
The Sheppard/Daniels left-wing pairing was ever-present throughout the 1927/8 season, with the exception of two League games (an away defeat and a home win), for which Wilbourn deputised in the flank position. He hadn't made the first team at Bramall Lane, but played seven times in the Third Division (North) for Halifax Town.

Failed trialist returned

HARRY Melbourne ***WILCOX*** *(1900-1901)*
b Dalston, Middx 17/1/1878
d Plymouth, Devon 21/7/1937
SL 29 (2), FAC 3 (2)
Bromsgrove Schools; Bromsgrove Rovers; Aston Villa Reserves; Small Heath (3/98); Watford (7/00); Preston North End (6/01); Plymouth Argyle (5/05); Leicester Fosse (5/06); West Bromwich Albion (11/07); Plymouth Argyle (£50 5/08 until cs 1920)
An unsuccessful trialist right at the start of Watford's professional era, he later returned to the club for a season during which he was ever-present at inside-right. He won a Second Division championship medal with Preston North End before rejoining Plymouth Argyle, where in 12 years' service he earned a formidable reputation as centre-half and captain, and twice represented the Southern League.

Crocked at Stoke

Fred ***WILKINSON*** *(1919-1921)*
b Bury, Lancs 1889
SL 35 (1), FL 37 (-), FAC 2 (-)
St Augustine's; Lancaster City (1907); Norwich City (5/10); Darlington (7/12); Blackpool (8/12); Newport County (9/13); Stalybridge Celtic (1914/5); Watford (£50 8/19); Stoke (free 6/21)
A first-team wing-half for nearly the whole of his two seasons at Cassio Road, he scored only once - in a 2-1 Southern League win at Swindon. Just before a knee injury finished his career, he made three appearances for Stoke early in the season in which 25 goals by Jimmy Broad (later of Watford), out of a total of 60, took them back into the First Division.

GILBERT George ***WILKINSON*** *(1927-1928)*
b Clandown, Somerset 20/4/1910
d Taunton, Somerset 1975
FL 9 (2)
Clandown; Watford (am 1/27, pro 4/27 until cs 1929); Sheppey Utd (loan 2/28 until 4/28); Taunton Town (pro, permit player 11/33); Taunton GWR (permit player 9/35)
Before his 17th birthday he'd played for Somerset, and also at centre-forward in the Third Division (South). He and Joe Groome (the latter for Northampton Town) made their League débuts in the same match, as amateurs. Both scored, and Wilkinson is still the youngest to have done so for Watford in the League, but his career was soon in decline.

The youngest scorer

John T. (JACK) ***WILKINSON*** *(1921-1923)*
b Durham City
FL 61 (7), FAC 4 (-)
Consett Celtic; Watford (8/21 until cs 1924)
Tommy Waterall's young replacement at outside-left, he was awkward and persistent, with good control. He was engaged immediately after playing in the first of the two 1921 pre-season trial matches, in which he impressed sufficiently to be put straight into the first team. Watford never lost a senior match in which he scored.

Tricky customer

PAUL ***WILKINSON*** *(1988-1995)*
b Grimoldby, Lincs 30/10/1964
FL 139+1 (51 inc 1p), FAC 8+1 (-), FLC 4 (1), FMC 6 (3)
Clee Juniors; Grimsby Town (sch 2/80, appr 7/81, pro 11/82); Everton (£250,000 3/85); Nottingham Forest (£285,000 3/87); Watford (£300,000 8/88); Middlesbrough (£550,000 8/91); Oldham Athletic (loan 10/95); Watford (loan 11/95); Luton Town (loan 3/96)
ENGLAND UNDER-21
A lean six-footer with little to his game except flick-ons and scoring goals - apart from claiming others of which has was no more than a close-range spectator. He did himself find the net steadily enough to top his club's scoring list in six successive seasons - three in a row for Watford (a club record) and then three more for Middlesbrough.

Chart-topper

ALAN ***WILLIAMS*** *(1965-1966)*
b Bristol, Glos 3/6/1938
FL 43 (4), FAC 2 (-), FLC 2 (-)
Bristol Schools; Gloucestershire Schools; Bristol City (am 6/55, pro 9/55); Oldham Athletic (£1,000 6/61); Watford (£5,000 7/65); Newport County (£3,000 11/66); Swansea Town (10/68); Gloucester City (free 6/72)
He joined Watford with over three hundred League games as a strong centre-half under his belt, and only a frozen pitch had deprived him of an Under-23 cap. He captained the RAF - and Oldham when they had their record 11-0 win *en route* to promotion to the Third Division. His son emulated him in playing for Bristol City, Swansea and Oldham.

Foiled by the weather

Conquered Europe

GARY **WILLIAMS** *(1990-1991)*
b Wolverhampton, Staffs 17/6/1960
FL 39+3 (-), FAC 3 (-), FLC 2 (-)
Aston Villa (sch 12/75, appr 7/76, pro 6/78); Walsall (loan 3/80); Leeds Utd (£235,000 7/87); Watford (free 1/90 until 11/91); Bradford City (12/91 until cs 1994)
A defensive player, performing mostly at full-back, he failed to score in 240 League appearances for Aston Villa, but later, astonishingly, hit an Associate Members Cup hat-trick for Bradford City. He helped Villa to win both the League championship and the European Cup, and in the latter achievement he's unique among Watford players.

Monopolised No 3 shirt

John Robert (JOHNNY) **WILLIAMS** *(1964-1975)*
b Tottenham, Middx 26/3/1947
FL 371+3 (2), FAC 26 (-), FLC 19 (-)
Bennetts End Youth Club; Watford (appr 5/62, pro 9/64); Colchester Utd (free 7/75); Margate (free 7/78)
The left-back position was almost exclusively his for a decade, but he still managed to accumulate over a hundred more League appearances after moving on to Colchester United. He shared in Watford's rise to the Second Division and their FA Cup semi-final run, and his only two senior goals came in the lowest-scoring season in the club's history.

KENneth **WILLIAMS** *(1947)*
FL 2 (-)
Watford (1/47 until cs 1947)
After being taken on halfway through the first normal post-war League season, he had a couple of successive Third Division (South) games in the No 10 shirt, in place of leading scorer Ralph Evans. An only-goal defeat at Exeter was followed by a 2-0 home win against Port Vale. He didn't appear again, and was released at the end of the season

Part of Watford's folklore

Reginald George (SKILLY) **WILLIAMS** *(1913-1926)*
b Watford, Herts 4/1/1890
d Watford, Herts 19/6/1959
SL 83 (-), FL 240 (-), FAC 17 (-), SCC 1 (-), WW1 58 (-)
Watford Juniors (by 1/09); Leavesden Mental Hospital; Watford (Reserves from 1910/1, pro 5/14); Brighton & Hove Albion (free 5/26 until cs 1929); Watford National (permit player 8/31); Watford Wanderers (by 9/39). Guested for West Ham Utd in WW1.
He came late to the professional game, but established himself as a legendary character in goal, renowned for courage, agility and geniality. He had also been highly successful as a centre-forward for Leavesden Hospital, and represented Herts in both positions. His son Reg, a prominent Watford player in wartime, became a First Division wing-half with Chelsea.

Thomas John (**TOMMY**) **WILLIAMS** *(1961-1962)*
b Battersea, London 10/2/1935
d Westminster, London 25/8/1987
FL 12 (6), FLC 2 (1)
Carshalton Athletic; Colchester Utd (9/56); Watford (£1,000 6/61); Gravesend & Northfleet (free 4/62)
His career as Watford's outside-right began with five goals in his first four games, including - remarkably, for he was under 5'8" - a hat-trick of headers in a 4-3 win at Torquay. It didn't last, and after a few more games his League career was over. He'd had a good run at Colchester, scoring 30 goals in 151 Third Division (South) appearances.

Unlikely hat-trick

William L. (**BILL**) **WILLIAMS** *(1936)*
b Swansea, Glam 1914
FL 1 (-)
Welsh amateur football; Southampton (pro 8/33); St Budeaux (permit player 11/33); Cork City (1935/6); Watford (7/36 until cs 1937); Gillingham (month's trial 11/37); Devon FA trainer (by 6/39)
A couple of home games at inside-left constituted his senior career at Vicarage Road. The first was Tommy Barnett's benefit match against Fulham (Williams scored in a 2-0 win), and the other a 2-1 League victory versus Clapton Orient. Just before war broke out he was a cricket professional at Helston in Cornwall, and also the Devon FA trainer.

Cricket pro in Cornwall

ROGER Christopher **WILLIS** *(1992-1993)*
b Sheffield, Yorks 17/6/1967
FL 30+6 (2), FAC 1 (-), AIC 1 (-)
Notts County Reserves; Dunkirk, Notts; Grimsby Town (5/89); Boston Utd (loan 1989/90); Barnet (£10,000 8/90); Watford (£200,000 10/92); Birmingham City (£120,000 12/93); Southend United (player-exchange 9/94)
ENGLAND SEMI-PROFESSIONAL
Following a brief taste of Third Division football with Grimsby, he became a member of the Barnet squad which got into the Football League and nearly earned further promotion at the first attempt. His one international cap came when he was a substitute for Paul Furlong, later a colleague at Watford, whom Willis represented in midfield and as a striker.

International sub

John (**JACK**) **WILSON** *(1896-1900)*
d Watford, Herts 23/3/1929 (aged 60)
SL 23 (-), FAC 1 (-), HSC 2 (-), BCCL 2 (-)
Middlesbrough Ironopolis; Royal Arsenal (3 seasons); Luton Town (1892/3); Wolverton LNWR; West Herts (am 11/95, trainer 1896 until cs 1900, pro 10/97 until cs 1900); also Crouch End (briefly 2/96)
Having served the club simultaneously as player and trainer, he settled in Watford and was later employed as a gateman at both Cassio Road and Vicarage Road. A clean-kicking full-back, he made a first-team friendly appearance as late as April 1903. He was fixed up with a job at Cassiobury House when he first came to the club in its amateur days.

Dual role

Years as a stand-in

*James Thompson (**JIMMY / TUG**)* **WILSON** *(1951-1957)*
b Middlesbrough, Yorks 15/3/1924
d Fulham, London 16/1/1987
FL 49 (12), FAC 2 (-), SFC 1 (-)
Fulham (am 4/41); Gravesend & Northfleet; Chelsea (6/47); Leeds Utd (a month's trial 8/50); Watford (12/50); Southend Utd (free 8/57 until cs 1958)
In six-and-a-half seasons as a forward or wing-half at Vicarage Road he never had a first-team run of more than nine games. The son of an outstanding Scottish international centre-forward, he scored for the Reserves in each of eight consecutive games towards the end of his Vicarage Road career. He was Bill Shipwright's best man.

Robert D. **WILSON** *(1923)*
FL 1 (-)
Watford (12/22 until cs 1923)
A young player who was registered for a trial period before being engaged in January 1923, he was picked at left-half for a League match at Southend when the club was having problems during the course of a three-match FA Cup tie with Cardiff City. His only other senior appearance was as a substitute in a friendly staged in aid of the Unemployment Fund.

One of four débutants

William **WILSON** *(1931)*
b Sheffield, Yorks
FL 1 (-)
Watford (3/31 until cs 1932)
Signed towards the end of 1930/1, he did well for the Reserves and was one of four who were given their League débuts in the final game of that season. He took Tommy Barnett's inside-right position, and helped the club to a 1-0 win at Norwich. He was a younger brother of a First Division wing-half with Sheffield Wednesday.

'Wildfire'

*Charles John (**CHARLIE**)* **WIPFLER** *(1937-1947)*
b Trowbridge, Wilts 15/7/1915
d Petts Wood, Kent 1/6/1983
FL 35 (8), FAC 3 (1), 3SC 3 (-), WW2 8 (1)
McCall's, Trowbridge; Bristol Rovers (am 8/34, pro 9/34); Heart of Midlothian (£800 7/35); Watford (£420 6/37); Frickley Colliery (6/39); Watford (6/46); Gravesend & Northfleet (free 6/47). Guested for Barnsley and Watford in WW2.
Shortly before his unusual transfer from the West Country to the Scottish League, he scored against Watford in the Final of the Third Division (South) Cup, which Bristol Rovers won 3-2 on Millwall's ground. During his two Vicarage Road spells he was used at both inside-left and on the left wing. They called him 'Wildfire' at Hearts.

Part Two

Richard Kingdon (DICK) **WISE** *(1896-1897)*
b Watford, Herts 1869
d Watford, Herts 29/3/1949
SL 5 (-), FAC 1 (-), FAAC 1 (-)
Colne Valley; West Herts (1894); also Watford Ramblers (1/96)
He played in one first-team friendly in each of the three seasons immediately prior to the club's entry to the Southern League, and continued to make the odd senior appearance - mostly at centre-half. He was appointed vice-captain of the Reserves for 1897/8. For a great many years he had a watch, clock and jewellery business in Watford High Street.

Harry (MICKY) **WOOD** *(1896-1901)*
b Bradford, Yorks 1878
d Watford, Herts, September 1921
SL 94 (9), FAC 10 (-), FAAC 2 (1), HSC 2 (2), BCCL 16 (2)
Watford Wanderers; West Herts (am 1895, pro 10/97 until cs 1901); Wapella, Canada (until at least 9/06); Indian Head, Canada (2 years)
When he made his last Southern League appearance he'd played in more such games than any other Watford player. A versatile wing-half or forward, he played in Canada with George Badenoch, and also fought near him in the trenches in the Great War, which cost both men their lives. Wood died from tuberculosis, caused by gassing.

War cost him his life

DAVID **WOODFIELD** *(1971-1973)*
b Leamington Spa, Warwicks 11/10/1943
FL 14+1 (-), FLC 1 (-)
Wolverhampton Wanderers (am 5/59, pro 10/60); Watford (£28,000 9/71, player-coach 6/73, coach until 5/75); Qatar national coach (cs 1975); coach in Saudi Arabia (by 7/76)
A product of the renowned Molineux youth set-up of the 1950s, he had a long career as a centre-half with Wolves (250 League games) before Watford paid their record fee. He immediately ran into injury problems which eventually ended his career, but remained as club coach until being sacked. He coached in Saudi Arabia with Bill McGarry.

Two blows at Watford

ALBERT *George* **WOODISON** *(1956-1958)*
b Fulham, London 22/5/1934
SFC 2 (-)
Colchester Utd (am 8/53)); Leyton Orient (pro 12/54); Watford (7/56); Folkestone (free 7/58 until at least 7/60)
During his first season at Vicarage Road he was unexpectedly - and successfully - tried as a full-back for the Reserves, having joined the club as an inside-forward. It was in the more familiar No 10 shirt that he made both his Southern Floodlight Cup appearances, the first of which was in a 4-3 defeat against his former club at Brisbane Road.

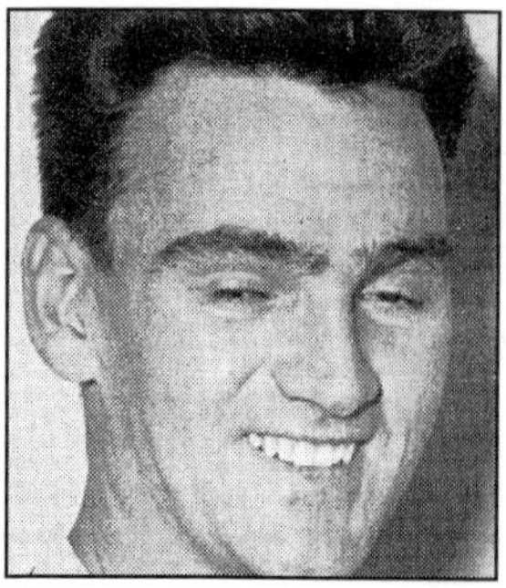

Played only under lights

Speed-merchant

LEWis Christopher **WOODROFFE** *(1947-1951)*
b Portsmouth, Hants 29/10/1921
FL 63 (6), FAC 1 (-)
Manchester City (am 10/45, pro 10/45); Watford (free 6/47 until cs 1951); Canterbury City (by 1953)
He was used both at inside-forward and on the right wing, being especially suited to the latter, where his speed (100 yards in even time) was an asset. His first-team chances came in short bursts throughout his four seasons, and he left the club whilst on the transfer list at £500. For Manchester City he'd had nine Second Division games (one goal).

Survivor at Ipswich

Charles Morgan Parkinson (CHARLIE) **WOODS** *(1970-1972)*
b Whitehaven, Cumberland 18/3/1941
FL 40+2 (3), FAC 1 (-), FLC 3 (1)
Keels Boys' Club; Cleator Moor Celtic; Newcastle Utd (£25 5/59); Bournemouth & Boscombe Athletic (£5,000 11/62); Crystal Palace (11/64); Ipswich Town (7/66); Watford (£9,000 5/70); Colchester Utd (loan 11/71); Blackburn Rovers (player/youth-team manager, free 7/72); Ipswich Town (reserve-team coach 3/73, first-team coach by 1982/3, assistant-manager cs 1983, chief scout 1/95)
After a trial with Aston Villa it was for Newcastle that he first played in League football. His two seasons as a left-winger on the Vicarage Road staff were undistinguished, the club's fortunes being at a low ebb. His career as coach and then assistant-manager at Ipswich went into a third decade, and as a golfer he represented Suffolk many times.

Two abandoned games

DENNIS James **WOODS** *(1962-1963)*
b Norwich, Norfolk 12/12/1936
FL 13 (2)
Norwich City (am 5/58); Cambridge Utd; Watford (£1,000+ 10/62); Wisbech Town (free (9/63)
In addition to his 13 games on Watford's right wing, he appeared in two abandoned Third Division matches within the space of a few weeks. His relatively brief flirtation with League football ended when he returned to the Southern League and to East Anglia, where his younger brother, Clive, was to become a long-serving winger with Ipswich Town.

Beds/North Herts man

H.A. (GAYLER) **WOODS** *(1909)*
SL 3 (-)
Dunstable Rangers (1898); Luton Town (am 1901); Victoria Works, Watford (12/03); Hitchin Town (1904 until at least 1908/9); also Dunstable Rangers (1904); also Luton Clarence; Watford (am)
Familiar in amateur circles a few miles to the north, he was given three consecutive Southern League games on Watford's left wing in February 1909, when the position was frequently changing hands. His début saw the club take their atrocious run of away form to 14 defeats and a draw in 15 games - but then he enjoyed two home wins.

ARTHUR **WOODWARD** *(1926-1945)*
b Watford, Herts 18/11/1906
d Harlesden, London 7/9/1984
FL 391 (16), FAC 29 (2), 3SC 12 (1), WW2 105 (3)
Watford St Mary's; Watford (am 7/26, pro 10/26); Scammells (1942); Watford (1944/5)
A tireless half-back whose wholehearted dedication to the Watford cause was in the Skilly Williams/Luther Blissett mould, all three players having been similarly revered by the local public. He came out of retirement when reserve-team fixtures were resumed in 1944, and even played a few more senior games - including two as an emergency goalkeeper.

Devoted to the cause

Joseph Henry **WOODWARD** *(1926)*
b Catford, London, February 1904
d Lewisham, London 1974
FL 2 (-)
Catford Southend; Watford (am 8/26, pro 9/26); Southend Utd (free 8/27); Clapton Orient (free 10/27 until 12/27); Queens Park Rangers (2/28); Merthyr Town (6/29 until cs 1930); Bexleyheath & Welling (permit player 1/31); Canterbury Waverley (permit player 8/32)
He was signed as Dave Russell's understudy with the club in the very unfamiliar position of having no established goalkeeper, following the release of Skilly Williams, one of three successive incumbents whose service had spanned more than two decades. Woodward had a couple of League games, but was then superseded by new signing Bill Yates.

ARTHUR **WOOLLISCROFT** *(1930-1933)*
(also known - incorrectly - as WOOLISCROFT)
b Salford, Lancs 17/2/1904
d Salford, Greater Manchester 1977
FL 63 (14), FAC 4 (2)
Salford; Manchester Docks; Manchester City (9/26); Caernarvon Athletic (cs 1928); Leicester City (£400 3/29); Watford (undisclosed fee 1/30 until cs 1933); Newport County (9/33); Northwich Victoria (7/34)
He reached Vicarage Road after failing to make Manchester City's first team, dropping briefly into non-League football, and then playing once in the First Division for Leicester City. A frustrating inside-forward who looked capable of more than he achieved, he was transfer-listed at £300 at the end of his fourth season, and didn't re-sign.

Flattered to deceive

John Edwin (TED) **WORRALL** *(1925)*
b Buxton, Derbys 2/10/1891
d Chesterfield, Derbys 24/7/1980
FL 4 (-)
The Comrades, Buxton (1908); Sheffield Wednesday (3/09); Fulham (6/19); Aberdare Athletic (5/23); Watford (1/25); New Brighton (6/25); Southport (5/27); Shirebrook (7/29); Ripley Town (1930 until 1931); Derbyshire Schools FA coach; Tottenham Hotspur scout. Guested for Chelsea and Tottenham Hotspur in WW1.

Uncle Sam was famous

A veteran full-back, he made only four League appearances for Watford, but then, in his mid-thirties, was ever-present for New Brighton in both the next two seasons. He'd been a First Division player before the Great War, in which he served in Mesopotamia, and joined Fulham on leaving the army. He was a nephew of the great goalie, Sam Hardy.

National-team manager

ERIC Senior **WORTHINGTON** *(1949-1950)*
b Sheffield, Yorks 29/12/1925
FL 24 (4), FAC 6 (-)
Queens Park Rangers (9/47); Watford (8/49); Dover (free 8/51); Bradford City (month's trial 9/53); Margate (by 12/59); Australia (head of coaching early 1970s, national team manager by 12/74)
One of the first footballers to play in contact lenses, he was at Loughborough College (where he became a PE lecturer in the 1960s) shortly before joining Watford as a versatile forward. He was a part-time professional, being employed simultaneously as a schoolmaster, and as soon as he left Vicarage Road he became a heavy scorer in the Kent League.

Trod the boards

William (WILLIE) **WRAGG** *(1901-1902)*
SL 18 (-), FAC 2 (-)
Notts Olympic; Newstead Byron; Hucknall Portland (pro 3/95); Stannington (12/95); Nottingham Forest (4/96); Leicester Fosse (3/99); Small Heath (1/01); Watford (8/01); Hinckley Town (8/02); Chesterfield Town (8/03); Accrington Stanley (8/04); Brighton & Hove Albion (9/05)
An FA Cup winner with Nottingham Forest little more than three years earlier, he spent only half a season or so as a wing-half or full-back in a Watford team that struggled in the Southern League First Division. He later worked in Fred Karno's show with Stan Laurel and Charlie Chaplin, appearing at the London Coliseum and elsewhere.

Bowling-club captain

Arthur (TICKER) **WRIGHT** *(1919-1920)*
b Watford, Herts
FL 1 (-). WW1 3 (1)
Watford (am 6/19, pro 11/20 until cs 1926)
His only League appearance was as an amateur. He'd played in three of the friendlies which marked the club's post-war resurrection, and also represented the county, and was later a stalwart reserve-team half-back with a great capacity for hard work. He became a member of the Supporters Club committee, and captain of North Watford Bowling Club.

Arthur Raymond L. **WRIGHT** *(1894-1897)*
b Gisburn, Yorks 1875
SL 1 (-), FAAC 1 (-)
West Herts (10/94); Apsley
With his brother Richard (they were sons of a Yorkshire vicar) he appeared in the forward line in the club's amateur era. After being elected a member of West Herts Club & Ground on the 2nd October 1894, he played regularly in the first team for a while. His later Southern League appearance, on the right wing, was in a five-goal defeat at Uxbridge.

John (JOCKY) ***WRIGHT*** *(1907-1908)*
b Hamilton, Lanarks 4/2/1873
d Southend, Essex 1946
SL 27 (-), FAC 1 (-), SEL 1 (-)
Hamilton Academical; Clyde; Bolton Wanderers (6/95); Sheffield Wednesday (11/98); Hamilton Academical (9/02); Bolton Wanderers (10/02); Plymouth Argyle (cs 1904); Watford (5/07); Southend Utd (5/08, reserve-team trainer cs 1913); Southend Transport coach
When he reached Cassio Road he was an experienced inside-forward of the brainy type, and had led Sheffield Wednesday's scorers with 24 goals when they took the Second Division title in 1899/1900, winning every home game. He had two sons who played League football - one of them also for England - and a grandson became a schools international.

Football in the family

NORMAN ***WRIGHT*** *(1935-1936)*
b Ushaw Moor, Co Durham 27/12/1908
d Newcastle-upon-Tyne, Tyne & Wear 30/1/1974
FL 21 (3), FAC 4 (2), 3SC 1 (-)
Esh Winning; Grimsby Town (2/28); Crewe Alexandra (6/30); Accrington Stanley (7/31); Manchester City (5/33); Watford (undisclosed fee 5/35); South Shields (free 7/36)
He was Watford's left-winger for the first 26 games of 1935/6, but didn't appear again. The club listed him at £200, but he was granted a free transfer by the Football League. He'd played briefly in the First Division for Grimsby Town, and also for Manchester City, where Eric Brook of England stood between him and a regular first-team place.

Couldn't get back

Richard Gane ***WRIGHT*** *(1894-1898)*
b Gisburn, Yorks 2/1/1877
d Cookham, Berks 27/10/1942
SL 13 (6 inc 1p), FAC 5 (2), FAAC 5 (4), HSC 6 (2)
West Herts (3/94 until 1898); also Casuals (1897/8); Cambridge University (1900 until 1903); Corinthians (by 3/01); Old Aldenhamians (1905 until 1906)
Arthur's younger brother was still at Aldenham School when he scored an FA Cup goal for the club against Tottenham Hotspur. He played for Herts, was three times a Cambridge blue, and was picked for the Amateurs of the South against the Professionals. He was centre-forward in the club's first Southern League game, and scored twice.

Schoolboy scorer

John (JACK) ***YATES*** *(1928)*
b Little Lever, Lancs 19/6/1904
d Heysham, Lancs 6/11/1980
FL 2 (-)
Little Lever; Watford (am 3/27, pro 4/27); Bangor City (cs 1928)
When he came to Vicarage Road on trial, his brother Bill was already playing in goal for the first team. Jack was taken on, and appeared at right-half in two consecutive

Joined his brother

League games. He was back in the town a decade later, as groundsman/cricket coach at the Grammar School for Boys, before returning north to work in a Radcliffe munitions factory.

County cricketer at 49

*William (**BILL**)* **YATES** *(1926-1929)*
b Little Lever, Lancs 20/3/1903
d Slough, Berks 13/10/1978
FL 47 (-), FAC 2 (-)
Little Lever St Matthew's; Bolton Wanderers (8/24); Watford (10/26 until cs 1929); Northfleet Utd (by 12/29); coach in The Netherlands (by 1931 until 1940)
The celebrated Dick Pym's understudy at Bolton, he went straight into Watford's first-team goal and didn't miss a game for a year. His coaching stint abroad ended when he fled the German invasion. He also had a succession of cricket-coaching appointments, was associated with Chesham CC for many years, and played for Buckinghamshire when he was 49.

G. **YOUNG** *(1908)*
SL 1 (-)
Hitchin Town; Watford (am 8/05)
A local amateur who represented the county, he turned out in the second 1905 pre-season public trial match. It was nearly three years before he made his only senior appearance, leading the forward line at Swindon in a fixture which brought Watford's only defeat in their last seven games of the season, as they improved their lowly Southern League position.

Broken leg

GEORGE **YOUNG** *(1946-1949)*
b Dundee, Angus 2/11/1919
d Ealing, London 1982
FL 43 (5), FAC 1 (-)
Forthill Athletic (am 5/36); Hibernian (12/36); Watford (7/46 until cs 1949); Headington Utd (briefly 3/50)
An eye-catching ball-player who, after a decade with Hibs, was one of Watford's inside-forwards when the normal Football League programme resumed in 1946. His three-season spell at Vicarage Road was marred by a long period out of action with a broken leg. His one game as a trialist for Headington was not a success, the injury probably having taken its toll.

Part Three

Wartime

COMPETITIVE football was played in both World Wars, but under conditions very different from those governing normal peacetime league and cup matches. Most significantly so far as the composition of teams was concerned, clubs were not restricted to the selection of their own registered players. Those who turned out for a club when not on its books were referred to as 'guest players'. Team changes were bewilderingly frequent, and it was normal for line-ups to include more than a sprinkling of other clubs' professionals who lived locally or were servicemen stationed in the area, or who possibly just happened to be at the ground near kick-off time when someone failed to turn up. Many amateurs were used also.

The following statistics are compiled from all matches played by Watford in the seasons when normal competitions did not take place, and 'Other Matches' include several which for various reasons were abandoned. The opening three Football League games of the 1939/40 season, which was aborted when war was declared, are treated as 'Other Matches'. In respect of 1945/6, when the FA Cup competition was resumed in earnest (one year ahead of the Football League), FA Cup appearances and goals are not included here, as they are incorporated in the players' career totals in Part Two.

Many of the guest players were previously or subsequently well-known in League football, but in some other cases the nature of the players' links with the clubs attributed to them is more difficult to establish.

*Names in **CAPITALS** indicate players featured in Part Two. Spare a thought for **William George McKenzie Law** and **Thomas William Postlethwaite**, whose only League appearances for Watford were nullified by the outbreak of war in 1939 and are listed below. (The matches in question were replayed at the beginning of 1946/7, the fixture list having been carried forward seven years.)*

a) The First World War

	LEAGUES & CUPS Apps	LEAGUES & CUPS Goals	OTHER MATCHES Apps	OTHER MATCHES Goals
W. Alderson (Coventry City)	1	1		
A. Alexander (amateur - Christ Church United)	4			
D. Allman (Croydon Common)			2	
C.B. or **E.B. Arnold** (OTC)	5			
W.G. ASHMOLE	5	3	1	
G.H. BARNES			1	1
- Berwick	1			
- Blackwell (Portsmouth)	1			
Pte J. Blagdon (Sherwood Foresters)	15		1	
- Bowler			1	
Company QMS Boyden (Grenadier Guards)	1			

	LEAGUES & CUPS Apps	LEAGUES & CUPS Goals	OTHER MATCHES Apps	OTHER MATCHES Goals
Cpl A. Boyle (Life Guards)	4			
G.G. Breed (amateur)	5			
Pte Brown (Sherwood Foresters)			1	1
J. Brown	1			
'J. Brown'	1			
R. Brown	1	1		
H.M. BULLING	1			
R. Cavanna (amateur - later Gillingham)	1	1		
F. Cheesman	1			
H. Cook (Sheffield United)	2			
G. Coomber (Brighton & Hove Albion)	61	6	1	
F. COTTERILL	1	1		
H.F. Couchman (amateur - Leavesden Mental Hospital)			2	
H. Crockford (Coventry City)	1			
Pte A. Crofts (Sherwood Foresters)	11			
H. CROWNSHAW	3			
W. Darby (Millwall)			1	
Pte Davies (Fulham)	1			
Sgt W. Dawson (a Guards regiment)	4			
J.A. Dorsett (Manchester City)	5			
Cpl G. Eames (Sherwood Foresters)	9	1		
G.W.N. EDMONDS	4	4	2	3
Air Mech W.F. Edwards (RFC - later Newport County)	28	14		
Air Mech W.J. Evans (RFC)	7			
H. Flannagan	1			
E. Frisby (RFC)	1			
R.W. Frith (Luton Town)	3			
G. FYFE			1	
Sgt H. Geeson (Life Guards)	4	1		
G. GEMMELL	1			
Pte Green (Sherwood Foresters)	2			
A. GREEN	9		1	1
C. Green (RFC)	1			
F. Green	1			
F.J. GREGORY	47	2	6	1
O.H. Gregory (amateur)	26	1	4	
V.F. GREGORY	41	2	2	
A. GRIMSDELL	1			
E.F. GRIMSDELL	30		1	
W. HASTINGS	24	1		
S.T. HATTON	2			
F. Hayes (RFC)	4			
T.E. Higham (Brighton & Hove Albion)	1			
W. Honeyborn (amateur - Wealdstone)	1			
J. Houghton (Norwich City)	28			
J. Johnson (Luton Town)			1	
Pte Jones	1			
'A. Jones'	1			
P. Kelso (son of the Fulham manager)	3			
R. Kennedy (Fulham)	5			
Pte J. Kenny	1			
Pte Ketch	1			

	LEAGUES & CUPS Apps	LEAGUES & CUPS Goals	OTHER MATCHES Apps	OTHER MATCHES Goals
T. Knighton (OTC - also guested for Tottenham Hotspur)	7	3 (1p)		
T. Langford (Wolverhampton Wanderers)	1			
W. Lawson	1			
Pte Leese (Stoke)	6		1	
- McKay (Portsmouth)	1			
W. McKee (Leytonstone)	17			
J.J.S. McLAUCHLAN	8	6 (3p)		
A.E. Mallett (amateur)	4		2	1
W.A. MARKLAND			4	
G.F. Meagher (amateur - St Albans City)	22	1	1	
G. Meekin (Derby County)	4	2		
J. Miller (Oldham Athletic)	2			
W. Miller (Brighton & Hove Albion)	1	1		
W. Miller			1	
F. Morris (West Bromwich Albion)	14	27 (4p)		
Sgt Moseley (Sunderland)	1			
E.W. or **C. Murray**	4			
Sgt A. Newman	4			
G.F. NIDD	1			
S. Norman (amateur)	1			
A.S. Owen (Leicester Fosse)	1			
Sgt Pamplin	1			
H.H. PANTLING	2	1		
Sgt Payne	1			
I.H. Price (Wrexham)			2	1
H.P. Roberts (Luton Town)	2			
Cpl N. Robertson or **Robertshaw** (Life Guards)	2	1		
E.R. Robson (signed from Gateshead, June 1914)	4			
A. Rogers (Leeds City)	6			
R. Routledge (Brighton & Hove Albion)	1			
A. Salter	1			
A.E. Sawyer			1	
C.D. Scorer (Newcastle United)	1		1	
Sgt Scraggins	1			
Sgt Smith			1	
H. SMITH	41	23	2	4
F. Spencer (Brighton & Hove Albion)	2			
G.W. Squire			1	1
A. SQUIRES	11			
W. Stanton (Rotherham County)	28	1		
Pte Stevenson (Tottenham Hotspur)	1			
A. STEWART	9			
E.H. Symes (amateur)	4		1	
J.H. Taylor (Barnsley)	14	9 (1p)		
F. Thompson (amateur)	1		1	
W. Thompson	1			
A. Tierney	2			
- Tilley (Portsmouth)	1			
G. or **H. Tilley** (amateur)	1			
H.W. Tilling (amateur - later Millwall)			3	
A.J. Tyler (Brighton & Hove Albion)	6	1		
Pte Walker	1			

	LEAGUES & CUPS Apps	LEAGUES & CUPS Goals	OTHER MATCHES Apps	OTHER MATCHES Goals
J. WALTER	1		2	
Pte J. Walton	1			
C.W. WHITE	41	6	3	4 (1p)
J. Wilde (South Shields)	2			
R.G. WILLIAMS	52		6	
A. Wood (Queens Park Rangers)	1			
A.B. Wood (Fulham)	4			
J. Woodhouse (Brighton & Hove Albion)	3			
A. WRIGHT			3	1
E.J. Wright (amateur)	49	8	1	
Pte J. Wright	1			

b) The Second World War

A.V. Aicken (Brentford)	2			
M. Allen (Southampton)	1			
J.C. Anderson (Portsmouth)	3			
G.R. Annis (amateur - Watford Boys Club)	2		1	
D.W.J. Anthony (amateur)	1			
J.H. ARMSTRONG	45		7	
R.J. Armstrong (Bristol City)	1			
C.W. Bacon (Chelsea)	1			
S.N. Baines (Northampton Town)	19	3	1	2
J. Barker (Aston Villa)	1			
T.A. BARNETT	89	22	10	4
R. Barnham (REME)	1			
J.W. Barrett (West Ham United)	1			
J.W. Barrs (Southampton)	1			
- **Basford** - see Blandford				
C.S. Bastin (Arsenal)			1	
W.H. BATES	1			
H.W. Bearryman (Chelsea)	1			
J. Beck (amateur)	1			
W. BECKETT	18	6		
S.J. Bennett (amateur)	1	1		
F.S. Biggerstaff (amateur - Chipperfield)	1		1	
A.G. Biggs (Aberdeen)	3	2		
T. Birkbeck (amateur - Kingley)	1			
G.P. BLAND	1			
- **Blandford** or **Basford** (Gainsborough Trinity)	1			
A.E. Bonass (Queens Park Rangers)	2			
F.P. Boulton (Derby County)	17		1	
J.C. Bowles (Stockport County)	1			
J. Brain (signed October 1943 - ex-Bristol City)	20	16		
N. Brand (Dundee United)	1			
F. Briggs (Wrexham)	8	1		
P.W. Bright	1			
- **Bristow** (Royal Navy)	1			

	LEAGUES & CUPS Apps	LEAGUES & CUPS Goals	OTHER MATCHES Apps	OTHER MATCHES Goals
C. **Broadhurst** (Manchester United)	3	1		
L. **Brook** (Huddersfield Town)	1			
F.H. **Broome** (Aston Villa)	1	1		
Sgt Brown	1			
A.R. **Brown** (Wrexham)	10	4		
G. **Brown** (amateur)	1			
H.S. **Brown** (Wolverhampton Wanderers)	18		2	
J. BROWN	17	4		
J. **Brown** (Motherwell)	1			
R. **Brown** (Millwall)	1			
W.H. **Brown** (Middlesbrough)	91	5	4	
J.H. **Browne** (Aston Villa)	3		1	2
R.J. **Browne** (Leeds United)	23		1	
H.A. **Bryant** (Shorts Sports)			1	
B. **Burley** (Chelmsford City)	1			
W.F. **Burnicle** (Aldershot)	2			
F.C. **Butterworth** (Leeds United)	1			
D.L. **Cock** (amateur - RAF)	1			
- **Cockburn**	1			
G.A. **Cooke** (amateur - Barking)	1			
A.D. **Cowie** (Aberdeen)	4			
E.C. **Crawford** (Clapton Orient)	1			
J.A. **Cringan** (Cardiff City)	17	1	2	
- **Croom** (Leeds United)	1			
R.G.G. **Croucher** (amateur - signed from Birmingham, December 1944)	1			
J. **Cruickshank** (Southampton)	2			
P.J. CURRAN	14	3	2	
B.E. DABBS	1		3	
D.B.L. **Davidson** (Bradford Park Avenue)	19			
J.W. **Davies** (Everton)	1			
W. DAVIES	114	50 (9p)	14	6 (3p)
- **Davison** (Blackburn Rovers)	5			
Lt Delaney	1			
S. **Denby** (Guildford City)	1			
C. **Dougall** (Burnley)	6	1		
G. **Dreyer** (Luton Town)	3		2	
C.J. DRINKWATER	45	4	1	1
A. **Driver** (Sheffield Wednesday)	4	1		
J.H. **Dugnolle** (Plymouth Argyle)	21			
A.J. **Duncombe** (amateur - Rickmansworth Town)	7	1	3	4
W.L. DUNDERDALE	8	5		
T.H. **Dunsmore** (Luton Town)	1		1	
- **Durman**	1			
T. **Dutton** (Rochdale)	4			
H. **Dykes** (amateur - Tottenham Hotspur)	1	3		
N.A. **Dymock** (amateur - Aylesbury ATC)			1	
M. **Edelston** (amateur - Reading)	1	1		
R. **Edwards** (Luton Town)	1			
G.D. **Egan** (Aldershot)	3	1		
E. **Embleton** (Doncaster Rovers)	3			
D.R. EVANS	5		2	1

	LEAGUES & CUPS Apps	LEAGUES & CUPS Goals	OTHER MATCHES Apps	OTHER MATCHES Goals
A. Farmer (Queens Park Rangers)	1			
A.L. FARNEN	1			
R.P. Farrant	1			
E.J. Feeney (amateur)	1			
H. Ferrier (Barnsley)	2			
W. FINDLAY	7		2	
A.M. Fitzgerald (Queens Park Rangers)	5			
P.J. Fitzsimmons (Queen of the South)	4			
F.F. Forder (amateur)	1			
S.R. Foss (Chelsea)	3			
A.J. Fowler (signed January 1944 - ex-Gillingham)	5		1	
J.L. Franklin (Middlesbrough)	1		1	
T. Galley (Wolverhampton Wanderers)	39	7 (3p)	2	
L. GALLIMORE	18		1	
P.H. Giddings (amateur - Leavesden Hospital)	11		1	
P. GILLESPIE	33		1	
G. Glaister (Blackburn Rovers)	3			
- Glynn	1			
H.A. Goodman (amateur - Chipperfield)	2			
R. GRAY	45	5 (2p)	1	
F.C. Gregory (Crystal Palace)	1			
H. Grey (Barnsley)	1			
J.E. Griffiths (Tranmere Rovers)	4	1 (1p)		
H.G. Groves (amateur)	1		1	
G. Guest (Rotherham United)	9	4	1	
R.V. Gunner (Queens Park Rangers)	1			
D. Halford (Oldham Athletic)	4	1		
A.E. Hall (Tottenham Hotspur)	1			
- Hamilton (Albion Rovers)	1			
W.T. HARRIS	68		5	
J. Hartshorne (Lincoln City)	3			
J. Harvey (Heart of Midlothian)	1			
J. Haver (signed December 1942 - ex-Coventry City)	3			
W. Haysman (amateur - Chipperfield)	2			
E.J. Haywood (Crewe Alexandra)	1			
B.J. Head (Torquay United)	9			
G.H. Henson (Sheffield United)	1			
R.W. Hipkin (Wolverhampton Wanderers)	8			
A.W. Hitchins (Tottenham Hotspur)	1			
H.H.F. Hobbis (Charlton Athletic)	1			
Sgt Major J.G. Hogg (amateur)	2			
- Holliday	1			
S. Hooper (Southampton)	1	1		
J. Horton			1	
J.S. Horwood (amateur - Bushey Swifts)	5		1	
F. Howe (Grimsby Town)	2			
T. Howshall (Stoke City)	5			
J. Hughes (from Irish football)	1	1		
S. Hughes (New Brighton)	2			
S. Hughes (Tranmere Rovers)	2			
G.H. HUNT	2			
H. Hutton (Halifax Town)	3	3		

	LEAGUES & CUPS Apps	LEAGUES & CUPS Goals	OTHER MATCHES Apps	OTHER MATCHES Goals
H. Jackson (Burnley)	47	27 (1p)	4	2 (1p)
A. Jeffries (Sheffield United)	1		1	
A. Jepson (Port Vale)	24			
B.A.G. JEZZARD	18	6		
J. Jobling (Charlton Athletic)	25			
T.H. Jobson (Ipswich Town)	1			
R.E. Johnson (Burnley)	11			
- Jones (Arsenal)	1			
E.N. Jones (West Bromwich Albion)	45	16 (4p)	1	1
F. Jones (Ipswich Town)	1	1		
F.R. Jones (signed September 1942 - ex-Birmingham)	8	2		
G. Jones	1			
G. Jones (Bolton Wanderers)	1			
H.J. Jones (West Bromwich Albion)	1			
T.J. JONES	221	25	20	4 (1p)
V. Jones (amateur)	1			
W.E. Jones (amateur - St Albans City)	10		1	
A. Kelly (amateur - Belfast Celtic)	1			
M. Killourhy (Doncaster Rovers)	17	7		
P. King (amateur - Croxley)	3			
F.J. Kurz (Grimsby Town)	17	8		
E.W. Lager (Coventry City)	5	4		
E.C. Lancelotte (Charlton Athletic)	1	1		
W. Lane (Carlisle United)	2	1		
W.H.C. LANE	1			
W.G.M. Law (signed from Stockport County, July 1939)			2	1
- Learmouth (Partick Thistle)	2			
D.J. LEWIS	62		10	
H.H. Lewis (signed Oct 1940 - ex-Queen of the South)	35	21 (3p)	1	
T.G. LEWIS	128	101	15	13
J. Liddell (Airdrieonians)	1			
G. Linsley (amateur)	1			
Flt Sgt B.C. Loom (amateur - RAF; also guested for Millwall)	3	4		
J.L. Loughran (Burnley)	8	1		
H.P. LOWE	4			
A.R. Lowes (Sheffield Wednesday)	1	1		
G. LUNN	1			
J. McCracken (amateur - Queens Park)	1			
A. McGivern (Belfast Celtic)	1			
J. McHUGH	67		12	
A. McIntosh (Wolverhampton Wanderers)	7			
P.M. McLachlan (signed March 1943 - ex-Clyde)	1			
D.A. McLeod (Motherwell)	6			
J. McNeil (Derry City)	1			
H. McTavish (signed Nov 1943 - ex-Leeds United)	1			
S.T. MALPASS	1			
N. Mansell (Army)	1			
R. March (Queens Park Rangers)	1			
D.K. Martin (Notts County)	11	7		
L. Martindale (Burnley)	2			
W.S. Mason (Queens Park Rangers)	23			

	LEAGUES & CUPS Apps	LEAGUES & CUPS Goals	OTHER MATCHES Apps	OTHER MATCHES Goals
G. Matthewson (Bury)	2			
R.C. Maudsley (Bolton Wanderers)	1			
G. MEE	26		1	
G.A. Merrett (amateur - REME)	1			
J. Milburn (Leeds United)	33	4 (3p)		
W.R. Millar (signed November 1942 - ex-Burnley)	4			
H.S. Miller (Northampton Town)	21	4	2	
J. Moffatt (signed March 1945 - ex-Rangers)	1			
P. Molloy (Bradford City)	1			
K.G. Moody (Grimsby Town)	2			
J. Morris (Stockport County)	21	6	1	1
R. Morris (Crystal Palace)	2			
T. Morris (amateur - RAF)	14	3		
S.H. Mortensen (Blackpool)	1			
F.W. Moss (amateur - RAF, ex-Birmingham)	1			
G. Moss (Notts County)	1			
T. Murray (signed October 1943 - ex-Motherwell)	7			
E. Muttit	1			
T.W. Naylor (Huddersfield Town)	1			
F.R. Needham (Stockport County)	1			
K.H. Nisbet (signed September 1944 - ex-Sunderland)	1			
R.V. O'BRIEN	54	4 (1p)	9	
J. Paterson (signed August 1945 - ex-Stockport County)	2			
R. Paul (Swansea Town)	4			
Capt A.L. Pease (Royal Artillery)	1	2		
L.A. Perkins (amateur - RAF)	1			
E. Perry (Doncaster Rovers)	1			
- **Pickering** (a Guards regiment)	1		1	
B. Poole (York City)	5			
T.W. Postlethwaite (free from Northampton Town, May 1939)			3	
R. Pugh (Cardiff City)	2			
H. Quinney (Coventry City)	1			
A.R. Ramsbottom (amateur - Norwich City)	1			
B. RATCLIFFE	1			
T.S. Reece	1			
A.G. REED			2	
- **Reeve** (Southend United)			2	
- **Reid** (Southampton)	2			
H.J. Rickett (signed October 1942 - ex-Southend United)	12			
F. Roberts (Luton Town)	3		1	
L.V. ROBERTSON	3			
T.S.E. Robinson (amateur - Wisbech Town)	10	4		
T.W. Robinson (Barnsley)	26	1		
R. ROSS	25	1		
H. Rothery (Bournemouth & Boscombe Athletic)	1			
A.T. Salltall (amateur - Bristol City)	1			
H.A. Sands (amateur - Berkhamsted Town)	1			
K. Saunders (amateur - Chipperfield; pro October 1944)	32	1	2	
W. Saunders (amateur - St Albans City)	9	2		

	LEAGUES & CUPS Apps	LEAGUES & CUPS Goals	OTHER MATCHES Apps	OTHER MATCHES Goals
W. Saunders (West Bromwich Albion)	41		2	
J. SHAW	97	1	1	
A.M. Sliman (Chelmsford City)	1			
J.R. Smeaton (Sunderland)	1			
- Smith	1			
- Smith	1			
C.J. Smith (Aberdeen)	1			
G.H. Smith (Charlton Athletic)	1			
J.C.R. Smith (Millwall)	2		1	1
T.W. Smith (amateur - Birmingham)	9	2		
T.W. Spencer (signed Nov 1943 - ex-Lincoln City)	3			
H. Staniford (amateur - ex-Tranmere Rovers)	1			
T. Stocker (Bournemouth & Boscombe Athletic)	2			
J. Stone (Sheffield United)	18	3	2	
H. SURTEES	1			
J. Sykes (Portsmouth)	1			
M.R. Tadman (Charlton Athletic)	1			
E. Taylor (from Portsmouth for £200, June 1939)	2		1	
E. Taylor (Southampton)	1			
J. Taylor (Norwich City)	1			
W. Taylor (Blackburn Rovers)	4			
Pte Thompson (Sheffield Wednesday)	1			
A. Thompson (Lincoln City)	2			
O.E. Tidman (Clapton Orient - later signed, Aug 1946)	1			
J. Tivendale (from Scotland - amateur Nov 1944, professional Feb 1945)	14	1	2	
- Wainwright (Manchester United)	1			
C.J. Walker (Sheffield Wednesday - ex-Watford)	2		1	3
G. Walker (signed from Crystal Palace, June 1939)			1	
S. Walker (Exeter City)	7	3		
H. Waller (Arsenal)	2	1		
Sgt PT Instr D. Walls (Clapton Orient)	1			
R. Walls (Cowdenbeath)	4	3		
K. Walshaw (amateur - later a Sunderland professional)	1	1		
T.C. WALTERS	30	14	4	2
- Ward	1			
H. Ware (Norwich City)	12	2		
L.H. Warner (Coventry City)	19	2		
Lt N. Watson Smith (amateur - Yorkshire Amateurs)	5			
D.S. Waymouth (amateur - Dulwich Hamlet)	3			
E. Weightman (Charlton Athletic)	3			
A. WEIR	21	4	1	1
D. Westcott (Wolverhampton Wanderers)	8	11		
A.S. White (amateur)	6	2		
- Whitfield (Bristol Rovers)	1			
W.P. Whittaker (Charlton Athletic)	1			
J.R. Whittle (Port Vale)	3			
F.V. Wicks (amateur - Croxley Green)	1			
C.E. Williams (Bristol City)			2	1
E.E. Williams (Grimsby Town)	7			
R.F. Williams*	124	9 (1p)	9	

	LEAGUES & CUPS Apps	LEAGUES & CUPS Goals	OTHER MATCHES Apps	OTHER MATCHES Goals
J. Williamson (signed September 1943)	1			
- **Wilson**	1			
- **Winstanley**	1			
D.T. Winter (Bolton Wanderers)	9			
C.J. WIPFLER	6	1	2	
A. Woodcock (Stockport County)	1			
J.T. Woodgate (West Ham United)	1			
A. WOODWARD	93	3	12	
J.L. Wrigglesworth (signed Sept 1994 - ex-Halifax Town)	12	10		
A.E. Young (Arsenal)	1			
L.G. Young (amateur - St Albans City)	3		1	
A. Younger (Partick Thistle)	1	1		

*** Reginald Frederick WILLIAMS**

b Watford, Herts 28/1/1922

Reg Williams, junior, was an amateur wing-half whose total of wartime appearances for the club was exceeded by only two players, and there was keen disappointment when he was tempted away by Chelsea, with whom he turned professional in October 1945, after five months on amateur forms. He was soon selected as an England reserve, but then ran into serious cartilage problems, and only the determination which was a hallmark of his game enabled him to accumulate 58 First Division appearances (13 goals) before he retired at the age of 29, in November 1951. He subsequently worked in the printing trade in Watford, in which he had been apprenticed, and also for a time was a publican. On the day he was born, his legendary father kept goal in an FA Cup tie at Tottenham attended by over 47,000 spectators - nearly double the biggest crowd at any previous Watford game.

Part Four

Other Matches

LISTED here are the players other than those featured in detail in Part Two who played in minor first-team competitions and/or friendly matches in the seasons from 1896/7 to 1914/5, 1919/20 to 1938/9, and 1946/7 to 1995/6.

*Names in **BOLD CAPITALS** indicate players who had played before 1896/7 and are therefore also included in Part One. Asterisks (*) indicate players who also represented Watford in wartime and are listed in Part Three. Underlined names are those of club managers (see Part Five).*

	First App	Last App
B. Andrews	1985	1985
- Ash	1904	1904
G.E. Aunger	1994	1994
A. Ayling	1973	1973
J. Barker	1966	1966
D.T. Bassett	1965	1965
J. Beach	1897	1897
- Beckley	1897	1897
H. Bennett	1954	1954
M. Brady	1984	1984
M.D. Brisbane	1963	1963
E.J. Bull	1899	1901
J. Burge	1901	1901
H. Campbell	1966	1966
A.J. Cheesewright	1965	1966
J.L. Cocks	1974	1976
W.S. COLES	1897	1897
J.W. Collins	1976	1977
J.O. CONQUEST	1896	1896
E. Corbridge	1960	1961
C.W. Cox	1921	1921
G. Davies	1923	1923
W. Dealey	1900	1900
C. Deane	1901	1902
J.F. Dixon	1899	1899
I.J. Douglas	1984	1984
W.E. Evans	1896	1896
F.W. Gilham	1910	1910
E.N. Gill	1951	1951
- Gilman	1966	1966
W. Glenister	1924	1924
E.A. Godman	1903	1903
J.P. Greaves	1976	1976
- Green	1907	1907
G. Hallam	1911	1911
- 'Hallett'	1898	1898
J.L. Hanson	1967	1967
A. Hardy	1921	1921
R.H. Harper	1966	1966
- Hartley	1904	1904
R. Hill	1898	1898
T.A.T. Hinton	1960	1961
F. HUGHES	1896	1896
H.G. Hughes	1896	1896
H.A. HUTCHINGS	1896	1900
G.H. Jacques	1899	1899
E. Jeffs	1897	1897
E.H. John	1974	1974
H. Jones	1967	1967
A.G. Judge	1994	1994
H. Kennedy	1964	1965
P.C. Kerlin	1978	1978
R. Lake	1935	1935
A.S. Lane	1897	1897
J.R. Lawton	1922	1922
- Lester	1973	1973
G. Lewis	1962	1962
J. McAloon	1979	1979
S. McClure	1911	1911
W.H. McGarry	1963	1964
K. McIntyre	1903	1903
- Mackenzie	1905	1905
A. Males	1911	1911
G.F. Meagher*	1915	1915

	First App	Last App		First App	Last App
R.C. Miller	1957	1957	J. Sheldon	1923	1923
D.S. Mitchell	1987	1987	A.B. Sleigh	1896	1896
P. Molloy*	1955	1958	K.P. Slinn	1994	1994
J.A. Muir	1957	1957	T.J. Stacey	1962	1962
J. MUNN	1897	1897	J. Stallard	1901	1901
C. Murray	1910	1910	C. Steel	1897	1897
C. Newlyn	1902	1902	S. Storm	1984	1984
- 'Newman'	1921	1921	W. Swain	1961	1961
P. Nolan	1913	1913	F.J. Taylor	1937	1937
M. O'Neill	1966	1966	G. Taylor	1983	1983
D. Ounsworth	1973	1973	P.J. Taylor	1992	1992
K. Owen	1971	1971	S.T. Thorne	1987	1987
A.D. Paris	1985	1985	C. Townsend	1956	1956
M.J. Pinner	1954	1954	J.H. Vernon	1897	1897
W. Pollock	1903	1903	C.J. Walker*	1937	1937
J. Price	1990	1990	J.W. Ward	1961	1961
S. Redwood	1977	1977	**H.E. WHITE**	1896	1902
J. Robertson	1968	1968	F.W. Whitehead	1956	1956
- Robinson	1926	1926	G. Wiffen	1897	1897
D. Robison	1992	1992	P.S. Wilkerson	1994	1995
- Rosson	1948	1948	D.H. Williams	1983	1985
F.A. SARGENT	1899	1899	P.D. Williams	1977	1977
P.B. Saunders	1977	1977	J. Wilson	1932	1932
- Scott	1965	1965	- Young	1968	1968
A. Scrivener	1897	1897			

Part Five

The Managers

UNTIL 1903, playing matters such as transfers and team selection were handled by the Committee, who appointed an honorary secretary to deal with routine administrative details, a professional trainer to keep the players fit, and a captain to lead the team on the field.

The club's first manager was the celebrated England inside-forward, John Goodall, but even he was denied anything like a final say in team affairs, and indeed it is only in modern times that the manager's decisions on football matters have been relatively free of boardroom interference.

Watford's first five managers spanned a period totalling 44 years, but then within the next nine years a further six incumbents had been both appointed and dismissed. Exactly half of the 22 managers also represented the club as players in the Southern League or Football League.

(In the results summary of each manager's term of office, 'W', 'D' and 'L' represent matches Won, Drawn and Lost, and the figures denoted 'Goals' and separated by a hyphen are the totals of goals scored and conceded, respectively. For a key to other abbreviations and an explanation of the format used in this section, see the introduction to Part Two.)

JOHN GOODALL *(1903-1910)*
b Westminster, London 19/6/1863
d Watford, Herts 20/5/1942
Watford career as a player (1903-1907):
SL 62 (14), FAC 7 (3), SEL 17 (17), UL 6 (2)
SL record as Watford manager:
W 90, D 63, L 93, Goals 347-358
Kilmarnock Burns Athletic; Kilmarnock Athletic; Great Lever (1883); Preston North End (1886); Derby County (5/89); New Brighton Tower (10/99); Glossop (2/01); Watford (player-manager 5/03, manager-trainer 6/09); Racing Club de Rubaix, France, player-manager (6/10); Mardy player-manager (5/12 until cs 1913)
ENGLAND FULL; FOOTBALL LEAGUE

Watford could have had no more distinguished figure as their first manager than this great inside-forward. He won 14 caps and was the League's top scorer in its first season, when he helped Preston to perform the Double. He also played First Class cricket, represented England at bowls, and was an excellent billiards player and a prize-winning cage-bird fancier. Forty years old when he arrived, he nonetheless for some time continued as a player. At 44 he became (and remains) the oldest player to have made a competitive first-team appearance for the club in peacetime, and he actually appeared occasionally in the Southern League for Mardy as late as 1913. His impact at Cassio Road was immediate, the championship of the Southern League's Second Division being won with spectacular ease. He had a cage-bird shop in Watford, and after leaving the game in 1913 lived in the town for the rest of his life, which included a spell as groundsman at West Herts Sports Ground. Although London-born (a son of a corporal in the Scottish Fusiliers), he spoke with a Scottish accent, having moved to Kilmarnock in infancy. His brother Archie was born in Ireland and represented that country as a footballer.

Henry ***(HARRY) KENT*** *(1910-1926)*
b Bedworth, Warwicks 22/10/1879
d Watford, Herts 22/12/1948
Watford career as a player (1909-1913):
SL 63 (6), FAC 6 (3), SCC 3 (-)
SL/FL record as Watford manager:
W 187, D 121, L 176, Goals 661-663
Notts County Reserves; Heanor Town (pro 9/00); Ilkeston Town (9/01); Newark (7/02); Brighton & Hove Albion (5/05); Middlesbrough (4/08); Watford (8/09, player-manager 5/10, manager until cs 1924, secretary-manager until 5/26)

Guiding the club to the Southern League championship, and a record term as manager in often fraught financial circumstances, testify to the astuteness of this taciturn, dignified and somewhat strait-laced man. He continued as the first-team centre-half for his first season of management, and his 16-year reign was broken only by absence on munitions work during the Great War. The 1914/5 Southern League title had been won only 12 months after relegation had been avoided by victory on the final day of the season, and in 1919/20 only goal average prevented a second successive triumph. Kent's incumbency was characterised by repeated close-season raids on the non-League clubs of the East Midlands, to recruit replacements for players released on free transfers. He received £239-19s-9d from his benefit game in 1921, and in his last two seasons carried out the additional duties of secretary, without addition to his salary. His resignation in 1926 marked a complete departure from the game, and from 1922 he spent the rest of his life as landlord of the *Wellington Arms* in Woodford Road. "A good man and a sportsman all his life", runs his epitaph in the Vicarage Road cemetery.

FRED PAGNAM *(1926-1929)*
b Poulton-le-Fylde, Lancs 4/9/1891
d Preston, Lancs 7/3/1962
Watford career as a player (1921-1927):
FL 144 (67 inc 6p), FAC 13 (7)
FL record as Watford manager:
W 45, D 28, L 53, Goals 204-239
Lytham; Blackpool Wednesday; Huddersfield Town (6/10); Southport Central (cs 1912); Blackpool (2/13); Liverpool ("big fee" 5/14); Arsenal (£1,500 10/19); Cardiff City (£3,000 3/21); Watford (£1,000 12/21, player-manager 5/26 until 5/29); Turkish FA national coach, Turkey (7/31); HVV, Netherlands, assistant-coach (1933); DWV, Netherlands, coach (1934); FC Haarlem, Netherlands, coach (1937 until 5/40); also De Volewijckers, Netherlands, part-time coach (1938); Lytham (during WW2). Guested for Arsenal and Blackpool in WW1.

A centre-forward whose goalscoring (including three League hat-tricks in five games) revived Watford's fortunes from the time he arrived for what was easily a club-record fee. In contrast to Harry Kent, here was a non-conformist whose quirky personality was not universally popular. Whilst still a player, he had to apologise to the directors for behaviour which had been the subject of complaint by his colleagues, and he retained his individual streak after taking charge. The son of a bank manager, he made a name for himself as a robust forward, and in 1917 gave evidence in a libel case in connection with a notorious Manchester United v Liverpool match-fixing scandal, testifying that he had been illegally approached but refused to participate. Having set up as a local publican (at the *Swan Hotel*, Rickmansworth) a few months after Harry Kent had done so, he perhaps eventually gave less commitment to his Vicarage Road duties than was expected of him, and his engagement was not renewed at the end of his third season as manager. His nine years of coaching overseas ended when he fled the Nazis with his Dutch wife in 1940, and he later returned to the licensed trade in Lancashire.

NEIL McBAIN *(1929-1937 and 1956-1959)*
b Campbeltown, Argyllshire 15/11/1895
d Ayr 13/5/1974
Watford career as a player (1928-1931):
FL 85 (5 inc 1p), FAC 9 (-)
FL record as Watford manager (two terms):
(W 137, D 71, L 128, Goals 591-516
(W 42, D 33, L 47, Goals 187-203
Campbeltown Academicals; Ayr Utd (5/14); Kilmarnock (4/15); Ayr Utd (4/15); Third Lanark (5/21); Ayr Utd (8/21); Manchester Utd (£4,600 11/21); Everton (£4,200 1/23); St Johnstone (£1,000 6/26); Liverpool (3/28); Watford (under £1,000 11/28, player-manager 5/29, manager 5/31 until 8/37); Luton Town (chief scout, manager 6/38 until 6/39); New Brighton secretary-manager (6/46); Leyton Orient (assistant-manager 2/48, manager 4/48 until 8/49); Chelsea scout; Estudiantes La Plata, Argentina, manager (3/50 until 8/54); Ayr Utd manager (4/55); Watford (manager 8/56 until 2/59, scout in Scotland 2/61); Ayr Utd manager (12/62 until 1963); Mansfield Town scout in Scotland (10/67); Everton scout. Guested for Portsmouth in WW1.

SCOTLAND FULL

He came to Watford as the suspended Frank Barson's replacement and continued at centre-half for nearly two seasons after becoming manager. Under his guidance the club was to begin its best period in Division 3 (South), but he was suddenly despatched for having adopted an individual approach to cash-handling. Re-engaged 19 years later, he had little to offer in his second spell, during which he brought in a succession of players from in and around his old Ayrshire stamping ground. He played no part in the signing of Cliff Holton in 1958, by which time his less-than-abstemious habits had dragged him down. Whilst with New Brighton he freakishly entered the record books by standing in for his goalie (who in bad weather failed to turn up at Hartlepool), to become the oldest player in Football League history. He was 51, and hadn't played for 16 years.

<u>William *(**BILL**)* **FINDLAY**</u> *(1937-1947)*
b Wishaw, Lanarks 17/2/1900
d Braunstone, Leics 11/6/1949
Watford career as a player (1932-1944):
FL 128 (6 inc 1p), FAC 9 (-), 3SC 4 (-), WW2 9 (-)
FL record as Watford acting-manager/manager:
W 50, D 25, L 39, Goals 179-152
Musselburgh Bruntonians; Third Lanark (6/23); Liverpool (£2,500 8/24); Leicester City (5/25); <u>Watford</u> ("substantial fee" 6/32, assistant-manager 4/37, acting-manager 8/37, manager 1/38 until 2/47); Edgware Town manager (5/47 until death)
SCOTLAND JUNIOR
An accomplished wing-half in his playing days, he was anything but flamboyant as a manager, but as something of a tactical thinker he maintained the club's consistency as one of Division 3 (South)'s best in the late 1930s. He was appointed Watford's first assistant-manager at the end of 1936/7, but unexpectedly began the next season in charge, although another four months were to elapse before he was confirmed in the post. His term of office encompassed the Second World War, during which he turned out occasionally in emergencies, and on the final occasion was nearly 45 years old. A sober, religious and undemonstrative man, he was still Edgware Town's manager, as well as a practising masseur and manipulative therapist, when he died on holiday at the age of 49.

<u>John *(**JACK**)* **BRAY**</u> *(1947-1948)*
b Oswaldtwistle, Lancs 22/4/1909
d Huncoat, Lancs 18/11/1982
FL record as Watford manager:
W 11, D 7, L 17, Goals 45-66
Clayton Olympia; Manchester Central (1928); Manchester City (£1,000 10/29, reserve-team player-coach cs 1946); <u>Watford</u> manager (3/47 until 1/48); Nelson coach (2/48 until 9/48). Guested for Birmingham, Blackburn Rovers, Nottingham Forest and Port Vale in WW2.
ENGLAND FULL; FOOTBALL LEAGUE
He was the first Watford manager who didn't also represent the club as a player. During his long engagement at Maine Road he'd been a member of winning teams in both League and Cup, and played six times for England as a constructive wing-half. With this pedigree and a positive approach to tactics and coaching, he might have seemed a good bet for successful management, but although he worked hard to try to introduce a youth policy at Vicarage Road. the short-term results at first-team level didn't come. He soon turned his back on the game for good, to concentrate on the sports-goods shop he'd opened in Lancashire.

Edris Albert (**EDDIE**) **HAPGOOD**
(1948-1950)
b Bristol, Glos 24/9/1908
d Leamington Spa, Warwicks 20/4/1973
FL record as Watford manager:
W 29, D 27, L 32, Goals 102-107
Kettering (cs 1927); Arsenal (£750 10/27); Blackburn Rovers manager (1/46 until 2/47); Shrewsbury Town player-coach (8/47); Watford manager (2/48); Bath City manager (3/50 until 2/56). Guested for Birmingham, Blackburn Rovers, Chelsea, Luton Town, Southampton, West Bromwich Albion and West Ham Utd in WW2.
ENGLAND FULL; FOOTBALL LEAGUE
One of the outstanding figures of football history, he was the highly influential left-back and skipper of Arsenal as they established their pre-eminence under Herbert Chapman. Hapgood's successes included five League championships, two FA Cup wins, and the England captaincy in most of his 30 peacetime and 13 wartime international appearances. His defensive know-how helped to produce a tight Watford defence (the 1949/50 sequence of eight League games without a single goal conceded is a club record), but an attitude less subservient than the board would have liked, and a personality clash with his senior player, Taffy Davies, brought about the assertive Hapgood's dismissal. Thereafter he twice took Bath City to the Second Round of the FA Cup, but he left football completely when he was 48. His son Tony became a Watford player.

Roland (**RON**) **GRAY** *(1950-1951)*
b North Shields, Northumberland 25/6/1920
Watford career as a player (1942-1946):
FL 16 (-), FAC 13 (4 inc 3p),
WW2 46 (5 inc 2p)
FL record at Watford acting-manager/manager:
W 13, D 15, L 28, Goals 63-93
Boldon Colliery; Sheffield Utd (5/38); Lincoln City (5/39 until cs 1940); Watford (9/42 until cs 1943); Notts County (9/43 until cs 1944); Watford (8/45 until 12/47, trainer 7/48, acting-manager 3/50, manager 6/50 until 8/51); Millwall (trainer 10/51, manager 1/56 until 1/58, and 1/61 until 11/63); Lincoln City manager (10/66 until 7/70); Ipswich Town chief scout (9/70 until at least 5/83). Guested for Aldershot, Grimsby Town and Millwall in WW2.
Deprived of a decent playing career - first by the war, and then by injury which left him finished at 26 - he was to become the youngest of all Watford managers. He was the youngest to depart, as well, for the club had to seek re-election at the end of his only full season in charge, and that was that. His career as a wing-half was abandoned on medical advice, 12 inactive months after he'd been injured on Boxing Day 1946. His one success as a manager came when he led Millwall to the 4th Division championship in 1962, but 18 months later he was shown the door after FA Cup defeat at the hands of non-League Kettering Town. At Sincil Bank he signed Graham Taylor for £1,300.

Adrian (**HAYDN**) **GREEN** *(1951-1952)*
b Greasley, Notts 18/3/1887
d Watford, Herts 8/2/1957
FL record as Watford manager:
W 16, D 11, L 27, Goals 70-95
Stanton Hill Victoria; Nottingham Forest (cs 1907); Manchester Utd (cs 1910); Aston Villa (3/12); Newport County (1913); Reading (5/14); Lincoln City assistant-manager (1920s); Ebbw Vale manager; Hull City manager (5/31 until 3/34); Bangor, Northern Ireland, manager; Guildford City manager (1936); Swansea Town manager (5/39 until 9/47); Watford manager (8/51 until 10/52)

More than twice the age of his immediate predecessor, he began with a 7-1 home defeat, but later sparked a burst of optimism, reflected in massive home attendances, at the start of the 1952/3 season, with what were, by the Watford standards of the day, big-name signings. The euphoria very quickly evaporated, however, and within weeks Green was sent packing, for taking backhanders in connection with the transfers of Jimmy Bowie and Frank Mitchell. He'd not endeared himself to the directors, whom he treated with disdain, and who found him a difficult employee to handle. As a forward and half-back he had an undistinguished career, but in management during the 1930s he had championship triumphs in Division 3 (North) (with Hull City) and the Southern League (with Guildford City). In his younger days he was a Powderhall sprinter.

Leonard Arthur (**LEN**) **GOULDEN**
(1952-1955 and 1956)
b Homerton, London 16/7/1912
d Plaistow, London 14/2/1995
FL record as Watford manager (two spells):
(W 52, D 39, L 45, Goals 210-198
(W 6, D 3, L 7, Goals 17-23
Chelmsford; Leyton (cs 1932); Dagenham; West Ham Utd (am 1931, pro 4/33); Chelsea (£4,500 8/45, coach cs 1950); Watford (manager 11/52, general manager 10/55, manager 2/56 until 7/56); coach to US forces in Germany (until 10/56); Watford coach (7/59 until cs 1962); coach in Libya (2 years); Banbury Town manager (1965 until 3/67); Oxford Utd reserve-team coach (1/69). Guested for Arsenal and Chelsea in WW2.

ENGLAND SCHOOLS and FULL; FOOTBALL LEAGUE

Can a person be "too nice", which was said of Len Goulden? In terms of what it takes to be a successful football manager, regrettably he can, and if the directors were seeking a quieter life after disposing of the abrasive Haydn Green, they picked the right man. There was a marked reluctance to replace him when the time came, and after a few months as 'general manager', while Johnny Paton was given responsibility for the team, he was recalled briefly before being sacked. He won 14 caps in the 1930s, and was at his peak as a creative inside-forward when war broke out, thereafter making a further five appearances for England in wartime. He also played in two wartime cup-winning teams at Wembley - for West Ham United and Chelsea, respectively.

John (JOHNNY) **PATON** *(1955-1956)*
b Glasgow 2/4/1923
Watford career as a player (1952-1955):
FL 84 (17), FAC 7 (-)
FL record as Watford manager:
W 2, D 6, L 7, Goals 16-28
Dennistoun Waverley (am 1/40); Celtic (5/42); Chelsea (loan 11/46 until 8/47); Brentford (£5,000 9/49); Watford (7/52, player-coach 6/55, manager 10/55 until 2/56); Arsenal (scout, 'A'-team manager 1961 for 6 years). Guested for Arsenal, Leeds Utd, Manchester City, Millwall and New York Americans, USA in WW2.
SCOTLAND SCHOOLS
The son of a prominent Celtic player, he was ATC welterweight champion of Glasgow, a prize-winning sprinter, and a schoolboy-international footballer. For a time he combined his career as a direct winger with that of a photographer with a national daily. After his promotion from the position of coach (the first such appointment at Vicarage Road), his brief spell in charge of team affairs included a 6-2 home defeat by Aldershot in the Southern Floodlit Cup, and elimination from the FA Cup by Bedford Town - the club's third at non-League hands in four seasons. He also had a spell in charge of the Herts FA's youth-coaching scheme. In the 1980s he took over the management of a snooker hall, and became a professional snooker referee and coach.

William Arthur **RON***ald* **BURGESS** *(1959-1963)*
b Cwm, Mon 9/4/1917
FL record as Watford acting manager/manager:
W 80, D 45, L 75, Goals 347-326
Cwm Villa; Tottenham Hotspur (5/36); Northfleet (loan circa 1937); Swansea Town (player-coach 8/54, player-manager 7/55); Watford (coach 12/58, acting-manager 2/59, manager 3/59 until 5/63); Hendon manager (1963); Fulham coach (cs 1965); Bedford Town manager (until cs 1967). Guested for Millwall, Nottingham Forest, Notts County and Reading in WW2.
WALES FULL; GREAT BRITAIN; FOOTBALL LEAGUE
An outstanding attacking wing-half and international captain, he made ten wartime appearances for Wales before winning 32 peacetime caps, and also represented Great Britain v The Rest of Europe. At club level he led Tottenham Hotspur on the field for eight years, which included an exhilarating period in which they stylishly won the Second and First Division championships in successive years. He was Watford's manager in the memorable 1959/60 season, but was less influential as a figurehead than his charismatic captain, Cliff Holton, and this was to lead to the latter's grotesquely ill-judged transfer. Burgess was eventually sacked with the side in serious decline.

William Harry (**BILL**) **McGARRY** *(1963-1964)*
b Stoke-on-Trent, Staffs 10/6/1927
FL record as Watford manager:
W 26, D 17, L 14, Goals 97-81
Northwood Mission, Hanley; Port Vale (6/45); Huddersfield Town (£10,000 3/51); Bournemouth & Boscombe Athletic player-manager (£2,000 3/61); Watford manager (7/63); Ipswich Town manager (10/64); Wolverhampton Wanderers manager (11/68 until 5/76); Saudi Arabia national coach (6/76 until 10/77); Newcastle Utd manager (11/77 until 8/80); Brighton & Hove Albion scout (1980); Power Dynamo, Zambia, coach; Zambia national coach (by 1/84); Wolverhampton Wanderers manager (9/85 until 11/85); coach in Bophuthatswana, South Africa (by 1993)
ENGLAND 'B' and FULL; FOOTBALL LEAGUE
Bill McGarry propelled the managership of Watford FC from near-feudalism into the modern era; there was no evolutionary period. Even his immediate predecessor helped with ground-maintenance work, but McGarry was nobody's lackey, and his style was confrontational, and based on strict discipline. A decade earlier, Haydn Green's attempt at the power game was always doomed, but the old order was changing rapidly, and McGarry's unexpected departure was a career move at his own wish, not the board's. His move to Watford had been resented by Bournemouth (they refused to relinquish his playing registration) and in his one season at Vicarage Road he took the club closer to Division 2 than it had ever been before. He subsequently led Ipswich Town back into the top flight, and Wolverhampton Wanderers to Wembley success in the League Cup. As a dour, gritty little wing-half he'd won four England caps, and played in the 1954 World Cup Finals.

KENneth **FURPHY** *(1964-1971)*
b Stockton-on-Tees, Co Durham 28/5/1931
Watford career as a player (1964-1968):
FL 95+6 (1), FAC 6 (-), FLC 4 (-)
FL record as Watford manager:
W 115, D 79, L 101, Goals 388-331
Everton (am 9/50, pro 11/50); Runcorn (12/51); Darlington (8/53, player/youth-team coach late-1950s); Workington player-manager 7/62); Watford player-manager (£1,000 11/64); Blackburn Rovers manager (7/71); also England Under-23 manager (1973/4); Sheffield Utd manager (12/73 until 10/75); New York Cosmos, USA, coach (1/76); Miami Toros, USA, coach (10/76); Ipswich Town scout; Detroit Express, USA, coach (3/77); Washington Diplomats, USA, coach (by 3/81); Bermuda manager; Cleveland Force, USA, manager; member of England manager's support team (9/90)
Although better-known as a manager, he made over five hundred appearances as a lower-divisions right-back. He came to Vicarage Road soon after leading Workington to their only Football League promotion, making 44 appearances himself, and continued in the dual role for nearly four years at Watford. The measure of his achievements, based on hard work, organisation and sound defence, is that the club was nearly 90 years old when it first won promotion to Division 2, and then reached its first FA Cup semi-final the following season. The financial input needed to strengthen the squad and consolidate at the higher level was not available, and further progress never looked likely. Furphy moved on to appointments with bigger English clubs, but without the success for which he seemed destined. In the United States he had some celebrated talent at his disposal, including Pele. He became a sports-shop proprietor in South Devon, and also a broadcaster there on local radio.

<u>*GEORGE KIRBY*</u> *(1971-1973)*
b Liverpool, Lancs 20/12/1933
FL record as Watford manager:
W 17, D 26, L 45, Goals 67-123
Longwen Juniors; Everton (am 8/50, pro 6/52); Sheffield Wednesday (3/59); Plymouth Argyle (1/60); Southampton (£17,000 9/62); Coventry City (£12,500 3/64); Swansea Town (10/64); Walsall (5/65); New York Generals, USA (6/67 until 9/68); Brentford (10/68 until 1/69); Worcester City (3/69); Halifax Town (coach cs 1969, manager cs 1970); <u>Watford</u> manager (8/71 until 5/73); Akranes, Iceland, manager; coach in Kuwait; Halifax Town manager (11/78 until 6/81); coach in Indonesia ($2\frac{1}{2}$ years to 12/85)

If ever a manager was on a loser, it was George Kirby, who was recruited immediately after performing the unlikely feat of taking Halifax Town to within a whisker of the Second Division in the only season of his first spell there, and then beating Manchester United's full star-studded side in the Watney Cup. Injuries, boardroom unrest, and a shortage of luck and money, conspired to produce two terrible winters consisting of one humiliating relegation and very nearly a second. He'd been a rumbustious centre-forward who, having been at Goodison Park for almost seven years - mostly as a reserve - spent the 1960s as a wanderer.

<u>*Michael Thomas* **(MIKE) KEEN**</u>
(1973-1977)
b High Wycombe, Bucks 19/3/1940
Watford career as a player (1972-1975):
FL 124+2 (5), FAC 5 (-), FLC 5 (1)
FL record as Watford manager:
W 67, D 48, L 63, Goals 237-236
Queens Park Rangers (am 5/57, pro 6/58); Luton Town (1/69); <u>Watford</u> (free 6/72, player-manager 6/73, manager cs 1975 until 4/77); Queens Park Rangers coaching staff (7/77 until 12/77); Northampton Town manager (2/78 until 3/79); Wycombe Wanderers manager (4/80 until 4/84); Marlow manager (cs 1985); Mike Keen Sports (player, by 5/85); Hamilton Academicals (Reading) Over-50s (by 10/95)

As a tall, stylish, all-round wing-half, he captained QPR to a unique double of League Cup and Third Division championship in 1966/7, which they followed immediately with further promotion. He retired as a player, after 664 League appearances, half-way through his spell as Watford manager, when the club dropped into the Fourth Division. He did introduce a pleasing footballing style at Vicarage Road, but without the discipline, drive and ambition which were soon to sweep the club into fantasy-land. His sacking was followed by one further crack at League management, which came to grief with Northampton Town languishing in the lower reaches of Division 4, but in 1983 he led Wycombe Wanderers to the Isthmian League championship.

<u>*GRAHAM TAYLOR*</u> *(1977-1987 and 1996)*
b Worksop, Notts 15/9/1944
FL record as Watford manager (two spells):
(W 191, D 105, L 132, Goals 692-544
(W 5, D 8, L 5, Goals 32-30
Scunthorpe Utd (am 11/60); Grimsby Town (am 7/61); England Grammar Schools Under-19; Grimsby Town (pro 7/62); Lincoln City (player-coach 7/68, manager 12/72); <u>Watford</u> manager (6/77 until 7/87); also England youth-team manager (10/82 until 5/83); Aston Villa manager (7/87); England manager (7/90 until 11/93); Wolverhampton Wanderers manager (3/94 until 11/95); <u>Watford</u> general manager (2/96)

The architect and builder of Watford's golden era. His career as a full-back was ended by injury, and at 31 he took Lincoln City to the 4th Division championship with a League-record haul of points. Drawn to Watford (Lincoln were paid £20,000 as compensation) by a persuasively ambitious chairman, Elton John, he took Vicarage Road by storm. Nobody can match his feat of taking a club from the 4th Division to be runners-up in both League and FA Cup, which he achieved within seven years. The exhilarating, direct style of his teams, which performed to high standards of conduct, was subject to some fatuous carping (not by those who attended Vicarage Road in unprecedented numbers), but little else about the Taylor decade was negative, and he generated a pioneering ethos of family and community involvement with the club which attracted widespread admiration. In 1987, sensing that his chairman's enthusiasm had waned, he left to revive Second Division Aston Villa, and within three years they were runners-up to League champions Liverpool. The success story ended with his appointment as manager of England and subsequently Wolverhampton Wanderers. He left both posts in the face of intense criticism, but there were few reservations at Vicarage Road about his return in 1996, to oversee efforts aimed at reversing nine years of decline both on and off the field.

<u>*David Thomas (DAVE)* **BASSETT**</u>
(1987-1988)
b Wembley, Middx 4/9/1944
FL record as Watford manager:
W 4, D 6, L 13, Goals 15-31
Hayes (8/61); Chelsea (am 8/62); Wycombe Wanderers (8/63); Hayes (1/64 until cs 1965); <u>Watford</u> (am 2/65); Hendon (12/65 until cs 1966); Walton & Hersham (8/68); Wimbledon (7/74, coach 1979, manager 1/81); Crystal Palace manager (8/84); Wimbledon manager (8/84); <u>Watford</u> manager (5/87 until 1/88); Sheffield Utd manager (2/88 until 12/95); Crystal Palace manager (2/96)
ENGLAND AMATEUR

Like Graham Taylor, he is one of very few managers to have taken a League club (in Bassett's case, Wimbledon) right through the divisions. That Taylor would be a hard act to follow was never in doubt, but the haste with which Bassett, a cheerful and confident character, rejected established standards and methods led to a catastrophic decline, and within a few months he had gone. Successful and popular elsewhere, he was the wrong man for Watford at that time, and in those circumstances. As a wing-half he recovered from a broken leg sustained in 1966 to win ten Amateur caps, and played in Walton & Hersham's Amateur Cup-winning team of 1973. With Wimbledon he won three consecutive Southern League championships and was their first Football League captain. Earlier he'd been on the books at Vicarage Road as an amateur, and his father-in-law, Tommy Carpenter, was once a Watford goalkeeper.

STEVEn John HARRISON *(1988-1990)*
b Blackpool, Lancs 26/12/1952
Watford career as a player (1978-1981):
FL 82+1 (-), FAC 9 (-), FLC 10 (-)
FL record as Watford manager:
W 36, D 29, L 35, Goals 127-111
Blackpool (sch 9/67, appr 8/68, pro 12/70); Vancouver Whitecaps, Canada (£20,000 3/78); Watford (£25,000 9/78); Charlton Athletic (free 7/81 until 4/82); Watford (coaching staff 6/82, reserve-team coach 7/85); Aston Villa coach (5/87); Watford manager (1/88 until 3/90); Millwall coach (7/90 until 10/91); also England coach on a match-to-match basis (8/90 until 10/91); occasional appearances for White Lion, Watford (by 1/91); Crystal Palace (reserve-team coach 10/91, first-team coach 5/93); Wolverhampton Wanderers coach (cs 1994 until 12/95); Preston North End assistant-manager (2/96)

At various times Watford's left-back, coach and manager, he admitted to being unhappy in the third role, but his aptitude for coaching, particularly of defensive players, led Graham Taylor to employ him four times. In his first full season in charge, Harrison did get Watford into the play-offs, but soon reverted to coaching appointments which offered freer reign to his extrovert personality. Perhaps a consequence of the pressures of management was his tendency to discard players (Bamber, Holden, Kuhl, Redfearn, Rimmer, Robson) not long after bringing them to the club. Much given to jocularity, he left his Millwall and England posts following a prank which was deemed well beyond the bounds of decency.

COLIN LEE *(1990)*
b Torquay, Devon 12/6/1956
FL record as Watford manager:
W 5, D 9, L 14, Goals 31-45
Bristol City (sch 7/71, appr 8/71, pro 7/74); Hereford Utd (loan 11/74); Torquay Utd (1/77); Tottenham Hotspur (£60,000 10/77); Chelsea (£200,000 1/80); Brentford player/youth-development officer (£17,500 7/87); Watford (youth-team manager 7/89, manager 3/90 until 11/90); Reading (youth-team manager 1991, assistant-manager 1992); Leicester City assistant-manager (12/94); Wolverhampton Wanderers assistant-manager (12/95)

Having been promoted from youth-team duties for the last few weeks of the 1989/90 season, he paid big money for a disappointing clutch of summer signings, and began the new season by losing the first seven home games. Soon after this he was replaced (by the manager who had taken him to Brentford), to become the only Watford manager who started and ended his term of office in the same calendar year. Thereafter he followed as assistant-manager to Mark McGhee as the latter moved from club to club in controversial circumstances. Lee began his playing career as a forward, and scored four goals on his début for Tottenham Hotspur. Chelsea turned him into a full-back, and he helped them to win the Second Division championship in 1984. Two years later, playing as a striker, he scored twice for them when they beat Manchester City 5-4 at Wembley in the first Full Members Cup Final.

*Stephen John (**STEVE**)* **PERRYMAN** *(1990-1993)*

b Ealing, Middx 21/12/1951

FL record as Watford manager:
W 42, D 35, L 44, Goals 140-151

Tottenham Hotspur (appr 8/67, pro 1/69); Oxford Utd player-coach (3/86); Brentford (player/assistant-manager 11/86, player-manager 1/87 until 8/90); Watford manager (11/90); Tottenham Hotspur (assistant-manager 7/93, acting-manager briefly 11/94); IK Start, Norway, coach (6/95); Shimuzi Pulse, Japan, assistant-manager (1/96)

ENGLAND SCHOOLS, YOUTH, UNDER-21 and FULL

At first a busy, perceptive little midfield player, he became an outstanding defender and captain of Tottenham Hotspur. His long service at White Hart Lane incorporated triumphs in the FA Youth Cup, the Football League Cup twice, the UEFA Cup twice, and the FA Cup twice. He also played in 655 League games for Spurs, leaving the club's previous record-holder (Pat Jennings) nearly two hundred appearances behind. That he won only one Full cap - and then as a substitute in what was in fact an England second XI - was an insult to a player more worthy than many with much longer international careers. As a manager he had less success. He failed to lift Brentford out of Division 3, and his main achievement at Vicarage Road was an excellent late-season run to avoid relegation. He resigned with the club merely treading water, and teamed up with his former playing colleague Ossie Ardiles, first at Tottenham and subsequently in the Far East.

GLENN *Victor* **ROEDER** *(1993-1996)*

b Woodford, Essex 13/12/1955

Watford career as a player (1989-1991):
FL 74+4 (2), FAC 3 (1), FLC 4 (-), FMC 1 (-)

FL record as Watford manager:
W 39, D 32, L 49, Goals 148-166

Arsenal sch (12/69 until 2/72); Orient (appr 8/72, pro 7/74); Queens Park Rangers (£210,000 8/78); Notts County (loan 11/83); Newcastle Utd (£125,000 12/83); Watford (free 6/89, player/reserve-team coach 7/90 until 8/91); Millwall Reserves; Leyton Orient (1/92 until 5/92); Purfleet (10/92); Gillingham manager (11/92); Watford manager (7/93 until 2/96)

ENGLAND 'B'

His leadership potential was apparent during his career as a footballing centre-half (he'd earlier been a midfield player), and the move into management came as no surprise. On the field he became known for the 'Roeder shuffle', a crowd-pleasing sleight-of-foot manoeuvre which left defenders comprehensively beaten as he surged upfield. He led QPR out at Wembley for the 1982 FA Cup Final, but missed the replay (which they lost) due to suspension. He was Watford's oldest signing for 24 years, and in 1991 left with the intention of chaperoning Paul Gascoigne in Italy, but subsequently withdrew from this unorthodox career move. After a managerial baptism at the grim end of Division 4, he was headhunted by Watford, who were later fined £10,000 for an illegal approach. Another £30,000 had to be paid as compensation to Gillingham. Not the least remarkable feature of his Vicarage Road incumbency was the use of 30 or more players in each of his three seasons. This total had been reached only once before in the club's entire Football League history. He left with the club adrift at the bottom of the table, and heading back to the lower divisions.

Part Six

Caps, Cups & Medals

International and Other Representative Honours

The following honours have been won by players whilst they were registered with Watford, up to the 17th June 1996:

FULL INTERNATIONALS

31		**K.F. Jackett** (Wales)
31	(18+13)	**J.C.B. Barnes** (England) - 3 goals
21		**G.J. Armstrong** (Northern Ireland) - 5 goals
20	(19+1)	**J. McClelland** (Northern Ireland)
9		**M.S. Watson** (Canada)
9	(5+4)	**L.L. Blissett** (England) - 3 goals
7	(3+4)	**G.P. Hodges** (Wales) - 1 goal
4		**D.J. Connolly** (Republic of Ireland) - 2 goals
4		**P. Nicholas** (Wales)
4	(2+2)	**M.J.G. Johnston** (Scotland) - 2 goals
3	(1+2)	**M. Allen** (Wales) - 1 goal
2		**F. Hoddinott** (Wales)
2		**P.A. Jennings** (Northern Ireland)
2		**A.S. Meola** (United States of America)
1		**S.J. Morrow** (Northern Ireland) - whilst on loan to Watford
1		**M.T. O'Brien** (Republic of Ireland)
1		**I.W. Roberts** (Wales)
1		**J.T. Walley** (Wales)
1	(0+1)	**L.M. Nogan** (Wales)

WARTIME INTERNATIONALS

1		**W. Davies** (Wales)

UNDER-23 INTERNATIONALS

2		**J.T. Walley** (Wales)
1		**P.A. Jennings** (Northern Ireland)
1		**B. Lewis** (Wales)
1		**M.S.G. Walker** (Wales)

UNDER-21 INTERNATIONALS

12	(10+2)	**G.M. Porter** (England) - 1 goal
10		**D.B. James** (England)
9	(7+2)	**N.I. Callaghan** (England)
7		**G. Lavin** (Scotland) - 1 goal

5		**N.J. Gibbs** (England)
5	(3+2)	**M.J. Gallen** (Republic of Ireland)
4		**R.J. Page** (Wales)
4	(3+1)	**L.L. Blissett** (England)
3		**J.C.B. Barnes** (England)
2		**K.F. Jackett** (Wales)
2		**M.J.G. Johnston** (Scotland)
1		**R.C. Thomas** (England)
1	(0+1)	**D.S. Bazeley** (England)
1	(0+1)	**D.G. Holdsworth** (England)
1	(0+1)	**L. Sinnott** (England)

'B' INTERNATIONALS

1		**L.L.Blissett** (England)
1	(0+1)	**N.I. Callaghan** (England)

AMATEUR INTERNATIONALS

1	**F. Fayers** (England)

YOUTH INTERNATIONALS

England: **D.J.T. Bond, F. Bunce, A.W. Currie, J. Drysdale, A.W. Fuller, N.J. Gibbs, J.M. Gilligan, D.G. Holdsworth, W.J. Jennings, G.M. Porter, S. Sheppard, J.R. Soloman, R.C. Thomas, P.A. Towler, R.E. Wignall, D.H. Williams, N.J.F. Williams**

Scotland: **G. Lavin**

Wales: **M. Allen, D.W. Evans, K.F. Jackett, R.J. Page, S. Pugh, I.W. Roberts**

SCHOOLS INTERNATIONALS

England: **N. Boachie, D.J. Elliott, G.R. Harrison, S. Sheppard, R.C. Thomas**

Northern Ireland: **A.D. Thirlby**

Wales: **S.J. Kendall, R.J. Page, N.S.C. Procter, S. Pugh**

FOOTBALL LEAGUE REPRESENTATIVE

2	**J. McClelland**

FOOTBALL LEAGUE, DIVISION 2

2	**J. Drysdale**

FOOTBALL LEAGUE, DIVISION 3 (SOUTH)

1	**M. Cook**

SOUTHERN LEAGUE

5	**V.F. Gregory**
1	**A. Squires**
1	**J. Webster**
1	**C.W. White**

Players Who Have Won International and Other Representative Honours and Also Played for Watford

The following honours have been won by players who have appeared in senior competitive matches for Watford in peacetime. Capital letters are used to indicate players who were honoured whilst with the club, and are listed above.

FULL INTERNATIONALS

Canada: **M.S. WATSON**

England: **J.J. Bagshaw, H.E. Banks, D.J. Bardsley, J.C.B. BARNES, F. Barson, L.L. BLISSETT, A.W. Currie, A.E. Devonshire, K.M. Dixon, A.T.B. Dunn, J. Goodall, A. Grimsdell, S.B. Hodge, A.E. Hufton, B.A.G. Jezzard, A. Lockett, H.H. Pantling, K. Richardson, L. Smith, K.G. Sansom, F. Spiksley, B.E. Talbot**

Ireland / Northern Ireland: **G.J. ARMSTRONG, C. Gallogly, R. Irvine, P.A. JENNINGS, J. McCLELLAND, S.J. MORROW** (capped whilst on loan to Watford), **M.T. O'Brien, P.J. Rice, E.E. Smith**

Republic of Ireland: **D.J. CONNOLLY, J.T. Gavin, T.J. Mancini, M.T. O'BRIEN**

Scotland: **M.J.G. JOHNSTON, N. McBain, T.B. Niblo**

United States of America: **A.S. MEOLA**

Wales: **M. ALLEN, R.H. Cumner, F. HODDINOTT, G.P. HODGES, K.F. JACKETT, T.J. Jones, P. NICHOLAS, W. Nock, L.M. NOGAN, I.W. ROBERTS, J.T. WALLEY, D. Ward**

WARTIME and 'UNOFFICIAL' INTERNATIONALS (excluding players who won Full caps)

England: **A.J. Elkes, F.W. Lock, F.R. Mitchell**

Wales: **W. DAVIES**

South Africa: **R.J.G. Oelofse**

'Team America' (unofficial match v England): **S.M.A. Scullion**

UNDER-23 INTERNATIONALS

England: **A.W. Currie, S. Ellis, A.G. Rankin, A.F. Stokes**

Northern Ireland: **P.A. JENNINGS, S.J. Morrow, P.J. Rice**

Republic of Ireland: **P.J. Morrissey**

Scotland: **J. Hamilton, R. Slater**

Wales: **B. LEWIS, M.S.G. WALKER, J.T. WALLEY**

UNDER-21 INTERNATIONALS

Canada: **M.S. Watson**

England: **J.C.B. BARNES, D.S. BAZELEY, L.L. BLISSETT, N.I. CALLAGHAN, K.M. Dixon, B.A. Dyer, N.J. GIBBS, D.R.L. Hill, S.B. Hodge, D.G. HOLDSWORTH, D.B. JAMES, N.B. Jemson, G.M. PORTER, C.D. Ramage, K.G. Sansom, T.A. Sherwood, N.J. Shipperley, S.F. Sims, L. SINNOTT, P.J. Suckling, B.E. Talbot, R.C. THOMAS, G.L. Thompson, P. Wilkinson**

Netherlands: **J.H.P. Lohman**

Scotland: **M.J.G. JOHNSTON, G. LAVIN, J. McLaughlin**

Wales: **G.P. Hodges, K.F. JACKETT, A.J. McCarthy, P. Nicholas, L.M.Nogan, R.J. PAGE**

'B' INTERNATIONALS

England: **L.L. BLISSETT, N.I. CALLAGHAN, A.P. Coton, A.E. Devonshire, T.C. Harmer, S.B. Hodge, D.C. Holdsworth, D.B. James, B.A.G. Jezzard,**

R.I. Jobson, G.V. Roeder, K.G. Sansom, T.A. Sherwood, S.F. Sims, A.F. Stokes, B.E. Talbot
Northern Ireland: J.W. Fraser
Wales: M. Allen, G.P. Hodges, A.J. McCarthy, L.M. Nogan, I.W. Roberts

AMATEUR INTERNATIONALS
England: E.E. Bennett, R.H. Brown, J.F. Crussell, R.A. Day, R.A. Dudley, F. FAYERS, G. Gemmell, E.F. Grimsdell, H.E.J. Miller, I.G. Sharpe
Wales: R. Davies, B.E. Jones, B.J. Jones, J.S. Morgan
Great Britain (Olympic Games): E.E. Bennett, R.H. Brown, I.G. Sharpe

YOUTH INTERNATIONALS
England: D.S. Allder, D. Barnes, D.J. Bardsley, M.J. Block, D.J.T. BOND, F. BUNCE, D.M. Caskey, S.R. Cherry, J.M. Cowen, A.W. CURRIE, M.O. Dalrymple, J. DRYSDALE, K.B.L. Dublin, D.J. Edmonds, M.P. Falco, G.E. French, N.J. GIBBS, J.M. GILLIGAN, A.C. Gregory, D.M. Heard, D.G. HOLDSWORTH, A. Horsfield, W.G. Houghton, W.J. JENNINGS, A.J. McCarthy, K.W. Nicholas, M. Patching, B.E. Pollard, G.M. PORTER, S.A. Rimmer, J. Sanchez, K.G. Sansom, R. Saunders, S. SHEPPARD, L. Sinnott, J.R. SOLOMAN, J. Stirk, P.J. Suckling, R.C. THOMAS
Netherlands: J.H.P. Lohman
Northern Ireland: P.A. Jennings, S.J. Morrow, P.J. Rice
Scotland: W.H. Falconer, A.J. Kennedy, G. LAVIN
Wales: M. ALLEN, K.F. JACKETT, M.J. Rees, R.J. PAGE, I.W. ROBERTS

SCHOOLS INTERNATIONALS
England: E.F. Bacon, D.J.T. Bond, D.M. Caskey, A. Farrall, A. Grimsdell, G.R. HARRISON, D.R.L. Hill, P.B. Holland, A.R. Low, D.J.R. Ludden (Under-18), W.A. Neill, K.W. Nicholas, H.S. Oliver, M. Patching, J.W. Rostron, J. Sanchez, K.G. Sansom, S. SHEPPARD, E.G. Steele (Under-18), R.C. THOMAS
Northern Ireland: J.W. Fraser, S.J. Morrow
Scotland: T.C. Anderson, W.H. Falconer, T. McCready, J. McLaren, L. Morgan, J. Paton
Wales: R.H. Cumner, G.G. Davies, O.H. Jones, P. Nicholas, R.J. PAGE

SEMI-PROFESSIONAL INTERNATIONALS
England: P.A.O. Agana, S. Butler, P.A. Furlong, A. Hessenthaler, R.C. Willis

'JUNIOR' INTERNATIONALS
Ireland: R. Irvine
Scotland: C.D.V. Birse, W. Findlay, J. Hill, W.J. Lees, J.F. Maxwell, J.Moffatt, J. Murray, B. Rowan, D.P. Russell, J. Tennant, P. Turner, A. Walker.
(**J.B. Barnes** and **V.H. White** both played against Scotland for the Birmingham FA, which represented England in 'Junior' International matches)

INTER-LEAGUE REPRESENTATIVE MATCHES
Football League: J.C.B. Barnes, A.W. Currie, A.J. Elkes, J.C. English, E. Fletcher, J. Goodall, A. Grimsdell, B.A.G. Jezzard, A. Lockett, J. McCLELLAND, K.G. Sansom, L. Smith, F. Spiksley, A.F. Stokes
Irish League: N. Case, W.G. Devan, R. Irvine, H.M. Matthew
League of Ireland: R. Hale, A. Weir

Scottish League: **J. Hamilton, L. Morgan**
Southern League: **V.F. GREGORY, A. SQUIRES, J. WEBSTER, H.M. Wilcox** (**L.T.A. Andrews, J. Broad, H.M. Matthew** and **C.W. WHITE** also represented the Southern League, but not against other leagues)

FOOTBALL LEAGUE, DIVISION 2 (v Italian League, Serie B): **J. DRYSDALE**

FOOTBALL LEAGUE, DIVISION 3 (SOUTH) (v Division 3 (North)): **M. COOK**

Other Players Honoured

The following players have represented Watford, but not in competitive first-team matches in peacetime. Each player is listed only once - under the first heading for which he qualifies - and the number in brackets after each name relates to the most senior level at which he played for Watford, as follows: (1) First team in wartime; (2) First-team friendly; (3) Reserves; (4) Reserve-team friendly; (5) Reserve-team friendly in private; (6) Youth team; (7) Under-16 team.

FULL INTERNATIONALS

Australia: **D.S. Mitchell** (2), **J.S. Polak** (3)
Australia (Olympic Games): **D. Seal** (4)
Canada: **G.E. Aunger** (2)
England: **J.W. Barrett** (1), **W.D. Barton** (6), **C.S. Bastin** (1), **F.H. Broome** (1), **T. Galley** (1), **J.P. Greaves** (2), **H.H.F. Hobbis** (1), **W.H. McGarry** (2), **H.S. Miller** (1), **F. Morris** (1), **S.H. Mortensen** (1), **S.J. Perryman** (3), **J.C.R. Smith** (1), **P.J. Taylor** (2), **G.W. Webb** (3)
Finland: **E. Pekonen** (4)
New Zealand: **V. Coveney** (3)
Northern Ireland: **R.J. Browne** (1), **D.K. Martin** (1)
Scotland: **G. Walker** (3)
Sweden: **J. Björklund** (5)
Wales: **B.J. Law** (3), **R. Paul** (1), **E. Perry** (1), **I.H. Price** (1)

(**R.P. Wilson**, a Full Scotland international, was registered with the Football League by Watford as a non-contract player, but did not make an appearances at any level. **G.O. Smith**, a Full England international, was reported to have been registered with the Southern League, but did not play for the club at any level.)

WARTIME INTERNATIONALS

England: **M. Edelston** (1), **D. Westcott** (1)
Wales: **D.T. Winter** (1)

UNDER-23 INTERNATIONALS

England: **J.H. Bloomfield** (3)

UNDER-21 INTERNATIONALS

England: **B.S. Horne** (3), **A.R. Impey** (6)
Netherlands: **S. Storm** (2)
Republic of Ireland: **M.J. Gallen** (3)
Wales: **D.W.T. Graham** (6), **S. Pugh** (3)

AMATEUR INTERNATIONALS

England: **D.T. Bassett** (2), **K. Harrison** (3), **W. McKee** (1), **A.S. Owen** (1), **M.J. Pinner*** (2), **T.J. Stacey** (2), **C. Townsend*** (2)
(***Pinner** and **Townsend** also represented Great Britain in the Olympic Games)
Wales: **R. Vale** (3)

YOUTH INTERNATIONALS

England: **A.J. Bayes** (6), **A.J. Cheesewright** (3), **A.J. Fuller** (3), **T.B. Gibson** (4), **R.H. Harper** (6), **J.D. Lee** (3), **E.M.S. Stein** (6), **P.A. Towler** (3), **R.E. Wignall** (3), **D.H. Williams** (2), **N.J.F. Williams** (3)
Northern Ireland: **W.J.J. McArthur** (6), **A.D. Thirlby** (7)
Scotland: **J. Taylor** (3)
Wales: **D.W. Evans** (3)

SCHOOLS INTERNATIONALS

England: **N. Boachie** (3), **S.R. Bowder** (3), **W.C. Cox** (3), **N.F. Edgar** (6), **D.J. Elliott** (3), **G.J. Heald (Under-18)** (3), **M.T. Spelman (Under-18)** (3)
Scotland: **W.B. Livingstone** (3)
Wales: **A. Emslie** (6), **M. Gardener** (3), **K.J. Hamer** (3), **S.J. Kendall** (6), **N.S.C. Proctor** (3)

INTER-LEAGUE REPRESENTATIVE MATCHES

Welsh League: **E.R. Robson** (1)

'JUNIOR' and SEMI-PROFESSIONAL INTERNATIONALS

England: **R.A.G. Codner** (3), **P.R. Gridelet** (6)
Scotland: **J.H.W.J. Tennant** (3)

Members of Championship and Cup-Winning Teams

The following players, all of whom represented Watford in competitive first-team matches in peacetime, made at least one appearance for a club in a season in which it won a League championship, or played in a final for a cup-winning team. (NB The competitions are listed without any temporary names by which they may have been known under commercial sponsorships.)

FOOTBALL LEAGUE (until 1991/2) and FA PREMIER LEAGUE

1888/9	Preston North End	**J. Goodall** (21 apps, 21 goals)
1889/90	Preston North End	**W. Hendry** (1 app)
1893/4	Aston Villa	**C.B. Hare** (10 apps, 7 goals)
1898/9	Aston Villa	**C.L. Aston** (13 apps)
1899/1900	Aston Villa	**C.L. Aston** (3 apps)
1902/3	Sheffield Wednesday	**F. Spiksley** (32 apps, 9 goals)
1912/3	Sunderland	**C.E. Gladwin** (27 apps)
1927/8	Everton	**R. Irvine** (9 apps, 3 goals)
1928/9	Sheffield Wednesday	**J. Trotter** (6 apps, 1 goal)
1929/30	Sheffield Wednesday	**T.J. Jones** (1 app)
1947/8	Arsenal	**L. Smith** (1 app)
1950/1	Tottenham Hotspur	**E.D.H. Uphill** (2 apps, 1 goal)

1952/3	Arsenal	**C.C. Holton** (21 apps, 19 goals)
"	"	**A. Shaw** (25 apps)
"	"	**L. Smith** (31 apps)
1961/2	Ipswich Town	**W.A. Baxter** (40 apps)
1970/1	Arsenal	**P.J. Rice** (41 apps)
1980/1	Aston Villa	**G. Williams** (21+1 apps)
1984/5	Everton	**K. Richardson** (14+1 apps, 4 goals)
"	"	**P. Wilkinson** (4+1 apps, 2 goals)
1986/7	Everton	**K. Richardson** (1 app)
"	"	**P. Wilkinson** (12+10 apps, 3 goals)
1987/8	Liverpool	**J.C.B. Barnes** (38 apps, 15 goals)
1988/9	Arsenal	**K. Richardson** (32+2 apps, 1 goal)
1989/90	Liverpool	**J.C.B. Barnes** (34 apps, 22 goals)
1991/2	Leeds United	**P.A.O. Agana** (1+1 apps)
"	"	**S.B. Hodge** (12+11 apps, 7 goals)
"	"	**J. McClelland** (16+2 apps)
1994/5	Blackburn Rovers	**T.A. Sherwood** (38 apps, 6 goals)

FA CUP

1881/2	Old Etonians	**A.T.B. Dunn**
1888/9	Preston North End	**J. Goodall**
1895/6	Sheffield Wednesday	**F. Spiksley** (2 goals)
1897/8	Nottingham Forest	**W. Wragg**
1914/5	Sheffield United	**J.C. English**
1919/20	Aston Villa	**F. Barson**
1920/1	Tottenham Hotspur	**A. Grimsdell**
1924/5	Sheffield United	**H.H. Pantling**
1938/9	Portsmouth	**L. Morgan**
1946/7	Charlton Athletic	**P.H.L. Croker**
"	"	**H.J. Phipps**
1966/7	Tottenham Hotspur	**P.A. Jennings**
1970/1	Arsenal	**P.J. Rice**
1974/5	West Ham United	**W.J. Jennings**
1977/8	Ipswich Town	**B.E. Talbot**
1978/9	Arsenal	**P.A. Jennings**
"	"	**P.J. Rice**
"	"	**B.E. Talbot** (1 goal)
1979/80	West Ham United	**A.E. Devonshire**
1980/1	Tottenham Hotspur	**P.R. Miller**
1981/2	Tottenham Hotspur	**P.R. Miller**
1983/4	Everton	**K. Richardson**
1988/9	Liverpool	**J.C.B. Barnes**

FOOTBALL LEAGUE CUP

1966/7	Queens Park Rangers	**M.T. Keen**
1970/1	Tottenham Hotspur	**P.A. Jennings**
1972/3	Tottenham Hotspur	**P.A. Jennings**
1986/7	Arsenal	**K.G. Sansom**
1988/9	Nottingham Forest	**S.B. Hodge**
1989/90	Nottingham Forest	**S.B. Hodge**
"	"	**N.B. Jemson** (1 goal)
1992/3	Arsenal	**S.J. Morrow** (1 goal)
1993/4	Aston Villa	**K. Richardson**
1994/5	Liverpool	**J.C.B. Barnes**
"	"	**D.B. James**

FULL MEMBERS CUP

1985/6	Chelsea	**J. McLaughlin**
1987/8	Reading	**N. Smillie** (1 goal)
"	"	**L. Taylor**
1988/9	Nottingham Forest	**S.B. Hodge**
1989/90	Chelsea	**K.M. Dixon**
"	"	**P. Nicholas**
1990/1	Crystal Palace	**G.L. Thompson** (sub)

ANGLO-ITALIAN CUP

1994/5	Notts County	**P.A.O. Agana** (1 goal)
"	"	**S.R. Cherry**
"	"	**D.W. White** (1 goal)

DIVISION 3 (SOUTH) CUP

1933/4	Exeter City	**S.C. Hurst**
1934/5	Bristol Rovers	**C.J. Wipfler** (1 goal)
1936/7	Watford (trophy shared	**J.H. Armstrong**
"	" with Millwall)	**T.A. Barnett**
"	"	**W. Black**
"	"	**D.R. Evans** (2 goals in 1st leg)
"	"	**L. Gallimore**
"	"	**H. Hawkins**
"	"	**T.J. Jones**
"	"	**D.J. Lewis**
"	"	**T.G. Lewis**
"	"	**J. McLaren**
"	"	**E. Morgan**
"	"	**R.V. O'Brien**
"	"	**D. Ovenstone**
"	"	**A.G. Reed**
"	"	**T.C. Walters** (1 goal in 2nd leg)

WATNEY CUP

1971	Colchester United	**E.R.C. Burgess**
"	"	**B. Garvey**
"	"	**B.E. Owen**

ANGLO-SCOTTISH CUP

1980/1	Chesterfield	**J. Stirk**

ASSOCIATE MEMBERS CUP

1985/6	Bristol City	**K. Waugh**
1986/7	Mansfield Town	**K.B. Cassells**
1995/6	Rotherham United	**N.B. Jemson** (2 goals)

FA AMATEUR CUP

1924/5	Clapton	**H.E.J. Miller**
1966/7	Enfield	**R.A. Day**
1969/70	Enfield	**R.A. Day**

FA YOUTH CUP

1960/1	Chelsea	**J.M. Cowen**
1965/6	Arsenal	**P.J. Rice**
1972/3	Ipswich Town	**J. Stirk**
1976/7	Crystal Palace	**P. Nicholas**
"	"	**K.G. Sansom**
1977/8	Crystal Palace	**P. Nicholas**
1981/2	Watford	**J.C.B. Barnes**
"	"	**F.J.A. Cassidy**
"	"	**P.L. Franklin**
"	"	**N.J. Gibbs**
"	"	**J.M. Gilligan** (1 goal in each leg)
"	"	**D.N.C. Johnson** (1 goal)
"	"	**N. Price**
"	"	**I.P. Richardson** (1 goal)
"	"	**W.R. Sterling** (1 goal)
1987/8	Arsenal	**S.J. Morrow**
1988/9	Watford	**B.J. Ashby**
"	"	**J. Drysdale**
"	"	**D.B. James**
"	"	**J.S. Meara** (sub)
"	"	**J.R. Soloman**
"	"	**R.C. Thomas** (1 goal)

FA TROPHY

1984/5	Wealdstone	**G. Donnellan**
1987/8	Enfield	**P.A. Furlong** (2 goals)
"	"	**P.J. Harding**

SCOTTISH FOOTBALL LEAGUE

1957/8	Heart of Midlothian	**J. Hamilton** (4 apps, 4 goals)
1959/60	Heart of Midlothian	**J. Hamilton** (27 apps, 7 goals)
1983/4	Aberdeen	**W.H. Falconer** (4+4 apps, 2 goals)
1984/5	Aberdeen	**W.H. Falconer** (10+6 apps, 4 goals)
1985/6	Celtic	**M.J.G. Johnston** (31+1 apps, 15 goals)
1986/7	Rangers	**C. West** (4+5 apps, 2 goals)
1989/90	Rangers	**M.J.G. Johnston** (36 apps, 15 goals)
1990/1	Rangers	**M.J.G. Johnston** (29 apps, 11 goals)
1991/2	Rangers	**M.J.G. Johnston** (10+1 apps, 5 goals)

SCOTTISH FA CUP

1887/8	Renton	**J. McNee** (1 goal)
1956/7	Falkirk	**R. Slater**
1984/5	Celtic	**M.J.G. Johnston**
1994/5	Celtic	**W.H. Falconer** (sub)

SCOTTISH FOOTBALL LEAGUE CUP

1953/4	East Fife	**J. Curran**
1958/9	Heart of Midlothian	**J. Hamilton** (1 goal)
1959/60	Heart of Midlothian	**J. Hamilton** (1 goal)
1962/3	Heart of Midlothian	**J. Hamilton**
1983/4	Rangers	**J. McClelland**
1984/5	Rangers	**J. McClelland**
1995/6	Aberdeen	**P. Hetherston** (sub)

IRISH FA CUP

1939/40	Ballymena United	**A. Weir**

FA OF IRELAND CUP

1938/9	Shelbourne	**A. Weir**

EUROPEAN CUP

1981/2	Aston Villa	**G. Williams**

EUROPEAN CUP-WINNERS CUP

1993/4	Arsenal	**S.J. Morrow**

UEFA CUP

1971/2	Tottenham Hotspur	**P.A. Jennings**
1983/4	Tottenham Hotspur	**M.P. Falco**
"	"	**P.R. Miller** (1 goal)

EUROPEAN SUPER-CUP

1981/2	Aston Villa	**G. Williams**

OLYMPIC GAMES

1912	Great Britain	**I.G. Sharpe**